SOCIAL MOVEMENTS II

Oxford in India Readings in
Sociology and Social Anthropology

GENERAL EDITOR
T.N. MADAN

SOCIAL MOVEMENTS II
Concerns of Equity and Security

edited by
T.K. OOMMEN

OXFORD
UNIVERSITY PRESS

OXFORD

UNIVERSITY PRESS

YMCA Library Building, Jai Singh Road, New Delhi 110 001

Oxford University Press is a department of the University of Oxford. It furthers the
University's objective of excellence in research, scholarship, and education
by publishing worldwide in

Oxford New York

Auckland Cape Town Dar es Salaam Hong Kong Karachi Kuala Lumpur
Madrid Melbourne Mexico City Nairobi New Delhi Shanghai Taipei Toronto

With offices in
Argentina Austria Brazil Chile Czech Republic France Greece Guatemala
Hungary Italy Japan Poland Portugal Singapore South Korea Switzerland
Thailand Turkey Ukraine Vietnam

Oxford is a registered trademark of Oxford University Press
in the UK and in certain other countries

Published in India
by Oxford University Press, New Delhi

© Oxford University Press 2010

The moral rights of the author have been asserted
Database right Oxford University Press (maker)

First published 2010

ISBN-13: 978-019-806328-5
ISBN-10: 019-806328-8

Typeset in Giovanni Book 9.5/11.5 by Jojy Philip
Published by Oxford University Press
YMCA Library Building, Jai Singh Road, New Delhi 110 001

Contents

Tables, Figures, and Box

TABLES

FIGURES

BOX

Preface

This book consists of fifteen chapters divided into three parts. Part One, with seven chapters, is on peasant and labour movements; Part Two, with five chapters, is on women and youth movements; and Part Three with three chapters discusses ecological and environmental movements. Of the fifteen chapters eight are contributed by sociologists/social anthropologists, three by political scientists, two by economists, one by two historians, and one by an ecologist. Thirteen chapters are already published; two in the 1960s, three in the 1970s, two in the 1980s, three in the 1990s, and three between 2000 and 2008. Two chapters are published here for the first time. Thus both the disciplinary and temporal distributions of the chapters are substantial.

In addition to contributing the general introduction and three sectional introductions as editor, I have authored three chapters (3, 12, and 15) in the book. Of the remaining 12 chapters, three are by late Kathleen Gough (Chapter 1), late S.M. Pandey (Chapter 5), and late Ranjit Dwivedi (Chapter 14). These are reproduced here with the permission of publishers. Of the remaining chapters, four are reproduced as they are: Chapter 4 by D.N. Dhanagare, Chapter 6 by Debashish Bhattacherjee, Chapter 7 by Supriya RoyChowdhury, and Chapter 11 by Philip G. Altbach. Three chapters have been condensed with the consent/cooperation of the authors: Chapter 2 by Partha Mukherji, Chapter 8 by Indu Agnihotri and Vina Mazumdar, and Chapter 13 by Vandana Shiva. Chapter 9 by Rajni Palriwala and Chapter

10 by Martha Alter Chen are published in this book for the first time in their current form. I thank all the authors for granting permissions to use their contributions, particularly those who helped to condense their chapters and those who consented to write fresh pieces.

Although I was initiated into research in sociology through my PhD thesis on the Bhoodan–Gramdan movement and sustained that interest in the last half-a-century, I never thought of editing a reader on social movements. The credit for persuading me to undertake this not-so-easy venture goes entirely to T.N. Madan, the General Editor of this series. It gives me great pleasure in thanking him for pressurizing me to undertake this task.

One of the reasons why Indian academics retreat from their research activities after their formal retirement is the inaccessibility of infrastructural facilities, particularly secretarial assistance. I am fortunate in my association with the Schumacher Centre for Development (SCD), New Delhi, as its Chairman where I am ably and most willingly assisted. I thank profusely Indu Ratra for her excellent and meticulous secretarial assistance and D.K. Giri, Director of SCD, for his unflinching support.

T.K. Oommen

Publisher's Acknowledgements

The publisher acknowledges the following for permission to include articles/extracts in this volume.

Economic and Political Weekly for Kathleen Gough, 'Indian Peasant Uprisings', 11 (32–4), August 1974, pp. 1391–412.

Economic and Political Weekly for Partha Mukherji, 'Study of Social Conflicts: Case of Naxalbari Peasant Movement', 22 (38), 1987, pp. 1607–17.

Thomson Press for T.K. Oommen, 'The Bhoodan–Gramdan Movement: An Analysis', in T.K. Oommen, *Charisma, Stability and Change: An Analysis of Bhoodan–Gramdan Movement in India*, New Delhi, 1972, pp. 26–44.

The Japan Center for Area Studies for D.N. Dhanagare, 'The New Farmers' Movement in Maharashtra', in Fumiko Oshikawa (ed.), *South Asia under the Economic Reforms*, Osaka, Japan, 1999, pp. 247–61.

Indian Journal of Labour Economics for S.M. Pandey, 'The Indian Labour Movement: Growth and Character', 9 (1), 1966, pp. 14–39.

Economic and Political Weekly for Debashish Bhattacherjee, 'Globalising Economy, Localising Labour', 14 October 2000, pp. 3758–64.

Economic and Political Weekly for Supriya RoyChowdhury, 'Labour Activism and Women in the Unorganized Sector', 28 May–4 June 2005, pp. 2250–5.

Economic and Political Weekly for Indu Agnihotri and Vina Mazumdar, 'Changing Terms of Political Discourse: Women's Movement in India, 1970s–1990s', 30 (29), 22 July 1995, pp. 1869–78.

University of California Press for Philip G. Altbach, 'The Transformation of the Indian Student Movement', *Asian Survey*, 6 (8), 1966, pp. 448–60.

Political Science Review for T.K. Oommen, 'Student Power in India: A Political Analysis', 14 (1 and 2), 1975, pp. 10–38.

Alternatives for Vandana Shiva, 'Ecology Movements in India', 11, 1986, pp. 255–73.

Sociological Bulletin for Ranjit Dwivedi, 'Parks, People and Protest: The Mediating Role of Environmental Action Groups', 46 (2), 1977, pp. 209–43.

Introduction
On the Analysis of
Social Movements

T.K. OOMMEN

S tudies on social movements are one of the late entries in
social science. One reason for this is that revolutionaries and
intellectuals had recognized the role of the masses in social
transformation only by mid-nineteenth century. Being a concrete
and complex phenomenon, social movements were an ideal field for
ideographic studies, and historians were the first to initiate them. As
political science is invariably involved in analysing contentions about
power it is natural for it to also social movements. Psychologists began
to contribute to the field with the rise of Nazism in Germany and
fascism in Italy as the study of authoritarian personality attributed to
those who led and participated in these movements became a popular
theme. Sociologists and social anthropologists were the last to enter
this field of analysis.

Broadly speaking there were three approaches to the study of social
movements: historical, psychological, and sociological. Historians
pursued the life-cycle approach and traced the career of movements;
they posed the question: how did movements get institutionalized
as conventional structures? Historical case studies focused on the
characteristics of participants and their motivations. But little effort
was made to extrapolate from case studies and formulate hypotheses
and theories. As Charles Tilly noted, historical analysis of movements
are concerned with motives and beliefs of crucial participants who
are taken to be an undifferentiated mass which can be mobilized

into collective action. But a sociological approach abandons the '... indiscriminate use of articulated beliefs as explanations of collective actions, and call attention to the necessity of analysing the development of an ideology, its function for the group which adheres to it, and more generally, the conditions under which a group will fight in the name of a set of beliefs'.[1]

The psychological approach views movements as expressions of individual participants' needs and discontents, its basic assumption is that the aspirations and frustrations of individuals provide motives for participation in movements. This approach focus on the neurotic and psychotic personality traits which prompts participation in movements. While social psychology can contribute to understand the behaviour of individuals and small groups *within* movements, its scope to understand the phenomenon of social movement is limited. The significant and immediate causes for joining movements will be found in the conditions of society rather than in the conditions of leaders' minds or in the pathology of their followers.[2]

A sociological analysis of social movements presupposes a theory of society because collective action is one of the possible responses to crises, which occur in society. Which is to say, in so far as there are different types of society and the structure of deprivations in them vary, a variety of movements emerge, crystallize and fade away in them. Despite this, the tradition of research on social movements is weak in sociology and social anthropology because the dominant paradigm of research in these disciplines was the structural-functional school whose obsession was with order and integration. In contrast, the concern of the study of social movements is change and conflict. Needless to say the structural-functional school did respond to this criticism gradually by including the field of social movement in its ken. But before elaborating on this response it is necessary to correct a widely shared perception that analyses of collective action were totally absent in classical sociology.

THE FOUNDING FATHERS AND THE RECENT TRENDS

It is true that none of the founding fathers—Durkheim, Weber, and Marx—put forward any neat and tidy theories of social movements or collective actions. And yet, it is evident to the discerning eye that incipient explanations of collective actions are ingrained in their analyses of society.

Émile Durkheim lived in a European society characterized by disintegrating social life, disoriented individuals, and extensive social conflicts. His seminal notions of collective conscience and collective representation undergird the idea of collective action; without the first collective action cannot be initiated and without the second the change brought about cannot be articulated. Durkheim first postulated a theory of collective action and that of social change in his *The Division of Labour in Society* (1893). Later in *Elementary Forms of Religious Life* (1915), Durkheim analysed the kind of solidarity that produced, ritualized, and approved forms of collective action. Thus he presents a society strained by a continuous struggle between forces of disintegration (rapid differentiation) and forces of integration (new and renewed commitment to shared beliefs). From this Durkheim derives three different kinds of collective actions—routine, anomic, and restorative.

Routine collective action takes place when development of shared beliefs is equal to or greater than the stress imposed by differentiation. When differentiation continuously outstrips the extent of shared belief anomic collective action is the expected manifestation. Restorative collective action mediates between routine and anomic collective actions and attempts to rescue society from anomic collective action into which it has slipped into from routine collective action. Durkheim's postulation prompts us to expect anomic and restorative collective actions to rise as differentiation accelerates. It leads us to anticipate and find segments of populations, which are newly emerging and/or displaced by differentiation engaged in collective actions. It predicts a close association among suicide, crime, violence and non-routine collective actions. It is clear that several theories of collective action, which were popular in the twentieth century, embody some version of the Durkheimian argument.[3]

Durkheimian argument largely neglects mobilization and subsequent institutionalization. Therefore we should expect a sharp discontinuity between routine and non-routine collective actions; their causes, content and consequences will differ significantly. Further, we should assume that faster and more extensive social change will lead to more widespread anomic and restorative forms of collective actions. Consequently, rapid industrialization and urbanization will necessarily produce exceptionally high levels of conflict and protest. We also need to admit that individual disorder and collective protest are closely tied to each other and sometimes even indistinguishable. Implied in this is the assumption that the more coherent and compelling a group's beliefs, the less likely it is to engage in disorderly behaviour. Logically, we have to admit that shifts in individual dissatisfactions and anxieties are the strongest and most reliable predictors of collective contestations. Some version of the Durkheimian formulation has been the dominant explanation of collective action for close to a century and it still appeals to many.

Max Weber portrayed collective action as the outgrowth of commitments to certain systems of belief. Weberians, like Durkheimians, tend to propose different explanations for routine and non-routine collective actions. In the non-routine form shared beliefs of the group have a strong, direct impact on the groups' collective action. While action routinizes, two changes occur: organizations crystallize to mediate between the beliefs of actors and group interests play a larger and more direct role in collective action. In Weber's view, groups commit themselves to collective definitions of the world and of themselves and the definitions, in turn, incorporate goals, entail standards of behaviour and include justifications of the power of authorities. Constituted authorities act on behalf of the groups based on their traditional, rational-legal or charismatic roles. Which of these bases that the group adopts goes on to affect its organization and its fate? In Weber's account then, the structure and action of the group as a whole spring largely from the initial commitment to a particular kind of belief system, which has its own logic and force.

According to Weber, religious and ideological leaders are continuously formulating new definitions of the world and of themselves.[4] Only a few of them, however, attract followers. In those cases where it happens, the followers commit themselves to the belief system, the charismatic leader and to the objects and rituals consecrated by those beliefs and the leaders. If more people find the new definitions as meaningful they join the existing group of followers and it expands. Then the group as a whole faces the problem of routinization of charisma.

Weber's discussion of routinization of charisma fits well into his general theory of social change. He postulates that traditional authority creates an equilibrium of social life if no disruption occurs. But two opposing forces of disruption are perennially present—the authority of rationality and the power of charisma. Bureaucratic rationality can be a revolutionary force against tradition, it revolutionizes through techniques. Charisma works exactly in the opposite way; first transforming the inner life of people and then inducing people to transform their worlds. Weber thus gives us a dramatic and compelling sense of social change as product of the eruption of charisma into history and diffusion of rationality through history. And yet he offers no theory of the circumstances under which charismatic movements arise. Consequently, Weber's followers had to complement their analyses of the life-courses of movements with non-Weberian explanation as to why people initiated and joined movements.

Weber, like Durkheim, suggests that rapid social change will produce widespread non-routine collective actions. However, Weber changes the course of his analysis by suggesting that there are two main categories of collective actors; those oriented to deviant beliefs and those oriented to beliefs, which are routinized and have won general acceptance. Accordingly, Weberian theory also suggests that commitment to a group is an incentive, rather than a barrier to participation in collective action, including non-routine collective action. Contemporary analysts invariably invoke Weberian explanations to understand collective actions of nation-states and complex organizations and they are less likely to apply Weber to the collective actions of political and revolutionary groups. This is so because the Weberian framework is largely silent on the issue of mobilization—a necessary aspect of social movements. Those who follow Weber[5] combine Weberian ideas with those of others, notably those of Marx. And yet, Weberians have pursued analyses of collective actions more persistently and effectively, than say, Durkheimians. On the other hand, all movements cannot be explained based on class inequality, as for example, movements which emanate from status deprivation. This explains the durability of the Weberian framework in understanding collective actions.

Karl Marx's analysis of collective action was more systematic, as compared with those of Durkheim and Weber. Notwithstanding a century of acute criticism the basic argument he proposed in *The Eighteenth Brumaire of Louis Bonaparte* (1852) and *The Class Struggles in France, 1848–50* (1895) stood the test of time. There are two aspects to the ideas propounded by Marx in this context. Implicitly, he divides the entire population into social classes based on their relationship to the prevailing means of production. Explicitly, Marx identified the major visible actors in politics with their class bases, pronouncing judgements about their basic interests, conscious aspirations, articulated grievances and readiness for collective action. Broadly, the tenor of the argument is that individuals and institutions act on behalf of particular social classes, save the case of those who run the state who may occasionally act in terms of their political interest ignoring class base.

In analysing the readiness to act, Marx attached great importance to the ease and durability of communication within the class and to the visible pressures of the class enemy. When political actors act, they do so out of common interests, mutual awareness and the internal organization. As compared to other analysts Marx attached little importance to generalized tension, momentary impulses and personal disorganization. However, it is not self-evident that social classes and their representatives are the principal actors in politics. Similarly, it is not true that prior organization is a prerequisite for a group's readiness to act; collective actions can be sudden and instantaneous. Finally, participants in mass movements may ignore their interest; they could be altruistic. That is, Marxian theory over-emphasizes the collective rationality of political action.

Although Marx's theory sounds familiar, even obvious to many now, in the nineteenth century it broke decisively with the prevailing accounts of mass action. Because the then theorists treated people as incapable of continuous and calculating pursuit of their collective interests and caricatured masses as responding mainly to impulses and to manipulation by the elite. Marx, on the contrary, believed in human beings' capacity for creative collective action. This faith in humanity, to be its own creator, is the chief merit of Marx's analysis.

Since Marx, interpretations about his analysis or school of thought have varied considerably in the relative weight and autonomy they have assigned to the variables that Marx had invoked. These analyses have also varied in recognizing the role and significance of collectivities other than classes—gender, religious, regional and caste groups. In fact, many who fall under the Marxist tradition do not qualify to be labelled as Marxists in the strict sense of the term. But they stand apart from the followers of Durkheim and Weber as they insist on the priority of material interests and in following the general logic of Marx's explanation of collective action. Two prominent examples are Moore Jr. and Wolf.[6] But neither of them analyses collective actions of industrial proletariat but those of peasantry.

In locating the seeds of collective actions in classical sociology it may be noted that Durkheimian structural differentiation and Weberian rationality assume the displacement of traditional collectivism with modern individualism and did not provide space for modern collectivism. In contrast, the two antagonistic classes and the collective actions evident in their confrontations as postulated by Marx produce modern collectivism. But they too did not account for the collective actions of non-class antagonistic social categories such as race, gender, generation, nationalities and the like. When 'post-class' and 'post-modern' movements whether feminist, youth, peace, environmental/ecological or national/ethnic crystallized in the West the existing frameworks within sociology could not explain them. Two theoretical responses surfaced in this context. One suggested that structural strain always existed in societies and that mobilization required both resources and a rational orientation to action. The participants in movements are not swayed by sentiments, emotions, and ideologies. The rational choice theory, as it came to be known, argued that collective action should be understood in terms of the logic of costs and benefits as well as opportunities of resource mobilization.[7]

The second response crystallized into the notion of new social movements (NSMs). The salient points upheld by theorists of NSMs are: (a) the social background of movement participants are structurally diffuse; (b) NSMs cannot be characterized in terms of ideology, they represent a variety of ideas and values; (c) the NSMs give birth to new identities or reinvent old ones; (d) in the case of NSMs the relation between the individuals is blurred, they often embody counter cultures; (e) NSMs are concerned with intimate aspects of human life such as dietary practices, dress patterns, sexuality and the like; (f) NSMs resort to new mobilization styles characterized by non-violence and civil disobedience; (g) NSMs interrogate the legitimacy and styles of functioning of traditional political parties and may give birth to new types of political parties (for example, The Green Party); and (h) NSMs tend to be diffuse, decentralized and segmented.[8]

DEFINING SOCIAL MOVEMENTS

Having identified the seeds of the theories of collective action in the writings of the founding fathers, it is imperative to understand the sense in which the notion of social movement is understood in contemporary sociology. This is necessary because as a term it is one of the most widely used and yet one of the least precise. For example, in the first textbook on modern social movements to be published in America,[9] a multitude of topics are included: Plato's republic, Thomas Moore's utopia, Marx's socialism, Mussolini's fascism, Gandhi's non-violence, and the cooperative movement, the labour movement, the peace movement, to mention but a few. The list includes not only movements (collective actions) but also idea systems. But the term social movement should be used more restrictively in referring only to collective actions. However, in doing so, a new problem may surface. Collective actions are of several types: panic responses, hostile outbursts and organized social actions.[10] The first two in the list above couldn't be labelled as movements, for they are relatively short-term, unorganized outbursts and are not necessarily inspired by an ideology or prompted by an issue. Therefore, only when an elementary collective action (the crowd behaviour, mass action) '…acquires organization and form, a body of customs and traditions, established leadership, an enduring division of labour, social rules and social values, in short—a culture, a social organization, and a new scheme of life', it becomes a social movement.[11]

A persisting source of confusion in using the term social movement emanates from the fact that it is possible to speak of 'general' social movements in which the participants have certain common interests and these are pursued in many different, even uncoordinated ways. Examples of such general social movements are the labour movement, the youth movement and the like. One can also use the term to refer to 'specific' movements within a general category as for example, the trade union movement and youth hostels' movement. Again, while on the one hand social movements are believed to be creative attempts to initiate social change they have also been perceived as pathological in character and those who belong to the movement (leaders and followers) are characterized as frustrated individuals.[12] Finally, the qualifying adjectives used to refer to social movements are too varied: 'radical', 'messianic', 'nativistic', 'fascist', 'non-violent', 'religious', 'socialist' 'secular' to recall some. Therefore certain measure of conceptual precision will be of great help to understand the phenomenon of social movement. Keeping this consideration in mind it is necessary (a) to discuss the characteristics of social movements; and (b) to identify the major components of social movements.

In order to identify the characteristics of social movements, the defining criteria of social movements as employed by ten writers have been used. The summary statement is presented in Table 1. The defining criteria employed by the selected authors are: goal, means, scope and content. To start with, it may be interesting to note that sociologists who have studied movements in their own or other 'complex' societies qualify them by the adjective 'political/social' (Abel, Blumer, Zald and Ash, Wendell King) and anthropologists who have studied movements in societies other than their own, which are usually 'simple' societies employ adjectives such as 'messianic' (Barber), 'nativist' (Linton), 'revitalization' (Wallace), and the like. Only Eisenstadt and Smelser speak of movements, which belong to different societies or cultures. While the former writes on 'nationalistic' movements in the New Nations, the latter refers to movements in a variety of societies. It appears that the labels used by these writers are conditioned by the nature of society in which they undertook investigations and the specific type of movements they have observed. For instance, all sociologists who have studied complex societies consider the goal of movements to be 'change' and all anthropologists speak of the goal as system stability, regeneration or maintenance. Even Wallace who considers social movements as change-orientated indicates that the goal is to revitalize the system. In contradistinction to this either/or (change/stability) position, Eisenstadt notes the possibility of nationalistic movements in underdeveloped countries simultaneously orientated to modern *and* traditional values thereby indicating that social movements may be oriented either to change, or stability and solidarity. Smelser distinguishes between norm-orientated movements and value-orientated movements and suggests that those who subscribe to a movement envision the restoration, protection, modification, or creation of social norms or values. That is to say, a movement may pursue either change *or* stability as its goal.

However, the observations regarding the differing orientations of sociologists and social anthropologists are applicable only when the latter study 'other cultures'. When anthropologists study their own societies/cultures the labelling invoked vary. For example, the Indian anthropologist Roy Burman[13] refers to proto-national and sub-national movements among tribal communities of India. Proto-national movements emerge when tribes experience a transformation from 'tribalism' to nationalism; it is a search for identity at a higher level of integration. In contrast, sub-national movements are responses to deepening disparities brought about by the ongoing process of development.

The second defining criteria of social movements used by the authors are the 'means' employed to attain their goals. It is surprising that not a single author referred to, made a systematic effort to distinguish and characterize movements based on the means employed; only two out of the ten writers refer to it at all. Moreover, there seems to be some confusion between means and content. For instance, Wallace speaks of religious and secular means. It seems, the religious-secular dichotomy is more appropriate in characterizing the content of movements. It is true that people, particularly in 'tribal' societies, resort to magical or religious means to achieve certain goals. But usually, it operates at the individual or family/kin-group level. At any rate, 'means' as used by Wallace cannot be meaningfully linked to the goal 'movements' pursue.

Abel refers to the 'new mode of procedure' (means) employed for goal-attainment as a distinguishing feature of social movements. However, he does not make it clear what is meant by a new mode of procedure. When one takes cognizance of the empirical situation one is struck by two types of means employed by social movements to pursue their goals: violent or non-violent. If one is to distinguish clearly between movements, which are orientated to total change of the system yet employing radically different means, we need to recognize the importance of the kind of means they employ, violent or non-violent.

Only five of the ten authors whose attempts to define social movements are presented in Table 1 employ the scope of the movement as a distinguishing criterion of social movements, and, of these, only

Table 1: Defining Criteria of Social Movements*

S. No.	Authors	Label Used	Defining Criteria Employed			
			Goal	*Means*	*Scope*	*Content*
1.	T. Abel[14]	Political	Change	Novel Means	Spatial & Societal	Not Employed
2.	B. Barber[15]	Messianic	Stability	Not Employed	Not Employed	Not Employed
3.	H. Blumer[16]	Social	Change	Not Employed	General/Specific	Not Employed
4.	S.N. Eisenstadt[17]	Nationalistic	Change/ Stability	Not Employed	Not Employed	Religious/Secular
5.	R. Heberle[18]	Social	Change	Not Employed	Societal	Not Employed
6.	R. Linton[19]	Nativistic	Stability/ Regeneration	Not Employed	Societal	Magical/Rational
7.	N.J. Smelser[20]	Norm-oriented and Value-oriented	Change/Stability	Not Employed	General/Specific	Secular/Religious
8.	Wendell King[21]	Social	Change	Not Employed	Not Employed	Not Employed
9.	A.F.C. Wallace[22]	Revitalization	Change	Religious/Secular	Not Employed	Not Employed
10.	M.N. Zald and R. Ash[23]	Social	Change	Not Employed	Not Employed	Not Employed

Note: * As noted earlier the first book on social movements was published in 1930. For one decade following that there was hardly any published account of movements. The 10 studies selected belong to the period 1941–66, that is, for quarter of a century.

Abel includes both the spatial and societal aspects in referring to the scope of movement. According to him, the greater the geographical coverage of a movement, the greater is its scope. Again, the more complex the society a movement tries to change, the greater its scope. Other writers refer to the scope of a movement only in terms of the aspects of the society the movement covers. It seems to be rewarding to recognize both the spatial and societal dimensions while referring to the scope of a movement. The scope of a particular movement may cover all aspects of society but may be confined to a limited locale. Another movement may concentrate only on one aspect of social life but may have a global spread. These movements would differ significantly in terms of their scope and hence it is important to recognize both the spatial and societal dimensions of a movement.

Content is employed as a distinguishing criteria only by three of the writers. All of them characterize movements either as religious or secular. (Linton's terms, magical and rational, are rough equivalents of religious and secular.) As has been pointed out earlier, one may consider the religious/secular orientation of a movement as an important criterion for distinguishing movements.

In the light of these considerations I suggest that social movements should be conceptualized as those purposive collective mobilizations, informed of an ideology to promote change or stability, using any means—violent or non-violent—and functioning within at least an elementary organizational framework.[24]

INDIAN CONTRIBUTIONS

There are some Indian authors who grappled with some of the theoretical and conceptual issues in the study of social movements but only after the period (1941–66) on which Table 1 focuses. For example, Mukherji classified movements based on the *quality* of change—accumulative, alterative and transformative—they pursue.[25] While accumulative changes are intra-systemic, the latter two are systemic changes; alterative change is geared to create new structures and transformative change aims at replacing the existing structure. But one creates new structures to replace or substitute the existing ones, therefore the distinction between the alterative and transformative change is ambiguous. Mukherji also distinguishes between three types of movements based on the nature of change they pursue: collective mobilization geared to alteration or transformation of the structures of a system is a *social* movement; collective mobilization aimed at wide ranging changes in the major institutional system is a *revolutionary* movement and collective mobilization aimed at change within the system is a *quasi-movement*. This postulation implies that (a) revolutionary means suit only movements, which pursue systemic changes, and (b) revolutionary goals can be pursued only through revolutionary means. But such postulations do not fit empirical realities. Revolutionary goals are pursued through non-revolutionary (non-violent) means and non-revolutionary goals could be pursued through revolutionary (violent) means. At any rate, Mukherji's analysis cannot account for movements, which have system stability as their goals.

Rao distinguishes between three levels of structural changes and on that basis three types of social movements—reformist, transformative and revolutionary.[26] Reform movements bring about partial changes in the value system, transformative movements aim at effecting middle-level (?) structural changes, and the objective of revolutionary movements is to bring about radical changes in the totality of social and cultural systems. These movements also vary in terms of the intensity of conflicts; conflict is least in reform movements, it acquires a sharper focus in transformative movements, and in the case of revolutionary movements conflict is based on class struggle.

There are several difficulties in the classification of movements as suggested by Rao. One, reform and revolutionary movements are distinguished based on the quantum of change, partial or total. Second, reform and transformative movements are distinguished in terms of where the change occurs; in the case of the former, change occurs in the value system and in the case of the latter it takes place at the middle level of the structure. Rao violates the principles of exhaustiveness and exclusiveness in classification (of movements) by shifting the defining criteria, which creates several problems. For example, if a movement pursues either partial middle-level structural change or total middle-level structural change, what would be its designation? How does one classify a movement, which aims at partial as against total change in the value system of a movement, or a movement that pursues revolutionary changes through non-violent means? How does one account for intense violent conflicts in the course of mobilizing primordial collectivities rather than classes? These and several other equally pertinent questions cannot be answered in the framework proposed by Rao.

Indian scholarship on social movements since the 1980s[27] largely falls in line with the existing conceptualizations/theorizations of social movements depending upon the theoretical orientations they adopt—structural-functional or Marxist. Although they do not make or claim any conceptual/theoretical breakthrough, they do make significant contributions towards a clearer understanding of the empirical situation in India. The prevailing consensus is that social movements cause/contribute to social change. While it is suggested that social movements aim to bring about an egalitarian and just society there is no consensus regarding what constitutes equity and justice. But the fact is that movements opposing equity and justice by the socially privileged especially when empowerment of the socially underprivileged is attempted, is not adequately taken cognizance of.

The first book on social movements in independent India by an Indian sociologist was by Oommen, published in 1972. He distinguishes between three ideal types of movements: ideological, organizational and charismatic, based on which the three crucial elements of a movement emerge—ideology, organization or leadership. This typology is based on the assumption that when societies or communities within them experience strain, mechanisms viz., formulating a new ideology, establishing a new organization or throwing up a new leadership are likely to emerge. Irrespective of which movement component emerges first, other components too will have to emerge subsequently if it has to become a social movement. However, one of the aspects—ideology, organization, leadership—will acquire primacy at different phases in the course of the career of all movements.

Through a case study of Bhoodan-gramdan movement, Oommen[28] interrogates Max Weber's theory of social change which invoked charisma as the force that triggered change. It has been argued that the attributes of charisma are not given forever; they are contextually determined. That is, charisma can be both a system changing and a system-stabilizing force, depending upon the context. While charismatic movements can, and do initiate change through collective actions, in translating movement goals into reality an organizational build-up becomes inevitable. In this process, there occurs considerable erosion of charisma and the movement may become a mechanism for pattern maintenance and tension management[29] experiencing erosion in its potentiality to bring about change.

Most books on social movements by Indian authors are case studies of particular social movements, except two,[30] which are state-of-the-art statements about movement studies. However, none of the Indian studies claim that they are making contributions to a general theory of social movements. But a later study[31] does make such a claim, and therefore it is necessary to examine briefly (for want of space) the validity of some of these claims.

First, Singh claims that abandoning the conventional conceptualization of society anchored to the classical Newtonian Physics and adopting the contemporary Einsteinian Physics, will provide a better understanding of society. But it is not made clear how this shift can equip the researcher to recognize the human agent's unique capacity to create and attribute meanings, that is, the ability to make symbols. In fact the field of Physics, which deals only with matter is simpler than even the field of biology, which analyses both matter and life. The field of social sciences, particularly sociology and social anthropology, which deals with culture, the crux of which lies in the ability to create symbols, cannot be modelled after material or life sciences, in spite of their vogue in social science.[32] Therefore, Singh's claim that 'reflexive empiricism' a methodological device he proposes can comprehend both nature and society equally well is untenable.[33]

Second, Singh commits a familiar mistake shared by most social scientists. He invokes the phrase 'Indian Society' ignoring the warning administered by Zygmunt Bauman[34] about the persisting tendency to conflate society and nation-state. In West Europe, the cradle of sociology and nation-state, where the two have intended co-terminality, this conflation is perhaps understandable. But the territory of Indian state is home to several 'nations' and societies. This is not to deny the over-arching unity of 'Indian civilization'. But the region of Indian civilization transcends the territory of the Indian state and encapsulates the whole of South Asia. Therefore, what are designated as 'regional', 'sub-national', 'linguistic', and 'tribal' movements by Singh, and most other sociologists as well, are actually national/societal movements.

A third difficulty in Singh's position emanates from the series of 'post-isms'—post-society, post-sociology, post-modernism—that he postulates. If these entities are 'post', logically, movements too should have a post phase! How, in the world of postisms, can movements alone retain their pre-post phase? Similarly, Singh refers to both 'old' and 'new' social movements. But this seems to be inadmissable in the Indian context.

Fourth, Singh suggests that conventional social movement studies in India have ignored everyday resistance, which I have called everyday protest.[35] However, everyday protest does not displace organized collective actions; they are not mutually exclusive but exist in different contexts and levels. Singh repeatedly insists that movements just happen, they are not created or led. Without subscribing to the idea of inevitability of heroes one can easily observe that leadership is a necessary component of movements. Even for everyday resistance to happen some amount of organization and initiative by grass-root leaders are prerequisites if they are not to remain ephemeral and individual and become continuous and collective.

Fifth, Singh argues rightly that a movement is engaged in the reproduction of society through conflict. However, it constitutes only one of the agencies for the reproduction of society; the cooperative dimension is also important to the reproduction of society. In fact cooperation is much more widespread, than conflict, although movement researchers do not focus on it. Society is the product of cooperation, which produces structures *and* conflict, which in turn produce movements. To assign the entirety of society to one of these—cooperation or conflict—is to mistake a part for the whole.

Finally, Singh argues that movements do not *cause* change; they are the very expression of change. The relationship between movement and social change is that between the proverbial chicken and egg, it is impossible to decipher which comes first. Without some social change, social movements cannot be triggered off, and social movements in turn accelerate change. This explains the relative absence of social movements in 'authoritarian' societies and their high frequency in 'democratic' ones. It should also be remembered that social movements could decelerate and prevent change, thereby causing social stability.

TOWARDS A TYPOLOGY OF MOVEMENTS

A multiplicity of groups coexist and mobilize themselves into collective actions to pursue their interests in most polities. In this endeavour, it is not unlikely that some of these collectivities would perceive a conflict between their goals and the 'national' interests. A classification of social movements should therefore take into account at least two factors: (a) the bases of group formation, that is, the type of collectivities, and (b) the nature of goals these movements pursue.

Group formations are based on a variety of factors. However, for the present purpose I propose to categorize them into 'biological' and 'spatial' collectivities (for example, gender, race, age and regional/local groups), 'civil' collectivities (for example, workers, peasants, students, professionals) and 'primordial' collectivities (for example, linguistic, religious, caste groups). The rationale of the three-fold categorization of collectivities—biological/spatial, primordial and civil—should be noted here; they can be placed on a fixed-flexible continuum. It is not suggested that the attributes of the biological collectivities are immutable; indeed they change gradually over time buttressed by socio-cultural factors, but as compared with other collectivities they are more stable. Similarly, particular individuals and groups may immigrate into and migrate out of a region but there will always be inhabitants who live in specific places and share common civic interests in maintaining the 'integrity' of those spaces. The attributes of civil collectivities are a product almost entirely of the socialization/enculturation process and amenable to quicker changes as compared with other collectivities. The attributes of primordial collectivities are ascribed and deeply internalized and hence slow to change. Given the relative fixed-flexible continuum, the possibility of crystallization of collective conscience also varies among these collectivities. In the case of biological/spatial collectivities, it is easier, and in the case of civil collectivities it is gradual and prolonged. The case of primordial collectivities comes in between.

The nature of goals that social movements pursue may be categorized into two: instrumental and symbolic. Instrumental goals are those oriented towards the reallocation of wealth and power, and symbolic goals are those that are geared towards the redefinition of status and privilege. Movements may pursue any one of these goals or they may combine both instrumental and symbolic goals.

Mobilization of a collectivity implies its active involvement and conscious participation in terms of the goals pursued. In turn, crystallization of collective consciousness is not only a precondition for mobilization, but takes place, as the very process of mobilization proceeds. The understanding of this intricate intertwining between the nature of attributes of a collectivity, the prospects of its mobilization and the shaping of its consciousness is of utmost importance for an adequate understanding of social movements. If we tabulate the two dimensions, collectivity types and nature of goals, a typology of movement emerges (see Table 2). However, these nine types of movements are not mutually exclusive. Thus, caste mobility movements may begin with symbolic goals (higher ritual status), but may later tend to pursue instrumental goals (political representation) as well. Similarly, a civil collectivity (for example, agricultural labour) may have a predominantly primordial base (that is, of SC origin) and hence may combine both instrumental (increase in wages) and symbolic (eradication of untouchability) goals. The point is that not only are there overlaps between the movements of a given collectivity but the goals they pursue may also undergo shifts over time.

The types of social movements as identified in Table 2 vary in terms of their consequences for the system. For example, movements which pursue exclusively symbolic goals (cases 1, 4, and 7) rarely question the basic values and principles involved in the prevalent distribution of goods and services, they only strive towards a change *in* the system. Similarly, movements, which pursue exclusively instrumental goals, (cases 2, 5, and 8) are also capable of bringing about change *within* the system only. But some of these movements may cause structural transformation, that is, change *of* the system, through an accretive process. For example, lowering the age at franchise can bring about a change in the distribution of political power in favour of the youth, if (a) they constitute a substantial proportion of the population, (b) political consciousness based on age crystallizes, and (c) exercise their entitlements to vote. Similarly, workers' movements for sharing of profit, if successful, can gradually undermine capitalism as a system.

Table 2: Types of Social Movements Based on the Nature of Collectivity and Goals Pursued

S. No.	Type of Collectivity	Nature of Goals	Typical Movements
1.	Biological	Symbolic	Movement for increasing/decreasing the age at marriage; right of admission to public places by women/blacks.
2.	Biological	Instrumental	Movement by women for equal wages; youth movement for lowering the age of franchise.
3.	Biological	Both Symbolic and Instrumental	Movement of a racial category for establishing a new nation-state.
4.	Primordial	Symbolic	Caste mobility movements; conversion or reform movements of religious collectivities; linguistic collectivities fighting for cultural identity.
5.	Primordial	Instrumental	Movement of religious/linguistic/caste/tribal groups for political representation, economic entitlements.
6.	Primordial	Symbolic and Instrumental	Secessionist movements by religious, linguistic, or tribal collectivities.
7.	Civil	Symbolic	Workers' movement to get May Day declared as a holiday.
8.	Civil	Instrumental	Students' movement for participation in university decisional processes; workers' demand for sharing of profits with owners.
9.	Civil	Symbolic and Instrumental	A large number of movements but particularly ecology/environment movements.

The case of movements, which combine both symbolic and instrumental goals is quite different. As for civil collectivities, such movements exist in large numbers but are rarely a threat to the polity although of course the governing elite could/may be replaced through such movements. In the case of biological collectivities only a racial group with regional concentration provides a basis for the emergence of movements, which combines symbolic and instrumental goals, can pose a threat to the polity. The possibility of the emergence of movements threatening the state is the greatest when the collective actors are constituted by primordial groupings such as religious, linguistic or tribal groups. Insofar as these collectivities are geographically concentrated and pursue both symbolic and instrumental goals simultaneously, secession is a plausible demand. The kernel of a state are its territorial integrity and political sovereignty. Any attempt to question its political sovereignty by the constituent units or any tendency towards extra-territorial loyalty by any section of its population is a sure indicator of a crisis of legitimacy that the state faces.

Among the biological collectivities neither gender nor age groups can fundamentally challenge the existence of a state, as they cannot form an alternate society. One cannot conceive of a state population composed exclusively of the male or the female, as the process of biological reproduction would come to a halt in such a society. This is despite the fact that separate settlements of men and women may exist as social isolates and a few babies could be produced by artificial insemination. Similarly, a particular age group—old, adult, youth—cannot constitute a self-perpetuating society and hence a state. Among the biological collectivities, only race with a territorial anchorage provides an adequate basis for the formation of a state, as noted above. On the other hand, even when race and territoriality coexist, these may not automatically lend themselves to state formation as in the case of Africa, wherein tribe or kinship are important elements of social organization.

The civil collectivities do not demand the formation of a separate state through a process of secession. Some of these collectivities (for example, industrial proletariat, peasantry, university students) may assume a vanguard role in bringing about radical social transformation, either through revolution (forceful capturing of political authority) or through reform (gradual displacement of old structures and values through a process of creating new structures and values). But these cannot be construed as threats to the state as an institution; they are attempts to redefine the existing values or to refashion the prevalent structures in favour of one or another civil collectivity within the state. This means that the real threat to the state emanates from primordial collectivities.

Because of these considerations, this book leaves out only movements, which are explicitly 'political', for example, movements that seek to establish a new sovereign state, such as anti-colonial or secessionist movements. However, some theorists invoke the notion of 'social movement' rather restrictively. For example, Touraine distinguishes between three conceptions of social movements.

The first of these conceptions is centred on the actor and his pursuit of his interest; the second is the functioning and, more especially, dysfunctioning of the political institutions for dealing with conflicts; the third on the central social conflict which takes shape around the appropriation of historicity and hence a society's capacity for development.[36]

Touraine insists that social movement analysts should follow the third conception and reject the first two. The implications of accepting this suggestion are far reaching. First, numerous movements which pursue the specific interests of participants cannot be included in movement analysis. Second, movements which are against political institutions will not qualify to be considered as movements. Third, social movements which are capable of bringing about change *of* the system are only social movements proper. This vein of defining social movement is too narrow and hence contested.[37] We need to follow an *optimal* view of social movements, that is, while excluding those movements, which explicitly pursue the political goal of establishing sovereign states, we should include all social movements which pursue change or stability of the system and in the system.

WHY DO MOVEMENTS EMERGE?

According to Davis, a social movement emerges to meet a 'new-felt need'.[38] Barber asserts that there exists a positive correlation between messianic movements and deprivations of various types.[39] Blumer contends that social movements arise out of 'undefined or unstructured situations', which cause stresses in the system.[40] Wallace opines that revitalization movements start only when the participants of a culture feel that the system is unsatisfactory.[41] Linton holds that nativistic movements are primarily attempts to compensate for the frustrations of the society's members.[42] Banks point out that social movements are functions of dissatisfaction with the existing order.[43] Abel argues that a movement is directed against something which it hopes to combat and eliminate, and the motivations behind the collective effort are the modifications to existing social arrangements.[44] All these writers note that, and, of course, many more can be added to the list, social movements emerge due to certain mal-integration in society. Therefore, it is necessary to discuss this proposition in some detail.

The structural–functional approach, for which role is the basic unit of analysis, views change in terms of three basic processes— structural differentiation, reintegration and adaptation. According to this sequential model of change, a movement may appear in any one of the stages depending upon certain system conditions. Thus, emergence of specialized and autonomous units, elaboration of division of labour and intensification of role specialization may release considerable stresses and strains in the system, depriving one or another social category, which in turn may inspire movements. But these movements are viewed as temporary aberrations, essentially pathological, indeed indicative of transient anomies. Movements are therefore incapable of effecting long term and continuous processes of change. In contrast, specialization permits maximum control of the system by assuming more effective roles and creating more efficient units. In this rendition, movements are products of tensions released by structural differentiation and tension-management mechanisms by specialized role incumbents. Since differentiation renders prevalent roles and norms obsolete, it is necessary to develop new mechanisms of reintegration, which follows a three-phase model. Due to dissatisfaction, individuals no longer perform roles adequately; this is followed by protests by the deprived that organize movements, and finally, new mechanisms of regulation and coordination, such as unions, associations and welfare agencies, are created to mobilize resources and commitments. A more flexible and specialized system inevitably emerges. Thus, movements are viewed as adaptive mechanisms in a period of rapid social change. With adaptation change is institutionalized.[45]

The basic flaws of this approach are three: one, it does not specify the source of deprivation; two, it considers human beings as mere creatures of societal determinism, sapping them of their creative vitality, and three, its unit of analysis namely role, is not appropriate for analysing movements. One can locate a variety of sources of deprivation in all systems but ultimately what disturbs people in egalitarian societies is their distance from the centre of the system. Insofar as they occupy positions on the periphery of a system, they may be deprived in terms of wealth, power or privilege, or of different combinations of them. In this sense, social movements are mechanisms through which human beings attempt to move from the periphery of a system to its centre. That is, movements are conscious efforts on their part to mitigate deprivation and secure justice. Second, while movements are conditioned by social-structural factors, it also implies voluntaristic action; participants create movements to achieve the goals they hold dear. Third, movements are perhaps the chief mechanism through which the deprived categories demonstrate their power. United by an ideology, they create organizational devices to fight the evils and redress grievances. Once a social category develops commitments to a movement's ideology and organization, their mobilization may be relatively smooth. Thus, movements emerge when human beings committed to a specified set of goals participate in protest-oriented, purposive collective actions. Therefore, its crucial aspects are mobilization and institutionalization. It seems then, that in order to analyse movements adequately, one has to focus on these aspects and not on roles.

One of the vexing issues in movement analysis is how participants develop commitment to a specified set of goals; to an ideology. It needs to be emphasized here that contrary to what Marx thought, while structural similarity may be a necessary condition it may not be a sufficient one for the development of shared consciousness. At any rate, given the multidimensionality of structural positioning of individuals and groups, those with a similar position in one dimension may not share the same position with regard to other dimensions. Therefore, it is necessary to recognize the importance of the divergence in structural positions of individuals and groups, the efforts needed to arouse their consciousness, the likelihood of conflicts crystallizing in the process of their mobilization, and the desirability of institutionalization of collective efforts to translate ideals into reality.

Mobilization of people into collective actions assumes the existence of a certain level of uniformity among participants based on their interests rooted in socio-economic background and ideas emanating from their political orientations and ideological commitments. Much of the problem in movement analysis stems from the presumed relationship or degree of correlation between these dimensions. While it is largely true that 'consciousness of kind' will not automatically follow the occupancy of similar structural positions, it seems that occupying comparable structural positions facilitates the crystallization of consciousness relatively easily. Thus, membership in ascriptive groups invariably facilitates the development of primordial collectivism due to the heavy weight of traditional values inculcated through the socialization process, the relatively stable character of their position in the social structure and the style of life associated with primordial collectivities. In contrast, membership in civil collectivities (the assumption here is that mobility is possible and that it does occur) may not easily facilitate the development of consciousness among the members of these social categories unless individuals and groups are made aware of their structural similarity. That is, civil collectivism is the resultant of not only objective conditions but also subjective perceptions. The point to be emphasized here is that mobilization of participants into collective actions is easier if certain of their structural attributes are undermined. Which of these attributes are of strategic significance in the mobilizational process is at least partly determined by the principles of social organization existing in that society.

Admittedly, system characteristics of a society affect the ethos and the style of functioning of social movements in that society. A 'pre-political' society may mainly express its values in a religious vocabulary; its mobilizational efforts may be based on 'communal' attachments. But with the emergence of a 'modern' state this vocabulary may be redefined to suit new conditions; it may be transformed into 'secular'. However, this is not to suggest that the transformation is neat and tidy and that communal and secular orientations will not co-exist. Similarly, mobilizational efforts may be increasingly anchored to civil collectivities as societies modernize. But, movements will neither have the potentialities to root out the features of the existing system completely nor will they succumb to the traditional structures entirely. Essentially then, social movements provide the stage for confluence between the old and new values, and structures.

It is widely acknowledged that there are different routes to change and collective action is but one of them. While recognizing this, it is necessary to ask and answer the question, why does a collectivity resort to mobilization as a route to change? One can certainly list a multiplicity of structural determinants, which facilitate the emergence of social movements, but it seems that the most critical factor is dissatisfaction about the conditions, which exist in society. Marx, for example, held the view that progressive degradation of the proletariat would finally reach the point of inevitable despair and revolt. But it is not those at the rock bottom who feel utterly deprived.[46] Second, dissatisfaction existed for centuries in societies but the phenomenon of social movement was not widespread. That is, only when dissatisfaction contains elements of deprivation, collective actions will emerge. Third, movements may trigger off when a short period of economic reversal follows a prolonged period of economic prosperity. That is a combination of high expectations and socio-economic setbacks leads to widespread frustration triggering collective actions.

Two points need to be underlined here. One, social movements are not always brought about by a decline from bad to worse. People who endured oppression for centuries may suddenly burst into collective action against the yoke, the moment it becomes lighter. Inevitable evils suddenly become intolerable once the idea of escape from them surfaces; that is, when political conditions change. Two, the baseline from which expectations emanate and where such expectations meet with increasing frustration is important. That is, the extent of the gap between expectations and satisfactions is crucial. If strains are accepted as facts of life there is no possibility of challenging the status quo. But when the belief that problems can be solved, through human actions, mobilization against the present arrangement becomes a possibility.

The foregoing discussion suggests that an adequate framework for the study of social movements should take into account the dialectics between historicity (past experiences), social structure (present existential conditions), and the urge for a better future (human creativity). That is, a theory of social movements implies not only a theory of social structure but also a vision about the future of society. I must hasten to add that the interlocking of the past-present-future implies that social movements reflect the confluence between the persistent, changing and evolving elements of a system. At a deeper level, the framework implies that people make history and constantly learn from their historicity. Movements are neither mere emotional outbursts nor entirely the resultants of manipulations by leaders and demagogues, but the consequence of conscious efforts on the part of participants to change the present societal arrangements in the light of their past experiences, avoiding pitfalls. Finally, the continuous triggering off of movements implies that human beings are not imprisoned by present structures and no moratorium on their creativity can be imposed.

The emergence of a movement starts with the crystallization of one of its components at the initial stage, and others later. Therefore, components of movements need to be identified. As Banks[47] pointed out, social movements have two important components, an ideology and an organization. But in the formative stage of a social movement either the ideology or the organization will appear first, depending upon a number of factors. Appearance of a new ideology itself is indicative of the strain in the system. Parsons[48] consider ideology as a device to ease situations of strain. In the process of absorbing strain, the existing patterns may be reinforced, if the forces of vested interest are strong, or change may come about, if the resistance is overcome. Zimmerman argues that ideologies arise as a result of differing viewpoints regarding the existing social arrangement.[49] Smelser too recognizes strain or mal-integration as the source for the emergence of ideology.[50] Given the fact that the strain in the system produces a new ideology and if a sufficient number of persons are attracted towards it, the emergence of an 'ideological' movement is a distinct possibility.

However, it is not necessary that an ideology should emerge first, for the birth of a social movement. Often it is observed that people come together and start an organization to deal with situations of strain. They may not always be clear about the ideology behind their organization in the beginning. The organization is launched as an instrument to fight an 'evil' or to eradicate certain social problems. As the organization develops, and grows, the ideology will be evolved or discovered. Such efforts may crystallize into an 'organizational movement' over a period of time, in that organization has primacy in such movements.

That is, situations of strain may give rise to two distinct kinds of social movements: ideological or organizational movements. A third possibility is the emergence of a charismatic leader. As Weber made it clear that charismatic heroes emerge from situations of strain.[51] Charisma represents the sudden eruption of novel forces from crisis. Since charisma is not only non-institutional but also anti-institutional, the possibility of an organizational build up is almost ruled out, especially in the initial stages. Yet, the charismatic leader can mobilize the deprived. The charismatic movement does not start with an ideology; what constitute the ideology of the movement are the pronouncements of the leader. Obviously, the ideology will crystallize and will be codified only after a period of time. Since, the primary inspiration of the movement springs from the charismatic leader, the ideology will have only secondary significance, especially in the formative stage of the movement.

Thus, a situation of strain within a society may be met through three distinct possibilities:[52]

1. Appearance of a charismatic leader, who comes with the promise of mitigating the evils at hand, and leading the people to a future utopia.
2. Emergence of a new ideology, which champions the cause of the disgruntled or dissatisfied section of the population.
3. Establishment of a new organization to deal with the problem at hand.

MOVEMENTS AND INSTITUTIONS

The relationship between movements and institutions needs to be underlined because of the intricate relationship between them. There is widespread tendency to conceptualize them as polar opposites and there are several reasons for it. First is the inadequate accounting of the time element in movement analysis.[53] The transformation of movements into institutions, and vice versa, is usually gradual, and seldom sudden. There is a social state between the two phases—movements and institutions—and social scientists have scarcely paid attention to this dimension of social reality. The attempts to view society as a process or an event would go a long way toward recognizing the interim social state between the 'solid state' (institutions) and the 'fluid state' (movements).

Second, movements are usually defined and perceived as large-scale or mass efforts. Be that as it may, most movements, however large they might become eventually, would usually have beginnings in the form of protests by small groups, associations or sects. That is, the formation of an institution or structure could be the starting point of a movement. Alternatively, a movement may emerge out of an event or happening. But soon an organization becomes a necessary accompaniment for pursuing the goal. That is, there exists a processual linkage between institutions and movements.[54] Thus, one can conceive of empirical situations wherein the intertwining between movements and institutions is perennially present and continuing.

If institutions do not 'produce' movements, that is, if they do not respond to the challenges posed to them periodically, they will become structurally and culturally obsolete; they will perish. Therefore, institutions require movements for their very survival through periodic replenishment. Movements provide institutions with the possibility of re-legitimation, if and when the latter experience an erosion of their legitimacy. On the other hand, unless movements provide institutional mechanisms, they will remain mere aspirations. That is, institutions are instruments of movements to translate ideology into programme, theory into praxis, without which they remain shells without substance. In fact, every movement is in search of a structure/institution, capable of translating its vision into reality.

The prevalent tendency to view movements and institutions as mutually antagonistic is essentially in line with the natural history or life-cycle approach to the analysis of social movements, by now obsolete in social science. The argument runs roughly as follows: the development of an organization, however rudimentary, is inevitable for the realization of movement goals. But the emergence of such an organization inevitably sets in motion influences, which defeat the very purpose which occasioned it. A paradoxical situation arises: that which is needed as an instrument—organization—for the translation of movement ideology into specific programmes often tends to become instrumental in frustrating the very purpose for which it emerged. Thus, the emergence of movement organizations leads to routinization of charisma,[55] development of bureaucratic structures,[56] persistence beyond the purpose for which it emerged,[57] all of which invariably leads to the institutionalization of social movements. In this strand of thinking, institutions are viewed as degenerate entities emerging out of movements.

In contrast, it is necessary to define and perceive institutions as vehicles of goal fulfilment of movements. As and when institutions become rigid and non-responsive to the purpose for which they emerged, it becomes imperative to challenge and de-legitimize them. That is, the relationship between movements and institutions is dialectical and multipolar. Second, there is no inherent tendency towards institutionalization of a movement and even when it occurs, it does not necessarily stop or even decelerate the process of mobilization which is so fundamental and primary to the very survival of a movement. In fact, mobilization and institutionalization coexist and, furthermore, the process of institutionalization provides new possibilities for mobilization. The institutionalization of a movement is believed to occur as the goals it pursued are achieved, or the elaborate machinery for the implementation of movement goals emerges, or associational proliferation takes place leading to the substitution of the movement by these associations. But empirical reality is at variance with this strand of thinking.[58]

The basic thrust of the present argument is that the process of mobilization and institutionalization are to be viewed essentially as two different dimensions of a movement rather than mutually inimical processes. However, the emphasis on different movement aspects would vary at different phases of a given movement (see Table 3).

In the final analysis, *mobilization is not displaced by institutionalization but both go hand-in-hand to a large extent and often the latter process may accentuate the former.* Admittedly, movements and institutions are to be viewed as processually linked. Institutions often trigger off movements; movements encapsulate within them seeds of institutions. Therefore, to characterize them in mutually exclusive terms is to create a wedge between concept and reality.

However, it is argued by some authors that the demise of a movement is inevitable.[59] The specific processes, which lead to the termination of a movement according to these authors are: repression, discreditation, co-optation and institutionalization. If a movement's goal poses a threat to the system and/or if it pursues its goal through violent means those who oppose it may attempt to unleash repression. The critical variable here is the collective conscience, which bestows legitimacy on the agent of repression and attributes illegitimacy to movement participants. That is, if the agent of repression is perceived by the society-at-large as a

Table 3: Characteristics of the Different Aspects of a Movement
at Two Phases

Aspects of a Movement	Mobilizational Phase	Institutionalization Phase
Ideology	Very important, emphasis on mass appeal, centres on issues of deprivation, stress on collective participation.	Not so significant, emphasis on translating movement ideology into specific programmes, stress on implementation.
Organization	Embryonic and rudimentary, leader–follower relationship emphatic. Stress on the movement functioning as a propaganda vehicle, emphasis on martyrdom.	Crystallized and complex, leader-follower relationship replaced by 'professional-client' relations, operate as interest groups, stress on administration of justice.
Strategy and Tactics	Stress on collective actions (agitations, strikes, *gheraos*, *satyagrahas*, demonstrations, etc.); emphasis on propaganda and communication of ideology to sensitize participants of their rights.	Interest articulation (bargaining, submission of memoranda, petition, lobbying for legislation), emphasizes the 'here and now' goal, namely, welfare of participants/social change.
Leadership	Professional revolutionary (typical roles: prophet, charismatic hero, demagogue).	Institutional entrepreneur (typical roles: manager, bureaucrat, bargainer, legalist).
Membership	Inclusive, expansive, undefined.	Exclusive and defined, clearer boundary demarcation.

legitimate authority, which should control the 'illegitimate' participants in a movement in the wider interest of the society, repression will lead to the termination of a movement. Conversely, if the agent of repression is perceived as illegitimate and the movement participants are defined as martyrs of a cause in the interest of society, repression will not weaken but strengthen a movement. It may however be cautioned that the argument holds mainly for democratic polities.

The two intermediary processes between repression and institutionalization, namely discreditation and co-optation, operate in different ways. Discreditation is indulged in by contending collectivities who are participants in movements which pursue inimical goals. The strategies of sacralization and demonization are commonly pressed into service. Participants in a movement are often prompted by the leadership to project an appropriate image about the movement to the wider world by their adherence to the movement ideology and pursuing the prescribed lifestyle. On the other hand, no effort will be spared to characterize the opponents/enemies of the movement in negative terms. If movements and counter-movements have adequate and appropriate resources it is very unlikely that discreditation will lead to their demise. As for co-optation the process is quite different in that it can take place only when the movements concerned have broadly similar means and goals. Therefore, co-optation does not lead to the termination of a movement but its enlargement through adaptation and accommodation with movement/s of similar orientation. To conclude, none of the four processes—repression, discreditation, co-optation and institutionalization—will herald the death-knell of a movement. Movements will survive if they have the required legitimacy and appropriate resources.

METHODOLOGICAL ISSUES

The discussion so far concentrated on the conceptual-theoretical as well as substantive aspects of social movements. It is necessary and useful to highlight some of the methodological issues in the study of social movements. The methodological problems in the study of social movements, are basically two: (a) the problems related to the *scale* of the movement, and (b) the issues related to the *units* and *levels* of observation.[60]

Three factors impinge on the scale of movements: (a) the number of participants, (b) the time-span of movements, and (c) the social composition of movement participants. Although the number of participants cannot be a defining criterion by which movements can be differentiated from non-movements, it cannot be ignored either. Nobody is likely to designate the mobilization of a handful of individuals as a movement. Therefore, it is obvious that movement participants should be of a substantial number. The number of participants can be defined as substantial both in terms of the universe, which forms the basis of mobilization as well as the absolute number of participants mobilized into collective action. For instance, even if only a small percentage of a specific category, industrial workers or farmers, for instance, are mobilized into collective action, one can legitimately label it a movement if they constitute thousands of persons. On the other hand, even when the participants are only a few hundreds insofar as they constitute a substantial proportion of the population which forms the universe of mobilization (as in the case of a tribe), such a mobilization can also be designated a movement.

At this juncture, however, one is likely to be faced by new problems related to the definition of participants. It is extremely tortuous to demarcate the boundaries of movements in terms of the nature and types of activities of participants. All movements are likely to have a set of core participants, the leaders at different levels, who can be differentiated in terms of the functions they perform; those who propound the ideology of the movement (the theoreticians), and those who translate these into actual programmes, through strategies and tactics (the men of action). Second, the rank and file who participate regularly in various kinds of mobilizational activities—picketing, *jatha*s, *Satyagraha*s, *gheraoe*s, strikes—and get arrested or killed and become martyrs of the movement. Third, there will be a set of peripheral participants who may identify themselves with movements, insofar as such involvement is not a risky venture perceived in terms of their life chances and immediate material interests. Typically, they participate in one or more of the following activities: attend the mass meetings organized under the auspices of the movement, read the documents produced by the movement, make occasional financial contributions to the movement. While it is extremely difficult to demarcate the active from the less-active participants, it is necessary to recognize this gradation among them. The problem becomes particularly vexing when one notes that several movements produce counter-movements by oppositional forces. Often those who are involved in counter-mobilizations are much more active and an adequate study of a movement should also take into account this category of persons who are usually taken to be 'outside' the movement. Since unions and associations often function as vehicles of movements it would be legitimate to view movements as a stream of associations/ unions operating parallely or in confrontation. In the final analysis, the number of persons mobilized into collective actions either for or against a movement becomes critical in understanding its scale.

The time-span of movements is one of the most critical dimensions, which defines the scale, yet it is one of the most neglected aspects in studies of movements. Thus, uprisings, rebellions, civil disturbances, revolts, insurrections, etc., are all indiscriminately and interchangeably referred to as 'social movements'. Some of these events may exist for a short period (say for a week) and others may continue for several months. This confusion emanates from an inadequate appreciation of the processual dynamic of movements. Rebellions, revolts and uprisings are specific events in the relatively long history of a movement. These events, which are often the more visible aspects of movements, are sustainable only for a short period and should not be mistaken for the whole of the movement.

Further, it is also likely that in the history of some movements these types of events may not take place at all because of their non-violent orientation. At any rate, whether or not a movement mobilized participants into violent collective actions would depend on the strategy and tactics that are perceived to be appropriate by the leadership and endorsed as legitimate by the participants at a given point in time. The methodological implication of this is that it is confusing to designate specific revolts or rebellions as 'movements'; rather, one should perceive them as specific links in the long chain of movements. Not only are violent revolts or rebellions specific events in the history of a movement, but they may even give birth to a non-violent movement. Alternatively, a violent revolt may ring the death-knell of a movement depending upon the intensity of violence it generates and its perceived illegitimacy by the state and the collectivity at large towards violence. Finally, some movements may have a natural demise as their goals are achieved, others would redefine their goals or add new goals so as to ensure continuity. Viewed from all these aspects, it is clear that the time-span forms an important dimension of the scale of a movement. Therefore, to designate specific events which occur in a limited range of time as movements is fallacious.

The third aspect of the scale of movement refers to the social composition of the participants. This dimension is discerned in terms of the number of potential participants a movement can mobilize into collective action. Thus, if a movement is oriented towards the interests of a primordial collectivity such as caste, tribe, religion or language, its optimum scale will be smaller as compared with another movement which champions the interests of civil collectivities such as workers, students or farmers. The case of biological collectivities would vary depending upon the size; gender-based mobilization having the highest potentiality. That is, the scale of a movement in the context of the social composition of participants is defined in terms of the heterogeneity/homogeneity of the social category under reference.

The problems bearing on the scale of movements is reflected in the very process of labelling movements. An examination of this (with reference to India, as most Indian authors are prone to do this) indicates that they are anchored around three factors: locality (for example, Bardoli, Telengana or Bihar movements), issues (for example, Tebhaga, anti-cow slaughter, regional development) and social categories (for example, peasants, workers, SCs and STs, Muslims). It is clear that in terms of the perspective followed here some of these are clearly not movements: they are but specific events in the long history of movements. Further, if the locality anchorage is too narrow, discerned in terms of the category involved (that is, peasants in Bardoli), or if the issue involved is too narrowly defined (as in the case of Tebhaga or cow slaughter), then mobilization emanating out of these situations or issues cannot be meaningfully designated as movements. But if the locality anchorage is large enough, Bihar, for instance, or if it potentially involves the entire population of the region as in the case of the Telengana separatist movement, or if it has the potentiality to mobilize a substantial size of the population as in the case of issue-centred movements (for example, movement against dowry) or category-based mobilization (for example, agricultural workers or STs), the term movement can be meaningfully employed as the scale of the movement is likely to be of a viable size.

The labelling of a movement based on the social categories largely determines its scale. Thus, if the collectivities are primordial, the movements are likely to be localized, usually confining their activities to a specific regional-linguistic area. However, this is not to suggest that such movements will not spread to other regional linguistic areas. Even as they do, they are likely to take a different orientation as the social categories of exactly the same attributes may not be found in other regions into which it spreads. In contrast, if civil collectivism provides the basis of participation in a movement the possibility of its simultaneous spread to a wider region exists if a centralized leadership provides the requisite ideology and an organizational structure crystallizes. The cases of labour, agrarian or student movements are illustrative of this. It is not suggested that these movements will simultaneously spread to vast geographic regions or that they will be of equal strength wherever they emerge, but such a possibility cannot be ignored. On the other hand, given the social diversity and regional-linguistic variations of a polity even class/occupation-based movements are usually confined to certain pockets.

The second basic methodological issue in the study of social movements relates to the units and levels of observation. I have already referred to the problem of boundary demarcation of movements from the perspective of differential involvement of participants in movement activities. The unbounded and open-ended feature of social movements throws up a critical problem when one looks for a viable unit of observation in an empirical analysis of social movements. Part of the problem is rooted in the varying intensity of mobilization at different phases in the life-cycle of movements and therefore, analysts of movements are prone to focus their attention on the phase of intense mobilization. Similarly, many movements that function as associational groups or have grown into organized bodies, has often meant that many studies of movements have also been analysis of associations. For these reasons most analysts tend to study either the intense mobilizational phase[61] or its institutionalized segment.[62]

The mobilized social category is invariably a deprived one and mobilization is always against an enemy. Even when movement ideologies get crystallized it may not be easy to understand the specific attributes of the enemy and there may be honest differences of opinion in this regard. Further, even when there exists consensus as to who is the enemy, the deprived social category may not perceive them due to their debilitating existential conditions—ignorance, illiteracy, poverty, powerlessness—or conversely because of the intimidating affluence, patronage and power of the enemy. Even when the enemy is identified and the deprived sections are aware of the same, there may be differences of opinion with regard to the manner in which the enemy is to be dealt with. Thus, those who attest the maxim, 'end justifies the means', invariably tend to liquidate the enemy, while those who are wedded to the principle of maintaining the purity of means may attempt to transform the enemy. This difference in approach is inevitably reflected in the mobilizational techniques—violent and non-violent—employed by different movements. Further, differences in value-orientation of movements get articulated in the perception of researchers, leading to varying emphases being given to different aspects of movements.

This brings one to the issue of the *level* of observation in movement studies. It seems that one of the fundamental methodological flaws of movement studies has been the exclusive emphasis on the macro-dimension, almost invariably ignoring the micro-dimension, thereby presenting a distorted picture. The usual tendency is to analyse movements in terms of their ideology, contained in the written records or oral pronouncements of the top leadership; the central movement organization, the machinery through which the ideology is sought to be propagated and communicated; the strategies and tactics devised by leaders, the specific procedures adopted to put movement ideology into practice. This emphasis on the macro-dimension cannot provide a picture of the actual functioning at the grass-root level, wherein one observes the filtration or accretion process to which the ideology is subjected in order to meet the specific needs of local conditions. Admittedly, there is a hiatus between the view from above and that from below. The ideological vision of the top leadership may not be meaningful to the grass-root participants unless it is translated into here-and-now issues, as experienced by them. And, those who have attempted to view movements from below often get a different picture, and can capture the 'inside story' of movements as different from the 'formal picture' which emerges from a study of the macro-dimension alone.[63]

I must point out here why analysts of movement are prone to concentrate on the macro-dimension. Rarely are on-going movements studied even by sociologists; typically, movement studies are undertaken after their assumed demise, at least after the period of intense mobilization and this is so for several reasons. First, ongoing movements continuously reformulate their ideology, restructure their organizational pattern and change their strategies and tactics to meet the challenges they face—movements live from moment-to-moment. This makes observation of ongoing movement processes hazardous. Second, the time-span of movements may be too long that a particular researcher cannot often invest his/her entire research time on the study even of a single ongoing movement. Third, movements are often triggered off suddenly and researchers may not be prepared to plunge into studies immediately. Fourth, since movements are invariably controversial in their orientation, it will be difficult to avoid taking value positions if one studies on-going movements. By the time a study is undertaken what is available to researchers is its documents containing the articulations of movement leaders. Even when participants are identified and information is collected orally, those consulted are invariably leaders. If one resorts to analysing records kept by law and order agencies about confrontations, the participants listed in these are likely to be those perceived as having a nuisance value by the local influentials as these records are often prepared on the basis of promptings by them. In the final analysis, an adequate capturing of the micro-dimension of movements is very difficult because of conventional research strategies and techniques in vogue. Therefore, unless a researcher makes deliberate attempts to view the movement s/he analyses from below, it is not possible to capture the grass-root processes involved.

Finally, in the origin and spread of movements one can discern two patterns: (a) independent local origin (at the micro-level) either simultaneously or sequentially, followed by their coordination by the movement leadership. In most of the movements in which the participants are identified based on their primordial identities, this seems to be the pattern; (b) simultaneous emergence in different regions through the inspiration of charismatic leaders or sponsored by macro structures such as political parties and civil society organizations. Most of the movements, which mobilize class/occupational categories, are of this type. Under both these patterns of movement crystallization, the ideology and organizational structure seem to be supplied by the top movement leadership in response to the prevalent political/cultural values and social policy measures. It seems therefore that the spread of movements is conditioned by two factors (a) when a society has to face an external enemy, unifying all the socially diverse categories, or (b) under the magnetic spell of charismatic heroes who transcend primordial attachments and who can mobilize the people against a commonly perceived enemy.

THE INDIAN EMPIRICAL SCENARIO

It is necessary to comment briefly on the nature and types of social movements in twentieth-century India, which is the focus of this book. I have already alluded to the general proposition that the historicity of context, the nature of social structure and the envisioned future in conjunction determine the nature and types of movements, which emerge in a society. To put it pithily, social movements in a society are conditioned by three factors: (a) Its core institutional order (CIO); (b) The principal enemy as perceived by the deprived; (c) The primary goal pursued by the society. Which is to say, the nature and types of social movements keep changing as these features change.

Twentieth-century India may be divided into three phases. The first half was the colonial period (1900–47), the referent here being the Indian subcontinent. The second phase, 1947–89, little over four decades, when the focus was nation-building/modernization and the third, that is the present phase (1990–) globalizing India. This is not to suggest that the earlier phases have been completely displaced by the later ones; to be sure modernization is still going on and streaks of colonialism reappear in new avatars.

During the colonial period the colonial state constituted the core institutional order, the principal enemy was the British colonizer, an outsider whose racial, religious and linguistic identities totally differed from those of the Indian 'subjects' and the singular goal pursued through the anti-colonial movement was to transform colonial subjecthood to citizenship of an independent sovereign state. An overwhelming majority of the people of Indian subcontinent perceived the colonizer as a common enemy, which facilitated the crystallization of a massive movement. Many analysts characterized the anti-colonial movement as a totality and ignored the specific interests and motivations of a wide variety of social categories. They have seen the wood but missed the trees. At any rate, they denied autonomy to the movements of women, peasants, youth, workers, religious communities, caste groups, tribes and other social categories.[64] I have designated this perspective as *macro-holistic*.

There is a diametrically opposite view, according to which, the movements of specific social categories were autonomous; even as they participated in the anti-colonial movement, they pursued their specific interests. This rendition missed the forest for the trees; it denied the existence of an overarching anti-colonial mobilization.[65] This perspective is *micro-individualistic* in its orientation in that the autonomy of specific social categories was highlighted ignoring their conjoint concern, namely, achieving political freedom. Admittedly, both these perspectives—macro holism and micro individualism—are partial and hence misleading. It is *not* true that movements of different social categories were mere tributaries of the anti-colonial movement and because they maintained a certain level of autonomy they were completely independent of it. That is, reciprocity and autonomy were implied in the relationship between the anti-colonial movement and the movements of numerous social categories.[66] Their relationship was buttressed by *situational interactionism*[67] and hence their reciprocity and autonomy varied across time, regions and communities. Only such a perspective will help us to understand as to why, those who claimed to represent the interests of the Hindus and the Muslims, and to a certain extent the Sikhs, demanded different 'nations'; why some categories (for example, Dalits) were less enthusiastic in their opposition to the British; why some others (for example, Leftists) were not very hopeful about the arrival of freedom because they perceived it as a mere transfer of power from the British colonizers to the Indian elite.

Once freedom arrived the primary goal became 'nation-building'; but not only did the 'nation' get divided, the meaning of nationhood also changed. The people who fought together against the British were divided into two 'nations'; secular India and Muslim Pakistan and became instant enemies. But national citizenship became the new central identity as against the erstwhile colonial subject-hood. After the arrival of freedom several movements were kept under suspended animation. For example, the undivided Communist Party of India stopped several mobilizations of peasants and workers to provide an opportunity to the national government to set things right; students were prodded to return to classrooms; the protest orientation of SCs and STs was partly contained by extending to them certain specific welfare entitlements. That is, there came about a sea change in the historicity of context, occasioned by the replacement of the colonial state by the national state.

The national state through the adoption of an innovative and progressive constitution, the launching of Five Year Plans, adoption of universal adult franchise, decentralization of polity and similar measures unleashed forces of social transformation. The national state became the core institution; fighting illiteracy and ill health, providing land to the tiller, rapid industrialization without ignoring the interests of labour that is, development with justice, became the new goals. Although equality became the central value its translation into reality remained a great challenge. In the meantime self-definitions of the constituting elements in the 'nation' changed with the exit of the colonizer. The idea of a common peoplehood gradually eroded, energizing the plurality of identities kept under suspended animation, manifesting in mobilizations of primordial groups—religious, regional, linguistic communities and caste and tribal groups. Most of the mobilizations by these categories combined the twin goals of equality and identity; they were directed against 'internal colonialism'.

However, there was another set of mobilizations focused primarily on equality piloted by/through civil collectivities. Movements of industrial workers, peasants and agrarian proletariat exemplify this. A third set of collectivity whose identity is rooted in biology—gender and age—started demanding equality; their identity is recognized but equality is denied to them. It is important to note that political parties through their front organizations initiate much of the mobilizations of civil and biological collectivities in independent India. And their primary purpose was to wrest equality and justice from the state and the dominant groups.

Till the declaration of internal Emergency during 1975–76, the state had considerable legitimacy in independent India as the initiator of social transformation and as the prime mover of economic development. From the latter half of the 1970s onwards the centrality of the Indian state came in for interrogation; Citizens' for Democracy, People's Union for Civil Liberty, People's Union for Democratic Rights and several other politically oriented non-governmental organizations emerged during this period. Paradoxically enough, the state also came to recognize the crucial role of welfarist NGOs in implementing development pro-grammes. This is evident from the importance accorded to NGOs in the Seventh Five Year Plan for the efficient delivery of development benefits.

There is yet another momentous development which occurred in the 1980s. The very idea of state-sponsored, capital intensive, high-tech driven model of modernization came in for questioning. This approach to development caused considerable displacement and deprivation particularly among the rural poor who sought refuge in urban India. The discontents of modernity unleashed a series of mobilizations, which highlighted the issues of deteriorating ecology and environmental insecurity. The net result of this is the erosion of legitimacy suffered by the state and the civil society gaining in importance—led to the crystallization of numerous mobilizations against the state by the civil society.

The second phase (1947–89) referred to earlier may be divided into two sub-phases from the perspective of understanding social movements in independent India. The movements of first sub-phase (1947–76) focused mainly on equality but those of the second sub-phase (1977–89) were concerned with equality and identity simultaneously. The widely held assumption that primordial identities will be dissolved in the cauldron of modernity was belied which necessitated this shift in emphasis.

The third phase (1990–) referred to above is the globalizing phase initiated by the liberalization of economy. The distinguishing features of this phase are: minimalization of the role of state in economic development, enlarged role of civil society in social transformation and centrality of market in the economy. If market becomes the core institutional order, the central identity will be that of the consumer, sidelining citizenship rights. This is so because the state is often incapable of ensuring citizenship rights against the rapacity of market. Understandably, human rights formulated by trans-state organizations will assume saliency. That is, discontents of globalization had started triggering off a new set of mobilizations.

The core institutional order of the global age being the market, both capital and consumer get privileged; capital is being enticed from rich foreign countries. The current protests against foreign capital, both from the Hindu nationalists and the political left, is to be situated in this context. The economic re-colonization of India through foreign capital has led to the reinvention of the *swadeshi* of the colonial times. Similarly, globalization is drastically influencing the lifestyles and consumption patterns, particularly of the middle class. This cultural invasion is perceived to be eroding the cultural specificity of India. Both these—economic re-colonization and cultural invasion—are inducing sporadic collective mobilizations in India, although not yet crystallized into sustained movements.

Finally, there was/is no archetype class movement in India; the equivalent of that was the anti-colonial movement. A large number of movements pursuing equality crystallized in independent India but these were movements aimed at gender, religious, tribal, caste and rural-urban disparity or environmental degradation. Also, these movements pursued equality and identity simultaneously. Therefore, they are compared to the new social movements of the West but their contexts are different.[68] This being so the designation NSM is not very appropriate for India.[69]

India has been and continues to be a classic land of cultural diversity. At the same time India had/has a unique system of inequality legitimized and institutionalized by tradition. This is a lethal combination. Republican India attempts to overcome this traditional deficit by bringing in the concept of equality to the centre stage. According to some, the principle of distributive justice recognized as an important aspect of planned economic development has been relegated to the background with the launching of globalization. These processes inevitably provide new grounds for protest and mobilization.

CONCERNS OF EQUITY AND SECURITY

Of the three issues—Identity, Equity, and Security—around which mobilizations of collectivities take place in contemporary societies, this book deals with the latter two. Therefore it is imperative to have a short discussion on equality and security before the general introduction is concluded.

Equality is a widely used notion in contemporary social science and yet it cannot be said that its meanings and connotations are well understood. Constitutions of democratic and socialist countries promise equality to all their citizens. This promised equality may be designated as ontological equality. But in order to translate the promise into reality it is necessary to provide for equality of opportunity to all citizens irrespective class, race, gender, age, religion, caste, language, rural-urban background and the like. Further, in order to enable citizens to avail of equality of opportunity it is necessary to create equality of condition that is, a level playing ground. In the process of creating equality of condition for the disadvantaged groups it is quite likely inequality among these groups may gradually emerge; that is equality of outcome cannot be ensured. Therefore creating equality of condition through measures such as affirmative action or protective discrimination and excluding those who have overcome their disadvantages (the creamy layer) from the purview of policies are necessary to ensure equity. These are contentious issues which create discontents among collectivities who experience both upward mobility as well as downward mobility.

These contentions and deprivations lead to the emergence of social movements based on class politics as well as identity politics. But there is no consensus among theorists regarding the route to be pursued to achieve movement goals. Even those who pursue class politics; it means either pursuing equality of opportunity or creating equality of condition in addition to assuring equality of opportunity. Further, for some if income disparities increase after providing for equality of opportunity it is acceptable, for others such tendencies should be moderated through distributive justice. These are the motives which drive the mobilizations of peasantry and industrial labour as well as those of the farmers and entrepreneurs. Even the radical groups are not arguing for equality of rewards these days because that will endanger incentives of human beings to work hard. Thus inequality which emerges in societies, after having provided for equality of opportunity and equality of condition, has come to be accepted as legitimate because it is perceived as the result of hard work and merit. That is, equity rather than equality is the motive force behind contemporary social movements.

The issue of equity is the concern of not only classes but also other collectivities such as gender and age-groups. But because women and youth are distributed across different classes, the basis of their mobilization cannot be based on class inequities. In the case of women inequity has been institutionalized and internalized through the values of patriarchy manifesting in sexual division of labour, differential wages for the same work, privileging exchange value as against use value (women being its principal producers), non-recognition of their crucial role in human reproduction, denial of access and privileges in the public spheres, subjection to violence even in the domestic space, to a list a few.

The youth, particularly the student youth, feel deprived because they are denied participation in the decision-making process in family and educational institutions not to speak of inadequate recognition in the public sphere. Even as they are denied equity the youth are prompted and persuaded to participate in mobilizations of all kinds by adult leaders. Thus although the youth are utilized as resources they are denied rewards causing frustration leading to alienation and aggression. That is to say inequity manifests in different contexts—income disparity, participation in decision making and denial of prestige, to list just three of them, all of which occasion protests and mobilizations.

Security has become a major concern in recent times because of organized non-state actors indulging in violent physical acts, referred to as terrorism in common parlance. While there is increasing evidence to show that collective conscience is getting disturbed due to this, there is no concerted effort from civil society to combat this manifesting in social movements. Analyses of comprehensive security are attempted with regard to several dimensions—military, political, economic, socio-cultural and environment. And five factors have contributed to the current concern to protect the environment.[70] They are: (a) the tremendous growth in population and the consequent unprecedent strain on planet earth; (b) the discrepancy between population growth and economic growth, population is galloping in the South while income is soaring in the North, prompting large-scale population shift from South to North; (c) the mismatch between the territory of nation-states and that of the geographic regions which requires inter-state cooperation in the protection of the environment; (d) the feared rapid decline of species diversity as well as ecosystem diversity; and (e) the consequences of reckless production and deployment of high technology to achieve rapid economic development which devastates ecology.

It needs to be underlined here that the most advanced technology is invariably used by the military and deployed as war technology. The deliberate destruction of the enemy's ecological system deploying high technology was done in Vietnam by the United States. Similarly ecological degeneration can occur because of the production and deployment of nuclear weapons and disposal of nuclear wastage. Whether ecological devastation takes place because of war strategies or because of the craze to achieve high-tech driven rapid economic growth, there is increasing and intense awareness in the contemporary world that '…people must have a fundamental human right to environmental security'.[71] This explains the rise and spread of ecology/environment movements which pursue the security of the environment.

NOTES

1. Charles Tilly, 'The Analysis of a Counter Revolution', *History and Theory*, III (1), (1963–4), pp. 25–47, especially p. 31.

2. R. Heberle, 'Observations on the Sociology of Social Movements', *American Sociological Review*, 14 (3), (1949), pp. 346–57.

3. C. Johnson, *Revolutionary Change* (Boston: Little Brown, 1966); T. Gurr, *Why Men Rebel* (Princeton: Princeton University Press, 1970).

4. M. Weber, *The Theory of Social and Economic Organization* (London: William Hodge and Company, 1947).

5. J. Gusfield, 'Social Structure and Moral Reform: A Study of Women's Christian Temperance Movement', *American Journal of Sociology*, 61 (27), (1955), pp. 221–32; M.N. Zald and J.D. McCarthy (eds), *Social Movements*

in an Organizational Society (New Brunswick: Transactions Books, 1987), pp. 321–47.

6. B. Moore (Jr), *Social Origins of Dictatorship and Democracy* (London: Penguin Books, 1969); E. Wolf, *Peasant Wars of the Twentieth Century* (London: Faber and Faber, 1971).

7. A. Oberschall, *Social Conflict and Social Movements* (New Jersey: Prentice Hall, 1973); Zald and McCarthy (eds), *Social Movements in an Organizational Society*.

8. J.L. Cohen, 'Strategy or Identity: New Theoretical Paradigms and Contemporary Social Movements', *Social Research*, 52 (4), (1985), pp. 663–716; B. Klandermans, H. Kriesi, and S. Tarrow, 'From Structure to Action', Vol. I, *International Social Movement Research* (Greenwich: JAI Press, 1988); G. McAdam, *Freedom Summer* (New York: Oxford University Press, 1988); A. Melucci, *Nomads of the Present: Social Movements and Individual Needs in Contemporary Society* (Philadelphia: Temple University Press, 1989); C. Offe, 'New Social Movements: Challenging Boundaries of Institutional Politics', *Social Research*, 52, (1985), pp. 817–68.

9. J. Davis, *Contemporary Social Movements* (New York and London: D. Appleton Century Company, 1930).

10. N.J. Smelser, *The Theory of Collective Behaviour* (London: Routledge and Kegan Paul, 1962).

11. H. Blumer, 'Collective Behaviour', in A.M. Lee (ed.), *New Outline of the Principles of Sociology* (New York: Barnes and Noble, 1951).

12. A. Green, *Sociology* (New York: McGraw Hill Book Company, Inc., 1956).

13. B.K. Roy Burman, 'Social Movements among Tribes', *Secular Democracy*, 4 (3 and 4), (1971), pp. 25–33; 'Challenges and Responses in Tribal India', in M.S.A. Rao (ed.), *Social Movements in India*, Vol. II (Delhi: Manohar Books, 1979), pp. 101–22.

14. T. Abel, 'The Pattern of a Successful Political Movement', in B.H. Stoodley (ed.), *Society and Self: A Reader in Social Psychology* (New York: The Free Press, 1962).

15. B. Barber, 'Acculturation and Messianic Movements', *American Sociological Review*, VI (3), (1941), pp. 663–9.

16. H. Blumer, 'Collective Behaviour', in A.M. Lee (ed.), *New Outline of the Principles of Sociology*, pp. 199–214.

17. S.N. Eisenstadt, 'Sociological Aspects of Political Development in Underdeveloped Countries', *Economic Development and Cultural Change*, V (4), (1957), pp. 289–307.

18. R. Heberle, 'Observations on the Sociology of Social Movements', *American Sociological Review*, 14 (3), (1949), pp. 346–57.

19. R. Linton, 'Nativistic Movements', *American Anthropologist*, 45(2), (1943), pp. 230–40.

20. Smelser, *The Theory of Collective Behaviour*.

21. W. King, *Social Movements in United States* (New York: Random House, 1956), p. 27.

22. A.F.C. Wallace, 'Revitalization Movements', *American Anthropologist*, 58 (2), (1966), pp. 264–81.

23. M.N. Zald and Roberta Ash, 'Social Movement Organizations: Growth, Decay and Change', *Social Forces*, 44 (2), (1966), pp. 327–41.

24. Cf. P. Wilkinson, *Social Movements* (London: Macmillan, 1971).

25. Partha Mukherji, 'Social Movement and Social Change: Towards a Conceptual Clarification and Theoretical Framework', *Sociological Bulletin*, 26 (1), (1977), pp. 38–59; 'Naxalbari Movement and the Peasant Revolt in North Bengal', in M.S.A. Rao (ed.), *Social Movements in India*, Vol. I (Delhi: Manohar Books, 1978), pp. 17–90.

26. M.S.A. Rao, 'Conceptual Problems in the Study of Social Movements', in Rao (ed.), *Social Movements in India*, Vol. I, pp. 1–15.

27. For a sample, see Dipankar Gupta, *Nativism in a Metropolis: The Shiva Sena in Bombay* (New Delhi: Manohar Books, 1982); D.N. Dhanagare, *Peasant Movements in India: 1920–1950* (New Delhi: Oxford University Press, 1983); M.S. Gore, *Social Context of an Ideology: Ambedkar's Political and Social Thought* (New Delhi: Sage Publications, 1993); Gail Omvedt, *Dalits and the Democratic Revolution* (New Delhi: Sage Publications, 1994).

28. T.K. Oommen, *Charisma, Stability and Change: An Analysis of Bhoodan-Gramdan Movement in India* (New Delhi: Thompson Press, 1972).

29. Ibid., p. 23.

30. See T.K. Oommen, *Protest and Change: Studies in Social Movements* (New Delhi: Sage Publications, 1990); G. Shah, *Social Movements in India: A Review of Literature* (New Delhi: Sage Publications, 1990).

31. Rajendra Singh, *Social Movements, Old and New: A Post-Modernist Critique* (New Delhi: Sage Publications, 2001).

32. T.K. Oommen, *Knowledge and Society: Situating Sociology and Social Anthropology* (New Delhi: Oxford University Press, 2007), pp. 8–12.

33. Singh, *Social Movements, Old and New*, p. 309.

34. Zygmunt Bauman, *Culture as Praxis* (London: Routledge and Kegan Paul, 1973).

35. T.K. Oommen, 'Erving Goffman and the Study of Everyday Protest', in S.H. Reggins (ed.), *Beyond Goffman* (New York: Mouton de Guytor, 1990 b), pp. 389–407.

36. A. Touraine, 'A Sociology of the Subject', in Jon Clark and M. Diani (eds), *Alain Touraine* (London: Falmer Press, 1996), p. 308.

37. See T.K. Oommen, 'Social Movements in a Comparative Perspective: Situating Alain Touraine', in Clark and Diani (eds), *Alain Touraine*, pp. 114–25.

38. J. Davis, *Contemporary Social Movements* (New York and London: D. Appleton Century Company, 1930), pp. 9–10.

39. B. Barber, 'Acculturation and Messianic Movements', pp. 663–9.

40. H. Blumer, 'Collective Behaviour', in A.M. Lee (ed.), *New Outline of the Principles of Sociology* (New York: Barnes and Noble, 1951), p. 130.

41. Wallace, 'Revitalization Movements', p. 256.

42. Linton, 'Nativistic Movements', p. 233.

43. J.A. Banks and Olive Banks, 'Feminism and Social Change: A Case of Social Movement', in George K. Zollschan and Walter Hirsch (eds), *Explorations in Social Change* (London: Routledge and Kegan Paul, 1964), p. 522.

44. Abel, 'The Pattern of a Successful Political Movement', in Stoodley (ed.), *Society and Self*, pp. 562–3.

45. See S.N. Eisenstadt, 'Sociological Aspects of Political Development in Underdeveloped Countries', pp. 289–307; Smelser, *The Theory of Collective Behaviour*.

46. See W.G. Runciman, *Relative Deprivation and Social Justice* (Berkeley: University of California, 1966).

47. Banks and Banks, 'Feminism and Social Change', in Zollschan and Hirsch (eds), *Exploration in Social Change*, pp. 547–69.

48. T. Parsons, *The Social System* (Illinois: The Free Press of Glencoe, 1951), pp. 289–97.

49. C.C. Zimmerman, 'Ideological Movements and Social Change', in Joseph Roucek (ed.), *Contemporary Political Ideologies* (New Jersey: Little Field Adams and Co., 1961), pp. 5–6.

50. N.J. Smelser, *Sociology of Economic Life* (New Delhi: Prentice Hall of India, 1965).

51. Weber, *The Theory of Social and Economic Organization*, pp. 358–73.

52. T.K. Oommen, *Charisma, Stability and Change*.

53. For an exception see F. Alberoni, *Movements and Institutions* (New York: Columbia University Press, 1984).

54. T.K. Oommen, 'Movements and Institutions: Structural Opposition or Processual Linkage', *International Sociology*, 5 (2), (1990), pp. 145–56.

55. T.K. Oommen, *Charisma, Stability and Change*.

56. S.M. Lipset, M. Trow and J. Coleman, *Union Democracy* (Illinois: The Free Press, 1956).

57. D. Sills, *The Volunteers* (Illinois: The Free Press, 1957).

58. T.K. Oommen, *From Mobilization to Institutionalization: The Dynamics of Agrarian Movement in 20th Century Kerala* (Bombay: Popular Prakashan, 1985).

59. G.R. Rush and R.S. Denisoff, *Social and Political Movements* (New York: Meredith Corporation, 1971).

60. T.K. Oommen, 'Sociological Issues in the Analysis of Social Movements in Independent India', *Sociological Bulletin*, 26 (1), (1977), pp. 14–37.

61. For example, see Dhanagare, *Peasant Movements in India*.

62. K.P. Gupta, 'Religious Evolution and Social Change in India: A Study of the Ramakrishan Mission Movement', *Contributions to Indian Sociology*, 8, (1974), pp. 25–50.

63. J. Pouchepadass, 'Local Leaders and Intelligentsia in the Champaran Satyagraha (1917)', *Contributions to Indian Sociology*, 8, (1974), pp. 67–88.

64. For example, see Bipin Chandra, *Nationalism and Colonialism in Modern India* (New Delhi: Orient Longman, 1979).

65. D.A. Low, *Congress and the Raj: Facets of the Indian Struggle 1917–1947* (London: Heinemann, 1977).

66. See M.H. Siddiqui, *Agrarian Unrest in North India* (New Delhi: Vikas Publishing House, 1978) for the case of peasantry.
67. For an elaboration of these approaches, see Oommen, *From Mobilization to Institutionalization*, pp. 9–10.
68. See G. Omvedt, *Reinventing Revolution: New Social Movements and the Socialist Tradition* (New York: M.E. Sharpe, 1993).
69. T.K. Oommen, 'Multiple Modernities and the Rise of New Social Movements: The Case of India', *Indian Social Science Review*, 3 (1), (2001), pp. 1–16.
70. T.K. Oommen, *Understanding Security: A New Perspective* (New Delhi: Macmillan India Ltd, 2006).
71. Peter Stoett, *Human and Global Security: An Exploration of Terms* (Toronto: University of Toronto Press, 1999), p. 71.

Peasant and Labour Movements

The focus of this section, with seven chapters, is on civil collectivities. The movements of civil collectivities are found in all 'democracies'. The two principal categories involved in social movements are the peasantry and the industrial labour. The proclivity of these collectivities to launch movements is conditioned by the situation that prevails in particular societies at different points in time, but their thrust invariably is equity.

Even today 70 per cent of India's population lives in rural areas and the Indian peasantry, that is, the agricultural labour and small land-holders are not simply economically deprived but acutely distressed. Understandably, land to the tiller, was a promise given by the leaders of the anti-colonial movement and upheld by the national state. Independent India has witnessed the passing of a large number of pro-peasant legislations, yet the agrarian issue remains basic and fundamental. Therefore it is but natural to expect frequent mobilizations by the Indian peasantry. While some have argued that the tradition of peasant movement has been weak in India because of the social fragmentation wrought by the caste system, Kathleen Gough argues in Chapter 1 that India has had a strong and enduring peasant movement.

There are two main reasons why an exaggerated count of peasant movements is found by Kathleen Gough. One, all varieties of peasant protests including transient rebellions which are but specific events in the course of peasant movements are designated as 'movements'. Second, ignoring the social background (religion, caste, region) of the peasants and focusing on their economic deprivation often meant relegating to the background the multiple deprivations of the participants and the multiplicity of goals pursed by movements.

Generally speaking peasant revolts broke out in India, when the state became oppressive, be it the Mughal or British. The national state attempted to eliminate through legislations the numerous layers of intermediaries between absentee landlords and the cultivators of land, but has not succeeded in fulfilling the promise of distributing land to the tiller because of the faulty operationalization of the notion of tiller. Small landowners and tenants were defined as tillers. But the first invariably drawn from the upper castes got the land tilled through agricultural labour drawn from the SCs. The tenants usually from the OBCs also did not always work the land directly but employed the SCs. Thus the rough caste–class congruence—landowners from upper castes, tenants from OBCs, and agricultural labour from SCs—rendered the empirical reality very complex in rural India.

Broadly speaking there are three routes to ameliorate the condition of the agrarian poor. Two of these—state-initiated legislative measures and violent peasant uprisings—are found universally, but the third— the non-violent approach to tackle the agrarian problem—is unique to India. This section discusses two types of peasant movements—violent and non-violent. While Chapter 1 provides a historical overview of peasant uprisings in India, in Chapter 2, Partha Mukherji presents a case study of the Naxalbari peasant revolt, the most well-known, widespread and persisting mobilization of its kind in India.

The agrarian front organizations of the Communist Parties—CPI, CPI (Marxist), and CPI (Marxist-Leninist)—are the most active in the field of peasant mobilization in India. The Naxalbari peasant uprising which started in 1967 actually pre-dated the formation of CPI-ML in 1969, but has come to be firmly identified with this party. The Naxalbari revolt has continuity with the Tebhaga movement in terms of goals such as zamindari abolition, distributing land to the tiller, prevention of tenant eviction and reduction of interest on loans. But the Naxalbari movement enlarged its goal as compared with the Tebhaga movement through forceful capturing/occupation of land, particularly of the rapacious landlords, its ultimate purpose being the forcible overturn of the State itself. Thus not only that the Naxalbari movement had added new goals but it pursued them through violent means. However, excessive violence led to the delegitimation of the movement in the eyes of not only the vested interest forces in society but also in the perception of the public at large. This provided the required legitimacy to the State to suppress the movement with an iron hand. In fact, dissensions crystallized even within the movement leading to its splintering into several factions. Eventually, some of the factions participated in the electoral process, abandoning the violent path. In its new incarnations the movement functions from different pockets of India following different means but retaining its revolutionary goal.

The non-violent Bhoodan (land gift) movement emerged in 1951, out of the womb of the violent Telengana peasant mobilization which failed to distribute land to the landless. Although started with the simple objective of receiving land donations from the landed and distribute land to the landless, the movement enlarged its scope to Gramdan (villages-in-gift). Gramdan not only aimed to establish villages in which land is owned by the community but also communitarian village republics in which the decision-making power is re-located from the village panchayat to the Gram Sabhas (village Assembly). Thus through non-violent means the movement hoped to establish radical social transformation. Gradually, not only the concept of Gramdan was recast into that of Sulabh Gramdan, which diluted the objectives of the movement but through invoking the notions of Prakhand Dan, Zilla Dan, Bihar Dan, and Bharat Dan, the very concept of *dan* was rendered into a mockery (see Chapter 3).

The ideology of the Bhoodan–Gramdan movement was drawn from the Gandhian notions of sarvodaya and antyodaya. In spite of its anti-bureaucratic stance, the movement gradually evolved an elaborate organizational set-up to implement its programmes. The combination of charismatic appeal and the lack of resistance from the vested interest forces, the landowners, facilitated the continuation of the movement for some time. But the required participation of both the haves (land donors) and the have-nots (the recipients of land) gradually unfolded the internal contradictions within the movement leading to its demise. It is argued by me in Chapter 3 that the Bhoodan–Gramdan movement initiated but could not consolidate and institutionalize change.

The accounts of the violent Naxalbari movement and non-violent Bhoodan–Gramdan movement demonstrate that both have failed in achieving their initial goal, namely distributing land to the tiller, not to speak of their ultimate goal of establishing a just society. If in the case of the former the failure can be attributed to excessive violence which made the movement illegitimate, in the case of the latter the total absence of regulation made it ineffective. It seems then a balance between legitimacy and coercion is a pre-requisite to institutionalize social change through social movements.

What are popularly designated as peasant movements in Independent India are the collective mobilizations of agrarian classes initiated by the front-organizations of different political parties. Rarely do analysts refer to the Bhoodan–Gramdan movement as a peasant movement in spite of its all-India spread and despite the fact it has collected and distributed more land than the government machinery through land ceiling measures. In the functioning of the front-organizations of political parties, caste, class, and party interest are inextricably intertwined. Admittedly, the objectives and style of functioning of different associations and unions varied; if the agricultural labour unions demanded land for cultivation, higher wages, parity in wages for men and women workers, stipulated working hours and the like from their employers, the farmers' associations demanded subsidized agricultural inputs and assured prices for their products from the state. In order to understand the formation and functioning of the farmers' associations we need to situate them in the context of Green Revolution.

The Green Revolution was introduced in India with the objective of making the country self-sufficient in food production which favoured the owner-cultivators. The emergence of what is designated as the 'new farmers' movement' by Dhanagare in the 1970s should be viewed in this context. While the Green Revolution brought prosperity, through subsidized inputs and assured prices provided by the State, to a section of farmers, it also had deepened the disparity between them and the agrarian poor. But ignoring this the leaders of the farmers' movement highlighted the old and continuing disparity between the inhabitants of rural India and urban India, characterizing the whole of the former as deprived as compared to the latter. The ideologues of the farmers' movement ignored the intra-rural inequities and insisted on subsidies from the Indian state.

Two important features of the farmers' movement need to be noted here. One, the party-movement link is tenuous in that the Left-parties are not very enthusiastic to support the demands of the new 'kulaks' of rural India. However, the parties with rightist orientation did often support their mobilizations even when they may not have direct links with these movements. Two, the leaders of farmers' associations are sharply divided on the issue of support to economic liberalization. While the majority of them interrogate and oppose the unfavourable trade practices recommended and indulged in by the Bretton–Woods institutions, some support them. Thus the value-orientation of the latter group unfolds a double contradiction; impervious to the immiserization of the rural proletariat in India and supportive of unethical trade practices obtaining at the global level as pointed out by D.N. Dhanagare in Chapter 4. The net result of this is the weakening of the bargaining power of farmers vis-à-vis the Indian State as well as the decline of cooperatives, the organizations which provided financial succor to farmers. The analyses in this section also unfold the peril movements face if they get closely identified with political parties and governments, thereby eroding their autonomy within civil society, the legitimate space to which they belong. What is common to these movements is that all the categories—agrarian proletariat, peasantry and prosperous farmers—are feeling deprived and demand equity.

The Indian industrial sector, though huge in absolute terms, is tiny as compared to the agricultural sector. Within the urban industrial sector an overwhelming majority of workers (92 per cent) are in the informal sector. It is the organized sector of the Indian labour which is conventionally involved in the labour movement through trade union activities. The Indian industrial labour movement surfaced in 1875 protesting against the deplorable conditions of women and children and demanding legislations to protect the interests of labour in general. In the 1920s there was only one all-India trade union but by the late 1940s there were at least four of them.

Right from the beginning the trade unions were intimately involved in anti-colonial mobilization and their political orientation was maintained through their strong attachment to political parties. The twin objectives—furthering the economic welfare of industrial labour and political interests of the sponsoring political parties—of trade unions in Independent India often conflicted. The fact that the leadership of the unions was drawn from the middle-class and upper-caste members of political parties created a further wedge. To complicate matters a multiplicity of unions functioned in the same plant; while they share economic interests their political objectives varied. This obstructs the realization of even their economic objectives. S.M. Pandey provides a general picture of the characteristics and growth of industrial labour movement in India in Chapter 5.

Chapter 6 by Debashish Bhattacherjee traces the story of the evolution of Indian industrial relations through two phases; 1950s to late 1970s and the 1980s to 2000, the first being exclusively that of planned economic development and the second phase includes the initial stage of structural adjustment programme (SAP). But each of these phases has two sub-phases. During the first sub-phase (1950 to mid-1960s) when State-driven industrialization was in vogue the labour movement was substantially regulated by the state. The second sub-phase (mid-1960s to 1979) is characterized by maximum industrial strife which manifested in fractured union voices. And yet, during this period, the public sector employees received considerable benefits. The third sub-phase (1980–91) witnessed increasing autonomy for the unions and polarization between organized and unorganized sectors. During the fourth sub-phase (1991–2000) the union membership in the organized industrial sector declined, the conflict of interests between industrial workers and consumers got articulated more clearly. In turn this led to decentralization of bargaining process, decline of collective mobilization and cleavages within the industrial labour movement.

The Indian labour movement was born in a political mould in the colonial times; it functioned as a tributary to the anti-colonial mobilization as noted above. After independence the labour movement operated as front-organizations of political parties and hence they operated as pro- or anti-state depending upon which political party they were attached to. With the adoption of economic liberalization and the gradual retreat of the state as an agency of economic development, the market forces started intimidating the labour force. Massive informalization of labour is increasingly castrating the unions of their bargaining capacity.

Informalization brings in its trail not only economic insecurity but also erosion of legal entitlements. The new efforts to 'organize the unorganized' had kept a conscious distance from political parties and the new activism has shifted its attention from class to community. The new activism is initiated not by political parties but by civil society organizations. However, it cannot be said that all segments of the community get adequate and relevant attention. Informalization of labour force and its feminization go hand-in-hand and the most neglected section are women. Chapter 7 by Supriya RoyChowdhury is a case study of women in garment industry in Bangalore which highlights the problems of women workers in the unorganized sector.

The three specific features of the garment industry are: (a) it is predominantly feminine; (b) the mainstream trade unions are apathetic to this new sector; and (c) the indifference of the state to implement labour regulations given the high export earning capacity. In spite of these, if unionization occurs, the strategy is to shift the manufacturing units to far-away sites which makes it extremely difficult, if not impossible, for women workers to commute to the work spots and in extreme cases even close down the factory.

Some of the interesting features of the new activism may be noted here. Instead of the old 'union-mode' associated with conventional trade unions attached to political parties which confronted the management, the philosophy of new activism is 'campaign-mode', which demands from the government to rectify legal deficits and once legislations are in place, insist that the prescribed legal norms are adhered to. The campaign-mode also trains and makes the workers aware—here, the women workers in the garment industry—about the problems specific to them and approach new institutional agencies (for example, the National or State Women's Commissions), to redress them. Finally, the highly export-oriented garment making manufacturing unit is but a part of a wide ranging economic chain and hence the new activism should also take into account the global context. The campaign-mode thus can appeal to the foreign consumer to boycott the product if the primary producers' rights are not protected or if non-eligibles are employed, for example child labour. Thus the new activism and the campaign-mode it invokes are qualitatively different from the old trade unionism, which are instruments to cope with both informalization and globalization.

The chapters of this section demonstrate that the movements in both agrarian and industrial sectors have changed substantially over a period of time. If they were conditioned by colonialism in the beginning, the impact of 'nation-building' initiated by the state and its regulations got imprinted on them gradually. And, with the onset of economic liberalization the movements are constrained to respond to the unfolding rapacity of the market. But the central thrust of these movements, namely the pursuit of equity, remains the same, in all the three phases.

ADDITIONAL READINGS

Sumanta Banerjee, *India's Simmering Revolution: The Naxalbari Uprising* (London: Zed Press, 1984).

Tom Bras (ed.), *New Farmer's Movement in India* (London: Frank Cass, 1995).

Harold Crouch, *The Indian Trade Union Movement* (Bombay: Asia Publishing House, 1966).

International Labour Organization, *Social Dimensions of Structural Adjustment in India* (New Delhi, 1992).

U. Kalpagam (ed.), *Labour and Gender: Survival in Urban India* (New Delhi: Vikas, 1994).

T.K. Oommen, *From Mobilization to Institutionalization: The Dynamics of Agrarian Movement in Twentieth Century Kerala* (Bombay: Popular Prakashan, 1985).

Suresh Rambhai, *Vinoba and His Mission* (Kashi. Akhil Bharat Sarva Seva Sangh, 1954).

M.S.A Rao (ed.), *Social Movements in India*, Vol. I (Delhi: Manohar Books, 1992).

CHAPTER
1

Indian Peasant Uprisings[*]

KATHLEEN GOUGH

Social movements among the peasantry have been widely prevalent in India during and since British rule. We may define a social movement as 'the attempt of a group to effect change in the face of resistance'[1] and peasants as people who engage in agricultural or related production with primitive (palaeotechnic) means and who surrender part of their produce or its equivalent to landlords or to agents of the state. This chapter is confined to social movements which (a) involved peasants as the sole or main force, (b) were class struggles against those who exacted surplus from peasants, and (c) undertook or were provoked to armed struggle in the course of their careers.

Generally, the scope and significance of India's peasant uprisings have been under-stressed. Barrington Moore, Jr, for example, in spite of acknowledging at some length instances of peasant revolts described in recent Indian writings, concludes that China forms 'a most instructive contrast with India, where peasant rebellions in the pre-modern period were relatively rare and completely ineffective and where modernization impoverished the peasants at least as much as in China and over as long a period of time'.[2] Moore attributes the alleged weakness of Indian peasant movements to; the caste system with its hierarchical divisions among villagers, the strength of bourgeois leadership against the landlords and the British, and the pacifying influence of Gandhi

* Originally published as 'Indian Peasant Uprisings', *Economic and Political Weekly*, 11 (32–4), August 1974, pp. 1391–412.

on the peasantry.[3] I would argue that peasant revolts have in fact been common both during and since the British period, every state of present-day India having experienced several over the past 200 years. Thus, in a recent brief survey I discovered 77 revolts, the smallest of which probably engaged several thousand peasants in active support or in combat. About 30 revolts must have affected several tens of thousands, and about 12, several hundreds of thousands. Included in these revolts is the 'Indian Mutiny' of 1857–8, in which vast bodies of peasants fought or otherwise worked to destroy British rule over an area of more than 500,000 square miles.[4] The frequency of these revolts and the fact that at least 34 of those I considered were solely or partly by Hindus, cause me to doubt that the caste system has seriously impeded peasant rebellion in times of trouble.

There does seem no doubt that, apart from the Mutiny, peasant uprisings in China usually had a wider geographical scope than those in India—at least since late Moghul times. The reasons for this may have included the political fragmentation as well as the diversity of language and culture among India's people. During the later decades of Moghul rule the country had already disintegrated into a number of virtually autonomous, mutually warring kingdoms and principalities between whose peasants there was little contact. The British conquered India piecemeal over a 100-year period from the mid-eighteenth to the mid-nineteenth centuries. Early revolts against their rule therefore tended to occur at different dates in different regions, although there was inter-regional coordination among the largest—for example, those led by Raja Chait Singh in Oudh and other areas in 1778–81, by Vizier Ali in Gorakhpur in 1799, and by the military chiefs (poligars) of Madras and Andhra in 1801–5.[5]

Shortly after the British had subdued most of India a huge uprising, widely backed by the peasantry, did sweep over most of northern and central India in the shape of the Mutiny, but even in this case resistance tended to be strongest in the areas more recently conquered, while those which had earlier had revolts that had been crushed played lesser roles.[6]

After the Mutiny, British rule and military preparedness became stronger than ever and the rural upper classes of landlords and princes were either crushed totally or co-opted by the British through concessions. At the same time, political disunity was perpetuated by the division of India into British provinces interspersed with 'native states' having separate judicial systems. Popular action was difficult to organize across these boundaries as well as across ethnic and linguistic lines. Between the Mutiny and independence the British government and army were also better coordinated than those of China, and besides, India was not disturbed by invasions. In these circumstances; political disunity, a despotic central government and opposition from their landed aristocrats, post-1858, peasants were able to engage only in regional uprisings led by religious figures or by local peasant committees until political parties began to form peasant unions in the 1930s. Even so, some of these revolts were impressive enough to force concessions out of the rulers. Since the mid-1930s, peasant uprisings as well as non-violent resistance by peasants have usually been, at least partly, guided by political forces at the level of the province and by the colonial and post-colonial state, than by the caste system or from peculiarities of the village structure. At least two Indian authors have, indeed, argued that the caste system provided a framework for the organization of peasant rebellions, since in many cases peasants were able to assemble quickly through the medium of their caste assemblies.[7]

When peasant uprisings figure in British literature, they are often obscured under such headings as 'communal riots'—between major religions or fanatical religious cults—or under the activities of 'criminal' castes and tribes. While the armed struggles of peasants have often had these characteristics, a large proportion of such movements have also, and primarily, been concerned with the struggles of tenants, agricultural labourers, plantation workers, or tribal cultivators, against the exactions of landlords, bureaucrats of the state, merchants, moneylenders, or their agents—the police and the military.

THE COLONIAL BACKGROUND

Information is limited about peasant uprisings and other forms of violence against the rich and powerful in pre-British times. Whatever the earlier record, revolts broke out in many areas during the seventeenth and eighteenth centuries, as the Moghul bureaucracy became more oppressive and exacted harsher taxes, as commercial relations penetrated the countryside, and as local rulers made increasing incursions into tribal hill territories.[8] Prominent among the peasant rebellions against the Moghuls were those of the Jats of the Ganges–Jamuna region from the 1660s–90s, and of the Satnami religious sect in Narnaul in 1672. In some, but not all, of the revolts against Moghul power, peasants placed themselves under the leadership of local princes or land managers (zamindars) who rebelled because the imperial land revenue pressed so heavily on the peasants that there was little left for these local dignitaries. In the eighteenth century, the rapid expansions of the Sikh and Maratha powers and the growth of Thuggee bands in the heartland of the empire owed much to the fervent support of peasants suffering under Moghul revenue exactions.[9] Outside the empire, peasant opposition to encroaching royal authority was felt in the revolts of the Maomoria movement against the kings of the Assam valley,[10] and in south India, in the resistance of the Kallar (literally, 'robber') tribes against the efforts of the rulers of Ramnad and Madurai to extract taxes from them in what were, traditionally, independent hill regions.[11]

As these revolts, movements spread throughout India, however, British rule gradually brought a degree of disruption and suffering among the peasantry which was, it seems likely, more prolonged and widespread than had occurred in Moghul times.[12] The effects of British rule came, of course, unevenly and in stages, but once operative, they created a structure of underdevelopment in the Indian countryside which became endemic, and which has been modified but never eradicated since independence. Although I cannot analyse this structure in detail here, the following seem to me to have affected Indian peasants during the 200 years between the beginning of British rule and the present time.

The early decades of rule by the East India Company saw outright plunder of the country's wealth coupled with ruinous taxation of the peasantry in some areas up to twice that imposed by the Moghuls. These no doubt contributed to the Bengal famine of 1770 in which a third of the people died. The collection of heavy revenues was subsequently regularized in the Permanent Settlements of Bengal, Bihar, and Orissa in 1793 and in comparably harsh settlements in other regions. Revenues in the early decades were used chiefly for government expenses, wars, private fortunes, remittances to Britain, and public works designed to increase imperial trade.[13]

In later decades, land revenue declined to a much smaller proportion of the crop than was exacted by the Moghuls, but by that time surplus was being removed from the peasants by other kinds of agents such as moneylenders, non-cultivating intermediary tenants, landlords, merchants, the new professional classes such as lawyers, and particularly, although less directly, by British firms engaged in export crop farming, banking, shipping, exports and imports, and internal trade.[14]

The British land settlements, for the first time, turned land into a private property of the capitalist kind. The new landlords included zamindars who had previously been revenue collectors under the Moghuls, a variety of princes or subordinate rulers, village headmen, military tenants, religious or secular functionaries of former governments, in some cases peasant cultivators who had hitherto merely leased land under customary regulation, and in other cases merchants or moneylenders who bought land rights, along with the right to collect revenue, in government auctions when previous revenue collectors proved unable to bring in the tax. While such persons gained private landownership, the lower ranks of cultivating tenants, village servants, and serfs lost their hereditary rights to work and to share the produce of village lands, and could be evicted if their landlords found them unnecessary, recalcitrant or unable to pay their rents.

During and since British rule, there has been increasing encroachment into tribal hill territories and oppression of tribes people by European and Indian planters, and by government agents. To the loss of large tribal areas was added exploitation in such forms as rack-renting, unequal terms of trade, usury, corvee and even slave labour, and the obligation to grow cash crops for little or no return.[15]

The British effected a reduction in the scale of at least some Indian handloom and handicraft industries, especially those meant for the production of luxury goods, through discriminatory internal and external tariffs. Such measures virtually destroyed India's export of manufactured goods and also obliged Indians to buy British industrial manufactures, notably cotton textiles.[16] Reports indicate that centres of manufacture such as Dacca and Agra, as large or larger than London in the mid-eighteenth century, shrank as a result of these and other British policies to a fraction of their former size.[17] Craftsmen deprived of their livelihood were driven back upon the land as tenants or landless labourers or joined the modern urban lumpen proletariat. Peasants had to sell their produce for cash, often to moneylenders in return for advance loans, in order to buy imported goods as well as to pay rents and revenues.

On balance, India was plundered through the export of capital to Britain by such methods as the repatriation of profits and salaries, debt services for colonial wars and public works, 'home charges' and adverse terms of trade with respect to raw materials exported from India and to imported manufactured goods.

In many regions various means were used to encourage or compel cultivators to grow industrial crops, and even food crops, for export. In addition to highland plantations for tea, coffee, cinnamon, and later, rubber, large areas of the plains were at different periods turned over to indigo, opium, cotton, oilseeds, jute, pepper, coconuts, and other export crops.[18] Landlords and local merchants profited from their sales to British export firms, and brought pressure on peasants to grow them in their roles as wage labourers, serfs, tenants or indebted smallholders. Despite the expansion of the total cultivated area, the production of export crops reduced the area available for subsistence farming in at least some regions such as Kerala.

Speculation and investment in land, by merchants, bureaucrats, landlords, and successful cash-crop farmers, made land sales increasingly common. The growth of absentee landlordism and of cultivation for private profit meant that traditional paternalistic relations of landlords and their tenants were disrupted in many villages, and that tenants and labourers were exposed to new and more alienating forms of exploitation, resulting in greater resentment on their part.

Population increase occurred, especially after 1921, as modern medical supplies and services reduced epidemics and infant mortality. Thus, the population of former British India more than doubled between 1891 and 1951. At the same time, industry developed very slowly, so that there came to be too many villagers for a palaeotechnic agriculture to feed adequately and large-scale unemployment or underemployment in the villages. In India as a whole, per capita agricultural output declined between 1911 and 1947.[19] Some of the consequences of 'agricultural overpopulation' were fragmentation of landholdings leading to dwarf-tenancies; competition for land among share-croppers and other tenants, which encouraged rack-renting; moneylending and chronic rural indebtedness; and the growth of debt bondage in some areas and of poorly paid day labour in others. Although the data are imperfect, it seems probable that there has been, both during and since British rule, a decline in the proportions of landlords, rich peasants and middle peasants and an increase in the proportions of poor peasants and landless labourers.[20] Today, India has overburdened villages and underemployed and ill-nourished villagers everywhere.[21]

From the 1850s with the building of the railways, the increased movement of goods and people had profound effects. It further undermined the unity and self-sufficiency of villages. The modern transport of foodgrains reduced the danger of severe regional famines; at the same time, by permitting grain stocks to be removed from prosperous areas it appears to have allowed the growth of chronic malnutrition throughout the country. Concomitantly, however, modern transport fostered the movement of ideas between town and country and created links between urban and rural people. Such links strengthened the Indian nationalist movement led by the bourgeoisie; they also permitted a degree of unity between peasants and urban workers in the more recent revolts.

The most brutal feature of the British period was the famines.[22] There were serious regional famines before British rule, notably in the Deccan in 1630–2 and in 1702–4. It seems certain, however, that the famines of the British period were more frequent. Thus, 14 major famines are known to have occurred between the early eleventh and the late seventeenth centuries. During the period of the East India Company government, by contrast, in addition to the catastrophic Bengal famine of 1770, there were 12 serious famines and four periods of acute scarcity before the Mutiny of 1857, while Indian peasants were being tormented by excessive revenue exactions. Still more devastating famines followed the Mutiny. The worst occurred between 1865 and 1899, and the most severe of all in 1896–7, when 97 million were seriously affected and at least 4.5 million died. Another 650,000 died in 1898, and a further 3.25 million in 1899. In the famines of the 1860s the principal victims were landless labourers and unemployed weavers, but by 1900 tenant cultivators formed the largest category employed in government relief works during famines in the Deccan and Gujarat, while landless labourers formed the next largest category, and weavers were still prominent. The data suggests that by the end of the century tenant cultivators had no reserves left and in famines they suffered almost equally with landless labourers and artisans thrown out of work by British industrial policies. Using figures collected by Bhatia, and selecting only those, which record the deaths of more than 100,000 people in any single famine year and region, I have calculated a total of 20,687,000 famine deaths in India between 1866 and 1943. Because of the omission of smaller figures this is undoubtedly far too low.

Probably thanks to improved transportation, no major famine occurred between 1908 and 1943, after which coupled with the stoppage of rice imports from Burma by the Japanese invasion and hoarding and speculation led to the Bengal famine in which 3.5 million died. Since 1947 no catastrophic famine has occurred in India proper (as distinct from Bangladesh), but unknown millions annually die untimely deaths as a result of illness compounded with chronic malnutrition. A United Nations report of 1963 charged that five million Indian children still died of malnutrition each year.[23] Severe shortages occurred in 1964–6, and since 1971 the situation has become increasingly critical, with famine deaths, suicides by starving people, food riots and other forms of agitation in many parts of India.

Since independence, and especially since 1954, foreign food loans have augmented India's food supply, but have also helped plunge the country hopelessly into debt.[24] India's own food production has roughly doubled since independence. This is no mean achievement, but even when combined with foreign imports the increase is barely adequate to meet the needs of a population which grew from 356 million in 1951 to 556 million in 1971. When combined with hoarding, speculation and widening inequality in incomes, it is not at all adequate.

Since independence, land reforms have removed some of the biggest landlords—the zamindars—and some of the non-cultivating intermediary tenants, but in general, laws on land ceilings have been evaded.[25] Before and after each act, landlords have evicted numerous tenants on the grounds that they needed the land for 'personal cultivation' and have created new paper owners to conform with the acts while leaving the real control undisturbed. At least in some areas, therefore, land reforms have resulted in an increase in the proportions of poor peasants working part-time for wages, of landless, and of both rural and urban casual workers and unemployed.[26]

During 1965–71 the 'Green Revolution' increased productivity in some regions. Reports indicate, however, that it tended still further to polarize agricultural incomes, for it enriched the larger owners while tenants and labourers gained little or no increase during a period in which they were also being affected by generalized inflation. As farms are consolidated and operate as industrial capitalist enterprises, the Green Revolution dispossesses some tenants, dis-employs some landless labourers and drives out of business small farmers who cannot afford the new technology and cannot compete.[27] In 1972–4, moreover, the gains of the Green Revolution have for the most part been wiped out by seasonal drought and flooding or, most recently, by shortages of fertilizers.

The above conditions form the background of agrarian revolt from the late eighteenth century until the present. Directly or indirectly, all of them have been either created or severely exacerbated by British colonial policies or by the policies of the Indian government, under the influence of imperialists, in the post-colonial period.[28]

A rough classification of the revolts during British rule yields five types of action in terms of goals, ideology, and methods of organization: (a) restorative rebellions to drive out the British and restore earlier rulers and social relations; (b) religious movements for the liberation of a region, or an ethnic group under a new form of government; (c) social banditry; (d) terrorist vengeance, with ideas of meting out collective justice; and (e) mass insurrections for the redress of particular grievances. (However, only the discussion on modern peasant uprisings are included in this chapter, editor.)

MODERN PEASANT UPRISINGS

Except for the early revolts to drive out the British and re-establish traditional principalities, the peasant uprisings were 'pre-political' or 'primitive' in the special sense that they were not addressed to the future of the nation-state and thus were doomed to failure when they aimed at revolution. These revolts were, however, politically progressive in that they sought a new state of peasant society, which would combine freedom from alien rule together with some traditional virtues and modern technology and popular government, rather than merely reverting to pre-British social structures. The revolts also amply illustrate the remarkable organizing abilities of the peasantry, their potential discipline and solidarity, their determined militancy in opposing imperialism and exploitative class relations, their inventiveness and potential military prowess and their aspirations for a more democratic and egalitarian society. The more impressive uprisings show that even in India, where inter-ethnic strife has produced some of the most tragic modern holocausts, peasants are capable of co-operating in class struggles across caste, religious and even linguistic lines to redress their common grievances.

Peasant revolts since the 1920s have been coordinated within the policies of oppositional political parties. They have formed two major types. On the one hand, there have been political movements or for national or regional autonomy among blocks of tribal peoples. The most notable of these have been the struggle for an independent state in Kashmir, the nationalist war of the Naga and Mizo tribal peoples, and the Jharkhand movement for the political autonomy of the Santhals, Oraons and other tribes. On the other hand, there have been peasant uprisings, which were primarily class struggles and were guided by one or another of India's communist parties.

Seven major peasant uprising or episodes of revolutionary struggle in the Indian countryside have occurred to my knowledge under communist guidance. The Communist Party of India conducted the first four before it split into two wings in 1964. These were the Tebhaga uprising in the north of Bengal in 1946, the Telengana peasant war in former Hyderabad state (now part of Andhra Pradesh) in 1946–8, a strike of tenants and landless labourers in eastern Thanjavur for several weeks in 1948,[29] and a series of short strikes followed by attacks on granaries and grain trucks in Kerala in 1946–8.[30] The other three uprisings were led by Maoist groups which began to break away from the Communist Party of India (Marxist) in 1967. They included prolonged peasant struggles involving land claims and harvest shares in 1966–71 led by the Andhra Pradesh Revolutionary Communist Committee; the uprising in Naxalbari in West Bengal in 1967; and the 'annihilation campaign' of the Communist Party of India (Marxist-Leninist) against landlords, moneylenders, police, and a variety of political enemies of party, especially in Srikakulam, Mushahari, and Debra-Gopivallabpur in 1969–70.[31]

Communist-sponsored uprisings differ in many respects from those of earlier periods. First, of course, they are led at least ostensibly by a vanguard party which recruits members from urban petty bourgeois, urban working class, or even landlord origins as well as from the peasants and which draws on the theories of Marx and Lenin as well as, more recently, Mao Tse-tung. In each uprising the party involved has had as its ultimate goal the revolutionary attainment of a people's democracy as a prelude to the transition to socialism throughout India.[32] Peasant revolts have been coordinated, and sometimes started, in accordance with current party policy, and have sometimes been stopped by the party because of national or even international changes in the party line.[33]

Nevertheless, just as modern tribal nationalist movements, in their goal of ethnic liberation, share common features with and may even draw experience and organizational strength from earlier tribal religious movements,[34] so various communist struggles among the peasants have had features in common with early peasant movements involving social banditry, terrorist vengeance with ideas of popular justice, or mass insurrections for the redressal of grievances.

The most successful communist-led peasant actions were those of Tebhaga in 1946, Telengana in 1946–8, Naxalbari in 1967, and Andhra Pradesh in 1969–71. All of them involved a large component of tribal people. All of these revolts began as strikes or other forms of popular action initiated by the peasants or with their willing consent for the redress of specific grievances. The Tebhaga revolt began with a demand for reduction of the occupying tenants' (jotedars)[35] rights in the crop from half to one-third and a corresponding increase in the rights of poor peasant share-croppers (adhiars or bargadars). It had been preceded in the late 1930s by a campaign on behalf of middle peasants (the better-off tenants) to abolish 'feudal' levies over and above the legal rents. In Telengana, too, the initial demands were for abolition of illegal exactions by the deshmukhs and nawabs—the feudal lords—and later on for cancellation of peasants' debts.[36] In Thanjavur, the demands were for halving the rents paid by cultivating tenants and doubling the wages of landless labourers. In Naxalbari the peasant unions began by taking over land, which the communist-led West Bengal government had already decreed should be removed from the jotedars, the former occupancy tenants who by the time had become outright owners of the land with the abolition of zamindari rights. The land act provided for this land to be distributed to the landless, but the proprietors refused to surrender it. Having driven out the landlords, the peasant unions then went on to distribute all the land among the peasants.[37] Similarly, in Warangal, Khammam and Karimnagar districts of Andhra Pradesh in 1969, the communist peasant unions began their armed struggle by occupying land which had been taken from them by neighbouring landlords and redistributing it among the tribal peasants.[38]

In all these struggles, much as in more successful of the traditional peasant insurrections referred to earlier, the peasant unions were able to secure temporary liberated zones, which they governed for several weeks or months through peasant committees, supervised by the Communist Party. In Thanjavur landlords, police and bureaucrats remained in the area but obeyed the village committees; in the other regions the peasants killed or drove out these figures during the period of the revolutionary government. The largest and longest revolt was that in Telengana, which is reported to have engulfed 2,000 villages in an area of 15,000 square miles, with a population of four million and a peasant army of 5,000. In the more recent Andhra Pradesh uprising of the late 1960s under the Andhra Pradesh Revolutionary Communist Committee, which took place partly in the same area, the revolutionaries claimed in mid-1970 a liberated area of 7,000–8,000 square miles with a population of 500,000–600,000.[39] Repression has since greatly increased and the movement appears to be temporarily crushed.

In contrast with these efforts, communist armed action has been less successful when it employed tactics suggestive of banditry or of terrorist vengeance, unaccompanied by mass insurrection or by demands for redressal of specific grievances and popular control by peasant committees. These tactics predominated in the party's struggles among the peasants in 1948–9 in Kerala and in those of the CPI (ML) in eastern India and elsewhere in 1969–72.[40] In the former instance the communists had earlier, in 1946, conducted successful mass strikes for higher wages among landless labourers and mass cultivation of the forest lands of big landlords. (As in Bengal, they had also successfully organized strikes of middle peasants against illegal levies during the late 1930s.) When, however, police reprisals became heavy and several communists and peasants were killed, the party went partly underground and squads of party members and peasant leaders began to rob grain trucks and ransack the granaries of landlords and distribute food to the people. Although poor peasants admired these exploits—much as they admire those of dacoits who pillage the rich and powerful—the peasants did not become organized through these actions and had no control over them. In the course of these actions the police and the armed goons of (Congress-supporting) landlords killed several leading peasants and party members and arrested most of the others, and the Communist Party became temporarily isolated from the villagers.

In the second instance, the CPI (ML) moving away from its earlier policy of mass struggle in Naxalbari and to some extent in Srikakulam, developed the policy of 'annihilation' of landlords, police, moneylenders, oppressive bureaucrats and enemies of other political parties by secret squads recruited from young party members and their associates in the cities, and, where possible, from the most oppressed groups of poor peasants and landless labourers in the countryside. Several dozens and probably hundreds of landlords in eastern India were assassinated in a three-year period. In their size, secrecy, primitive weaponry, utter devotion and in the fact that they tended to operate some distance from home, these revolutionary squads resembled those of the Moplah peasant insurgents who carried out acts of terrorist vengeance in Malabar in the nineteenth century—and no doubt were also similar to other Indian terrorist groups in urban uprisings of the early twentieth century. While commanding admiration in many villages, the squad tactic, unaccompanied by mass organization around specific economic grievances, isolated the cadres and exposed a defenceless populace to police and later to military reprisals. The annihilation policy, along with other shortcomings, was criticized in a letter from the Chinese government in November 1970, and helped provoke a split in the party in 1971. Since the death of Charu Mazumdar, the party chairman and the main exponent of the annihilation tactic, in July 1972, it has been repudiated by most of the party's remaining leaders.[41] By 1974, most of the CPI (ML)'s cadres appear to have been arrested, or to have left the party, or to have been killed in action or in jails.[42]

* * *

Indian peasants have a long tradition of armed uprisings, reaching back at least to the initial British conquest and the last decades of Moghul government. For more than 200 years peasants in all the major regions have risen repeatedly against landlords, revenue agents and other bureaucrats, moneylenders, police and military forces. The uprisings were responses to relative deprivation of usually severe character, always economic, and often also involving physical brutality or ethnic persecution. The political independence of India has not brought surcease from these distresses, for imperial extraction of wealth from India and oppression by local property owners continue to produce poverty, famine, agricultural sluggishness and agrarian unrest. Major uprisings under communist leadership since British rule not unnaturally show a continuity of tactics with earlier peasant revolts. Of these, the more successful have involved mass insurrections, initially against specific grievances, and the less successful, social banditry and terrorist vengeance. Both in the case of communist revolts and in that of earlier peasant uprisings, social banditry and terrorist vengeance, when they occurred, appear to have happened in the wake of repression of other forms of revolt.

Although revolts have been widespread, certain areas have an especially strong tradition of rebellion. Bengal has been a hotbed of revolt, both rural and urban, from the earliest days of British rule. Some districts in particular such as Mymensingh, Dinajpur, Rangpur and Pabna in Bangladesh, and the Santhal regions of Bihar and West Bengal, figured repeatedly in peasant struggles and continue to do so. The tribal areas of Andhra Pradesh, and the state of Kerala, also have long traditions of revolt. Hill regions where tribal or other minorities retain a certain independence, ethnic unity, and tactical manoeuvrability, and where the terrain is suited to guerilla warfare, are of course especially favourable for peasant struggles, but these have also occurred in densely populated plains such as Thanjavur, where rack-renting, land hunger, landless labour and unemployment cause great suffering.

The more successful revolts of the recent period occurred under irregular conditions, which are unlikely to be repeated. The Tebhaga revolt took place three years after a famine had killed three-and-a-half million Bengalis, leaving a labour shortage. The British government was nervous of offending the peasantry because of the Japanese invasion; it failed to move against the rebels until the Japanese had been defeated and the proportions of the rebellion had become alarming.[43] In Telengana, in 1946–7, the change of government created an Emergency, as the Nizam of Hyderabad refused to accede to the Indian Union, and it was some time before the Indian government decided to invade the state and mop up both the Nizam's forces and the communists. In Thanjavur in 1948 the government was occupied in invading Hyderabad and did not immediately institute repression.

Today, the Indian government is more heavily militarized than it has ever been. It has the experience of crushing recent peasant struggles, of years of police repression in West Bengal, and of the invasion of Bangladesh. It also has the example of methods of repression used by the United States in Indo-China.[44] The increasing poverty, famine, and unemployment make it seem certain that India's agrarian ills can be solved only by a peasant-backed revolution leading to socialism, but the struggle will be very long and hard.

NOTES

1. David F. Aberle, *The Peyote Religion among the Navaho* (Wenner-Gren Foundation for Anthropological Research, 1966), p. 315.

2. Barrington Moore, Jr, *The Social Origins of Dictatorship and Democracy* (Beacon Press, 1966), p. 202.

3. Ibid., p. 383. Moore is actually equivocal about the effects of caste on peasant unrest, for example, see, p. 382.

4. S.B. Chaudhuri, 'Civil Rebellion in the Indian Mutinies, 1857', in S.B. Chaudhuri (ed.), *Civil Rebellion in the Indian Mutinies, 1857–1859* (Calcutta: World Press, 1957), p. 32.

5. See ibid., pp. 56–8, 74–5, and 125–32 for accounts of these revolts.

6. Punjab appears to have been an exception. Although recently conquered, the Sikhs in particular provided soldiers loyal to the British.

7. See E.M.S. Namboodiripad, *The National Question in Kerala* (Bombay, 1952), pp. 102–3; Irfan Habib, *The Agrarian System of Moghul India* (London: Asia Publishing House, 1963), p. 332.

8. The formerly 'primitive tribes' of India number about 45 million and form about one-twelfth of the population.

9. For peasant revolts in the Moghul period see Habib, *The Agrarian System of Moghul India*, pp. 330–3, 337–51. See also Ramkrishna Mukherjee, *The Rise and Fall of the East India Company* (Berlin: Veb Deutscher Verlag der Wissenschaften, 1957), p. 217. Information on the Thuggee is taken mainly from an unpublished paper by the late Saghir Ahmad, 'Thuggees: Rebels or Criminals?', which is being edited for publication. Major sources include W.H. Sleeman, *History and Practices of the Thug* (Philadelphia, 1839); W.H. Sleeman, *Reports on the Depredation Committed by the Thug Gangs of Upper and Central India* (Calcutta, 1840), Francis Tuker, *The Yellow Scarf* (London, 1961); and John Masters, *The Deceivers* (London, 1960).

10. Stephen Fuchs, *Rebellious Prophets: A Study of Messianic Movements in Indian Religions* (Asia Publishing House, 1965), pp. 143–4.

11. W. Francis, *Madras District Gazeteers* (Madura: Madras Government Press, 1906), pp. 88–91.

12. See, for example, Michael Barratt Brown, *After Imperialism* (Heinemann, 1963), pp. 58–60; Amiya Kumar Bagchi, 'Foreign Capital and Economic Development in India: A Schematic View', in Kathleen Gough and Hari P. Sharma (eds), *Imperialism and Revolution in South Asia* (Monthly Review Press, 1973), for analysis.

13. Chaudhuri (ed.), *Civil Rebellion in the Indian Mutinies*, p. 15.

14. See, for example, Brown, *After Imperialism*, pp. 174–7; and Bagchi, 'Foreign Capital and Economic Development in India', in Gough and Sharma (eds), *Imperialism and Revolution in South Asia*.

15. See, for example, Martin Orans, *The Santal* (Wayne State University Press, 1965), pp. 30–6; Rupert M. Moser, 'The Situation of the Adivasis of Chota Nagpur and Santal Parganas, Bihar, India', International Work Group for

Indigenous Affairs, Document No.4 (Denmark: Frekderiksholms Kanal 4, 1972); Chaudhuri, *Civil Rebellion in the Indian Mutinies*, pp. 51–3.

16. The century-old dispute regarding the extent, or even the occurrence, of 'deindustrialization' in nineteenth century India has not abated. Most writers acknowledge that there was certainly a decline in the proportion of Indian craftsmen relative to the total population in the first half of the nineteenth century, and some that the decline continued throughout the century. The argument regarding the earlier period, in particular, seems unquestionable in view of the staggering decline in exports of Indian craft goods and the staggering increases in Indian exports of raw materials and in British imports to India of manufactured goods. For evidence and figures see Brown, *After Imperialism*; Bagchi, 'Foreign Capital and Economic Development in India', in Gough and Sharma (eds), *Imperialism and Revolution in South Asia*; B.B. Misra, *The Indian Middle Classes* (Oxford University Press, 1961); and Daniel Thorner, 'Deindustrialization in India', *Land and Labour in India* (Asia Publishing House, 1962), chapter VI. Ramesh Chandra Dutt's classic study, *The Economic History of India under Early British Rule*, 1757–1837 (Routledge and Kegan Paul, 1963), first published in 1901, is still of great value, especially pp. 176–200. Dharma Kumar, who is mainly concerned about stressing the existence of landless labour in India from pre-British times, nevertheless points out that the agriculturally dependent population increased from about 60 to 69 per cent between 1800 and 1901. It had reached about 75 per cent by 1951 (*Land and Labour in South India* [Cambridge University Press, 1965], p. 181). In Kerala and Thanjavur in the 1950s I found many families in castes traditionally designated as weavers, goldsmiths, traders, tile-makers, high-class potters, oil-mongers, basket and mat-makers, or other craftsmen, who became unable to ply their crafts at some time during British rule and who became tenant farmers, landless labourers, or casual workers in towns. Saghir Ahmad found the same in West Punjab (see 'Peasant Classes in Pakistan', in Gough and Sharma (eds), *Imperialism and Revolution in South Asia*, pp. 203–21). Morris D. Morris has argued more strongly than other recent writers against 'deindustrialization', but I believe his arguments to have been ably answered by several Indian authors. See Morris D. Morris (ed.), 'The Indian Economy in the Nineteenth Century: A Symposium', Indian Economic and Social History Association, Delhi School of Economics (1969).

17. The population of Dacca is reported to have fallen from 150,000 in 1757 to between 30,000 and 40,000 in 1840. In 1787, the exports of Dacca muslins to England amounted to three million rupees, but in 1817 they had ceased altogether. Muishidabad, Surat, Agra, and also southern cities such as Thanjavur suffered correspondingly (Mukherjee, *The Rise and Fall of the East India Company*, pp. 337–9).

18. Opium, for example, was the chief agricultural crop in Malwa and lower Rajputana in 1817–8 (Chaudhuri, *Civil Rebellion in the Indian Mutinies*,

p. 217), and this was still true in 1860–80. Indigo in Bengal and Bihar, cotton in the north–west provinces, central India, and Karnataka, jute and sugarcane in Bengal, and tea, tobacco, and coffee in northeast and south–east India were among the export crops that were greatly expanded in the first-half of the nineteenth century. In Bombay province in 1834–45 cotton occupied 43 per cent of cultivated land in Broach and 22 per cent in Surat but the cultivators were reported to receive little or no profit (B.C. Dutt, *The Economic History of India in the Victorian Age, 1837–1900* [Routledge and Kegan Paul, 1960], p. 98). Today about 40 per cent of the land in Kerala state is devoted to export crops and Assam is similarly dominated by a plantation economy; export crops occupy at least one-fifth of the cultivable land of India as a whole (A.K. Gopalan, *Kerala: Past and Present* [Lawrence and Wishart, 1959], pp. 79–96). In addition to the expansion of industrial crops for export, India also exported increasing amounts of foodgrains during the nineteenth century, in spite of the growing population and the virtual stagnation of subsistence agriculture. Thus, India exported 1.25 million tons of foodgrains in 1879–80, whereas it had exported only 0.65 million pounds sterling worth in 1842, 3.58 million in 1860 and 27.26 million in 1880 (B.M. Bhatia, *Famines in India, 1860–1965* [Asia Publishing House, 1967], p. 38).

19. For a detailed treatment of trends in both commercial and subsistence agriculture during British rule, see George Blyn, *Agricultural Trends in India, 1891–1947* (Philadelphia, 1966).

20. There is uncertainty about the exact proportions of the different classes of peasants and agricultural workers in various decades because of imperfect records and differences in modes of classification. Dharma Kumar rightly points out that there was a substantial class of agricultural labourers at the beginning of British rule, usually enslaved and mainly untouchable. She estimates its size at about 10–15 per cent of the total population. Although she emphasizes continuities in the agrarian structure of India in the nineteenth century, Kumar notes that, agricultural labourers had increased to an estimated 15–20 per cent of the total population in the period between 1871 and 1901. Landless labourers were estimated at 28 per cent of the total workforce in 1951 and 26 per cent in 1971. It is also relevant to estimate the proportions of agricultural labourers in relation to the total population dependent on agriculture in the various periods, and the latter in relation to the total population of India. Rough estimates are as follows. Dharma Kumar estimates the agriculturally dependent population at 60 per cent of the total population in 1800 or even less. Agricultural labourers were probably about 17–25 per cent of the agricultural population. In 1901 the agricultural population was about 69 per cent of the total with agricultural labourers about 27–9 per cent of the agricultural population. In 1951 the agricultural population was about 75 per cent of the total population and agricultural labourers about 38 per cent of the agricultural population. In 1971 the agricultural population had declined again to 69 per cent of the total; agricultural labourers still

formed about 38 per cent of the agriculturally dependent population but a larger proportion of them were probably totally landless than were in 1951. (See Dharma Kumar, *Land and Caste in South India* [Cambridge University Press, 1965], especially pp. 168–93; Charles Bettelheim, *India Independent* [Monthly Review Press, 1969], p. 25; and Government of India Censuses for the various decades.) In some states where the agricultural population's density is very high, the number of agricultural labourers has risen quite rapidly in recent decades. In Thanjavur district, for example, they increased by 60 per cent between 1951 and 1961. (See, for example, Mythily Shivaraman, 'Rumblings of Class Struggle in Thanjavur', in Gough and Sharma (eds), *Imperialism and Revolution in South Asia*, p. 252). When middle and poor peasants lose their lands, moreover, not all of them show up in the category of landless labourers. Some, like a few former landless labourers, are forced to migrate to cities, where they often join the lumpen proletariat of beggars, casual labourers and underemployed craftsmen or service workers. The urban population increased from about 25–31 per cent of the total between 1951 and 1971.

21. See, for example, V.M. Dandekar and Nilkantha Rath, 'Poverty in India: Dimensions and Trends', *Economic and Political Weekly*, 2 January (1971), pp. 106–46. The authors estimate that in 1960–1, 38–40 per cent of India's rural population and about 54 per cent of its urban population received inadequate diet by United Nations standards, even with respect to number of calories. By 1967–8, consumer expenditure among the poorest 5 per cent of villagers had declined slightly, while the poorest 20 per cent in the rural areas had stagnated. In towns, partly as a result of the migration of the rural unemployed to the cities, consumer expenditure had declined among the bottom 40 per cent between 1960–1 and 1967–8. Using a different criterion of a minimum of Rs 15 per month per capita for consumer expenditure, Bardhan estimated that the rural population living below the poverty line was 38.03 per cent in 1960–1, 44.57 per cent in 1964–5 and 53.02 per cent in 1967–8 (P. Bardhan, 'Green Revolution and Agricultural Labourers: A Correction', *Economic and Political Weekly*, 2 January (1971), pp. 25–48. Male agricultural labourers can find work for an average of only 190 days a year and females for only 120 days a year (Bettelheim, *India Independent*, p. 30).

22. See Bhatia, *Famines in India*, for the following information, especially pp. 10–13, 239–42 and 308–39.

23. *Newsweek* (17 June 1963), reporting on the World Food Congress held in Washington, D.C. under the auspices of the United Nations.

24. P.L. Eldridge, *The Politics of Foreign Aid in India* (New Delhi: Vikas Publishing House, 1969), especially pp. 112–16. India imported only 2.6 per cent of its foodgrains in the First Five Year Plan (1951–5) period, but this was increased, chiefly under US Public Law 480 loans, to 4.9 per cent in the Second Plan and 7.5 per cent in the Third.

25. For the impact of land reforms, see, for example, Bhowani Sen, *Evolution of Agrarian Relations in India* (New Delhi: People's Publishing House, 1962);

Grigory Kotovsky, *Agrarian Reforms in India* (People's Publishing House, 1964); and Bettelheim, *India Independent*, pp. 146–233.

26. See Hari P. Sharma, 'Green Revolution in India: Prelude to a Red One?', in Gough and Sharma (eds), *Imperialism and Revolution in South Asia*, pp. 88 and 94. Observations in Kerala in 1964 convinced me that these processes were widely at work there, partly as a result of landlords' reactions to successive land reform acts. In one north Kerala village, for example, I found that whereas in 1948 poor peasants, landless labourers and casually employed non-agricultural day labourers, having no land or only one small garden, were 72.1 per cent of the population, by 1964 they were 88.2 per cent.

27. See, for example, Francine Frankel, *India's Green Revolution: Economic Gains and Political Costs* (Princeton: Princeton University Press, 1971), for the increasing gap in incomes brought about by the Green Revolution and the fact that it chiefly benefits the larger farmers. Mohan Ram (*Maoism in India* [New Delhi: Vikas Publishing House, 1971], pp. 185–6) and Shivaraman, 'Rumblings of Class Struggle in Thanjavur', cite increases in landless labourers and unemployed.

28. See Hamza Alavi, 'Imperialism, Old and New', *The Socialist Register* (Monthly Review Press, 1964), pp. 104–26; and Bagchi, 'Foreign Capital and Economic Development in India', in Gough and Sharma (eds), *Imperialism and Revolution in South Asia*, for characteristics of neo-imperialism in India since independence, and for comparisons and contrasts with the period of British rule. Alavi's later essay, 'The State in Postcolonial Societies: Pakistan and Bangladesh', in Gough and Sharma (eds), *Imperialism and Revolution in South Asia*, pp 145–73, is also in many respects highly relevant to India.

29. See John F. Muehl, *Interview with India* (New York: John Day, 1950), pp. 249–92.

30. See E.M.S. Namboodiripad, *Kerala: Yesterday, Today and Tomorrow* (Calcutta: National Book Agency, 1967), pp. 193, 196.

31. For all of these actions see Mohan Ram, *Maoism in India*, pp. 38–163. See also Mohan Ram, 'Five Years after Naxalbari', *Economic and Political Weekly*, Special Number, 7 (31–3), August (1972), pp. 1471–6.

32. For differences in ideology and strategy among the Communist Party of India (Marxist), the Communist Party of India (Marxist-Leninist) and the Andhra Pradesh Revolutionary Communist Committee, see Mohan Ram, 'The Communist Movement in India', *Bulletin of Concerned Asian Scholars*, 4 (1), Winter (1972), pp. 32–42.

33. The Cominform intervened in 1951 to induce the Communist Party of India to abandon armed struggle. See Mohan Ram, *Maoism in India* (New Delhi: Vikas Publishing House, 1971), p. 34.

34. The movement originally started by the Kacha Naga religious leader Jadonang in 1929 and carried on intermittently by his woman disciple Gaidiliu into the 1960s seems in particular to have been a forerunner of the Naga nationalist movement although confined to one tribe, and much smaller in scale (see Fuchs, *Rebellious Prophets*, pp. 147–56).

35. By the time of the Tebhaga rebellion the zamindar or landlord retained rights to only a small proportion of the produce and the *jotedar* or occupying tenant received most of the surplus. By the time of the Naxalbari revolt the zamindars had been removed and the *jotedars* were the landlords.

36. Hamza Alavi, 'Imperialism, Old and New', in Gough and Sharma (eds), *Imperialism and Revolution in South Asia*.

37. Kanu Sanyal, 'Report on the Peasant Movement in the Terai Region', *Liberation*, 2 (1), November (1968). For the circumstances surrounding the Naxalbari rebellion and for the attitude taken towards it by the Communist Party of India (Marxist), which was then in power in a coalition government in West Bengal, see *People's Democracy*, weekly organ of the CPI (M), 3 (23–30), (1967). See also Mohan Ram, *Maoism in India*, pp. 38–71.

38. Ram, *Maoism in India*, pp. 165–9.

39. Ram, 'The Communist Movement in India', p. 42.

40. Ram, *Maoism in India*, p. 163; 'The Communist Movement in India', p. 41.

41. *Frontier*, 5, 4 November (1973), pp. 15–16.

42. Several massacres of Naxalites or supposed Naxalite supporters have been conducted in the streets by police or gangs of hired hoodlums. In May 1974 about 45,000 revolutionaries were still in jails in India, many of them under the legal classification of criminals rather than of political prisoners. Many have been held for four or more years without being brought to trial.

43. See Hamza Alavi, 'The State of Postcolonial Societies: Pakistan and Bangladesh', in Gough and Sharma (eds), *Imperialism and Revolution in South Asia*.

44. On 1 March 1971, the Government of India sent about 10,000 paramilitary personnel into the districts of Warangal, Khammam and Karimnagar in Andhra Pradesh and subdued the revolutionary struggle there. Something similar to the Vietnamese strategic hamlet plan has been attempted in Srikakulam district, people of scattered villages being herded together in camps at three mile intervals so that food supplies to the guerillas are cut off. No civilians are allowed out after dusk. Some 50,000 tribes people were still confined in these hamlets in April 1974. See Ram, 'The Communist Movement in India', p. 42; *Frontier*, 5, 27 January (1973), p. 8; and *Economic and Political Weekly*, 9 (17), 27 April (1974), p. 666.

Naxalbari Peasant Movement*

PARTHA MUKHERJI

The genesis and evolution of the Naxalite movement by 'communist revolutionaries' seeking fundamental changes in the Indian society, is inextricably tied to the peasant uprising that took place in and around Naxalbari[1] ever since the communist movement experienced its first split in 1964. The formation of the Communist Party of India-Marxist (CPI-M) out of the undivided Communist Party of India (CPI) was a manifestation of the disengagement of the pro-Soviet and pro-Chinese ideological divide within the communist movement. In the space of three years, the contradiction between the more radical pro-Chinese groups and the larger body of moderates within the CPI-M became intensely antagonistic and by April 1969 the Communist Party of India (Marxist-Leninist) (CPI-ML) was formed with avowed revolutionary objectives. By 1973 nearly 40,000 of its members were reportedly languishing in jails and many were 'eliminated' in encounters. The party was banned, its publications confiscated, its activities deemed as insurrectionary. Strangely enough, the application of such force by the established ruling party did not lead to the dissolution or dissipation of the movement, but rather to its multiplication and dispersion. From a single party practicing Naxalism,

* Originally published as 'Study of Social Conflicts: Case of Naxalbari Peasant Movement', *Economic and Political Weekly*, 22 (38), 1987, pp. 1607–17. The study is based on primary data from fieldwork. The extract has been subjected to extensive editing by Partha Mukherji, especially for this volume.

the politics of Naxalism now embraced countless political groupings operative in various parts of the country. Many of these would prefer to maintain with puritanical zeal their ideological position shying away from a reconsolidation under a bigger party organization.

It is in this perspective that the significance of the study undertaken can be viewed. The Naxalbari peasant uprising in 1967, continuing until about 1972, gave rise to spontaneous structural responses all over the country involving large numbers of youth endowed with intellect and courage fired by a revolutionary idealism. The mobilization was the only one of its kind after the nationalist struggle for independence.[2] The Naxalbari peasant revolt gave rise to a radical agrarian movement, which in course of time, was expected to surround, overwhelm and overpower the urban citadels of power for bringing about a revolutionary socialist transformation of the state and society. Naxalbari is the only region which experienced the phases of revolt and revolutionary mobilization. It was felt that a study of the movement in the Naxalbari region would be of considerable significance in the understanding of structure and change and in the analysis of theory and practice.

It is in the Phansidewa, Naxalbari and Khoribari regions in the Siliguri sub-division[3] of the Darjeeling district of West Bengal that the peasant uprising took place. It covered an area of roughly 274 square miles with a population of about 1,67,000 at the time of the movement.[4] The area was covered by 32 revenue units (*mouzas*) including 90 settlements (*jotes*).[5]

METHODOLOGY

The study is based on intensive and extensive fieldwork. The universe was the Siliguri Sub-Division of the northern district of Darjeeling in West Bengal, including the Naxalbari, Khoribari and Phansidewa regions. The units of enquiry in this research were the partisans, anti-partisans and non-partisan households in relation to the movement as it involved or affected them. The selection of units followed the logic of linkages as they became apparent with the progress of the enquiry. The data goes into longitudinal depth. Depth interviews which involved oral histories through case studies were controlled only by an interview guide. Hence the data is of an intensely qualitative nature providing valuable insights into the structure and functioning of the agrarian social system, revealing the contradictions that provided the basis for social mobilization and change.

AGRARIAN STRUCTURE

The agrarian structure of this region cannot be adequately comprehended without a close look at the predominant mode of organization of the agrarian social system of the Rajbansis. The social organization of production of the *jotedari* system has been likened to that of a farm in comparison to the traditional village economy. Structurally, this was a two-tier system of the *jotedar-adhiar* or the *ticcadar-adhiar*,[6] forming a complex of social and economic relationships. Normally, if an 'average' *jotedar* owned lands in excess of what could be cultivated by his family labour, he would parcel out portions of his lands to fixed-rent tenants (*ticcadars*). In the rest of the lands he would settle up to 10–15 families of *adhiars* who would be given lands to cultivate on a crop-sharing basis of 50 per cent gross produce. The limited number of *adhiars* settled on such lands, was a pervasive phenomenon. This followed some latent notion of an outer-population-limit of settled *adhiars*, beyond which it would be difficult to maintain a patrimonial-feudal, quasi-extended 'familial' structure. This was generally the case in the farms of resident *jotedars*. Variations from this modal central tendency generally occurred in the case of substantial non-resident *jotedars* who preferred fixed rent tenants. There were, however, many substantial *jotedars*, who even after exhausting these arrangements were left with surplus uncultivated or barren lands. In such situations special efforts were made to attract *adhiars* and *ticcadars*. Since tenurial arrangements with *adhiars* were not legally guaranteed, and *ticcadars* were bound by annual contracts, there was continuous and large-scale turnover in these categories. Thus if a *jotedar* was able to attract a more efficient *adhiar* he could easily compel a 'lazy' *adhiar* to pack. The unemployed *adhiar* would then seek for another *jotedar* whose marginal efficiency level of production at that point in time permitted an additional recruitment. One septuagenarian erstwhile *jotedar* likened these turnovers to retrenchments and dismissals in tea gardens or factories (*adhiar chhantai*).

The central value which guided this mode of organization was an assurance of loyalty by the *adhiar* to the *jotedar* (respectfully called *giri*). To insure such loyalty the *adhiar* was expected to seek for paddy loan for household consumption from his master at the end of each harvest, *even if he did not need it*. He would, in all probability, begin his tenure with a paddy loan. This eating-out-of-the-granary of the *jotedar* was regarded as a symbol of *adhiar* loyalty and *jotedar* munificence. The other side of the coin was the exploitative character of this credit relationship. The interest payable on such loans was 50 per cent. The recovery of interest at the time of harvest ensured that the *adhiar*s net take-home crop-share fell by six to nine months of his annual household consumption, compelling him for the next round of paddy loan. Perpetual indebtedness was built into the system, nay it was institutionalized.

This loyalty was reciprocated by providing the *adhiar* with free supply of materials for construction of his house. He would be allotted on an average anywhere between approximately 5–15 acres of land depending upon an assessment of the size of the family and its labour productivity. The supply of seeds, plough-cattle and other instruments of production would be free of charge. With the passage of time, rentals in kind were imposed for supply of seeds and plough-cattle, and the cost of the seeds was shared equally. This indicated a trend towards a firmer grip over the *adhiar* with a larger labour supply. The increase in exploitation of labour was somewhat compensated by a minimal 'medical insurance' of sorts for the *adhiar* household.

A unique feature that distinguishes the *adhiar* from a sharecropper in the classic sense of the term, is the 'single-master' configuration of the *jotedar-adhiar* relations of production. The tenancy market was thus culturally restricted in the sense that the sharecropper remained continuously 'attached' to a 'single master'. This delicate balance of perpetual indebtedness and loyalty was disturbed when the *adhiar* accumulated debts in disproportion to his repayment capacities. In such circumstances the *adhiar* fled on his own without the *jotedar* pursuing him and intimidating him legally or physically for settlement of dues. He was allowed to settle down with another *jotedar* even if he was traced by his previous employer; nor would the relationship between the two *jotedar*s necessarily sour on this account. Flights, even 'thefts' of *adhiar*s were either condoned or settled or left unchallenged. 'Theft' of an *adhiar* happened when a *jotedar* had an eye on him for his qualities and would like to employ him, even as he was serving another master. He would then lure him and organize his flight. The matter would be settled between the two *jotedar*s either by a settlement of his debts, or overlooked, depending upon the power equations between the *jotedar*s.

Apart from the crop-sharing and crop-advance content of the economic relationship, the *adhiar* was expected to contribute free labour towards repairing his master's house, his granary, his irrigation channels, and so on for which he would only be entitled to free meals.

The practice of *haoli* or voluntary contribution of the collective labour offered by a group of *adhiar* households in others' fields during sowing and harvesting seasons, took two forms. The *adhiar* families of a *jotedar* would provide voluntary labour to the labouring family members of their master's family. In no instance was it found that the *jotedar* family members reciprocated this cooperation. The other form involved voluntary exchange of labour on a reciprocal basis amongst *adhiar* families themselves.

The *jotedari-adhiary* system did not generate a class of agricultural labourers. However, well-to-do *jotedar*s kept *naukar*s (domestic servants) on long-term basis. Neither the domestic labour nor the *adhiar* sharecropper was 'free' in the labour market. Nonetheless it is interesting that in the Darjeeling *tarai* (foot hills), perpetual indebtedness did not reach the extremes of bondage or slavery as in many other parts of the country. The reproduction of the *jotedari-adhiary* system assured a comfortable subsistence and a general health insurance for the *adhiar*, for which the premium of perpetual indebtedness was the price. In essence the system was sustained by a patrimonial-feudal culture of the Rajbansis.

The otherwise sharp class exploitation was matched by *culturally* egalitarian social relationships amongst the average Rajbansi *jotedar*s. The Rajbansi *adhiar* had free access to the inner sanctums of his master's house participating and helping in all the social ceremonies willingly. Just from looks one could hardly distinguish between a *jotedar* and his *adhiar*. In the event of a marriage taking place in an *adhiar* household, the *jotedar* family's participation was clearly visible. Exchange of gifts flowed both ways, the larger flow from the *jotedar* to the adhiar.

Cases of *jotedar*s without male offsprings bringing eligible *adhiar*s into their families as sons-in-law, though not frequent, were an institutionalized practice. Even in such cases when it came to paddy loans, it came with a 50 per cent interest tag. The economic content of loyalty remained unsparingly uniform.

Barring exceptional cases of very prosperous *jotedar*s attracted by the glamour of urban consumption styles, giving into ludicrous display of wanton spending, the average well-to-do *jotedar* lived a very simple life. Surprisingly, his savings were not entrusted to the custody of banks. Gold currency in the form of gold guineas, and ornaments would be kept hidden under the floor, or in specially devised receptacles in roof thatching. The concept of a monetized market economy had hardly penetrated this region, much less the Rajbansi community. Cases of a *jotedar* settling his long-standing dues with a shopkeeper or an employee, by transferring a *jote* or a part of it, were not very frequent but known occurrences. For example, the grandfather of a prosperous Bihari *jotedar*, had once served as a *chowkidar* (watchman) to one of the large Rajbansi *jotedar*s without drawing any salary continuously for about 15 years. He was rewarded with the gift of a *jote*. This is illustrative of the large-heartedness of the Rajbansi culture which had no clear cognition of the operation of the land market.

The Rajbansis combined economic prosperity with social backwardness to a degree that is difficult to fathom. Surprisingly, the prosperous generations up to the 1940s had remained largely illiterate or hardly crossed elementary education! None had gone through the college. All this was by choice rather than compulsion.

The social organization of agricultural production in the Darjeeling *tarai* was highly institutionalized with the indelible imprint of the Rajbansi culture. So high was the degree of self-regulation of the system that it required no coercive apparatus for social control. Unlike the feudal landlordism practiced in parts of eastern India, *jotedar*s did not employ muscle-men, or *sepai*s,[7] and did not have their '*kutcherries*' (or courts). There was not a single instance of an *adhiar* house being razed to the ground, or his woman violated, for his 'crime'. Incredible as it might sound, the two largest landowners (blood brothers) with estates totalling about 10,000 acres, owning countless *jote*s all over Phansidewa, Khoribari, Naxalbari areas, utilized the services of a single manager, a couple of *sepai*s who were sent on rent collection errands from *sherwan*s.[8] There was no conspicuous evidence of any serious dispute or resistance in the operation of this system. The *jotedari-adhiary* system established by the Rajbansis expanded to include non-Rajbansis who entered the land market. Finding the system so smooth in its functioning, investment in land became attractive, safe and very good. The British were more than content to protect a peacefully self-regulated system that yielded good land revenue with minimum cost of governance.

Given their culture and lifestyle, the Rajbansis applied selective discrimination to distinguish themselves from other ethnic groups. This became conspicuous with the entry on a large scale of the tribal population into the tenancy (*adhy*) and land-lease (*ticca*) markets in north Bengal, via the tea plantations.[9] A change in the agrarian system began with Rajbansi *jotedar*s now recruiting the more labour productive tribal Oraon, Munda, Santal as *adhiar*s and *ticcadar*s, in preference to their own caste men. Though economically more productive, they were culturally marked as 'polluted' communities with whom social interactions were guided by strict observance of commensal restrictions on inter-dining and inter-marriage. Tribal *adhiar*s were not allowed to draw water from their wells and entry into their households was restricted to the outer veranda. Social discrimination was practiced along with the economic exploitation, which was already embedded in the *jotedari* system. The 'strain' within the system was introduced, on the one hand, by the entry of non-Rajbansi Bengalis and other professionals[10] who entered the land market in increasingly large numbers, on the other, by the encouragement provided by the Rajbansi landed interests themselves to the tribals to participate in increasing numbers in the tenancy and land-lease markets.

The decade of the 1940s and the 1950s witnessed two cataclysmic events in this region: (a) the Partition of India, and consequently of Bengal, resulted in a massive influx of population from across the border of eastern Pakistan (the then East Bengal); and (b) the promulgation of the West Bengal Land Acquisition Act of 1953 involved large-scale appropriation of surplus lands affecting suddenly and mainly the Rajbansi landowning population. Subsequently through a series of land reforms, including ceiling on land and protection of tenancy rights, the economic power of the Rajbansis suffered a disastrous decline.

Shorn of their previous economic status, lacking in education and political consciousness without any class organization and identity, the predominant mode of organization of the preponderant community crumbled before the forces of market. The tea plantations did not attract the Rajbansi, Mech or Dhimal labour, so it reached out to the traditional reserves for such labour in the tribal areas of Bihar and West Bengal. They were inducted by the British in large numbers. The understanding of *this overall context of historical evolution of agrarian relations in the tarai is a prima facie requirement for a proper assessment of the Naxalbari movement in store for the future.*

NAXALBARI MOVEMENT: MOBILIZATION

The Tebhaga movement[11] in Bengal which had raged in the adjacent districts of Jalpaiguri and Dinajpur, in the years from 1945–7, had not affected the Siliguri area in the district of Darjeeling. Charu Mazumdar, the architect of the Maoist movement in India, while still a fresher in college, received his first field training in the Tebhaga movement under the leadership of Sachin Dasgupta, who had sacrificed a brilliant career in medicine, to become the president of District Committee of the Communist Party of India of Jalpaiguri. Mazumdar came from a prosperous *jotedar* family, which had an enviable record in the national struggle for independence led by the Congress Party. His father was learned, well known and admired for his qualities of both the head and the heart. He had married into a *jotedar* family and agreed to become a part of his father-in-law's family on request. He was disenchanted with the property bequeathed to him, when, after the demise of his father-in-law, he faced unsavoury behaviour from his other surviving in-laws.

The bohemian, don't-care-a-damn attitude, that Charu Mazumdar developed, and his strong alienation against the class of *jotedar*s in which he himself grew up, can partly be attributed to this environment in which he was brought up.

Even as the Tebhaga movement petered out in the districts of Jalpaiguri and Dinajpur, the first peasant committee formed by the communist workers in the Darjeeling District was established in the Siliguri sub-division in a place called Patharghata in 1946, under the leadership of the three brothers Atin, Nripen and Souren Bose, and the tribal leader Bandhan Oraon. They invoked Tebhaga the peasant struggle by making forcible demands for two-thirds of the crop-shares for the *adhiar*s on the threshing floors (*khamar*s) of *jotedar*s. Possibly the first instance related to one Bhagwan Daya Singh, a big *jotedar* who hailed from the Hindi-speaking state of Uttar Pradesh. The police made seven arrests, and the leaders were forced to sign a bond under Section 107 of the Indian Penal Code undertaking to refrain from such illegal activity in that region.

The slogans of Tebhaga and its front organizations—the *Krishak Sabha* (peasant association) and *Krishak Samiti* (peasant committee)—were the programmatic and organizational instruments with which activists like Kanu Sanyal, Jogen Mukherji, Chunilal Goala, Panchanan Sarkar, and some others made their first entry amongst the exploited peasantry. The initial slogans too were a carry-over from the Tebhaga movement. These were demands for *zamindari* (landlordism) abolition, for land to the tiller, against tenant eviction, for a reduction of interest to 25 per cent on paddy loan, followed by a call to the peasants not to surrender their lands under threat. The earliest contacts with the peasants were established in weekly or bi-weekly village markets (*haat*s). They were not welcome to the *jote*s nor could they enter these without attracting notice of the *jotedar*s.

The first general elections in 1952 witnessed the humiliating defeat of their candidate Bandhan Oraon. This prompted the determined band of workers to step up their activities and efforts. They shifted their venue for their next Krishak Sabha meeting in 1952 outside Siliguri town to Ambari for their first major conference. An estimated 2,000 peasants reportedly attended. A coordination committee was formed consisting of Panchanan Sarkar, Jogen Mukherji, Chunilal Goala, Mujibur Rehman, Khokon Mazumdar, Keshab Mazumdar, Keshab Sarkar who were assigned to Khoribari, Buraganj, Naxalbari, Hatigheesha and Champasuri areas respectively. Kanu Sanyal presided as coordinator.

Henceforward, peasant organizational strength went on gaining with every struggle that yielded result. I shall mention three significant struggles that changed the course of events. Soon after the conclusion of Ambari conference news reached the Krishak Samiti that an *adhiar* had been evicted in Buragunj by one Harihar Singh a *jotedar* hailing from Bihar. The Krishak Samiti made its presence felt in full strength settling for nothing less than his reinstatement. This was a totally unanticipated and alien experience. A bewildered, shocked and completely shaken Harihar Singh was quick to oblige. Krishak Samiti's maiden effort was the taste of its first easy victory.

Two other incidents in the 1950s against Mitin Lal and Serket Singh involved large-scale mobilizations of peasants and a proper trial of strength between Rajbansi *jotedar*s and peasants (*adhiar*s). In the case of Mitin Lal more than a thousand peasants surrounded his house and forcibly reinstated the evicted tenants. Later on, through legal procedures Mitin Lal was able to sustain their eviction. But in the case of Serket Singh the fight was over Tebhaga share. The fierce outcome resulted in the loot of his entire granary followed by a massive display of armed procession of peasants. These three incidents broke the power and morale of the *jotedar*s who at most took recourse to courts of law where occasionally their claims were upheld.

Programmatically, the Krishak Samiti began with their crusade against tenant eviction. Subsequent to the 1953 Act their role expanded to counter attempts by *jotedar*s to circumvent the land ceiling laws. *Ticcadar*s and *adhiar*s were asked not to share their crops unless the *jotedar* produced bona fide documents of ownership claim over the lands they were tilling. The next step was to free peasants from 'extra-economic coercion', namely, produce rents on the maintenance of *jotedar*'s bullocks (*panudan*), free labour for repair of *jotedar*s households, etc. Tebhaga or two-third crop-share (which was now legislated tenancy law) was pursued with vigour until the *adhiar* himself found out that the terms and conditions associated with equal crop-share was working out better. Peasant mobilizations were stepped up during periods of food scarcity.

As mentioned earlier, the Sino-Indian border clash in 1962 affected the Communist movement. The Siliguri and Jalpaiguri units of the party pronounced the Government of India guilty of expansionism. This issue led to a rift within the Communist Party and to its subsequent split in 1964 that witnessed the birth of the pro-Chinese CPI-M. The Siliguri sub-divisional committee in course of time took up an even more radical pro-Chinese stand within the CPI-M to which they now belonged. This belligerent attitude was spearheaded by Charu Mazumdar, who, subsequent to his electoral defeat in the 1966 by-election to the West Bengal Legislative Assembly, circulated a series of documents calling for an armed struggle for revolutionary transformation. This was met with approval by the Siliguri sub-divisional committee of the peasants which was largely guided by the unquestioned peasant leadership of Kanu Sanyal.

Soon differences between Charu Mazumdar and Kanu Sanyal began to surface when the former insisted on fighting *economism* by scaling down the role of peasants and workers organizations, which had supposedly got habituated to making only economic demands, and hence were deemed inappropriate instruments for bringing about any qualitative structural changes. Kanu Sanyal, on the contrary, felt that the long established tradition of peasants and workers struggles so assiduously built over two decades could be propelled towards achieving revolutionary objectives. Mazumdar denounced the parliamentary institutions and likened them to pig sties, whilst Sanyal held that these institutions should be utilized for their political ends and their ultimate overthrow.

In the first phase of this inner party debate in Siliguri, Kanu Sanyal's view prevailed. The elections to the Legislative Assembly in March 1967 were taking place under conditions of a bad harvest. Jangal Santhal, the tribal leader, was made the official candidate of the CPI-M from this constituency. The peasant committee relentlessly went on a de-hoarding and confiscation spree alienating many landed interests. Jangal Santhal lost to the Congress Party, but the Congress Party in the state lost to CPI-M and its United Front allies.

Now that their party was in power, prompted the peasant leaders to step up their de-hoarding drive, give the green signal for forcible seizure of lands with dubious ownership claims (*benami*), and to declare that in the prevailing period of acute food scarcity not one single peasant would be allowed to starve as long as there were paddy stocks. The militancy of the peasants led many Rajbansi *jotedars* flee their homes for safer refuge. An embarrassed CPI-M leadership in power, unable to persuade their more radical comrades, finally resorted to police action to gain control. Most, if not all, the peasant leaders sooner or later found themselves behind bars. Charu Mazumdar was not one of them.

The determined vigour with which the party members rebelled against their central leadership was further fuelled by the Chinese declaration that Naxalbari revolt was the spring thunder over India and that soon the whole country would be engulfed by a prairie fire of revolutionary struggles. This provided an unprecedented legitimacy to the pro-Chinese activists, for whom a Chinese certification overrode all other considerations. During this period the United Front government had been dissolved, and CPI-M and its allies were returned to power with a larger mandate. More firmly straddled in power, the CPI-M adopted an attitude of let-bygones-be-bygones, releasing the imprisoned Naxalbari leaders. No sooner Kanu Sanyal was released on 8 April 1969, the formation of the CPI-ML was announced by him on 22 April in Kolkata.

The political work leading to the formation of the new party was carried out by Charu Mazumdar whilst Kanu Sanyal and other peasant leaders were languishing in jails. He was able to create within a remarkably short period of time a completely new set of leadership drawn from amongst the youth, which replaced maturity with a spirit of revolutionary adventure. The new leadership was almost entirely urban middle class and subject only to the authority of Charu Mazumdar. Released from their incarceration the veteran comrades from Jalpaiguri and Siliguri found in them new faces who had now been privileged with direct access to the leader, Charu Mazumdar, who in the meanwhile, had assumed the position of revolutionary authority. Orders issued from this single source. The peasant leaders were suddenly confronted with these new unfamiliar comrades now lodged in their agrarian bastions issuing orders and demanding protection and sustenance from the peasants. The seeds of inner party contradictions were sowed no sooner than the CPI-ML was formed.

The pattern of events from 1969 onwards stood in sharp contrast to those that took place in 1967. The conspiratorial style of execution of the so-called 'class enemies' by guerilla squads replaced the involvement of peasant masses in collective struggles; agrarian issues receded in the background; and targets for annihilation seemed to include many betrayers from the poorer classes; and finally, with the peasant leaders again taken into custody within a very short period of their release, left the agrarian terrain free for the new leadership. The new revolutionary élan rejected the semi-feudal, imperialist, comprador state and its institutions and sought for their destruction by revolutionary violence. The involvement of the urban middle-class youth carried terrorism into the towns and cities totally upsetting the instruments of social control. In course of time a nonplussed, alienated peasantry became indifferent or withdrew support from the movement, even as state power mounted offensive determined to carry on to a bloody finish. By 1972 the second phase of agrarian revolution came to an end in the Naxalbari region.

NAXALBARI MOVEMENT: ANALYSIS

We are now in a position to attempt an analysis of the movement. Before the advent of the British the two-tier agrarian social system in the *tarai* was largely an arrangement within a single community—the Rajbansis. Presumably the Meches and Dhimals at the same time practiced their egalitarian mode of production. Under the British, with the introduction of railways, the growth of urban centres like Darjeeling and Siliguri, the establishment of tea plantations, the penetration of the market in a basically non-market economy had their consequences. It introduced investment in land by commercial and professional people who came to seek their fortunes in the promising town of Siliguri. These interests were quick to sense the value of the Rajbansi style of organization of agricultural production that fitted quite well their economic interests, and sought not to disrupt it. For both the British as well as the urban investors the peaceful, stable exploitation of labour was welcome. The British, for whom the borders were sensitive areas, did not propose a permanent land revenue settlement, instead they preferred to lease out lands for specific periods of time. In doing so they took care not to disrupt the stable agrarian system by providing for hereditary rights in the lease contract system, a somewhat unusual practice. The commercial and professional interests were conscious of the fragility of this delicate structure. That the unlettered wealthy Rajbansis were oblivious of the dangers that could destroy them was very well perceived by them. Consequently, they tried quite hard to create a class organization of the *jotedar*s so that their own interests too would be safeguarded. The formation of the Jotedar Association and the Tarai Mangal Samiti were such efforts. In the face of total Rajbansi apathy neither of these two organizations took off. When the Congress Party entered the scene it got the Tarai Mangal Samiti dissolved to integrate it with the peasant wing of the party.

As long as land was plenty and labour scarce, the *adhiar* was assured of a comfortable subsistence. The power structure of the *jotedari-adhiary* system was represented by ever so many small 'pyramids' with the *giri* and his *adhiar*s and *ticcadar*s. The power did not extend very much beyond their boundaries. That is why *adhiar* flights and thefts were left to go by default. In fact only later do we find some evidence of *jotedar*s from Bihar or Uttar Pradesh employing strong arm men. As long as the social relationships between Rajbansi *adhiar*s and *jotedar*s blurred the exploitation of *adhiar*s, the system went on reproducing itself smoothly. The entry of the tribal population as *adhiar*s and *ticcadar*s to Rajbansi *jotedar*s signalled the beginning of a new contradiction, that of social discrimination. The consciousness of being looked down upon as of low status unworthy of social interaction with their Rajbansi masters, when their Rajbansi counterparts enjoyed unfettered access into their households, provided a social contradiction so direct that it developed into an antagonistic relationship in course of time. During this period the tribal population had generated a stratum of self-cultivating rich and middle peasants who had entered into the land market by dint of their own industry and hard labour through savings from the plantation labour. The juxtaposition of these two phenomena prepared the ground for the maturation of an antagonistic relationship embedded in the tenancy structure of exploitation.

This is clearly explained by the fact that the earliest to be mobilized by the peasant leadership were from amongst the tribals both in the plantations and in the agrarian fields. The militant culture of the tribals made their armed mobilizations easily possible. The extraordinary mobilization of the peasants and plantation workers that took place in 1955 demanding for bonus for plantation workers can be explained. Plantation labour was exclusively tribal. The peasants mobilized were predominantly tribal ranging from rich to poor peasants. Savings from plantation labour provided the basis for tribal peasantization. Tribal peasant support for tribal worker demand for bonus meant a reinforcement of the process of tribal peasantization through increased savings leading to further investment in land. The close-knit tribal organization provided a ready-made base for the invocation of tribal solidarity.

It is true that Rajbansi *adhiars* joined the movement as time progressed but it would not be a misplaced perception to state, that generally speaking, whilst the tribal peasant responded against exploitation, the Rajbansi *adhiar* was lured by the prospect of greater gain. They had hitched themselves with the wagon of tribal peasantry.

It is interesting to note that Rajbansi *jotedar*s did not develop a consciousness of class. The one time prosperous Rajbansi *jotedar*s bemoan the fact that they could never unite in strength to counter the challenge of the Krishak Samiti threat. Leading Bengali lawyers with outstanding professional credentials as owners of *jote*s sought to give leadership to the Rajbansi *jotedar*s but failed. It is significant that most of the targets of the movement were Rajbansi *jotedar*s as non-Rajbansi Bengali *jotedar*s were non-residents. In a few cases tribals were targets, but almost invariably they were Christians. Even as the class organization of the Rajbansi *jotedar*s weakened, the peasant classes grew from strength-to-strength.

Incredible as it may sound, the 1953 Act had disastrous consequences for many Rajbansi *jotedar*s out of their sheer ignorance. They had not cared to distribute their landed assets among their next of kin, even to the extent permissible within the ceiling laws. This was another blow to their already dwindling power.

While so far the analysis has followed ethnic-class logic, it is instructive to look at it from the perspective of the movement. The peasant associations had clearly set secular goals for combating exploitation, based on the principal contradiction located in the exploitative tenancy relationships. Tactically, the peasantry, initially, could not but be organized through tribal peasant solidarities. Thus ethnic mobilization was sought for achieving secular goals. The party itself sought to secularize the movement by attracting to its fold Rajbansis and other communities. The peasant leadership was able to maintain universalistic values within their organization guided primarily by secular principles. The Ambari conference in 1952 saw 2,000 peasants cooking their own food in 22 different hearths. By the 1960s their conferences were catered to by single kitchens. Such has been the long-term impact of this secularization process, along with other factors, that today it is almost inconceivable that they can once again be mobilized in the same fashion. They are now fragmented in different trade unions and peasant associations all of which are now competing against each other recruiting from the same social bases.

When these massive peasant mobilizations took place, the agrarian social system was less evolved and simply stratified. Between the *jotedar* and the *adhiar* there were no intervening class categories, hence exploitation and/or discrimination was directly and consciously perceived. Such a system is vulnerable to class polarization. The alliance of middle and poor peasant classes was not difficult to form, as they had nothing to lose. They did not get their lands cultivated by *adhiars*. So their support could be sought against the landlord. It can be safely hypothesized: in the present circumstances in which classes do not stand in sharp and direct relationship with each other; when a two-party political confrontation (CPM and Congress Party) is replaced by multiple Marxist and non-Marxist parties competing with each other; when any number of voluntary organizations are extending their clientele; class contradictions cannot be sharp enough to bring about a polarized class mobilization for structural changes as in the past.

Finally, a look at the movement dynamics. In the initial phase of the movement the peasant association sought to bring about a series of quasi-structural changes. It sought to obtain for the *adhiar* better and less exploitative terms with the *jotedars*. The claim for Tebhaga crop-share and the struggle against all other forms of extractions from his legitimate crop share are illustrative of these. The means adopted were combinations of legal and non-institutional (or 'illegitimate') means that involved several trips to the jails every year by the leading peasant leaders and their followers. Thus intra-systemic changes were sought through non-institutionalized and legal means. This vulnerability of the system towards change continued until 1967 when the mobilization was stepped up with a call for forcible seizure of land by the actual tillers of the soil. The movement had now started making demands for systemic change through a more intense use of non-institutionalized violent means. This resulted in a counteraction by the State and its support to the counter-movement by the first ever manifestation of class consciousness among the Rajbansis. In 1969, the movement stepped up non-institutionalized means, and took a plunge for a revolutionary transformation, by inactivating the quasi-movement structures.[12] This resulted in invoking the much larger might of the state, on the one hand, and a loss of legitimacy for the movement from its quasi-movement base. The loss to the movement has since been irretrievable in Naxalbari.

NOTES

1. Situated in the northern district of Darjeeling in the eastern state of West Bengal.
2. The massive mobilization for a total revolution on neo-Gandhian lines was to come up five years later resulting in the declaration of national Emergency and the subsequent fall of India's prime minister and the ruling Congress Party.
3. The Siliguri sub-division was a sensitive frontier region bordering Nepal, Sikkim and close to Bhutan, Tibet and China. Hence the British declared it a non-regulation area, meaning that the legislative decisions taken in Calcutta did not become laws in this region. Its administration was directly under the governor of Bengal. Apart from agricultural crops, the cultivation of tea in plantations was extensive. This chapter discusses only the agrarian structure.
4. Census of India, *West Bengal Part X-A+B Directorate of Census Operation,* Series 22, Government of West Bengal (1971).
5. *Mouza*s are strictly defined boundaries of an area which is the smallest unit of revenue collection in the rural areas. The *jote* is the native term of an identifiable cluster of households. The original settlement pattern of a *jote* differed from the more dispersed villages. One *mouza* can include one or more than one *jote*.
6. The *jotedar* could be a large, middle or even a lesser landowner, who would rent out land to *adhiar*s (rentiers). They could also lease out land on contractual terms to *ticcadar*s. Exactly 97 of the 535 *jotedar*s had practically no lands under direct cultivation. These naturally included all non-resident *jotedar*s. This number was 53 in 1987, indicating a rise in landlordism.
7. *Sepai*s constitute the functional equivalent of the 'police' in the landlord's governing structure.

8. *Sherwan*s were selected from among the *jotedar*'s most loyal *adhiar*s to act as inspectors of weighments of crop during harvest and supervise the share due to *adhiar*s. As an extra consideration for his services the *jotedar* could go to the extent of rewarding him with additional land allotments, and at times, even rent-free land.
9. The first tea garden in the area was established in 1862.
10. These included *marwari*s, pleaders, merchants, etc. who had acquired the holdings by moneylending, who were rent receivers and whose tenants were the actual tillers of the soil; *nijjote* literally translated means 'own *jote*', that is, *jote* under personal cultivation.
11. The fierce agrarian tenant share-croppers movement was for a demand of two-third crop-share instead of the prevailing equal share between the landlord and the tenant.
12. Partha Nath Mukherji, 'Social Movement and Social Change', *Sociological Bulletin*, 26 (1), (1977), pp. 38–59.

The Bhoodan–Gramdan Movement*

T.K. OOMMEN

Though the Bhoodan–Gramdan Movement was initiated only in 1951, three years after the death of Gandhi, the ideology of the movement may be traced back to him. Gandhi pursued two major objectives: Swaraj, broadly understood as independence, and Sarvodaya (literally, 'uplift of all') the ideal society, the non-violent social order, which Gandhi wanted to evolve. After independence, Sarvodaya became the primary Gandhian objective, and it was towards this ideal that he and other leading Gandhian disciples, continued to work.

Even before the attainment of independence there was a rift between Gandhi and his followers, which culminated in his 'retiring' from Indian National Congress, the political organization which he led in the fight against the British. Before disassociating himself from the Congress, Gandhi made a statement wherein he had noted the reasons for his action and the relevant ones are noted below[1]:

1. The failure of Congress intelligentsia to practice hand-spinning (Gandhi had insisted on personal, daily hand-spinning as a prerequisite for membership in Congress instead of a nominal fee).
2. The method of approaching the problem of untouchability (Gandhi

---

* Originally published as 'The Bhoodan–Gramdan Movement: An Analysis', in T.K. Oommen, *Charisma, Stability and Change: An Analysis of Bhoodan–Gramdan Movement in India*, New Delhi: Thomson Press, 1972, pp. 26–44.

advocated complete touchability-orientation, that is, completely avoiding the practice of untouchability).
3. Inadequate recognition by congressmen of the fundamental importance of the creed of non-violence.
4. The means-end controversy (Gandhi insisted on the purity of means, that means should be absolutely non-violent).
5. The growing corruption in Congress ranks.

The reasons that Gandhi listed for his retiring from the Congress organization indicate the gap between the ideals it upheld and the practice. Soon after independence Gandhi had suggested the dissolving of the Congress and wanted that congressmen should become a band of devoted social workers (*lok sevaks*). His suggestion was not heeded then and before he could give it any concrete shape he was shot dead. Soon after his death, the 'constructive workers' (the Gandhian followers engaged in social reconstruction on the lines suggested by him) met at Sevagram in March 1948, in Wardha where Gandhi's Ashram is situated and decided to start a Sarvodaya Samaj, a brotherhood for the upliftment and welfare of one and all, a brotherhood of those believing in the practice of truth and non-violence in all aspects of their life.[2] A Sarvodaya Samiti was formed to organize annual *melas* (meetings), *sammelans* (conferences) and to maintain a register of *sevaks* (servants) and for correspondence in India and abroad with persons interested in the Sarvodaya ideal. Thus, Sarvodaya Samiti emerged as an organization without any challenging objectives or programmes, constituted by a large body of 'unemployed' constructive workers.

The first conference of the members of this organization was held in 1949 near Indore (Madhya Pradesh) where Vinoba Bhave, the leading Gandhian disciple had elucidated the principles of Sarvodaya and the aims of the Samaj. The Akhil Bharat Sarva Seva Sangh was founded to carry on the activities of the Samaj. It is this organization with its headquarters at Kashi, which coordinates the activities undertaken on Gandhian line, including those of Bhoodan–Gramdan movement, in India. The second session of the Sarvodaya Samaj was held in 1950 in Orissa and the third session in Hyderabad (in Andhra Pradesh) in 1951. Vinoba went to Hyderabad to attend the conference from Sevagram Ashram and had planned to walk back to the Ashram after the conference. The objective of this Padayatra was to acquaint himself with the conditions, which existed in rural areas particularly in Telengana. Telengana had just come out of violent peasant riots. It was Vinoba's quest to solve the problem of landlessness through non-violent means, which took him to Telengana where he secured the first land donation, which marked the beginning of the Bhoodan-Yagna (Land Gift Mission).

TELENGANA PEASANT RIOT

As early as in 1947 a revolutionary peasant movement had slowly been forming, led by communist leaders in Telengana.[3] Telengana was the eastern half of the erstwhile princely state of Hyderabad, comprising eight districts having an area of 44,000 sq. miles, populated mainly by the Telugu-speaking people. Under the Nizam a notoriously semi-feudal agrarian system had been perpetuated and the peasantry was ripe for radical leadership. On the eve of independence Hyderabad became a large question mark in the heart of India, being a Hindu majority area, entirely in the hands of a Muslim ruler and managed by Muslim elites. An extremist Muslim sect, the Razakars, demanded the integration of Hyderabad with Pakistan. The Congress and the Communists in temporary alliance, went into underground operation. In September 1948, the Indian government forcibly marched into Hyderabad and the Nizam gave way. When the interim Congress government was set up in Hyderabad after the merger with India, the Communists refused to surrender their arms and went into underground operation against the government. The Communists set in motion an indigenous mass campaign against the landlords mainly in the districts of Nalgonda and Warangal. The armed Communists emerged at night to murder the landlords and to divide their lands among the poor. According to Communist claims, a total of 3,000 villages had been Sovietized, and one million acres of land had been seized by the peasants during that period. A large number of men were killed by the Communists and police during the riots.

Indian Communist leaders claimed that the Telengana peasant riot shook for the first time 'the main bastions of feudal orders in India to its very foundations' and 'blazed the path of Indian peoples Democratic Revolution'.[4] Terror and insecurity prevailed in Telengana from 1948–50.[5] It was this depleted Telengana that Vinoba visited after his Sarvodaya conference in Hyderabad in 1951. On his way back to Wardha by Padayatra he reached Pochampalli village where 40 Harijan (the name Gandhi used for 'untouchables', meaning the children of God) landless families requested him to secure some land for them. Vinoba conveyed this desire of the landless lower castes in a meeting held in the village and the first land gift or Bhoodan of 100 acres came forth.[6] Thus the Bhoodan–Gramdan movement was born out of a crisis.

THE EVOLUTION OF THE MOVEMENT

The initial objective of the Bhoodan movement when it started in 1951 was to secure voluntary donations of land and distribute it to the landless with a view to remove the bitterness existing between the land-owners and the landless. However, the movement soon came out with a demand for one-sixth share of land from all landowners. In 1952, the movement had widened into Gramdan (literally, village-in-gift) and had started advocating the collective ownership of land.

The first village to come under Gramdan was Mangroth in Hamirpur district of Uttar Pradesh. It took more than three years to get another village as a gift. The second and third Gramdans took place in Orissa and the movement started spreading with emphasis on securing villages in gift.

The process of Gramdan starts with an awakening of social consciousness of collective will among the villagers (Gram Bhavana). This is to be followed by Gram Samkalpa, the creation of community determination to accept the Gramdan way of life. It is believed that Gram Samkalpa will result in the generation of Lok Shakti (peoples' power) and this in turn will give birth to a people's polity (Lok-niti). Thus a new environment is hoped to be created where the centre of all activities and efforts, will be individuals.

A village should take three interlinked steps before it earns its title: Gramdan village: (a) the villagers who opt for Gramdan should agree to transfer the title deeds of all their land in favour of a legally constituted village assembly (Gram Sabha); (b) a pre-condition for this being that the village assembly should be constituted beforehand; and (c) creation of a village fund (Gram Kosh) meant for social welfare measures and economic development.

The basic phases of Gramdan are Prapti (receiving), Pushti (completion) and Nirman (reconstruction). During the first phase people are persuaded to make a declaration that they have voluntarily decided to sign away the ownership of land in favour of their village assembly. During the second phase, the community is expected to implement the primary conditions of Gramdan, that is, re-distribution of land, formation of Gram Sabha and the constitution of a village fund (Gram Kosh). Then starts the phase of reconstruction (Nirman) with the active cooperation of the entire village population.

It is necessary at this stage to acquaint ourselves with the changes that the concept of Gramdan has undergone. Though the notion of Gramdan emerged in 1952, the first systematic attempt to define it was made by the Prabandh Samiti of the Akhil Bharat Sarva Seva Sangh, at its meeting in September 1957. Gramdan and gram parivar (village family) were defined as follows:

If about 80% of landowners of a village are prepared to give up the right of ownership of their land and not less than 51% of the total land had come under its purview, the village was to be considered as Gramdan. If, due to scarcity of land, the landless people and their families who have got very small size of land are prepared to similarly gift away their other incomes then it should be considered as 'Gram Parivar'.

The notion of Gram Parivar, thus extended the scope of donation from land to other kinds of wealth (Sampati Dan). Other types of *dans*, such as Shrama Dan (donation of labour), Budhi Dan (gift of intelligence), Jeevan Dan (gift of one's life), etc., too were introduced in order to secure the cooperation of men with varying resources and dispositions.

In the beginning, the term 'village' was meant to refer to a revenue-village and the donation of 80 per cent of the persons owning 51 per cent of the total land was necessary to deem it to be Gramdan. It may be noted here that most villages have hamlets (*tola, patti*, etc.) attached to them and these hamlets were also considered independent villages for purposes of Gramdan donations which also created a number of problems.[7]

After a village was declared Gramdan it was expected that the land in the village should be distributed equally amongst the households taking into account the number of persons in each household. However, such a measure was not welcomed by the landed in general and the richer landlords in particular. Redistribution of land on an equal basis hardly took place anywhere. In order to narrow the gap between the ideal and the actual, the concept of Gramdan was redefined in 1965. Instead of an equitable distribution of land it was thought to be satisfactory, if all landowners parted with only one-twentieth of their land, for distribution to landless. The landowners were permitted to retain 19/20th of their land with permanent heritable rights. The new arrangement was designated as Sulabh Gramdan. Though the leaders of the movement rationalize this goal reversal as, 'one step backward in order to secure two steps forward', in effect, the notion of Sulabh Gramdan amounts to a substantial change in the goal orientation of the movement; a tendency towards the decline of the movement.

The concept of Sulabh Gramdan called for a clear-cut distinction between ownership and possession of land. While a person joining Gramdan was expected to surrender his ownership in respect to his entire land, he can possess 19/20th of the land with permanent hereditary rights. Though it can be argued that theoretically individual ownership of land is abolished through Sulabh Gramdan, practically each owner continues to have the benefits of ownership.

It is felt, by the workers of the movement, that exclusive emphasis of the movement on securing land donation and distribution, narrows down its scope. Consequently, it was decided to work towards an enlarged goal of Gram Swaraj (village republic) in 1963. Therefore, along with Gramdan, the programme of building a Shanti Sena (the peace brigade) and developing village-orientated Khadi too were included, all within the scope of the movement. This came to be known as the Triple programme (Trividh Karyakram). Vinoba declared that the best way of paying homage to the memory of Gandhi during his centenary year in 1969 would be to lay the foundation for Gram Swaraj in every village in India through the movement by that year.

The concept of Sulabh Gramdan as it is understood now insists on four basic conditions:

1. A minimum of one-twentieth of cultivable land should be donated by all landowners in the village for distribution to the landless.
2. The ownership of the entire land in the village should be vested with Gram Sabha (village assembly). The landowner's heritable right with regard to 19/20th of his land will continue. To take loan from the government and cooperative bank one can mortgage the land in possession with the permission of the Gram Sabha and one can sell the land to the Gram Sabha or to any family, which has joined Gramdan.
3. After paying the land revenue and distribution of the crops, one has to contribute to Gram Sabha one-fortieth of the produce of the land for Gram Nidhi (village fund). Those who are landless and have other sources of income will contribute one-thirtieth of it to the village funds either in cash or in labour. The Gram Nidhi is to be used for the maintenance of orphans and destitutes, for extending educational facilities and for the economic development of the village.
4. A Gram Sabha will be constituted by drawing one member from each family (household). The Gram Sabha is expected to function either with unanimity or consensus.

The triple programme for village reconstruction which was accepted in 1963 by the movement could not be implemented with much vigour and failed to maintain the expected tempo. To accelerate the pace of the movement Vinoba gave a call for Gramdan Toofan in 1965. The movement was concentrated in the state of Bihar. There are 70,000 villages in Bihar and if one-seventh of it could be brought under Gramdan within six months, it would have created a conducive environment for the movement.

In order to avoid possible pitfalls while operating on a mass-scale four basic conditions were laid down, for a village to be declared as Gramdan.

1. The village, where 75 per cent of landowners and 75 per cent persons residing in that village have signed the declaration form for surrendering ownership will only be considered a 'pledged' Gramdan.
2. The individual Samarpan-Patra (document surrendering the owner-ship right in land) should be filled in at the same time as one has signed the declaration form (Gramdan Patrika).
3. If one-twentieth part of the village land has been distributed to the landless and Gram Sabha constituted, a village will be considered 'active'.
4. Only after the registration of a Gramdan village by the government, it will be regarded as a 'declared village'.

The number of Gramdan villages were inflated due to the tendency on the part of the workers of the movement to bring smaller villages or hamlets into Gramdan, usually leaving out big villages with a more complex social structure. This situation compelled Vinoba to give a call for Prakhand Dan, that is gift of Blocks (in Rural India a number of villages are grouped under a Community Development Block and they are treated as a unit for purposes of development). Moreover, it was hoped that Prakhand Dan will facilitate reconstruction work, for it is an economically viable unit for developmental purposes.

The first block-gift came from the Tirunelveli district in Tamil Nadu by early 1966. Initially it was thought that only if all the villages in a block are bought under Gramdan that it should be considered to be Prakhand Dan. But later on (April 1966) it was decided that when at least 75 per cent of the total population in a block, excluding the urban population, or 85 per cent of the revenue villages of the block have come under Gramdan, the whole block should be declared as Prakhand Dan.

When all the blocks in a district declare Prakhand Dan, it is deemed as a Zilla Dan. The first Zilla Dan came from the Durbhanga district of Bihar in early 1967.

The state-wise distribution of Gramdans, Prakhand Dans and Zilla Dans is shown in Table 3.1:

Table 3.1: State-wise Distribution of Gramdans, Prakhand Dans, and Zilla Dans as on 20 January 1969

S. No.	States	No. of Gramdans	No. of Prakhand Dans	No. of Zilla Dans
1.	Andhra Pradesh	4,200	10	–
2.	Assam	1,489	1	–
3.	Bihar	39,085	335	7
4.	Delhi	74	–	–
5.	Gujarat	803	3	–
6.	Himachal Pradesh	17	–	–
7.	Jammu and Kashmir	1	–	–
8.	Kerala	418	–	–
9.	Madhya Pradesh	4,242	18	1
10.	Maharashtra	3,126	12	–
11.	Mysore	570	–	–
12.	Orissa	9,348	40	–
13.	Punjab and Haryana	3,694	7	–
14.	Rajasthan	1,021	1	–
15.	Tamil Nadu	5,302	50	1
16.	Uttar Pradesh	12,675	77	2
17.	West Bengal	644	–	–
	Total	86,709	554	11

With this new development the Sarvodaya leaders hope that the movement would influence the political processes in the districts, state and the nation.[8] By late 1960s the movement started focusing on Bihar and strives towards Bihar Dan. The next logical step being talked about is Bharat Dan (Gift of India)!

We have attempted to trace the evolution of the movement from its origin to the present stage. Our main interest was to highlight the goal transformations of the movement, which had widened into an attempt to establish communitarian or collective settlements to effect radical social changes. Faced with the difficulties in this context, the movement had thinned down its target in terms of quality and enlarged its scope to facilitate a wider geographical coverage. The ultimate aim is to envelop the idea of the entire Nation in dan.

CHARISMATIC TRAITS OF THE MOVEMENT

Several social scientists[9] characterize the movement and its leadership as charismatic and popular writers describe the movement as a 'social miracle' and refer to its leader, Vinoba, as a 'saint'[10] and his achievements as 'superhuman'.[11] Notwithstanding such labelling of the movement no systematic attempt has not yet been made to examine its charismatic traits. We propose to undertake this task in this chapter. We have already noted above that the movement emerged out of a crisis situation: the Telengana peasant riot.

The manner in which the first land donation came forth confirms the charismatic characteristic of the movement. When the *harijan* landless families had requested him for land, Vinoba assured them that he would try his best to obtain the same for them. A meeting of the villagers was convened. 'For a minute there was utter silence. Vinoba seemed engrossed in deep meditation. Shortly, after he raised his head and inquired whether there were some land holders also in the lot sitting before him'.[12] The answer was in affirmative and then he had asked, 'If land is not provided by the government or if it takes time, cannot something be done by the village people themselves?' Then came the first donation of 100 acres of land. 'Vinoba passed a sleepless night. He went over the days' incident again and again. He spent the night in prayer. He felt convinced that there was God's hand behind all that and that he wanted to use him as His instruments in that work'.[13] Thus the first land donation came forth in an atmosphere of awe and meditation, inner inspiration of the donor and the faith of the leader in God.

Vinoba's faith in God is deep. He says 'On that day (the day of the first land gift) God gave me a sign. I meditated on it the whole of the following night and ended up by finding out what I had to do…. Without this hint on His part I should never have made up my mind to *Bhoodan*'.[14] This aptly fits in Bittner's[15] observation that in order to ensure the acceptance of the pronouncements of the charismatic leader it needs to be shown that he had received his command or message under the most unusual circumstances, that he 'knows better' thanks to his 'unique experience'.

Vinoba's utterings stand testimony to the fact that his is a movement operated through the 'Gift of the Grace'. 'None except God is the owner of land. We mortals can only be His children'.[16] He urges people to realize that '…God wants this land (India) to make a successful experiment in a non-violent social and economic revolution'.[17] He asserts that 'It (Bhoodan–Gramdan) is a phenomenon inspired by God'.[18] The 'Gift of the grace' so much innate to the charismatic leader is profusely acknowledged by Vinoba and conspicuously present in the movement. Thus the movement derives its inspiration from supra-empirical sources.

The difficulty in labelling a leader's power as charismatic arises due to the absence of adequate empirical indices. The behaviour of the followers does not always indicate the nature of the power possessed by the leader. Friedland suggests that, knowing that a given leader has no claim to legal or traditional authority, it is by intuition that the observer designates his authority as charismatic.[19] But the reason why we label Vinoba as a charismatic leader is far beyond this, for, as Parsons had pointed out 'Charisma is not a metaphysical entity but a strictly empirical observable quality of men and things in relation to human acts and attitudes'.[20]

Vinoba, the initiator of the movement is viewed as a 'saint' by the masses. Drawing upon the goodness of human nature, moving from village-to-village on foot, dressing, eating and behaving like a typical Indian sadhu he operated in a manner which generated tremendous mass appeal. Vinoba dressed in loin cloth, which normally kept only his waist covered, usually lived on five cups of milk a day, and when he ate he used banana leaf instead of plates. He used to get up at 4 AM, operated the charkha regularly, prayed both in the morning and evening, spend time in meditation and thus lead the most simple and disciplined life. Vinoba's appearance, behaviour and conduct created awe and respect in men and women and he was regarded as a 'holy man'.

The Bhoodan–Gramdan movement aims at the total transformation of contemporary Indian society. While this broad vision is the long-term goal, re-structuring the agrarian society in the country is its immediate objective. In fact, the movement had emerged as a response to the agrarian unrest, as we have noted in the beginning of this chapter.

It is important to note that while only rarely revolutionary movements were initiated to tackle agrarian unrest, the agrarian problem is deep-rooted and widespread in India. This is so, in spite of the fact that the land reform laws enacted in India since independence 'constitute the largest body of agrarian legislations passed in such a short period in any country'.[21] India became independent only in 1947 and the Bhoodan–Gramdan movement was started in 1951. It is unrealistic to expect from a new government to make its impact on a deep-seated problem, so quickly. But '...in terms of their announced aims, the land reforms...have by and large failed...and the agrarian problem remains basic, serious, and deeply rooted',[22] and 'the great wave of land reform in India from the agrarian point of view...has turned out to be a fairly conservative process'.[23] That the Bhoodan–Gramdan movement continues to operate in spite of all these legislations goes to indicate that the legislative weapon had failed to grapple with the situation and the fact that the movement is an alternative approach to tackle the agrarian unrest is confirmed.

It is clear that the immediate objective of the movement is economic and ameliorative in character. To this extent the charismatic colour of the movement is faded. However, it is significant to note here that Vinoba insists that the objective of the movement is moral. He asserts: 'Mine is not so much to provide food to the hungry as is to bring it home to the people that before they take their food they must share it with others. I want to create an atmosphere of giving in this age of taking so that non-possession and co-operation in place of ownership and competition, may be the basis of life'.[24] Essentially, then, the movement is a 'mission' and not a mere economic or ameliorative programme.

Notwithstanding the claim made by the leadership in regard to the nature of the movement it is important to know how the collectivity views it and what is the motivating influence that prompts people to participate in the movement. Our data indicate that most of the participants in the movement are motivated by material benefits. This is perhaps inevitable due to the ameliorative programmes of the movement.

The charismatic movement should come forward with new ideas. These ideas may be new goals or new means to achieve the goals which are hitherto pursued through other means. To a large extent the Bhoodan–Gramdan movement emerged due to the failure of land reform legislations and violent agrarian mobilizations to tackle the land question. The distinctive character of the movement is to be found in the means or the mode of procedure it employs. Though it preaches the maxim 'land for society', communalization of land is a notion by no means novel.[25] Agrarian reforms and institutional innovations are attempted through the mechanism of law or through violent revolutions, all through history. None relied on voluntary gift of land, wealth and intelligence for bringing about all-sweeping changes in the structure of the society. It is the uniqueness of the means advocated by Vinoba which adds to the charismatic appeal of the movement.

Our discussion on the nature of Bhoodan–Gramdan movement confirms its charismatic character. It is time to turn to an analysis of the ideology and organization of the movement.

THE IDEOLOGY AND ORGANIZATION OF THE MOVEMENT

Daniel Bell[26] argues that in the contemporary West there is a rough consensus among intellectuals on vital political issues such as the acceptance of a welfare state; the desirability of decentralization of power; a system of mixed economy and political pluralism. To a large extent this consensus is a reaction to the atrocities of the mass society, ushered in by urban-industrialism.[27] Interestingly enough, while intellectual debates on ideology are said to be exhausted in the contemporary West, the new nations of Asia and Africa are shaping new ideologies; those of industrialization, modernization and nationalism. The ideologies of the nineteenth century were universalistic, humanistic, and fashioned by intellectuals. The mass ideologies of Asia and Africa are parochial, instrumental, and created by political leaders. The driving forces of these ideologies were social equality and, in the largest sense, freedom. The impulsions of new ideologies are economic development and national power.[28] Matossian[29] makes the same point; industrially backward countries have two problems: (a) the need to change traditional institutions and values, and (b) the challenge of the modern West. Due to the contact with the industrial West, the native intelligentsia, mostly Western educated, vote for large-scale industrialization and modernization.

It is against this background that we must try to understand the unique nature of the Sarvodaya ideology which is the basis of the Bhoodan–Gramdan movement. We have no intention to attempt an elaborate treatment of the ideology; we will only attempt a sketch of the ideology in its bare rudiments.

Sarvodaya attempts to re-define Indian society in terms of Varna, Ashrama and Dharma, the three basic tenets of Hindu social organization. The value pattern of Sarvodaya is based on certain cardinal principles such as Ahimsa (non-violence), Satya (truth), Asteya (non-accumulation), Sarir-Srama (physical labour), Aswad (regulation of taste), Sarvatra Bhaya Varjan (total fearlessness), Sarva-Dharma-Samanatve (equal reverence for all religions), Swadeshi (using indigenous products), Sparsh Bhavana (complete touchability orientation). These values are sought to be inculcated through the institution of dan, defined as equal sharing (Sama Vibhagh). The notions of Bhoodan, Gramdan, Sampati Dan, Budhi Dan and Jeevan Dan are already developed and in operation. Those subscribing to the Sarvodaya ethic must keep a pot (Sarvodaya-patra) at home to keep contributions in the form of cash or kind to be handed over for the maintenance of Sarvodaya workers, who pledge to offer their life in service of the people. The movement bases itself on the basic ideas of Sarvodaya namely trusteeship, collective ownership and basic democracy (Gram Swaraj).

Sarvodaya aims to evolve a society keeping in line with the genius of India on the one hand and on the other it is referred to as the 'Third Way', an attempt to manufacture a Vishwa Manav, a man with world loyalty. It is a synthetic ideology, which partakes universalistic and humanistic principles and in a limited sense parochial, for, the social laboratory in which the man with world loyalty is to be manufactured is village republic, thus orientated to a limited locale in its vital aspects. It disapproves the revolution of unbridled rising expectations and ceaselessly emphasizes the need for voluntary restriction of wants. Its commitment to industrialization is not unqualified, nay it approves only a minimally industrialized society. It does not vote for an economy of abundance but advocates an economy of self-restraint and frugality. Modernization is not rejected totally while tradition is accepted partially. It purports to avoid the 'evils' of mass society and strives for the retention of primary group relations: it hopes to evolve a communitarian society, a society in which the group has primacy over the individual. It visualizes a polity where all adult members of the society are incorporated into the decision making process, which is designated as a participatory democracy. In order to realize the world of its conception it prefers village republics which plan for themselves while having tangential dependence on wider territorial units encircling it: Districts, States, Nations. The social system visualized through Sarvodaya ideology is neither traditional nor modern: its acceptance of the modern or the rejection of the tradition is not total. For want of a better term we call the Sarvodaya social order a Civic Society.[30] Thus the Sarvodaya ideology is distinctly different from the prevalent ideologies in the new nations. The simultaneous slant given both to tradition and modernity attracts both revivalists and moderns to its fold.

The peculiar character of its ideology renders the Bhoodan–Gramdan movement slightly different from an ideal-typical charismatic movement which thrives mainly on the charismatic appeal of the leader. So far as the movement and its ideology promises a different destination than the one officially sponsored or championed by other ideological streams, it attracts at least some persons who are ideologically orientated and this enhances the possibility of pursuing the goal of the movement independent of the charismatic leader.

We have suggested above that an ideal charismatic movement should operate without any organization, bureaucracy and 'Office'. The position taken by the leaders of the movement in regard to its organizational aspect is proximate to this. Vinoba pleads for the creation of Swatantra Janashakti or the self-reliant power of the people. He believes that the power of the people is admittedly superior to that of the state. Having rejected the power of the state as channelled through law he advocates (a) Vichar Shasan or peaceful conversion of people to one's views, and

(b) Kartrittya-Vibhajan or distribution of work among individuals without creating an administrative bureaucracy.[31]

Vichar Shasan implies the readiness to understand other's point of view and to persuade others to accept one's viewpoints. It rules out the imposition of one's view on others. It insists that one should accept a viewpoint only after getting convinced of its correctness. This position rules out the dominance of rational-legal authority, the instrument of law and coercion in the context of change conceived by the movement.[32] Kartrittya Vibhajan calls for the investing of power in the community and the abolishing of state and its bureaucracy.

Notwithstanding the categorical disapproval of organization and bureaucracy, soon after the first donation a 'trust' constituting the donor, Bhoodan workers and village chiefs was formed to administer the distribution of land. As the movement became widespread the number of Bhoodan workers also steadily increased. As Bhoodan had widened into Gramdan the necessity for several organizations to look after the welfare of Gramdan villages arose. The activities of several villages in a given region needed coordination and a number of regional-local organizations were established at the village, district and state levels. The activities of the movement at the all-India level are coordinated by Akhil Bharat Sarva Seva Sangh. This development confirms our analysis in regard to the life cycle of a charismatic movement.

An organizational base is a prerequisite for pursuing the programmes of the movement. However, it reduces the charismatic orientation of the movement, resulting in routinization of charisma. In addition to this, the problem of leadership at the local level is very important in the case of the movement as it operates at the grass-roots level. While the top-level (national) leadership of the movement is charismatic, the local (the district and village level) leadership may be devoid of charismatic attributes. Nevertheless, we need to recognize the possibility of vertical dispersion of charisma[33] or charisma through contact.

In our attempt to examine the characteristics of the Bhoodan–Gramdan movement, we find that while the movement is predominantly charismatic it has certain non-charismatic traits too. The strong ideological moorings and the fairly well-knit organizational base of the movement, reduce the charismatic content of the movement. Two special features of the Bhoodan–Gramdan movement, add to its atypicality as a charismatic movement. We now turn to an analysis of these characteristics.

SPECIAL FEATURES OF THE MOVEMENT

Unlike other social movements the ideals of Bhoodan–Gramdan movement can be actualized only if men with diverse, in fact, opposing interests simultaneously 'participate' in the movement.[34] So far as the entire accent of the movement is on voluntary donations (of land, wealth, labour, skill and life) by the people, the 'haves' should 'participate' in it for the success of the movement. In fact, it is frequently alleged that many donors donate only uncultivable land and many are motivated to donate, in order to escape the legal measures brought forth to prune the size of their holdings. To this extent the haves develop a vested interest in the continuance of the movement, for, it helps to perpetuate their interests. The danger of the movement becoming a system-maintaining device and the possibility of its revolutionary vitality being sapped looms large in this context.

The continuance of the movement, it appears, is at least partly due to the active connivance and acquiescence of the forces of vested interests in the society. More than once, Vinoba despaired in public that the movement was a failure and he would retire to his Wardha ashram. But with the subsequent injections of official patronage by the government and the local Congress leaders and landlord, it regained its momentum. The official patronage was aimed to confirm its commitment to a socialistic pattern of society. The landlords pledge support, for they despair the repetition of Telengana and are afraid of the alternative course that might confront them. Frequently, Vinoba exhorted people that if they do not give voluntarily the alternative would be Communism. Perhaps it may not be too vulgar a suggestion that the perpetuation of the movement is made possible, to a large extent, due to the combination of the vested-interest forces and the charismatic character of the movement.

An unanticipated consequence of the simultaneous participation of both the haves and have-nots in the movement is to envelop men of divergent motives and interests in it. In order that a movement may succeed the constituent elements should share common interests and pursue common objectives. In the case of Bhoodan–Gramdan movement the 'participants' are drawn from diverse, and to some extent, groups with inimical interests and, therefore, the possibility of goal attainment is likely to be reduced.

Charisma is not only non-institutional but also anti-institutional. The association of charismatic movement with the rational-legal authority (government), will, therefore, reduce the charismatic content of the movement. We have referred to the governmental association and participation in the movement. So far as the movement's immediate aim is to bring about a radical change in the agrarian relations in the country, the official position finds much in common with the movement. In addition to this, since the movement is based on the Sarvodaya ideology which is derived from Gandhi, to whose ideas the Congress Party profusely pays lip-sympathy, the government feels obliged to associate itself with the movement. Third, so far as the movement has arisen as a response to the failure of land legislations initiated by the government, it cannot entirely alienate itself from the movement. In fact the government looks upon the movement as a complementary effort to tackle agrarian problems. In the final analysis the government 'uses' the movement as a legitimizing instrument for its pitfalls, as a tension-management mechanism, and as a diversionary therapy for the masses.

The official patronage given to the movement and the recognition accorded to Vinoba Bhave is considerable. In 1957 Pandit Nehru, the then prime minister of India invited Vinoba Bhave to Delhi to get counsel for his government on certain vital issues. Ministers at the state level invariably accompany the team of padayatris when the latter move about in their respective states. Central ministers approved of the movement by inaugurating the All-India Sarvodaya Conferences, by participating in Padayatra or by issuing appreciative statements. The government also passed special legislations to legalize the donations made under the auspices of the movement. Finally, material incentives in the form of special loans and grants are given to Gramdan villages. All these have led to the stepping up of donations, particularly Gramdan donations. Both the leaders of the movement and the government see much in common between the officially sponsored Community Development Programme and the Bhoodan–Gramdan movement. The officials of the ministry of Community Development and Akhil Bharat Sarva Seva Sangh try to work in coordination.[35]

For the present purpose the consequences of the governmental association with the movement is more important than its motivations. An important latent function of the governmental association with the movement is in directing the people's motivation to material benefits and utilitarian purposes. This is antithetical to the interest of a charismatic movement. Though the leaders of the movement claim that it is essentially a moral movement, we have noted above that the ameliorative programmes of the movement reduces its charismatic content. In addition to this, the governmental association with the movement and the consequent expectation of material benefit that the participants develop, results in a further erosion of charisma from the movement.

We have examined the nature of Bhoodan–Gramdan movement in order to unfold the potential it has for change. We suggest that a purely charismatic movement is incapable of any sustained change process due to its weak ideology and feeble organizational base. While we found that the Bhoodan–Gramdan movement possesses several of the characteristics of a charismatic movement its strong ideological moorings and well-knit organizational base may act as change-propelling forces. Nevertheless these very features of the movement may pose serious dilemmas for the actualization of its goals. Because of the simultaneous emphasis of the Sarvodaya ideology both in terms of tradition and modernity, the persons attracted to its fold may be of divergent backgrounds. This, to some extent, is likely to be inimical to the interests of the movement. The organizational build-up of the movement may facilitate the efficient implementation of its programmes. At the same time, since the movement operates at the grass-root level the 'quality' of local leadership is crucial to its success. So far as organizational positions obtain at the local levels and no specific 'qualifications' are prescribed for recruitment to these positions, they are likely to be filled by disgruntled, frustrated or vested-interest elements. The filling up of organizational positions by such may check the change process.

The ameliorative programmes and the governmental association with the movement might considerably influence the motivations of the collectivity for participating in the movement. Many of them may associate themselves with the movement only for material benefits. Finally, since both the haves and have-nots participate in the movement the constituents are necessarily drawn from different backgrounds. Therefore, it is likely that the rich and the poor, the ideologues and the bureaucrats, the frustrated and the power-oriented, the revivalist and the modern—all seek 'shelter' in the movement. The Sarvodaya ideology is diffuse in character and each of these groups may interpret and invoke it to its advantage. This is likely to render the movement nebulous, amorphous, and a shell without any substance. Inevitably the movement may become incapable of initiating any sustained change process.

NOTES

1. D.G. Tendulkar, *The Mahatma* (Bombay: Vithalbhai K. Jhaveri and D.G. Tendulkar, 1952), Vol. III, pp. 362–7.
2. See Suresh Rambhai, *Vinoba and His Mission* (Kashi: Akhil Bharat Sarva Seva Sangh, 1954), pp. 26–7.

3. For details of Telengana peasant riots see, Gene, D. Overstreet and Marshall Windmiller, *Communism in India* (Berkeley: University of California Press, 1959), especially pp. 246–67 and 300.

4. G. Adhikari, *Resurgent India* (Bombay: People's Publishing House, 1956).

5. For an official version of Communist Party of India on Telengana, see, Information Document No. 7 (1950) (place not given) and Zamindari-Police Terror in Andhra (place and date not given). For an account of governmental version, see *Communist Violence in India* (New Delhi: Ministry of Home Affairs, 1954).

6. It may be interesting to note here that Ramachandra Reddy, the first donor of land to Vinoba, was a man of high idealism. His two brothers Madhusudan Reddy and Narayan Karam Reddy taught philosophy at the Osmania University and the former had obtained his doctoral degree in the philosophy of Aurobindo. Himself a graduate, Ramachandra Reddy too was highly influenced by the doctrines of Aurobindo. His antagonism towards the Communist Party and communists in general was so much that he contested against Ravi Narayana Reddy (his brother-in-law) the famous communist leader (who was also one of the top leaders of the Telengana peasant riot) in the Third General Election. It is indeed interesting to probe into the motivation behind Shri Reddy's donating the land: his conviction that the problem of land can be effectively met through this non-violent approach, or his hatred for violence as it happened in Telengana and the consequent recalcitrant reaction against communists? Or due to his sense of insecurity and despair that the landlords will not be allowed to keep more than a specified area of land? While we recognize the complexity of motivations involved, it is beyond the scope of the present study to pursue its analysis.

7. For a discussion on this, see T.K. Oommen, 'Problems of Gramdan: A Study in Rajasthan', *Economic and Political Weekly*, 17 (20), (1965), pp. 1035–40.

8. Monthly Newsletter of Akhil Sarva Seva Sangh, Varanasi (September, 1968), pp. 22–3.

9. See for example, Milton Yinger, 'Religious Change and Social Change', in Milton Singer (ed.), *Religion, Society and the Individual* (New York: Palgrave Macmillan, 1957), p. 305 and M.C. Sekhar, *Social Change in India* (Poona: Deccan College, 1968), pp. 280–357.

10. Daniel P. Hoffman, *India's Social Miracle* (California: Nature Graph Co., 1961).

11. Hallam Tennyson, *Saint on March* (London: Victor Gollanez, 1955). Also see, H.H. Stevens, 'India's Newest Saint', foreword to Hoffman, *India's Social Miracle*, p. 4.

12. Suresh Rambhai, *Vinoba and His Mission*, p. 39.

13. Ibid., p. 40.

14. Lanza Del Vasto, *Gandhi to Vinoba* (London: Rider and Company, 1956), p. 85.

15. Egon Bittner, 'Radicalism and the Organization of Radical Movement', *American Sociological Review*, 28 (6), (1963), pp. 936–7.

16. Hoffman, *India's Social Miracle*, p. 46.

17. Ibid., p. 24.

18. Suresh Rambhai, *Vinoba and His Mission*, p. 44.

19. W.H. Friedland, 'For a Sociological Concept of Charisma', *Social Forces*, 43 (1), (1964), p. 22.

20. Talcott Parsons, *Structure of Social Action* (Illinois: The Free Press of Glencoe, 1940), pp. 668–9.

21. Daniel Thorner and Alice Thorner, *Land and Labour in India* (Bombay: Asia Publishing House, 1962), p. 63.

22. Ibid., p. 5.

23. Ibid., p. 3. That the implementation of the enacted land legislations is ineffective, is a point made by other students of agrarian reforms in India. See for instance, M.L. Dantwala, 'Prospects and Problems of Land Reform in India', *Economic Development and Cultural Change*, 6 (1), (1957), pp. 3–11.

24. Suresh Rambhai, *Progress of a Pilgrimage* (Kashi: Akhil Bharat Sarve Seva Sangh, 1958), p. 43.

25. Of the several reformers who have argued for agrarian socialism and for the maxim 'land for society' Henry George is the most outstanding. See his *Progress and Poverty* (New York: The Modern Library, 1879). Leo Tolstoy, John Ruskin and Thomas Paine upheld similar conceptions about the ownership in land. The Fabians in the early phase, upheld, 'public property in land is the basic economic conditions of socialism', see Bernard Shaw, *Fabian Essays* (London: Allen and Unwin, 1948), (Jubilee edition), p. 24.

26. Daniel Bell, *The End of Ideology* (Illinois: The Free Press of Glencoe, 1960), p. 373.

27. Bell, *The End of Ideology*, pp. 21–36.

28. Ibid., p. 373.

29. M.Matossian, 'Ideologies of delayed industrialization', *Economic Development and Cultural Change*, 6 (2), (1958), pp. 217–18.

30. Following the lead given by Edward Shils, Almond and Verba had defined civic culture, which '...is neither traditional nor modern but partaking of both; a pluralistic culture based on communication and persuasion, a culture of consensus and diversity, a culture that permitted change but moderated it'. Gabriel A. Almond and Sidney Verba, *The Civic Culture* (Princeton: Princeton University Press, 1963), p. 8. We have described the Sarvodaya social order almost in a similar vein. It is keeping these considerations in mind that we propose the term civic society to refer to the Sarvodaya social order.

31. Rambhai, *Progress of a Pilgrimage*, p. 5.

32. Not withstanding the disapproval or very cautious approval of law as an instrument of social change by Sarvodaya leaders several legislations have been passed to accelerate the movement, though antithetical to the very spirit of a charismatic movement. However, the exclusive dependence on voluntaristic action without introducing reinforcement mechanisms such as law, seem to be as much dangerous as the introduction of law without

the creation of appropriate social climate. Though interesting this point is a diversion from our argument and hence not pursued further.

33. Shils argues that the dispersion of charisma from the political and religious segments to the economic segment is a prerequisite for economic growth. Obviously the reference is to horizontal dispersion. We suggest that vertical dispersion of charisma is equally important. In the present context vertical dispersion is viewed as a prerequisite for the effectiveness of charismatic leadership. See, Edward Shils, 'The Concentration and Disperson of Charisma: Their Bearing on Economic Policy in Under-developed Countries', *World Politics*, 2 (1), (1958), pp. 1–19.

34. Vinoba is aware of this problem. He says: 'If I can be the agent of both the rich and poor I shall be glad. For the poor I am striving to win rights. For the rich I am striving to win moral developments'. See, Tennyson, *Saint on March*, p. 69.

35. For details, see, *Gramdan Movement* (New Delhi: Planning Commission, Government of India, 1964).

The New Farmers' Movement in Maharashtra*

D.N. DHANAGARE

The new farmers' movement in India gathered momentum in the 1970s. Its reverberations were first felt in Tamil Nadu, down South, where the Vivasayigal Sangham (farmers' association) had launched a series of agitations demanding fair prices for agricultural produce. Its leader Ramaswamy Naidu mobilized impressive support from the farm sector for its 'road-blocking' and similar types of agitations. The Kisan Union in Punjab was equally restive. It demanded higher remunerative price for wheat in 1973 itself and had even asked farmers to boycott *mandi*s (market-yards) and not to sell wheat to any government agency. The Shetkari Sanghatana's emergence in Maharashtra in 1979 was with a big bang. It first agitated for remunerative price for onion—a perishable produce whose prices dropped dramatically during the 1978–9 consecutive harvest.[1] The rise of the Karnataka Rajya Rayyat Sangha (KRRS) under Professor Nanjundaswamy's leadership was almost simultaneous.[2]

The spate of farmers' mobilizations in different parts of India appeared almost as a well-orchestrated action, though it was really not so. Similarity of problems the farmers faced in Maharashtra, Punjab, Karnataka, and Tamil Nadu was very striking though. Agitations

* Originally published as 'The New Farmers' Movement in Maharashtra', in Fumiko Oshikawa (ed.), *South Asia under the Economic Reforms*, Osaka, Japan: The Japan Center for Area Studies, 1999, pp. 247–61.

everywhere were marked by spontaneity and similarity in the forms of protest, as well as in the state response to them. As elsewhere the movement in Maharashtra was sustained by repeated protests against low sugarcane prices (1980–1), followed by those on tobacco (near Nipani on the Maharashtra–Karnataka border), milk, wheat and cotton (in Vidarbha area) from 1981–5 or so. Numbers of those joining these agitational protests, by the Shetkari Sanghatana were swelling constantly. Barring the agitation over milk-prices, on all other agricultural produce, Sanghatana agitations had paid off rich dividends. The state government conceded to most of its demands and with that the base of the new farmers' movement widened in the countryside, specially in Maharashtra in the early 1980s as new enthusiastic supporters joined their ranks.[3] Its visibility and media coverage were equally important factors that sustained the farmers' movement initially.

Generally, the turbulence amongst the farmers in the 1970s and 1980s must be understood as an offshoot of two contradictions unleashed by the Green Revolution in rural India in the post-High Yielding Varieties Programme's fairly successful implementation. First, whereas the agricultural productivity had been substantially increased, thanks to the adoption of new seeds, fertilizers that is, 'green-revolution' technology, agricultural profitability did not keep pace with high productivity. Ideologues of the farmers' movements all over India argued that agriculture was, and continued to be, a losing proposition unless the State came forward to offer support prices for farm produce to ensure that prices at least covered the cost of production.[4] The second contradiction was better portrayed by the growing proportion of population below the poverty line in India as a sharp contrast to the prosperity champions of the Green Revolution often claimed it had brought in.[5] What is significant is that productivity and general prosperity brought about by the Green Revolution had not resulted in reduction of poverty, specially in rural India.

The main achievement of the farmers' movement in Maharashtra has been that it brought the farm issues to the centrestage of the political and ideological discourse in India. The movement's principal ideologue Sharad Joshi translated the technical jargon of the 'Terms of trade' between industry and agriculture into a comprehensible idiom of 'India vs. Bharat'. Anchored in Rosa Luxemberg's theoretical contributions on 'internal colonialism',[6] Joshi argued that the unevenness in the development of the industry and underdevelopment of agriculture could be removed only by a single panacea, that is, remunerative prices for farm produce. This would generate some profits to farmers and augment the process of capital accumulation in the countryside.

Streaks of economism and populism were then evident in the ideology of the Shetkari Sanghatana as it believed that all sections of 'Bharat', that is, farmers in rural India would stand to benefit and hence they must unite under its banner.[7] The industry-agriculture (that is, India vs. Bharat) contradictions were projected as primary and hence the movement tended to relegate 'rich farmers-landless labourers' internal contradiction in rural India (Bharat) to a minor position.

The ideological interpellations by Sharad Joshi helped the farmers' movement in the 1980s to bring together most of their organizations working in different states. An Interstate Coordination Committee (ICC) was set up with membership from all the states. Key partners in ICC belonged to the Bharatiya Kisan Union (BKU) led by Mahendra Singh Tikait—a Jat clan leader from western Uttar Pradesh, BKU from Punjab, the Shetkari Sanghatana from Maharashtra and the Gujarat Khedut Sangh. The KRRS led by Professor Nanjundaswamy was no doubt, formally a part of the ICC but always felt that ICC was an uneasy coalition. Some partners obviously found Sharad Joshi's domination in the ICC repulsive. In fact, despite some ideological differences with Joshi, Professor Nanjundaswamy's KRRS joined the ICC primarily to contain Joshi and restore balance-of-power both within the farmer's movement and in the changing political power equations at the all-India level.[8] In a public interview Professor Nanjundaswamy is reported to have said:

Sharad Joshi does not believe in ideology. We differ with his one-point programme. He says that the prices are not scientifically calculated. If the prices (are) given all the problem will be automatically solved. It does not happen. Multipronged solution has to be formulated to set right the rural economy. This is the basic ideological difference with Sharad Joshi.[9]

Such simmering differences within ICC surfaced openly around 1990. The reasons are not far to seek. In the formative years of the Shetkari Sanghatana, Sharad Joshi repeatedly used 'one-point programme' (the demand for support prices, or cost-linked agricultural prices) and harped on 'India vs. Bharat' catchwords to captivate the rural masses. He was reticent over several polemical issues such as state policy on agricultural exports and imports, debureaucratization of measures, withdrawal of state subsidy to farmers using irrigation, electricity and fertilizers as well as loans. However, first under Indira Gandhi and later during Rajiv Gandhi's regime the process of economic liberalization had set in and had been accelerated. After Indira Gandhi's return to power in 1980, a conscious policy was adopted to gradually open the doors of Indian economy for multinational corporations to invest in India and to relax fiscal policy and rules. The rigidities of the 'license permit raj' were sought to be removed substantially to facilitate investments by foreign companies. It was truly in June–July 1991 when the Narasimha Rao Government came to power that India took strides towards drastic revision in its economic policies and favoured aligning these policies with global economic trends on the one hand and contemporary economic realities in India on the other.[10]

As Dunkel proposals were being debated all over the world in the early 1990s and India was getting ready to sign the draft as well as to join the World Trade Organization, further liberalization of the Indian economic policies of the Nehruvian era was inevitable. During the 1991–6 period, after years of intense debate, serious rethinking of Indian economic and policy planning has resulted in deregulation of industrial investment activities, an expanded role for private sector and privatization, as against the hitherto much pampered public sector, import liberalization, disinvestments of a part of government equity in public sector undertakings, increased investment in agriculture and social sectors—such as health and education so as to ensure minimum protection and social security to the more vulnerable sections.[11]

The new economic reforms and the policy of liberalization, entailed by the Dunkel Draft, was bound to sharpen the internal differences within the new farmers' movement all over India, especially in Maharashtra and would have set in a kind of process of polarization of various organizations which were held together in the ICC for some time. Any psychologism attempting to reduce the explanation of the fissions within the movement to personalities of leaders like Sharad Joshi, Tikait or Nanjundaswamy would not lead us anywhere in understanding divergent responses of the new farmers' movement to globalization. The political economy of globalization and reforms ought to be looked into if an understanding has to emerge as to why liberalization led to polarization within the farmers' movement.

A quick glimpse at the Dunkel proposals on agriculture and as they were seen to be affecting Indian agriculture whether favourably or adversely would not be out of place in this context.

DUNKEL-GATT PRESCRIPTIONS ON AGRICULTURE

Broadly speaking the Dunkel Draft provided for two sets of measures—those concerning general applications, the draft expected (a) that domestic support to agricultural production be reduced by 20 per cent by 1999; (b) that export, that is, direct subsidies shall be subject to commitment for reduction by 36 per cent and 24 per cent in 1993 and

1999, respectively; and (c) that tariffication or ordinary customs duty be reduced (on an average basis) by 36 per cent by 1999; maximum rate of (prescribed) reduction was expected to be 15 per cent for each tariff line.[12]

As for the developing countries—such as India—the Dunkel text stipulated (a) that countries where aggregate support (in the form of a variety of subsidies) is up to 10 per cent for individual agricultural product, shall not be required to reduce subsidy. (For instance, Indian government's subsidy is less than 10 per cent; hence this clause would not affect Indian farmers adversely in the near future.) (b) Investment subsidies provided to poor and marginal farmers would be exempted completely from the purview of the reduction commitments.

Table 4.1: Agricultural Subsidy as Percentage of the Price Received by Producers from Different Countries (1985–6)

Countries	Subsidy (in per cent)
Argentina	–38
China	–34
Pakistan	–22
Egypt	–6
India	–2
Brazil	+21
Mexico	+43
Australia	+10
New Zealand	+19
United States	+26
EEC	+37
Japan	+72

Table 4.2: Increase in Agricultural Subsidy in Developed Countries

Countries	1979–81 (in per cent)	1986–8 (in per cent)
United States	16	39
Canada	24	46
EEC	37	49
Japan	57	75

Source: S. Brahme, *Dunkel Prastav-Bharatiya Shetiwar Halla* (Dunkel Proposals—An Attack on Indian Agriculture) in Marathi, Pune: Shankar Brahme Granthalaya, 1993, p. 18 (both tables).

In India more than 56 per cent of the landholders held less than one hectare (or 2.5 acres) of holding and were classified as 'marginal' landholders in 1981. Another 18 per cent of landholders had less than two hectares.[13] Therefore, nearly three-fourths of the cultivators would be less likely to be affected adversely by the reduction commitments as per the Dunkel Draft prescriptions. (c) Developing countries with non-convertible currencies, which have balance of payments restrictions would (have been) exempted from the purview of tariffication of non-tariff measures.[14]

Available statistics clearly show that for many years now, some of the advanced countries have been subsidizing their agricultural production heavily thereby distorting and offsetting the world trade completely. Figures given in Table 4.1 clearly bring out the high levels of subsidy in many developed countries as against subsidy levels in some of the developing countries.

Facts presented in Table 4.2 tell us that over the 1979–88 decade, agricultural subsidies were hiked in the United States, Canada, European Economic Community (EEC) and Japan. On the contrary, countries like India, Pakistan, and China offer minus subsidies suggesting that subsidies are hopelessly inadequate (Table 4.1). As per the Dunkel text the developed countries will have to reduce their export subsidy on farm products by 36 per cent in value, and by 21 per cent in volume by the year 1999. Correspondingly, countries like India ought to increase agricultural subsidies. Protagonists of Dunkel proposals in India have argued that once subsidies are reduced in developed countries, prices of their agricultural produce will rise by about 10 per cent in the world market and consequently Indian farmers would get some benefits. Due to a comparative price advantage, for instance higher sugar prices in the world market will directly benefit Indian farmers. One apprehension, however, is that it will have an adverse impact on poor countries which are required to import food, at least in the short run.

So far as reduction in subsidy is concerned, Indian agriculture, it is argued, does not have to worry as the maximum subsidy permissible under the Dunkel proposals is Rs 30,000 crores whereas presently it stands at Rs 11,300 crores for Indian agriculture.[15] Hence, in the near future Dunkel-GATT proposals were not likely to reduce subsidies to the farm sector in India.

Sometimes Indian farmers harbour fears that once the Dunkel regime starts they will not be allowed to use their own seeds for the next year's sowing operations. In reality though, the Dunkel proposals assume that those farmers who cultivate land for cereals, and not for seed production *per se* would be allowed to keep a part of the seeds to be used next year. Such seeds could be given to others in the neighbourhood as a part of exchange relationships. However, the only stipulation here is that a farmer must not produce new kind of seeds in the majority of his land for sale under his own brand. If any farmer innovates new seeds, he has to abide by the Dunkel rules and will have to get them duly patented.

More optimistic supporters of GATT foresee a good deal of scope for seed development and production activity in India. Even a major biotechnological application and gene revolution is anticipated by some people. Similarly, under GATT's mandatory provision of 'minimum access of domestic markets of developed countries to farm produce from outside' an opportunity for export of Indian agricultural products to Europe, Japan, South Korea, etc. seems possible.[16] Thus, theoretically at least, Indian farmers can make the best use of this opportunity to export their produce.

The Shetkari Sanghatana ideologue Sharad Joshi shared this optimism over what the GATT would spell out for the Indian farmers. He, therefore, openly supported GATT and the entire package of economic liberalization and globalization though not without discomfiture to other partners in the Interstate Coordination Committee of the farmers' organizations. Joshi highlighted four major features of GATT to be most favourable to Indian farmers. They are:

1. It proposed to remove all levy and compulsory procurement from farmers. If the government wanted to regulate the supply of cereals through a public distribution system, it must buy grains from the open market and not impose a levy to procure them from farmers at cheaper rates.

2. It wanted such a restructuring of farm economy whereby the pressure of poor surplus labour power on agriculture would be reduced eventually. Agriculture must not be labour intensive as it had been in the traditional agricultural economy that suited pre-industrial India.

3. It expected member nation-states to remove all restrictions on export of farm produce even when agricultural production declined in a particular year due to unfavourable season.

4. Although it wanted member-states (of GATT/WTO) to progressively reduce the subsidy to agricultural sector up to 10 per cent, this would affect nations like Japan, France and the United States where governments offered very high farm subsidies ranging from 36–90 per cent. Hence, this proposal would not affect Indian farmers since the level of subsidy in India is –25 per cent.[17]

About trade-related intellectual property rights (TRIPS) on which the Dunkel Draft has an exhaustive chapter, Sharad Joshi argues that their immediate implications will be two-fold: (a) Patent rights will be extended to food, chemicals, medicines, biotechnology research etc.; and (b) the duration of protection has to be 20 years uniformly. Accepting these conditionalities as fair, Joshi has ridiculed Indian intelligentsia—scientists, researchers, etc. who are opposing the extension of patent laws because these handful of elites had all along been thriving by copying or through plagiarism. Those who have exploited farmers so far have now started 'crying wolf' that Indian farmers will have to buy seeds, fertilizers, medicines, and so on, at an exorbitant price, or that 'our biodiversity will be ruined forever'. Such elitist apprehensions have been termed as hoax by Joshi. Finally, he has expressed his robust optimism in the capabilities of Indian farmers to make new seeds and compete well under the 'free market access regime'.[18]

Such an unqualified advocacy of GATT by an ideologue of the farmers' movement needs to be subjected to closer scrutiny so that any one-sided exaggerations, often built into an ideological discourse,

Table 4.3: Proportion of World's Food Production and Population
(A Comparison between the Developed and the Developing
Countries/Continents, 1990)

Country/Continent	World's Food Production (in per cent)	Population (in per cent)
North America	20.2	8.1
Europe	14.4	9.4
Former USSR (now CIS)	11.9	5.4
Africa	4.7	12.1
Asia	43.9	58.8
South America	3.5	5.6
United States	15.6	4.7
India	10.4	16.1

Source: D. Desai, Bharatiya Sheti anti Dunkel Niti (Indian Agriculture and Dunkel Policy) in Marathi, Pune: Samajvigyan Academy, November 1993, p. 6.
Note: Some figures have been left out in this tabular presentation as they were not very relevant for the discussion here.

could be brought out clearly. First of all, it needs to be stressed that the sharp contrasts between social and economic realities in the developed as well as in the developing world have been overlooked by supporters of Dunkel and GATT. Sharad Joshi and his Shetkari Sanghatana are no exceptions. A simple comparison of the proportion of world's food production in different continents as against the percentage of the world's total population that these continents help subsist, would be quite revealing. The data presented in Table 4.3 bring out these contrasts.

It is quite evident that the proportion of food produced in United States as percentage of total food production of the world is 15.6 per cent, while the population percentage is just 4.7 per cent. In contrast, India has 16.1 per cent of world's population but produces only 10.4 per cent of world's total food output. Although GATT has placed certain restrictions and imposed some obligations and conditionalities on both the developed and the developing countries entering world trade, their proposed equalization through GATT measures remains at the theoretical level only often raising sceptical reactions. In practice, trade in agricultural produce between the two can be an exchange between two unequals. The fact that the unequal relationship between the North and South, between developed and developing countries has been historically determined, has been more or less glossed over by the framers of GATT and its supporters (in developing countries) whose political stakes are high. What is significant is that an ideologue of a farmers' movement, like Sharad Joshi, also chose to overlook the basic inequalities among trading partners.

Often a romanticized, rosy picture is painted about the prospects of export and the outlet Indian agricultural produce will have in the world market. Economists seem to be divided in their assessments of export prospects for Indian farmers flowing from the GATT measures. Supporters of GATT and Dunkel highlight the advantages which India would derive in agricultural exports, further arguing that this will more than make up for the negative consequences of the new intellectual property regime under the World Trade Organization. However, Usha Menon[19] has argued that such an export optimism is not really warranted by the GATT proposals.

Although GATT rules stipulate that developed countries must reduce agricultural subsidies, the desired results of such a measure are offset by the way the subsidy system actually operates. For instance the EEC, which has adopted the common Agricultural Policy, has guaranteed high price to farmers by protecting them from external competition. EEC does this by means of variable duties, which neutralized the difference between international and high domestic prices. In addition, farmers are given 'export subsidies' (not debarred by GATT) to ensure that their products could be sold at cheaper prices prevailing in the international markets.[20]

Theoretically GATT regime would entail reduction commitments on the part of developed countries, which would pave the way for making the world market accessible to more enterprising, and competitive exporters from developing countries like India. However, these hopes are founded on 'heroic' assumptions that new GATT regulations would necessarily lead to reduction of subsidies offered in the developed countries. The GATT rules refer to direct subsidies only. They leave loopholes whereby the developed countries could continue to support domestic farmers in a form that would not be counted as 'subsidies', such as (a) the direct payments to farmers, not necessarily related to the levels of production—called 'decoupled income support', (b) environment-related subsidies, and (c) subsidies for backward regions.[21] Under the present GATT rules these payments to farmers can neither be disallowed nor termed as 'subsidies' to agriculture. To quote Usha Menon:

…from 1995–6 onwards cereal growers (in EEC) will be (are being) paid ECU (European Currency Unit) 207 a hectare (about Rs 8,000 a hectare) and oilseed growers will be (are being) paid ECU 359 a hectare (Rs15,000 a hectare)….
.With this kind of subsidy European farmers will be able to compete effectively in the international market, even if the export subsidies are withdrawn. It is because of this level of indirect subsidy paid on the basis of holdings that EEC is able to reduce its target price for cereals to ECU 100 a tonne. In fact, this could make their cereals even cheaper than India's.[22]

The protection promised to developing countries like India under the 'balance of payment crisis' clause in GATT is again not everlasting. Once this cover is lifted, Indian farmers would have to face stiff competition with cheap, subsidized foodgrain imports (since a certain percentage of domestic food requirements, as per GATT, will have to be met by imports). Moreover, India will be constrained from imposing countervailing duties to prevent food imports because according to Article 13 of GATT, indirect subsidies (offered in developed countries have been considered as 'non-actionable'.[23]

Finally, although Sharad Joshi and other protagonists of the GATT regime feel that the right of farmers to save seeds will not be assailed,[24] it is safeguarded only in the immediate future (that is, say up to 1999). Two possibilities thereafter cannot be ruled out: (a) the Indian farmers right to save seeds can be taken away after the review of the relevant clause at the end of the first five years of the GATT regime, (b) likewise, the introduction of plant breeders' rights (PBRs) (very much demanded by the original Dunkel proposals),[25] if it materializes, can bring, in a form of monopoly rights quite similar to patents, made applicable to seeds. In that case, Indian farmers would end up paying heavily for seeds and the farm-seeds industry in India would stand to lose.

An elaborate resume of the critics of GATT and Dunkel proposals has been given above to provide a balanced view of the arguments and counterarguments. Intricacies of such a technical discourse can be infinite. Our purpose here is to show that the promised integration of Indian agriculture into the world market, as envisaged by the new world trading regime is really not as rosy and attractive as its protagonists would like to paint it. On the other side, the pitfalls of that integration may not be as devastating for Indian agriculture as its critics often make it out to be. The real question is, once integrated fully with WTO would Indian agriculture have the freedom to selectively link with, and delink itself from, the GATT rules.

It is really unlikely that ideologues like Sharad Joshi of the new farmers' movement are unaware of the dangers inherent in the global regime, integration with the world market and in new economic reforms. In spite of that, ideologues often choose to selectively appropriate an advantageous part of an economic argument to sustain both the spontaneity of their protest movement and their leadership. The ideologues of the farmers' movement in India since mid-1980s onwards (Joshi, Professor Nanjundaswamy or Tikait) chose to respond differently to GATT and the new economic reforms. As stated earlier, Joshi came out with an unqualified, unbridled advocacy of the GATT regime, whereas the responses of Tikait in Uttar Pradesh was exactly the reverse, as he opposed the Dunkel proposals. And so did Professor Nanjundaswamy in Karnataka where the KRRS took an aggressive stand against any excessive penetration of the Indian economy by the multinationals—such as on the Kargil issue.[26] In Punjab GATT created factions within BKU as one group led by Bhupinder Singh Mann supported the liberalization and GATT while the faction led by Rajewal opposed.[27] In this context it is important to note that Bhupinder Singh Mann was nominated to the Rajya Sabha (Upper house of the Indian Parliament) by the V.P. Singh-led Janata Government which had also appointed Sharad Joshi as an advisor to the Ministry of Agriculture with the status of a cabinet rank minister. The farmer's movement in Maharashtra was not free from fissions and internal divisions. A group led by Anil Gote deserted the Shetkari Sanghatana and joined the Samajwadi Janata Party—a new national-level political formation.

Sharad Joshi's own position on GATT has since then become more qualified, now that his new political party—called Swatantra Bharat Party, set up on the eve of the Assembly Elections in Maharashtra in March 1995 and which also contested seats in parliamentary elections in Maharashtra in March 1996, met with its 'Waterloo'. One thing is absolutely clear that the new farmers' movement, specially its leadership, was divided on Dunkel and GATT right from the beginning. Such a scenario was bound to lead to an inevitable fragmentation of a movement that was reasonably well coordinated till 1985 or so.

The argument we wish to advance here is that the differential response of the farmers' movement to new economic reforms and globalization cannot possibly be understood purely in terms of the economic reasoning or rationality. Justifications offered for supporting or for opposing GATT by the leaders of the farmers' movement are only partly guided by economic consideration, but also they are partly dictated by political compulsions. Hence, the focus of our analysis ought to be shifted to power politics, changing political equations and fragmentation of political processes at the national and state levels. Here, this chapter is confined to the understanding of the Shetkari Sanghatana and its politics in Maharashtra under Sharad Joshi's leadership vis-à-vis economic reforms.

POLITICS OF POWERS: SHETKARI SANGHATANA'S RESPONSE TO GATT

An organization like the Shetkari Sanghatana, that claimed to have mobilized 70 per cent of farmers and peasants, could not possibly have remained apolitical. A leading activist of the movement like Vijay Javandhia, a former president of the Interstate Coordination Committee of Farmers' Organizations, has all along been a known supporter of the Sanghatana's involvement in electoral politics since 1980 itself. Sharad Joshi was still undecided at that stage about the Sanghatana's strategy and tactics vis-à-vis mainstream party politics in India. Even in 1983 at the Sanghatana workers' meeting, held in Manmad, conflicting views were expressed by participants about their role in party/electoral politics. A sizable group of them were in favour of active political participation, in the form of Sanghatana activists contesting elections to Panchayats and to cooperative societies, banks or sugar cooperatives. In fact between 1984 and 1988 Sanghatana workers did contest these local-level elections in the areas of their stronghold.[28]

In the 1980s Sharad Joshi's Sanghatana preferred politics of alliance, but its frequently shifting partners in the alliance often raised doubts about the exact political and ideological stance of the Sanghatana and its leaders. At the assembly elections in Maharashtra in 1985, Sanghatana had declared the ruling Congress (Indira) as its 'enemy No.1'. Hence its first electoral alliance was with the Socialist Congress led by Sharad Pawar who was then outside the Congress as a rebel against the dynastic culture prevalent in the party. At a farmers' rally, held in Rahuri (district Ahmednagar) during the electoral campaign, Sharad Joshi shared the platform with Choudhary Charan Singh (then leader of the Bharatiya Kranti Dal), Datta Samant (a trade unionist from Bombay), and Sharad Pawar. In the election campaign the Sanghatana activists then openly canvassed for candidates of the Progressive Democratic Front led by Sharad Pawar.

By 1989–90, however, the Janata Dal had regained its lost ground after the collapse of the post-Emergency Janata Government. A substantial part of the credit of the Janata revival in 1986–7 onwards must go to the V.P. Singh–Rajiv Gandhi rift over the Bofors issue. This had led the former to step down as the Defence Minister from the Union Cabinet and to join the Janata Party. As elsewhere political equations changed dramatically as a sequel to V.P. Singh's exit. In 1990, the Lok Sabha (Parliamentary) elections and Maharashtra State Assembly elections coincided; the Sanghatana workers contested as the Janata Party candidates in more than 25 constituencies and managed to get six of them elected to the State Assembly. However, its tactics of multiple alliances in the parliamentary elections proved to be a miserable failure as they were confusing, and to some extent intriguing to many of its workers, let alone to the voter at large.

The outcome of Sanghatana's fickle minded politics in 1989–90 was only to be expected. At the parliamentary elections in Maharashtra, out of the total 48 seats, Sanghatana decided to support the Congress on nine seats and Janata and other opposition parties (such as the Republican Party and Peasants and Workers Party) on the remaining 39 seats. Sharad Joshi's strategy was incomprehensible to many voters. Sanghatana supported candidates were routed in the 1990 Parliamentary elections in Maharashtra. After such a dismal performance that gave the Sanghatana leaders a rude shock, the political survival of Sharad Joshi was possible only through 'rehabilitation' under the patronage of V.P. Singh[29] who then led the Janata Government at the centre with the support of the Bharatiya Janata Party (BJP), from outside.

In the V.P. Singh Government in Delhi, Choudhary Devi Lal was given the post of Deputy Prime Minister (the no. 2 position in the government) in addition to the charge of Ministry of Agriculture. Devi Lal who was himself aspiring to be the prime minister could never reconcile to his subordinate position to V.P. Singh both in the party and in the government. Given his social background and political upbringing, Devi Lal was less likely to studiously involve himself in the agriculture ministry which otherwise is both a demanding and an absorbing portfolio to hold. The Janata Dal's electoral manifesto had offered to the rural voter and farmers a rosy dream—the promises of not only fair prices to agricultural produce but also substantial subsidies to the farm sector besides implementation of the Mandal Commission's recommendations and an increase in the share of agriculture in the plan allocation to 50 per cent.[30] In order to redeem these pledges made to the voter, the V.P. Singh Government needed a star performer to draft its agricultural policy. Sharad Joshi was therefore inducted in the agricultural ministry as an advisor (with the rank of a cabinet minister). It served dual purposes for V.P. Singh. First, the task of preparing a draft agricultural policy, as well as of deciding such technical matters like agricultural prices and costs of production, which had suddenly acquired significance. This work could be handled by Sharad Joshi with finesse and sophistication. Second, at the same time Joshi could be expected to keep a vigilant check over Devi Lal who might have otherwise succumbed to populist pressures and taken all the liberty to announce populist concessions to the farm sector. Such measures would entice rural voters alright, but for any government the financial burden on the state treasury was unaffordable.

To cite only one example, political parties and leaders of all persuasions were vying with each other to woo the farmers. Waiving farm loans was their most favourite populist measure in late 1980s and early 1990s. In the V.P. Singh Government, Devi Lal was quite adamant on loan-waivers since the BJP governments in the states of Uttar Pradesh, Madhya Pradesh and Rajasthan had used this measure successfully to capture power by offering fabulous concessions to the farm sector.[31]

In the politics of state power Sharad Joshi was seen in 1990 as a protege of V.P. Singh, as he had been inducted by the latter in the agriculture ministry with a definite purpose. V.P. Singh's Government also faced one of the worst crises of foreign currency reserves and the balance of payments. Joshi was, therefore, left with no option but to oppose Devi Lal's populism as an unprincipled and expensive measure. Therefore, Joshi's subsequent swing in favour of the world market, competitive ventures or enterprises by farmers, their export-oriented farming, and so on, has to be understood as primarily a political compulsion. His pro-Dunkel/WTO politics since 1990 could be seen as a post-facto theorization of an essentially 'anti-farmer' stand he was compelled to take being an insider to the V.P. Singh Government.[32]

By the time the Sanghatana leader could carry his convictions over the newly acquired pro-Dunkel policy to the people, the V.P. Singh Government had collapsed in November 1990 due to power-tussles and factionalism within the Janata Party. Devi Lal had joined hands with Chandrashekhar who had managed to occupy the prime ministerial post for about six months (November 1990–May 1991) with the support of the Congress. Following Rajiv Gandhi's assassination in 1991, the Narasimha Rao Government took office in June 1991. The new government adopted the policy of globalization, economic reforms and structural adjustments without making much ado of its adieu to Nehruvian policies and to socialism. The process of integration of the Indian economy in the global market via multinationals and also through IMF/World Bank loans has been on the Congress agenda since Indira Gandhi had been returned to power in 1980. The Narasimha Rao Government only carried forward that process without any ideological inhibitions or hangovers of socialism. Quintessentially then Sharad Joshi's advocacy for free world market and unbridled competition had drawn him closer to the Congress. As one of his critics had said, the post-Rajiv Congress had found in him a Congress campaigner but under the Janata mask.[33]

* * *

The polemical position taken by Sharad Joshi on the Dunkel, GATT, and economic reforms under the global market regime has led to divisions and fragmentation in the farmers' movement not only in Maharashtra but also all over India. This development is to be seen as inherent in or an integral part of the faction formations in a fragmented polity. The political space in India, or even in the constituent state, is no longer dominated by a single party. The one-party domination syndrome of 1960s had given way long ago and has been replaced by political sharing through constantly shifting alliances. So long as Sharad Joshi's movement stayed away from party and power politics, it operated within the space of civil society and its leader held almost a charismatic sway on the farmers' movement. From the mid-1980s, when its priorities shifted from civil society to the state and power politics, the movement found its topsy-turvy stand vis-à-vis politics as unavoidable, though often garbed under the euphemism of 'political pragmatism'. We finally argue that the divergent responses of farmers' movement to globalization and economic reforms have to be understood as a logical extension of that pragmatism. Though GATT regulations were in fact perceived differentially as beneficial, or detrimental to certain class interests in the Indian countryside, these perceptual differences within the farmers' movement in themselves do not adequately explain its fragmented, often incoherent, responses to GATT and globalization or economic liberalization. They need to be explained, at least partly in terms of the national as well as regional level politics of power and shifting political alignments.

NOTES

1. For details, see D.N. Dhanagare, 'Shetkari Sanghatana: The Farmers' Movement in Maharashtra—Background and Ideology', *Social Action*, 40 (4), October–December (1990), pp. 347–69.

2. The farmers' movement in Karnataka has been well documented and analysed by M.V. Nadkarni, *Farmers' Movement in India* (New Delhi: Allied Publishers, 1987).

3. See V. Parulekar, *Yoddha Shetkari* (Peasant warrior) (in Marathi) (Pune: Rajhans Prakashan, 1983).

4. Sharad Joshi, *Prachalit Arthavyawasthewar Nava Prakash* (A New Light on the Contemporary Economic System) in Marathi, no. 2 (Alibagh: Shetkari Prakashan, 1982), pp. 18–39.

5. These two contradictions have been discussed elaborately in D.N. Dhanagare, 'Green Revolution and Social Inequalities in Rural India', *Economic and Political Weekly*, 22 (19–21), May (1987), pp. 137–44.

6. Reference here is to: Rosa Luxemburg, *The Accumulation of Capital* (London: Routledge and Kegan Paul, 1963), pp. 348–54.

7. See, for example, Sharad Joshi, *Bharat Speaks* (Bombay: BUILD Documentation Centre, n.d.).

8. M.H. Assadi, *Peasant Movement in Karnataka, 1980–94* (Delhi: Shipra Publications, 1997), pp. 137–40.

9. This quotation is taken from Assadi, *Peasant Movement in Karnataka*, 1997, p. 141.

10. See Manmohan Singh, 'India: The Unfinished Agenda of Economic Reforms', 28th Jawaharlal Nehru Memorial Lecture, New Delhi, 13 November 1996.

11. Ibid., p. 3.

12. For details, see *Dunkel's Draft Text: Indian Agriculture* (New Delhi: NWGPL, 1992).

13. *Agricultural Census* (India) (1981).

14. These details have been taken from Nalini V. Dave, 'Dunkel Proposals and India', *Yojana*, 381 (8), 15 October (1994), pp. 20–1.

15. Ibid., p. 21.

16. For instance, see F. Klaus, G. Fischer, and K.S. Parikh, 'Would Developing Countries Benefit from Agricultural Trade Liberalisation in OECD Countries', in *Agricultural Trade Liberalisation: Implications for Developing Countries* (Paris: OECD and World Bank, 1990).

17. Sharad Joshi, 'Dunkel Prastav Shetkaryanchaya Hitacha' (Dunkel Proposals Beneficial to Farmers) in Marathi, *Kirloskar* (a Marathi magazine) (July 1993), pp. 3–9.
18. Ibid., pp. 8–9.
19. See, U. Menon, 'False Hopes: Where are the Farm Exports?', *Frontline*, 11 (9), 6 May (1994), p. 130.
20. Ibid., p. 130.
21. Ibid.
22. Ibid.
23. Ibid., p. 132.
24. See, for example, Joshi, 'Dunkel Proposals Beneficial to Farmers', pp. 3–9; and also, Dave, 'Dunkel Proposals and India', pp. 20–4.
25. For details, see Klaus, Fischer, and Parikh, 'Would Developing Countries Benefit from Agricultural Trade Liberalisation in OECD Countries'.
26. Assadi, *Peasant Movement in Karnataka*, pp. 275–6.
27. For the background of the Bharatiya Kisan Union in Punjab, see Nadkarni, *Farmers' Movement in India*.
28. D.N. Dhanagare, *Shetkari Sanghatana ani Pakshiya Rajakaran* (Shetkari Sanghatana and Party Politics) in Marathi, *Samajshastra Samshodhan Patrika*, (1986).
29. For a perceptive critique of Sharad Joshi's shifting political alliances, see V. Javandhia, 'Shetkari Sanghatanecha Bolka Rajakeeya Prawas' (A Self-explanatory Political Journey of Shetkari Sanghatana) in Marathi, *Daily Loksatta* (Pune edn), 5 August (1996), p. 6.
30. See, Gail Omvedt, *Reinventing Revolution—New Social Movements and the Socialist-Tradition in India* (New York: M.E. Sharpe, 1993), p. 261.
31. Javandhia, 'A Self-Explanatory Political Journey of Shetkari Sanghatana', p. 6.
32. Ibid., p. 6.
33. Ibid.

The Indian Labour Movement
Growth and Character[*]
S.M. PANDEY

The Webbs, after examining the history of the labour movement of Britain in the eighteenth and nineteenth centuries defined a trade-union as 'a continuous association of wage earners for the purpose of maintaining or improving the conditions of their working lives'.[1] Implicit in this definition is the idea that a union is not likely to be successful in achieving its goals unless it can win, and maintain on a permanent basis, an adequate and stable membership. It is this notion of continuity through time, which distinguishes a trade-union from a demonstration. The degree of continuity of membership is a function of the composition and stability of the working force. The workers who have just left a primitive form of subsistence agriculture and have not adjusted themselves well to the new environment of the urbanized industrial community, may not be able to form a stable and permanent rank and file of a trade union. The labour movement of a developing country, therefore, has to pass through various stages before it can reach the stage of continuity and stability.

The purpose of this chapter is to identify some of the more salient characteristics of the Indian labour movement in different stages of its growth and to attempt at identifying some of the factors responsible for them.

[*] Originally published as 'The Indian Labour Movement: Growth and Character', *Indian Journal of Labour Economics*, 9 (1), 1966, pp. 14–39.

ITS GROWTH AND CHANGING CHARACTER

The history of the Indian labour movement may conveniently be divided into three main stages, according to the structural developments and changes in the movement's character: (a) Origin and Temporary Organization (1875–1917); (b) Beginning of the Organized Labour Movement (1918–46); and (c) Relatively Continuous Organization and Political Involvement (1947–63).

Origin and Temporary Organization (1875–1917)

The origin of the labour movement in India during the later-half of the nineteenth century may be traced in terms of the attempts to protest against the deplorable conditions of work and employment, mainly of a large number of women and children. Alternative hypotheses have been advanced regarding the initiation of the agitation for the factory legislation in India. According to one view, the initial cause of the origin of labour movement in India was the rivalry of the Lancashire textile magnates. It was because of the protest lodged by the Lancashire textile manufacturers that the First Commission for the investigation of factory conditions in 1875 was appointed.[2] On the other hand, it is held that the movement for factory legislation was humanitarian in origin, and it was at a later stage that the trade jealousy of Lancashire became a contributing factor.[3] Both the hypotheses seem to be partly correct. Thus, while the First Factory Commission was appointed in 1875 as a result of agitation in England, no action was taken by the government to enact any legislation. Therefore, to focus attention on the working conditions in the factories, S.S. Bengalee started a fresh agitation for factory legislation in India. He drafted a Bill on Child Labour in April 1878 to be introduced in the Bombay Legislative Council, permission to which was refused. The movement for factory legislation was completely humanitarian so far. Later on, however, the course of action was changed and Bengalee appealed to Manchester for support, which led to a fresh agitation in England ultimately resulting in the enactment of the Factories Act of 1881.[4] N.M. Lokhanday founded the Bombay Mill Hands Association and represented the workers' viewpoint through memoranda, memorials and commissions.

Born out of philanthropy, the motive force of the movement was sympathy.[5] Short-lived associations were formed for passing the legislation. There was no continuity in these associations which were disbanded as soon as their immediate demands were met. The Bombay Mill Hands Association was disbanded after some of its demands were conceded to by the Mill Owners' Association and later codified in the legislation of the Bombay Presidency. Even before it disbanded, the Mill-Hands Association was described as non-existent as an organization: 'The Bombay Mill Hands have no organized trade-union....the (Mill Hands') Association has no existence as an organized body, having no roll of membership, no funds and no rules....Mr Lokhanday simply acts as voluntary adviser to any mill hand who may come to him'.[6]

Beginning of the Organized Labour Movement (1918–46)

The second stage of the development of the Indian labour movement marked the beginning of organized labour movement and was characterized by the rise of somewhat continuous trade-unions, coordinative efforts and political activities. A start was made by B.P. Wadia who formed in 1918 the Madras Labour Union. Wadia himself was a politician and journalist with radical leanings. This union was successful in removing some grievances of the workers: 'The success was unexpectedly quick after the establishment of the union; the midday salutory interval of half an hour for food was lengthened by the employers; It had an extraordinary effect on the workers....Encouraged by this small concession, they joined the union in their thousands....'.[7]

During 1918–20, a large number of the unions sprang up all over India. Most important factors contributing to the growth of labour movement during this period were: (a) increasing economic hardships of industrial workers due to rising prices; (b) awakening of class-consciousness among the workers; (c) upsurge of feeling of nationalism and struggle for national independence; (d) success of the Soviet Revolution (1917); and (e) the formation of the International Labour Organization (ILO).

As can be seen from Table 5.1 the index numbers of wholesale and consumers' prices increased tremendously from 1914 (beginning of the World War I) to 1918 (end of the War).

Table 5.1: Index Numbers of Prices and Wages[8]

Year	Index of Whole Sale Prices 1948–9=100	Index of Cost of Living 1900=100	Index of Mean Wages 1900=100	Index of Real Wages 1900=100
1914	26.8	130	128	98
1918	47.2	200	153	77
1919	52.5	228	160	70
1920	54.2	238	182	76

The money wages could not keep pace with the rising cost of living and therefore the real wages declined. The situation deteriorated further in 1919. Obviously, therefore, the industrial workers willingly participated in strikes and other protests to better their conditions. The money and real wages increased from 160–82 and 70–6, respectively within one year, 1919–20.

At the all-India level, the All India Trade Union Congress (AITUC) was formed in July 1920 with three-fold objectives: (a) to coordinate the activities of growing number of trade unions all over the India; (b) to achieve a greater degree of control over the urban industrial masses; and (c) to get representation at the ILO Conferences. Several all-India organizations were formed and dissolved during the period. This period was most eventful from the point of view of growth of the Indian labour movement. Three most significant events that affected the Indian labour movement were: (a) Indian Trade Unions Act, 1926; (b) Meerut Trial, 1929; and (c) the formation of Congress ministries, 1937–8.

Before the passage of the Indian Trade Unions Act, 1926, there was no trade union legislation and the old conspiracy principles of Common Law applied to workers' organizations.[9] In order to remove this difficulty N.M. Joshi prepared a Trade Union Bill in 1921 which resulted in the passage of the Indian Trade Union Act, 1926. The Act dealt exclusively with the requirements of unions, which wish to become and remain registered under the law and with the rights of registered unions. It permitted a trade union to be registered by seven or more members. The only protection a union was guaranteed through the registration was immunity for its members and officers from criminal conspiracy proceedings and from civil suits growing out of trade disputes. The Act contributed to the growth of the labour movement by encouraging the formation and registration of unions.

The Meerut trial, in which 31 leading trade-unionists were arrested on 20 March 1929 was in fact, directed against the organized labour movement with the intention to crush the rising upsurge of the working class and to prevent the European working class movement from giving any help to Indian labour movement.[10] The Meerut trial, which lasted for about four years, dealt a heavy blow to the immediate prospects of the movement. 'This led to difficulties in the growth of trade union movement, specially in view of the earlier split.'[11]

In 1937–8, Congress ministries were formed in seven out of nine provinces in India. The greater freedom enjoyed by the workers during the period and the sympathetic attitude of the Congress ministries paved the way for a remarkable growth of the trade unions. The number of industrial disputes suddenly increased from 157 in 1936 to 379 in 1937, and 399 in 1938: the number of registered unions increased from 241 in 1935–6 to 420 in 1937–8 and 562 in 1938–9; and the number of workers involved, mandays lost in industrial disputes, and the membership of the unions submitting returns also increased considerably. A number of Labour Enquiry Committees were appointed and Acts introduced for the amelioration of the working conditions of workers. However, with the outbreak of World War II, the Congress ministers had to resign. Thereafter, the labour movement was again faced with a pro-employer government.[12]

Table 5.2: Growth of Trade Unions in India (1928–46)

Period	Average No. of Unions on Register	Average No. of Unions Submitting Returns	Average Total Membership ('000)
1927–8	29	28	100.6
1929–31	99	87	214.2
1932–4	263	143	227.1
1935–7	242	205	271.4
1938–40	549	396	433.4
1941–3	722	476	590.8
1944–6	904	574	844.8
Absolute Variations	+875	+546	+744.2
Per Cent Variations	3017.24	1950.00	742.71

Table 5.2 reveals that during the period 1927–8 to 1944–6, the number of registered trade unions experienced a tremendous increase (3,017 per cent). The membership could not keep pace with the increase in the number of unions: which indicates that a large number of small-sized unions were formed.

This stage of Indian labour movement was characterized by a number of new developments. The philosophy of the movement was influenced by radical and militant nationalism and its structure was loose and unsound. It underwent a variety of new experiences: 'moderation', 'radicalism', splits, mergers and continuous political orientations. The leadership of the movement was mainly drawn from the political parties, which was, in a sense, necessary because of the then prevailing conditions of the working class. Consequently, the apex organization, AITUC did not have an ideologically homogeneous leadership but from the very beginning, it was subject to ideological rifts and organizational splits. The formation of the trade unions on local level, in most cases, was a result of the discontent among the workers, which was effectively used by the leadership to unite and organize the workers into trade unions. This stage of the movement was transitional during which it evolved and consolidated itself, acquired an all-India and international character, and passed through the early period of political unionism. The organizational base of the union was, however, limited to only a few major industries.

Relatively Continuous Organization and Political Involvement (1947–63)

In the immediate post-World War II period, the strike activity was intensified. Number of strikes went up from 658 in 1944 to 820 in 1945, 1,629 in 1946 and 1,811 in 1947. This may be attributed to three main factors: first, during the war the real wages of workers experienced a continuous decrease while the profits went up. The cost of living index increased from 100 in 1939 to 269 in 1945 and 323 in 1947; the index of real wages decreased from 100 in 1939 to 75 in 1945 and 73 in 1946; and the index of industrial profits increased from 100 in 1939 to 334 in 1945. Therefore, the workers demanded restoration of pre-war real wages and share in war-time profits. Second, the workers' expectations were high on the eve of independence. These expectations were not fulfilled and their condition deteriorated further due to the continuous rise in cost of living. Third, political parties were so far busy in the struggle for independence. Now with independence close-at-sight there was increased pressure of divergent political parties in the labour field, with the clear objective to gain control over the working classes.

When the Congress leaders were released from jails in 1946 to form an interim government, the labour movement was mainly in the hands of the communists and Royists who had favoured the war efforts. The Congress leaders first tried to recapture the AITUC failing which they formed the Indian National Trade Union Congress (INTUC) in May 1947.[13] Later, the socialists also seceded from the AITUC and formed Hind Mazdoor Sabha (HMS) in December 1948. This was followed by the formation of yet another organization—United Trade Union Congress (UTUC)—by the revolutionary socialists of Bengal. Further developments in the national politics has led to the emergence of several more all-India organizations.[14]

As a result of all these developments, the trade unions multiplied during this period. Workers' grievances and discontent on the one hand, and increased interest of political parties and their labour wings helped this process. Table 5.3 shows the growth of trade unions during the period 1947–63.

Table 5.3: Growth of Trade Unions in India (1947–63)

Period	Average No. of Registered Unions	Average Number of Unions Submitting Returns	Average Total Membership ('000)
1947–9	2,547	1,489	1,652
1950–2	3,914	2,135	1,853
1953–5	5,782	3,155	2,122
1956–8	8,785	4,599	2,549
1959–61	10,624	6,382	3,848
1962–3	11,375	6,961	3,630
Absolute Variations	+8,828	+5,472	+1,978
Per Cent Variations	342.97	367.50	119.73

In the pre-independence period, the labour movement was much influenced by nationalism and the union goals were regarded, to a great extent, subsidiary to the main political current of the period—India's struggle for independence. The freedom of association existed only in name and there was practically no recognition of trade unions by the employers.[15] In the post-independence period, trade unions were in many cases, recognized by the management, though no suitable provision of compulsory recognition could be made. The Five Year Plans have stressed the need of encouraging the development of a full-fledged labour movement. The scheme of workers' participation in management was introduced. The rapid expansion of the public sector and, therefore, the emergence of the State as an employer, created some conflicts between the government and the unions. On the other hand, development planning under the Five Year Plans has put the government as well as trade unions in a sort of dilemma. The government has been trying to reconcile between trade union rights and economic development. The unions have assumed the twin role of maintaining and improving the deteriorating conditions of the workers on the one hand and contributing to the process of economic development of the country, on the other. Consequently, the unions and the employers at the 16th Indian Labour Conference, 1958, adopted the code of discipline, Model Grievance Procedure and Inter-Union Code of Conduct. But, rising inflation and introduction of various rationalization schemes have led the trade unions to adopt a militant defensive character.

PRESENT STRUCTURE AND CHARACTER

The above account of the labour movement in India serves only a part of our purpose. For a correct understanding it is essential to focus attention on the 'physical' structure of the unions. Unions in India are generally amorphous and fragmented, they lack a sound and common structure; finances are insufficient; inter-union and intra-union rivalries prevail; outside leadership dominates; and collective agreements are rare. One of the chief problems in structuring the Indian labour movement has been how to weld together the numerous units at the local level into centralized coordinating federations. At present there are about 15,000 unions of workers in India of which nearly 40 per cent fail to submit their returns under the Indian Trade Union Act, 1926. Most of these unions are very small in size.

Table 5.4 reveals that in 1950, about 59 per cent of the unions submitting annual returns had on their rolls less than 300 members, covering only 7 per cent of total membership. About 70 per cent of the unions had membership less than 500 members, covering about 12 per cent of total membership. In 1960, the situation worsened further. The percentage of unions with less than 300 membership increased to 73 per cent and that of unions with less than 500 members to 82 per cent;

Table 5.4: Percentage Distribution of Union and Membership by Size

Membership Group	1950–1		1959–60	
	Number of Unions	Membership	Number of Unions	Membership
Below 50	13.0	0.4	22.8	1.1
50–99	15.1	1.1	20.5	2.5
100–299	30.7	5.8	29.5	8.5
300–499	10.9	4.5	9.4	6.1
500–999	14.4	11.2	9.0	11.2
1,000–1,999	7.6	11.0	4.6	10.5
2,000–4,999	4.8	15.7	2.6	13.1
5,000–9,999	1.7	11.9	0.8	8.4
10,000–19,999	1.0	13.9	0.5	12.5
20,000 and above	0.8	24.5	0.3	26.1
Total	100.0	100.0	100.0	100.0

these two groups covering about 12 per cent and 18 per cent of total membership, respectively. On the other hand, only about 3.5 per cent unions had on an average more than 5,000 members on their rolls in 1950, covering more than 50 per cent of total membership. In 1960, only 1.6 per cent unions had more than 5,000 members with 47 per cent of total membership. Thus two different trends emerge. On the one hand, there is a tendency of small-sized unions springing up in large numbers at local level. On the other hand, there are some well organized unions (like Textile Labour Association, Ahmedabad) with a large and stable membership.[16] On the whole, however, a picture of weak and small unionism emerges. The picture is further complicated by a high turnover rate among Indian unions. According to a very rough estimate, unions in India are subject to infantile mortality, about 10 per cent of the registered unions cease to exist every year.[17] On the other hand, small locals equal or more in numbers are created each year. This high rate of turnover and fragmentation is attributed to the Trade Union Act of 1926 which permits any seven workers to for a union and get it registered. There is, therefore no proper incentives for the stable unions to develop at an industry level.

Financial debility is characteristic of Indian unionism. The average yearly income of the unions in India (Rs 2,300) is too inadequate to build up strong unions and to enable them to undertake welfare programmes for their members.[18] The above figure of average income presents an overestimated figure because there are some rich unions as well. In recent years, though the total income of the unions has increased, the per union membership could not keep pace with it due to unchecked growth of small and rival unions. About half of the so-called organized union members in India do not pay their dues regularly. Yet the contribution from the members accounts for about 73 per cent of total union income from various sources.

The item-wise distribution of expenditure of the unions shows that 'salaries and allowances to the office-bearers' and 'establishment expenses' constitute about 50 per cent of total expenses. On the other hand, expenditure on compensation to members for loss due to trade disputes, funeral, old age and other benefits to members and educational benefits is only 6 per cent of the total. Thus, most of the unions cannot afford full-time officers and staff-members, undertake welfare programmes and carry out organizational campaigns for unorganized workers as well as other regular union activities.

Multiple and rival unionism is another characteristic of the Indian labour movement. This phenomenon is rooted in the history of the labour movement. Splits and creation of rival organization on ideological

Table 5.5: Period-wise Average per Union Membership[19]

Period	Average Membership per Union
1927–8	3,594
1929–31	2,515
1932–4	1,621
1935–7	1,337
1938–40	1,095
1941–3	1,242
1944–6	1,473
1947–9	1,141
1950–2	873
1953–5	680
1956–8	514
1959–61	603
1962–3	548
Absolute Variations	(–3,046)
Per Cent Variations	847.52

and political grounds have been its peculiar features. After independence the competition between political parties has intensified, resulting in an increasing tendency on the part of political parties to have their own organizations in the labour field. As we noted earlier, presently there are more than half-a-dozen central trade union organizations in India. The existence of different competing or rival organizations with divergent political orientations, but without much differences in their objectives from the point of view of the workers, is held responsible for inadequate and unsound growth of labour movement in India. Within a single organization also are found groups and factions comprising of 'insiders' and 'outsiders', 'new-comers', 'moderates' and 'radicals' and 'high caste' and 'low caste' workers. This, in turn, helps in creating breakaways and small unions. The attitude of the government and the employers are also said to have helped in creating rivalry.

In the absence of any suitable indicator to measure probable impacts of inter-union and intra-union rivalry on labour movement, we may hypothesize, on the basis of our own observations regarding the practice of unions at local level, that such rivalries have undermined the strength and solidarity of the workers by encouraging the formation of weak and small unions with no or very little bargaining capacity. The

following figures of average membership of the unions may be cited in
support of this hypothesis.

Table 5.5 reveals a continuously declining trend in the average
per union membership. From 3,594 in 1927–8 (pre-split period),
the average membership came down to 2,515 in 1929–31 (period of
first split), 1,621 in 1932–4, 1,337 in 1935–7 and 1,095 in 1938–40
periods mostly characterized by disunity. It increased from 1,095 in
the period preceding the merger of the NTUF and the AITUC (1938–
40), to 1,242 in 1941–3 and 1,473 in 1944–6 (period of unity). After
independence (period of continuous splits and rivalry), the per union
membership has experienced a steady decline. The only exception
to this trend was the period 1959–61 when the inter-union code of
conduct was publicized and practiced with full vigour. This is not to
argue, however, that the inter-union rivalry necessarily reduces the
average membership of the unions and weakens their bargaining
power in all circumstances. It can only be said that the break-up of
the labour movement in India and resulting rivalry, has been one
important factor in this phenomenon.

The character of a labour movement is closely related to the pattern
of its leadership. The leadership of trade unions in India, as in many
other developing countries, has been mostly from the outside. The trade
unions[20] it is frequently argued both by the INTUC and non-INTUC
union leaders that the government policy regarding the recognition
of unions and selecting a representative union on the one hand, and
employers' policy of not recognizing any one union for bargaining
purposes and their encouragement to the formation of rival unions
(company unions) on the other, are contributing to the inter-union
rivalry. The unions were organized by the intellectuals and social workers
who saw a need for it and possessed necessary skills which were lacking
in the majority of the working force because of mass illiteracy. These
outside leaders found the labour movement as a method for mobilizing
masses for the independence movement. In the post-independence
period, these leaders found it as a media of communicating political
ideas to the workers. Now, most of the unions in India have become
subordinate organizations to political parties or factions to which their
leaders belong. Naturally, then, the decisions taken by the leadership
do not necessarily represent the desires of the workers.

The continuance of outside leadership in the labour movement
is justified on various grounds. The illiteracy of the workers and the
fear of reprisal, increasing legal orientations of trade union functions,
differences of caste, region and religion are said to be the factors
which necessitate the continuance of outside leadership to facilitate

the trade union organization on efficient lines.[21] While there can be no two opinions about the fact that outside leaders have bridged the gap between leadership supply and demand, such leaders generally perform both political and trade union activities. Many of them enter the labour movement to further their own personal and political ambitions. Generally, therefore, it leads to multiple, rival and weak unionism, chaos at the local level, and lack of collective bargaining, which characterize our labour movement today.

Strong and stable unionism is a pre-condition for the success of collective bargaining. The characteristics of the Indian labour movement described above did not allow the system of industrial relations based on collective bargaining to grow. The aforesaid weaknesses of the trade unions have rendered the collective agreements ineffective and collective bargaining in the real sense as non-existent. Other reasons for the failure of collective bargaining to take hold in India are: too much government intervention; the presence of temporary workers in large numbers who are competing for jobs and thus weaken the bargaining power of the unions by not staying out during the strikes etc.; and the refusal by the management to deal with the unions in good faith. The government intervention in labour management relations has usurped much of the area of collective bargaining. The statutory regulation of wages, 'Conciliation' and 'Compulsory Arbitration' are said to have exerted a negative influence on collective bargaining by not leaving any incentives for the union to unite and become strong.[22] Despite all these weaknesses, however, the labour movement has contributed a good deal in economic, political and social betterment of workers and of the country as a whole.[23]

THE LABOUR FORCE AND THE LABOUR MOVEMENT

The labour movement of a country is the function of its labour force. In India unionization is confined mainly to the organized industrial sector. Therefore, it is only an increase in the size of the non-agricultural labour force which leads to an increase in the union membership. Total non-agricultural labour force in India increased from 36,394,000, in 1931 to 42,218,000 in 1951 and 57,425,000 in 1961. Total membership of the unions also increased from 219,000 in 1931 to 1,750,000 in 1951 and 4,002,000 in 1961. Consequently, the degree of unionization also increased from 0.62 to 1931 to 4.14 in 1951 and 6.97 in 1961. One more important aspect of the relationship between the labour force and labour movement is the effect of labour force on the character of the movement. Viewed from this angle, most of the characteristics of

Indian labour movement can be explained in terms of nature of labour force itself.

The migratory character of the bulk of our workforce poses a serious problem. Workers are both 'pushed' from the overcrowded and stagnating agricultural areas and 'pulled' by the newly industrializing cities. These workers find it difficult to adjust to the social and psychological requisites of an industrial and urban environment. This is reflected in the form of a very low level of commitment to the factory system and urban life. This low degree of commitment on the part of workers, in turn, is variously manifested and gives rise to a number of other problems: absenteeism, turnover, low level of productivity, poverty, and sporadic strikes. All these characteristics of Indian labour have influenced the growth and character of the labour movement in different ways:[24]

1. The workers who leave an industrial centre in short spells of time, and are frequently changing their employment, are less inclined to organize themselves into any kind of union. This results in a very low degree of unionization.

2. Such workers, even if they join trade unions, under some pressure or persuasion, are less inclined than more committed workers to maintain a constant interest in that organization. They look upon the union in terms of demonstration; as something to join in order to obtain immediate wage increases or remedy some injustice, which is glaring and obvious. When this is achieved, the members frequently lose their interest in the union. This is reflected in the form of unstable membership.

3. The illiterate workers, burdened by their debt, poverty, and high prices, consider even a small subscription and union dues, a 'waste'. This makes unions financially weak and dependent upon the outside agencies for financial and political support. This discourages the system of collective bargaining to evolve.

4. The workers who were not fully employed and adequately paid had enough energy and leisure and were often motivated to take up activities outside their workplace. This results in the absence of active trade unionists from among the workers and encourages outside leadership.

5. Another difficulty arises from the division among the workforce which run across the lines on which trade unionism must develop. Differences in language, religion, caste, etc., are disintegrating factors, and to these is generally added the opposition of the employees and employers to any thing similar to a horizontal organization.

Thus, the nature and character of the labour force has shaped the growth and character of the Indian labour movement. What is surprising is that no material change in the situation has been noticed since 1930 when the Royal Commission on Labour submitted its report.

Table 5.6: Landmarks in the Indian Labour Movement

Year	Event and Cause	Result	Existing Organizations
1920–8		The AITUC was the only representative of Indian labour.	AITUC
1929	Split at Nagpur Session: 'Radicals' passed resolutions on total boycott of ILO and Royal Commission on Labour, Affiliation of the AITUC to Pan-Pacific TU Secretariat, etc.	'Moderates' led by N.M. Joshi, seceded from the AITUC and formed the All India Trade Union Federation (1930–2).	AITUC and AITUF
1931	Split at Calcutta: Because of the differences regarding the representation of the Girni Kamgar Union.	The extreme communists led by S.V. Deshpande and B.T. Ranadive seceded from the AITUC and formed the Revolutionary Trade Union Congress (1931–5).	AITUC, AITUF, and Revolutionary Trade Union Congress (RTUC)
1933	Unity between AITUC and All India Railway Mens' Federation.	A new organization namely National Trade Union Federation was formed (1933–8).	AITUC, RTUC and NTUF
1935	Merger of NTUF into AITUC.	(AITUC+RTUC)= AITUC.	AITUC
1938	Provisional unity between the AITUC and NTUF.	Affiliation of NTUF to AITUC.	AITUC+1

Year	Event and Cause	Result	Existing Organizations
1940	Merger of NTUF into AITUC.	AITUC became the sole representative of Indian labour.	AITUC
1942	Split: The AITUC adapted a neutral attitude towards World War II: M.N. Roy supported the War efforts of the government.	M.N. Roy and his group seceded from the AITUC and formed Indian Federation of Labour (1942–8).	AITUC and IFL
1947	Split in the AITUC: Congressmen failed to re-capture it.	Non-Communists (mainly Congressmen) seceded from the AITUC and formed the Indian National Trade Union Congress.	AITUC, IFL and INTUC
1948	Split in the AITUC: Socialists opposed the Communists' dominance.	Socialists seceded and formed the Hind Mazdoor Sabha. IFL merged into it.	AITUC, INTUC and H.M.S.
1949	Further split in the AITUC: Bengal-group opposed the AITUC leadership.	M.K. Bose and others seceded from the AITUC and formed United Trade Union Congress.	AITUC, INTUC, HMS and UTUC

* * *

The labour movement in India has passed through different stages of its development as is evident from Table 5.6. The pattern of growth and character of the movement in different periods was shaped by the existing social, economic and political characteristics of each period. In the pre-World War I period, the labour movement took a political character. Under the influence of nationalism, the labour movement played a vital role in the freedom movement. During this period, the area of labour's protest encompassed the entire spectrum of political and social needs. In the post-independence period, the character of the labour movement further changed. On the one hand, competition for political power among the parties has led to the formation of union organizations on a political basis. On the other hand, the planning for rapid national development has necessitated a rethinking on the part of union leadership about their activities. While they are committed to the development planning, conflicts have arisen, sometimes related to the means achieving the goals but mostly reflecting struggles for power.

The union-structure is weak and there is no proper coordination of activities between the local unions and federations. The weakness of the unions is demonstrated by their small-size, low degree of unionization, unstable-membership, multiplicity, inter- and intra-union rivalries, poor finances, limited programmes for the members and dependence on the outsiders. The character and composition of the labour force and political environment of the country are, to a great extent, responsible for the above weaknesses. A large number of the unions is either only on paper or too weak to be called as continuous organizations of workers with stable membership. Out of about 15,000 unions in India, only a few are strongly organized—having regular and continuous membership and welfare programmes.

The dynamics of economic growth and social change requires the labour movement to face dynamic tasks; to be able to contribute in the processes of economic development on sound lines, free from its present weaknesses and structural deficiencies. The Third Five Year Plan document has observed:

There is need for a considerable re-adaptation in the outlook, functions and practices of trade unions to suit the conditions which have arisen and are emerging. They have to be accepted as an essential part of the apparatus of industrial and economic administration of the country and should be prepared for the discharge of the responsibilities which attach to this position. Trade-union leadership has to grow progressively out of the ranks of the workers, and this process will be greatly accelerated as the programme of workers education gathers momentum. At present, the trade unions are in most cases labouring under the handicap of insufficient resources and are not in a position to obtain all the help and guidance that they used.[25]

Unfortunately, however, no significant progress seems to have been made in this direction ever since the Plan was drafted.

At the end, it needs to be emphasized that this chapter was designed to present only a synoptic review of growth and character of the Indian labour movement. Different aspects of characteristics discussed above need more careful and detailed analysis. In this connection, some exploratory studies on the origin, growth, and character of trade unionism in important industrial centres of India will be fruitful.

NOTES

1. Sidney Webb and Beatrice Webb, *History of Trade Unionism* (London, 1950), p. 1.
2. R.K. Das, *The Labour Movement in India* (Berlin, 1923), p. 7.
3. Ahmad Mukhtar, *Factory Labour in Punjab* (1929), pp. 11–13 as quoted in G.K.Sharma, *Labour Movement in India* (Jullundur, 1963), p. 50.
4. See V.B. Singh, 'Trade Union Movement', in Singh (ed.), *Economic History of India: 1857–1956* (Bombay, 1965), p. 564.
5. 'The trend of the Indian labour movement....was characterized by a tendency to petition, memorialize and seek redress of grievances through mild pressure'. See S.R. Gurtu, *Jagjivan Ram on Labour Problems* (Delhi, 1951), p. 38.
6. The Report on the Working of the Factory Act in Bombay for 1892, quoted in R.P. Dutt, *India Today* (Bombay, 1949), p. 375.
7. The Government of Madras had previously interned him with Annie Besant and another colleague for their advocacy of home rule for India. See B.S. Rao, *Industrial Worker in India* (London, 1939), p. 13.
8. J. Kuczynsky, 'Condition of Workers', in Singh (ed.), *Economic History of India*, pp. 634–5.
9. B.P. Wadia and his associates were summoned to the Madras High Court as a result of legal action taken by the employers. The High Court restrained these leaders from taking part in union activities and ordered that they pay a fine of Rs 75,000. See Sharma, *Labour Movement in India*, p. 91.
10. See Singh, *Economic History of India*, p. 581. For a readable account of the Meerut Trial, see Hutchinson, *Conspiracy at Meerut* (London, 1935).
11. Singh, *Economic History of India*, p. 884.
12. 'If the Congress Government had continued in office during the War Years…, there is absolutely no doubt that the wages of the industrial workers would have been substantially increased'. Moreover, 'the Congress, could have fought the British reactionary elements by continuing in office…Apart from this being a political blunder, the Congress deserted the working classes and left them to fight their own battle', see, K. Dwarkada, *Forty-Five Years with Labour* (Bombay, 1962), pp. 54 and 64.
13. See The Proceedings of the INTUC Inaugural Session (3 and 4 May 1947), pp. 12–16.
14. Socialist Party (now SSP) formed Hind Mazdoor Panchayat (HMP); Jan Sangh has created Bharatiya Mazdoor Sangh (BMS); Swatantra Party and DMK—are also reported to have formed their separate organizations.
15. See Government of India, *Labour Investigation Committee* (Main Report–1946), p. 372.
16. In 1960–1, the membership of the TLA was 1,04,046. See the TLA, *Annual Report 1960–61* (Ahmedabad, 1962), p. 4.
17. See Charles A. Myres, 'India', in Walter Galenson (ed.), *Labour and Economic Development* (Wiley, 1959), p. 37.
18. See, *Indian Labour Statistics 1965*, table 65, 9 (1), April (1966), p. 121.

19. See, *Indian Labour Year Book 1946*, table XXIII, pp. 114–15; *Indian Labour Year Book 1950–51*, Table LIX, p. 161 and *Indian Labour Statistics, 1965*, Labour Bureau, Government of India.

20. It is frequently argued both by the INTUC and non-INTUC union leaders that the government policy regarding the recognition of unions and selecting a representative union on the one hand, and employers' policy of not recognizing any one union for bargaining purposes and their encouragement to the formation of rival unions (company unions) on the other, are contributing to the inter-union rivalry.

21. For example, in his study of Cotton Textiles Unions in Delhi, K.N. Vaid observed:

    Unionism has been strong where consistent outside leadership has been available over a long period of time. This outside leadership has been available over a long period time. This outside leadership has mainly been made available by the political parties.

    See, *Growth and Practice of Trade-Unionism* (Delhi, 1962), p. 45.

22. For the effects of compulsory arbitration on trade union, see Van D. Kennedy, 'The Conceptual and Legislative Frame Work of Labour Relations in India', *Industrial and Labour Relations Review* (July 1958).

23. See, Singh, *Economic History of India*, p. 598; Asoka Mehta, 'Dynamics of the Labour Movement', Presidential address to the Indian Labour Conference (Varanasi, 29 December 1965), pp. 12–13; and Van D. Kennedy, *Labour and Indian Development*, no. 3 (Bombay: United Asia, 1960) pp. 220–4.

24. See, Government of India, *Report of the Royal Commission on Labour* (Main Report, 1931), p. 321.

25. Government of India, Planning Commission, *Third Five Year Plan*, p. 255.

Changing Trends in Industrial Relations
India, 1950–2000*

Debashish Bhattacherjee

During the first three decades of planned industrialization in India (1950s to the mid-1970s), national government played a determining and strategic role in guiding outcomes both in the labour market as well as within the organized labour movement. The industrial relations (IR) system was largely characterized by tripartite centralized bargaining between well-defined (and fairly homogeneous) employer groups, government agencies (like the Bureau of Public Enterprises in the case of public sector bargaining), and large national trade union federations. The latter were almost invariably trade union wings of well-established parliamentary political parties. Wage determination and the structure of bargaining mostly took place at the centralized or at the industry (or regional) level often with the use of bureaucratically administered wage boards. This highly centralized configuration suited the economic administrators, as it was relatively easy to plan for and execute a national-level IR system, especially since the overall labour legislative framework made it easier to do so. Given that regional economic disparities and differentials were not significant during the first two decades of planned development in India (that is, the 1950s and the 1960s), the maintenance and the reproduction of a 'national' IR system was not only viable and necessary, but also to a large extent was fair and efficient.

* Originally published as 'Globalising Economy, Localising Labour', *Economic and Political Weekly*, 14 October 2000, pp. 3758–64.

With the onset of economic liberalization in the early 1980s under the then prime minister Rajiv Gandhi, and later, under the World Bank–IMF-initiated 'structural adjustment reform programme' in the early 1990s, the Indian economic landscape changed considerably in response to both increased domestic and international competition. Regional differences in terms of economic development have become large and significant and this has clearly affected the behaviour of employers, unions, individual workers, and most importantly, has altered the strategic decision-making of local and state governments. Each state/region now actively lobbies, and hence competes for, both national and international capital investments. The erstwhile 'national' IR structure, whose ideal model was a curious mix of the competitive pluralism of the Anglo-Saxon IR system and a form of state-dominated corporatism, has begun to give way to a myriad variety of 'local' and state-level IR models across the country that vary not just by region, but also by type of enterprise (public versus private, domestic versus foreign, small versus large, etc.). Generally, tripartism has given way to mutualism and bipartism, decentralized bargaining structures are slowly but surely replacing centralized political lobbying, the local/ state governments are now playing a greater role in dispute resolution than the central government, and centralized union structures are giving way to decentralized employees' unions and non-governmental organizations at the regional and local levels. In this current context, where the Indian state seems to have considerably retreated from its prior dominant role in the IR system, it seems unlikely that the concept of a 'national' IR system is viable in the contemporary epoch of decentralization and globalization.

The purpose of this chapter is to trace the above evolution through a succinct historical analysis in terms of two distinct phases of industrial relations. The first phase (1950–late 1970s) refers to the pre-liberalization era where I discuss the movement from a 'national' state-controlled IR system to its crisis of legitimacy. The second phase (1980–2000) represents the post-liberalization era that reflects the search on the part of both capital and the state for greater labour market flexibility (that is, both wage and employment flexibility). The essential argument here is that the spread of market principles and its effect on the widening of regional economic differentials in India has led to several local-level IR systems with their own distinct textures of labour-management relations. In addition, I intend to show, using the above historical sketches, that the 'transformation' of the Indian IR system is considerably determined by endogenous political economy variables, rather than exclusively by exogenous globalization considerations (even though the latter have hastened the changes). In the absence of a national consensus on major labour law reforms, with the large trade union federations divided on several issues, and given that coalition governments at the centre have come to stay, it seems unlikely that a viable national IR system is likely to emerge, at least in the foreseeable future.

CRISIS OF 'STATE PLURALISM'

The first part of this phase (1950 to the mid-1960s) represents the period of 'national' capitalism: a state-led industrialization strategy with an import-substitution policy that resulted in the formation of the large, employment-intensive public sector enterprises. Effective protection through these rigid policies guaranteed a captive domestic market and hence provided a stimulus to private sector investment. The growth and development of these public enterprises led to robust growth rates in employment during this period.[1] Public sector employment quite naturally led to the formation of public sector unionism. The number of 'registered' trade unions increased rapidly from 4,623 in 1951–2 to 11,614 in 1961–2 and their membership more than tripled during this period.[2]

While the communist-led All India Trade Union Congress (AITUC) continued to consolidate its position from its pre-independence days in the private sector, the growing public sector during these initial years provided a new terrain for large-scale unionization. It is here that the nationalist Indian National Trade Union Congress (INTUC) made early inroads. Unlike the communist AITUC that arose from within the rank and file, the nationalist INTUC was in a critical sense imposed from above; there were no ambiguities in the chain of command, it flowed from the party to the union.[3] As nearly all IR functionaries were government appointed, management officials were often requested or pressurized to assist INTUC unions to establish themselves or defeat rival unions.[4] This relationship of patronage tied in nicely with the provisions of the Industrial Disputes Act of 1947 and the Trade Union Act of 1926. There were no provisions to determine the representative union (such as through 'secret ballot') even though it allowed for any seven workers to legitimately form a union. And as employers were under no legal obligation to bargain with unions, there were no built-in incentives for either party to engage in collective bargaining. Early writings on Indian IR consistently pointed to these aspects of the law that impeded genuine collective bargaining.[5] Even though there were some articulated attempts in the 1950s at enacting a labour legislation that would have promoted genuine collective bargaining, none was enacted; many commentators have interpreted this abortive attempt as a major setback to the development of a mature IR system during these early years.[6]

State intervention in the determination of wages and working conditions was the effective norm during the first part of this phase. Wages were determined by political and institutional considerations.[7] Specifically, wages were set by central and industrial wage boards by adjudicators when wage demands were in dispute, by ad hoc industrial awards, and by the bureau of public enterprises for public sector enterprises. The structure of bargaining was largely centralized, and the Indian experience of wage determination was referred to in the literature of the time as 'tripartism' and 'political bargaining'.

In terms of the movement of real wages of industrial workers, India was held out as an example of the Lewis model of growth at work, with both product and consumption wage growing slower than labour productivity. Low unionization rates, inter-union rivalries sharpened by political affiliation, excess supply of labour and state intervention of a complex type contributed to a wage lag.[8] The IR regime was one of promoting 'responsible unionism' subject to the maintenance of industrial peace.[9] By the mid-1960s, there were further splits in the trade union movement: the socialists within the Congress broke away and formed their own union, as did the radicals within the Communist Party.

The first stage of this phase then represented the period of a state-driven industrialization and accumulation regime that required the state to guide, or more strongly, to control the direction of the trade union movement. At the level of the enterprise, the paradigm that dominated the capital-labour relationship was a paternalistic labour relations system that was premised on the belief that the 'state knew' more about workers themselves. In this way, the state appropriated and aggregated the various 'union voices' for the 'collective' purpose of rapid industrialization with minimum industrial strife. In the public sector enterprises and services, internal labour markets generated social efficacy, if not economic efficiency, with the cooperation of trade unions. It is no wonder that scholars have characterized these years as a form of 'state pluralism' and 'limited pluralism' in the IR system. Industrial pluralism was not a strategic option, since the 'contingencies of underdevelopment rather than the authoritarian nature of the regime *per se* might make state pluralism imperative'.[10]

ECONOMIC CRISIS

The second part of this first phase (mid-1960s to 1979) is characterized by the economy facing severe industrial stagnation with high rates of inflation, especially in food prices.[11] During this period the economy suffered two oil price shocks (1973 and 1978), and it is during these years that actual growth rates of industrial production were far below plan targets.[12] Average annual growth rates in employment fell from 2.2 per cent during 1967–9 to 1.8 per cent during 1974–9 and unemployment rates nearly doubled.[13]

These structural changes in the economy had an effect on union activity, collective bargaining practices, industrial labour markets, and labour relations in general. As employment elasticities fell and labour markets got tighter, the number of disputes (both strikes and lockouts), the number of workers involved in these disputes, as well as the number of mandays lost, increased phenomenally between 1966 and 1974.[14] New forms of worker protest, such as the *hartal* (the go-slow), emerged during these turbulent years, frequently resulting in considerable violence. Disillusionment with the government union's (INTUC) internal practices and its ineffectiveness at the shop-floor level led to the proliferation of unions affiliated to other, more radical, political organizations, as workers sought more skilled and committed activists and negotiators to lead their struggles. The number of strikes as a result of inter-union rivalries increased substantially during this period. These uncertainties within the organized labour movement finally culminated in the all-India May 1974 railway workers' strike that paralysed the economy at the time. According to Rudolph and Rudolph, 'It was the first political challenge by a trade union to the central government at the national level. The strike, by a multi-million member union in the state sector revealed the weakness of established industrial relations doctrine and practice and the state's vulnerability to a unified national challenge'.[15] The strike was eventually smashed by the then prime minister Indira Gandhi who then went on to declare a national Emergency that lasted nearly two years (1975–7). During the Emergency years, there were attempts at imposing from above a kind of corporatism that tried to spuriously substitute bipartism for tripartism.

After the Emergency years, silent but significant changes began to take place in the IR arena. To bypass government intervention in the determination of collective bargaining outcomes, in many instances, a form of coalition bargaining between multiple unions and employers took place, so as to arrive at a binding legal settlement.[16] Since the states could add on labour legislation to the central labour statutes ('labour is a concurrent subject in India', that is, it is a joint responsibility of the union and state governments), several states in the early 1970s (such as Maharashtra, Gujarat, Rajasthan, and Madhya Pradesh) enacted their own laws regarding trade union recognition, laws that 'laid down procedures for compulsory recognition of trade unions seeking representative status on the basis of majority established under statute'.[17] In the state of Maharashtra, not to bargain with the (newly defined) representative union became an unfair labour practice. The crisis in the centralized state-controlled IR system slowly began to manifest itself in terms of specific regions trying to enact their own 'rules of the game'. This tendency is further exhibited in the segmented way in which workers' wages began to move.

It was found that since the mid-1970s, whereas 'low paid' workers in the older and declining sectors of economic activity faced diminishing, or at best stationary, wage growth, 'high paid' workers in the more modern and advanced sectors of production made substantial real wage gains.[18] It could be argued that segments within the union movement shifted their goals from those of 'rights', to those of 'interests', this distinction roughly corresponding with the value unions place on centralized lobbying ('rights') vis-à-vis decentralized collective bargaining ('interests'). There were several factors that conditioned such a shift: (a) An uneven development of firms within an industry, as well as spreading inter-industry differentiation, led to some sites being considerably more profitable than others. The unions in these sectors quickly cashed in on this increased 'capacity to pay' during collective bargaining, while unions in the declining sectors had no such opportunity. (b) Workers and their unions in the profitable sites were aware of their firm's financial condition through their informed bargaining practices and/or through management's willingness to share this information more readily with unions in these enterprises. (c) Workers in these units realized that the leadership in many of the traditionally party-based unions was averse to intense decentralized bargaining, due in part surely to their party commitments and their more national concerns.

Thus, the second part of this pre-liberalization phase reflected two crises: one, an objective crisis of accumulation in industry under the state-led industrialization regime; and two, a subjective crisis of legitimacy of the 'state pluralism' model in the existing IR system. This mode of regulation precipitated fractionalization within the organized labour movement; indeed, the growth of the Left-wing trade unions reflected alternate voices; and in many instances at the local level, employers found them easier to deal with in spite of their greater militancy. A fractionalization occurred both within capital and labour. Whereas in the growth sectors the labour-management relationship increasingly turned to an informed decentralized bargaining mode, in the declining sectors, the government and the large centralized trade unions found themselves enmeshed in the web of the 'state pluralism' mode.

The IR system in India, just prior to economic liberalization, was characterized as a form of 'involuted pluralism'.[19] The term 'involution' was used 'as a metaphor for a decline or loss of vigour that results from a replication of units whose increase in number is accompanied by a decline in effectiveness'.[20] They refer of course to the massive multiplicity of trade unions in India: in 1950–1 there were 2002 'registered' trade unions, whereas in 1979 there were 10,021 such unions. According to these authors, organized labour in India has totally been unable to challenge the state's centrist ideology and politics, that is, whether to mount or support a Left class-based party.

LABOUR MARKET FLEXIBILITY

The second phase also represents two distinct stages. The first stage of this phase (1980–91) reflects the period when domestic economic policies significantly changed to increase both internal competition and export growth. It witnessed a gradual retreat of the state from not only the economic arena, but also from the IR arena. This stage is also associated with considerable political turmoil (Indira Gandhi's comeback in 1980, her subsequent assassination in 1984, the landslide victory for the Congress Party with her son Rajiv as prime minister, and his assassination in 1991). The second stage (1991 to the present) represents the 'structural adjustment reforms' period and beyond. During this period a whole range of economic reforms affecting financial and capital markets, industrial licensing, international trade, etc., were put into place; however, labour law and labour market have not been formally reorganized. Despite this institutional inertia however, silent and significant changes continue to take place affecting the quality of labour-management relations at the level of individual firms, specific industries and services, as well as in specific geographical domains.

The first stage is characterized by 'jobless growth'. According to Ghose: 'The most striking fact is that the 1980s have been the best decade in terms of economic growth but the worst decade in terms of employment generation'.[21] As employment elasticities declined rapidly in major sectors, especially services, labour markets concentrated in urban and semi-urban locales got tighter.[22] Employers, stifled by rigid employment security provisions, curtailed the hiring of permanent labour and in many instances technologically upgraded their enterprises. Between 1980–1 to 1988–9, while employment growth declined, the capital-labour ratio and labour productivity increased at 8 per cent and 7.5 per cent per year, respectively.[23] The search for labour market flexibility in Indian manufacturing led labour-intensive firms and those engaged in the production of consumer non-durables to subcontract and outsource their production to the unorganized sectors.[24]

In the organized and more profitable sectors, unions, often 'independent' unions, managed to secure a part of these productivity increases through militant bargaining and/or by signing generous productivity bargains, a consequence of this being deceleration of employment growth in these sectors. In the relatively unorganized and in the less profitable sites, workers and unions lost out. While organized sector employment as a percentage of total employment in manufacturing fell from 24.5 per cent in 1972–3 to 17.4 per cent in 1987–8, real wages of workers and 'other employees' in organized manufacturing increased at a rate of 5.8 per cent and 4.1 per cent, respectively, whereas, 'low paid' workers actually suffered declining wages.[25] As the union wage effect increased significantly in the profitable sites of production, firms cut back on further hiring and actually started the retrenchment process (through generous separation payments) and increased the capital-labour ratio that in turn increased labour productivity. Thus, according to this scenario, the faster growth in real wages in the 1980s did play a role in slowing employment creation.[26]

These are two alternative explanations for the observed wage increase with employment slow-down. Nagaraj, using data from the Occupational Wage Surveys and sharply distinguishing between the wage rate and earnings suggested that earnings per worker increased primarily as a result of an increase in the number of man-days per worker, that is, an intensification of the labour process.[27] The latter to him is indicative of a decline in union power. In addition, Jose examined earnings, employment, and productivity trends for 19 industry groups for the period 1970–88, and found that technological changes led to a rise in wages and productivity and a decline in employment growth.[28] Whatever the reasons, the first part of this phase was characterized by the increasing segmentation within the organized labour market in terms of profitability, union structure(s), and the patterns of IR. In a stylized characterization that combined macroeconomic and IR variables, Bhattacherjee and Datta Chaudhuri showed that since the mid-1970s 'high paid' workers often represented by decentralized 'independent' unions secured real wage gains and there were positive returns from striking, whereas, in the 'low paid' sectors, centralized unions found themselves short of new strategies and employers lowered wages by imposing lockouts.[29]

Employment inflexibilities as embedded in the Industrial Disputes Act were the key focus of attention of labour researchers. The 1982 Amendment required the employer of a firm employing more than 100 workers to get state government permission before they could lay off or retrench workers. The study by Fallon and Lucas actually showed how employment would have been higher in several industrial sectors in the absence of these restrictions.[30] Mathur recommended that these restrictive provisions be deleted from the act and suggested the need to define an economically and socially acceptable exit policy for workers employed in unprofitable, often state-owned, enterprises.[31]

To remedy several of the limitations of the Industrial Disputes Act and the Trade Union Act, from both the unions' and the employers' points of view, a number of changes were proposed in these acts. Among other things the changes proposed would reduce the fragmentation and multiplicity of unions, define the bargaining agent clearly by providing for a secret ballot, promote internal trade union leadership, set up state-level industrial tribunals, force employers to set up all-encompassing bargaining councils to facilitate internal grievance settlement, and so on. After considerable debate and deliberations however, 'the bill was given a burial at the 29th session of the Indian Labour Conference in April 1990 because of controversy over the definition of "industry"'.[32]

In the union and IR arena, the first stage of this phase is marked by two major strikes. The first is the massive public sector strike in Bangalore during 1980–1 which involved the giants of Indian public sector enterprises (like Hindustan Machine Tools, Hindustan Aeronautics, Electronics Corporation of India, Indian Telephone Industries). According to Subramaniam, 'the public sector strike was not so much a conflict that occurred within the prescribed rules of the game as a conflict that occurred over the very rules of the game, the fundamental process of rule making itself.'[33] The second and more significant event during the first stage of this phase was the two-year old Bombay textile strike of 1982 that effectively challenged state controlled bargaining in the industry by throwing up an independent trade union movement.[34] What started as a wage and bonus issue in a few mills in late 1981, soon developed into an industry-wide strike that ultimately went on to become the longest strike in post-independence labour history. The textile strike ended in a whimper somewhere around late 1983; many workers returned to their villages, employers restructured their mills, and the credibility of the government-sanctioned union in the industry declined to levels from which it could never recover.

Another important feature of this stage of the second phase is the rise and proliferation of 'independent' plant-based unions operating in major industrial centres and competing with the traditional party-affiliated trade unions. Segmented and uneven development in the industrial sector tied workers' earnings like never before to the fortunes of the plant in which they were employed. As Bhattacherjee and Datta Chaudhuri put it: 'In this changed environment, plant-specific unions in the dynamic sectors of production thrived by negotiating productivity bargains, whereas in the declining sectors, traditional union structures whose survival largely depended on sustaining employment growth found the environment increasingly hostile'.[35] An analysis of plan-level contracts from western India revealed that, ceteris paribus, the 'independent' unions delivered a higher wage and fringe package than did the affiliated unions during the late 1970s and early 1980s.[36] In sum, the gradual withdrawal of the state from the economic and IR arena during the internal liberalization period generated considerable structural changes within the organized labour movement as well as in the nature of urban and industrial labour markets.

Finally, this stage is marked with increasing inter-regional, interstate, and intercity variations in the nature of labour-management relations. In an important study of labour-management relations in four Indian cities (Mumbai, Calcutta, Chennai, Bangalore), Ramaswamy points to significant inter-city differences in the texture of the labour-management relationship. According to him, 'The driving forces of the Bombay labour movement are union leaders who disclaim allegiance to political parties and their trade union federations. What we find here is the most evolved Indian version of business trade unionism', and 'the city has witnessed the steady decline, if not eclipse into oblivion, of ideological trade unionism.'[37] This clearly has something to do with the fact that private and multinational firms dominate the urban and economic landscape in Mumbai. In sharp contrast is the case of Calcutta, where a highly politicized IR regime prevails with the dominant trade union federation (the CITU) under the close watch of the dominant political party (the CPI-M). This has created considerable inflexibilities for management and hence industry is reluctant to invest here. Bangalore, a city where both private and public sector enterprises thrive, especially those in the high technology areas, has witnessed the rise of plant and firm-based unions with shop floor leaders representing a highly educated and skilled workforce. These inter-city differences, attributable no doubt to different political, social, and urban histories, emphatically suggest the inherent difficulties involved in trying to generalize about an 'Indian' IR system. With the onset of 'structural adjustment' reforms in the early 1990s, attempts at this kind of generalization have become increasingly difficult.

In terms of the 'monopoly versus voice' framework, the labour market and IR evidence from this first stage of the second phase of industrial relations seems to suggest that some monopoly effects dominated over the all-encompassing voice effects, and that the proliferation of 'independent' unions and their micro-economic success may have created negative spillover effects on less organized labour markets. In the private corporate sector, firms attempted 'efficiency wage' strategies, usually with the cooperation of unions, but often changing the nature of plant or firm-level unions in the process. In public sector internal labour markets, unions often got enmeshed into unproductive activities while managing these enterprises. In terms of IR strategy, not only did the actors operate with considerably more choices and options than before, but at the extreme, one could even suggest that segments within the economy operated with their own strategy, insulated as it were from outside forces. Thus, effective 'gainsharing' resulted from efficient bargaining in some sectors, whereas in the unorganized sectors, the not-so-invisible hand of a free market regime prevailed.

REFORMS AND BEYOND

On average, the Indian economy grew at 5.3 per cent during the first five years of the reforms (1992–6); with the tertiary sector growing the fastest at about 6.8 per cent per year.[38] While early into the reforms there were considerable apprehensions that government expenditure on the social sector will decline significantly, Nagaraj's findings suggest that social spending, averaged over four years since the reforms did not suffer; most of the cuts took place in defence. Again, contrary to earlier expectations, investment performance in India actually improved since the reforms, with the private corporate sector emerging as India's leading' sector. Transnational companies, as expected, have reacted very favourably to the new economic policy in terms of their entry and growth that has been accelerated through extensive mergers and acquisitions.[39]

On the employment front, the available data seems to suggest that the initial impact of economic reform has led to an increase in rural poverty and a decline in urban poverty.[40] Although the initial stabilization years took a toll on organized manufacturing employment the subsequent structural adjustment process led to employment growth at around

2.3 per cent between 1992 and 1995.[41] According to the authors, if this rate continues for the next few years, 'employment in the factory sector would be about 12 per cent higher at the turn of the century than in 1990-1'.[42] However, even under the most optimistic employment growth scenario, given declining employment elasticities in organized manufacturing and given the unlikely expansion of employment in the public sector, it is quite evident that 'a large majority of the nearly 80 million persons who will join the labour force during 1999–2000 will have to find work as self-employed or casual workers'.[43] In the light of the latter, it seems imperative to considerably expand on the existing public employment schemes.

One of the main objectives of the economic reform package is the restructuring of unprofitable public sector enterprises that are large drains on the public exchequer. These units were given the freedom to reduce their excess human resources through voluntary retirement schemes (VRS) assisted through the National Renewal Fund that was instituted by the government.[44] The objective of this fund was to serve as a generous 'safety net', by providing assistance to cover the costs of retraining and redeployment of employees resulting from modernization, technological upgradation, industrial restructuring, and possible closure. In 1993–4, Rs 7 billion was allocated for the implementation of voluntary retirement schemes in the various central public sector enterprises; of this, nearly Rs 4.9 billion was allocated to the textile sector alone.[45]

While new recruitment was all but frozen in government-run establishments (especially at lower levels), the government also froze the centralized wage bargaining process for the public sector enterprises for the first few years after 1992. It opened the negotiation process subsequently and attempted to decentralize the bargaining process by announcing that any wage increase will have to be absorbed by the specific enterprise as these increases now cannot be passed on to final output prices (as they used to be earlier). In other words, the new policy clearly stated that any additional wage burden would not receive budgetary support.[46] To what extent the government subsequently actually monitored the above is not clear at this time.

The need for tripartite consultation relating to the various issues concerning labour matters under economic reform was felt during the initial years and many such meetings were carried out. Mathur documented the experience of consultation during the early phase of structural adjustment in India (1990–2), and suggested that although the government partly diffused possible tension through its consultative approach, unions had 'serious misgivings about the adequacy of consultation at (the) industrial or enterprise level'. [47]

It is during this second stage that the public has become acutely aware (thanks largely to the print and visual media) that trade unions in India today represent a declining 'sectional interest group'. Bhaduri and Nayyar point this out in no uncertain terms: 'The government also needs to protect consumers against sectional interests of many unrepresentative trade unions. While the trade union rights of workers must also be respected in any democracy, the government must also ensure, perhaps through secret ballot, that no union harasses ordinary consumers.' They go on to add: '…recognition of workers' rights must go with appropriate regulations for recognizing these rights. All such rules of the game need to be set transparently and without partisanship.'[48]

The government announced in January 1999 that the second National Labour Commission would be set up (the first was set up 30 years ago). The terms of reference lay down that the Commission should suggest rationalization of existing labour laws in the organized sector and recommend an 'umbrella' legislation to ensure minimum protection for unorganized workers. The Commission will have a two-year term and will comprise of representatives from government, trade unions, and industry. As of now, trade unions feel that there is little in the existing laws to protect workers from the whims of errant management, and that any tinkering of these laws would only add to managerial power. For example, the proposal to relax contract labour laws to generate more contract jobs in the unorganized sector is interpreted by the unions as a move to undercut permanent unionized jobs. More recently, proposed changes in the Industrial Disputes Act will make it difficult for trade unions to call flash (wildcat) strikes and these amendments will dilute the need for government approval before declaring lockouts, while at the same time giving more teeth to the tribunals so that they can penalize errant employers.

In terms of labour market and IR reforms, the continuation of economic liberalization programmes would undoubtedly lead to greater employment flexibility, a movement towards greater decentralization in bargaining structures (and hence lesser governmental intervention in the bargaining process), fewer strikes, and a possible halt to the cleavages within the union movement. From the positive side, all this could imply more employment, and a more efficient union voice developing both at the micro and macro level with industrial pluralism being strengthened. On the negative side, continuing economic reforms could lead to an increase in managerial power and accelerate the growth of the non-union sector both leading to a decline in the power of organized labour. While at the micro-enterprise level, in many instances, unions of all political hues are cooperating with management in the economic restructuring process (often, because they have no other choice), at the macro-level, the organized labour movement is by and large critical of the globalization and reform process. From a strategic viewpoint, trade union federations of different political affiliations will have to forge a united front at the macro-level so as to ensure their continuing growth as 'all encompassing' organizations. The latter will have to mean organizing the unorganized.

The necessary IR reforms that are required to facilitate economic restructuring with a 'human face', have been discussed and written about in seminars, journals and newspapers ever since the reforms were initiated way back in 1992. However, cleavages and differences within the centralized trade unions, the political parties, and state governments, have indefinitely delayed the passage of these much-required changes. A lack of consensus, and political instability at the centre (in terms of several coalition governments being unable to complete their full terms) since 1992, has led to an inertia in the political will required to carry out these reforms. A terribly worrying negative fallout (of this inability to arrive at a national consensus on labour market and IR reform) is the future effect of the heightened inter-state competition to attract domestic and foreign capital on regional labour markets, and labour relations in general. In the absence of these nationally legislated reforms, various states may attempt the 'levelling down' of their labour market institutions by offering several incentives to capital flows into their state. The latter will have a profound effect on inter-regional variations in labour standards. As these divergent trends will make it difficult for the centralized trade union federations to act on a national level, it is in their immediate interest to press for IR reform. Indeed, one of the most important concerns troubling social scientists in India today is the effect economic liberalization will have on inter-state variations in human development and social productivity. States with a poorer, if not non-existent, history of an organized labour movement, if controlled by pro-capital state governments, may attempt to attract capital with implicit promises of a union-free environment. Ruling state governments in other states with long histories of proletarian politics are desperately attempting to change their signals. These attempts are now not only creating considerable confusion within the union movement, both among the leadership and the rank and file, but are also leading to chasms between political parties and their affiliated unions. In several instances, temporary or issue-based alliances have been formed between unions affiliated to opposition parties, especially with regard to privatization of public sector services and utilities.

* * *

This chapter traced the evolution of the Indian IR system. This was undertaken by truncating the time period into two phases. The first phase reflected the era of state planning in the economic domain with a state-dominated pluralism in the IR arena. Towards the end of this phase, economic crisis and political turmoil severely tested the legitimacy of this state-dominated pluralism in the IR arena. The second phase reflects the internal and external liberalization periods with the state gradually withdrawing from both the economic and IR domains. During this latter phase, the decentralization of bargaining structures accompanied the growth of 'independent' trade unionism in certain regions and sectors. However, the procedural environment required for competitive industrial pluralism to work at its best is still absent from the Indian IR system (that is, the absence of a secret ballot, the absence of a single bargaining agent, the absence of third-party arbitration, and strong restraints on 'legal' strikes) due to the lack of any consensus among, as well as within, the actors in the IR system. Consequently, the effects of economic liberalization, and later globalization, has led to the rise of 'local' and the 'specific' in terms of sectors and regions/cities in the IR landscape, and a gradual decline in the importance of the 'national'. These IR 'transformations' have resulted from both endogenous (political economy) and exogeneous (globalization) factors. An artificial attempt on the part of the central government to exogenously impose an anachronistic 'national' IR system, without the necessary level of consensus among the concerned parties, will not only be resisted but will, in all probability, not work.

With the onset of the economic liberalization process and its consequent effects on inter-regional variations in the level of economic activity, it appears that struggles over labouring conditions will be increasingly fought at the local and regional levels. Trade unions will have to forge deep links with neighbourhoods and communities, urban movements, environmental groups and an array of region-specific non-governmental organizations to enhance their effective power. Ultimately it all depends on 'public action', the participation by the public in the process of social change. The organized labour movement in India today can trigger off this much needed 'public action' through broad-based alliances with other subaltern groups.

NOTES

1. T.S. Papola, 'Employment Growth and Social Protection of Labour in India', *Indian Journal of Industrial Relations*, 30, October (1994), pp. 117–43.

2.   C.S. Venkataratnam, 'Industrial Relations in India', paper presented at a seminar on 'Labour Markets and Industrial Relations in South Asia: Emerging Issues and Policy Options' (New Delhi: India International Centre, 18–20 September 1996).

3.   R. Chatterjee, *Unions, Politics, and the State: A Study of Indian Labour Politics* (New Delhi: South Asian Publishers, 1980).

4.   V.D. Kennedy, *Unions, Employers and Government* (Mumbai: Manaktalas, 1966).

5.   Ibid.

6.   E.A. Ramaswamy, *Power and Justice* (New Delhi: Oxford University Press, 1984).

7.   A.J. Fonseca, *Wage Determination and Organised Labour in India* (New Delhi: Oxford University Press, 1964); D.A.S. Jackson, 'Wage Policy and Industrial Relations in India', *Economic Journal*, 82, March (1972), pp. 183–94.

8.   L.K. Deshpande, 'Institutional Interventions in the Labour Market in Bombay's Manufacturing Sector', in T.S. Papola and G. Rodgers (eds), *Labour Institutions and Economic Development in India*, Research Series No. 97 (Geneva: International Institute for Labour Studies, 1992).

9.   C.K. Johri, *Unionism in a Developing Economy: A Study of the Interaction between Trade Unionism and Government Policy in India, 1950–65* (Mumbai: Asia Publishing House, 1967).

10.   Chatterjee, *Unions, Politics, and the State*, p. 8.

11.   D. Nayyar, 'Industrial Development in India: Growth or Stagnation?', in A.K. Bagchi and N. Banerjee (eds), *Change and Choice in Indian Industry* (Calcutta: K.P. Bagchi, 1981); V. Joshi and I.M.D. Little, *India: Macroeconomics and Political Economy, 1964–91* (The World Bank, 1994).

12.   I.J. Ahluwalia, 'Productivity and Growth in Indian Manufacturing', Centre for Policy Research (1991) (mimeo).

13.   Papola, 'Employment Growth and Social Protection of Labour in India'.

14.   A.K. Sengupta, 'Trends in Industrial Conflict in India (1961–87) and Government Policy', Working Paper Series No. 174–92 (Calcutta: IIM, 1992).

15.   L.I. Rudolph and S.H. Rudolph, *In Pursuit of Lakshmi* (Mumbai: Orient Longman, 1987), p. 274.

16.   B.R. Patil, 'Coalition and Convertive Bargaining', *Indian Journal of Industrial Relations*, 18, October (1982), pp. 241–62.

17.   A.N. Mathur, *Employment Security and Industrial Restructuring in India: Separating Facts from Folklore—The Exit Policy Controversy* (Calcutta: IIM, 1992), p. 48.

18.   B.K. Madan, *The Real Wages of Industrial Labour in India* (New Delhi: MDI, 1977); B. Tulpule and R.C. Datta, 'Real Wages in Indian Industry', *Economic and Political Weekly*, 23, October (1988), pp. 2275–7.

19.   Rudolph and Rudolph, *In Pursuit of Lakshmi*, p. 259.

20.   Ibid., p. 269.

21.   A.K. Ghose, 'Economic Restructuring, Employment and Safety Nets: A

Note', in *Social Dimensions of Structural Adjustment in India* (New Delhi: ILO-ARTER, 1992), pp. 94–102, see especially p. 95.

22. Papola, 'Employment Growth and Social Protection of Labour in India'.

23. Ahluwalia, 'Productivity and Growth in Indian Manufacturing'.

24. K.V. Ramaswamy, 'The Search for Flexibility in Indian Manufacturing: New Evidence on Outsourcing Activities', *Economic and Political Weekly*, 34, February (1999), pp. 363–8.

25. Ghose, 'Economic Restructuring, Employment and Safety Nets'.

26. Ahluwalia, 'Productivity and Growth in Indian Manufacturing'.

27. R. Nagaraj, 'Employment and Wages in Manufacturing Industries: Trends, Hypothesis and Evidence', *Economic and Political Weekly*, 29, January (1994), pp. 177–86.

28. A.V. Jose, 'Earnings, Employment and Productivity Trends in Organised Industries in India', *The Indian Journal of Labour Economics*, 35, July–September (1992).

29. D. Bhattacherjee and T. Datta Chaudhuri, 'Unions, Wages and Labour Markets in Indian Industry, 1960–86', *Journal of Development Studies*, 30, January (1994), pp. 443–65.

30. P.R. Fallon and R.E.B. Lucas, 'The Impact of Changes in Job Security Regulations in India and Zimbabwe', *The World Bank Economic Review*, 5, September (1991), pp. 395–413.

31. Mathur, *Employment Security and Industrial Restructuring in India*.

32. Ibid., p. 50.

33. D. Subramaniam, 'Bangalore Public Sector Strike, 1980–81: A Critical Appraisal', *Economic and Political Weekly*, 32, April (1997), pp. 767–78, see especially p. 767.

34. D. Bhattacherjee, 'Unions, State and Capital in Western India: Structural Determinants of the 1982 Bombay Textile Strike', in R. Southall (ed.), *Labour and Unions in Africa and Asia* (London: Palgrave Macmillan, 1988), pp. 211–37.

35. Bhattacherjee and Chaudhuri, ' Unions, Wages and Labour Markets in Indian Industry, 1960–86', p. 446.

36. D. Bhattacherjee, 'Union-type Effects on Bargaining Outcomes in Indian Manufacturing', *British Journal of Industrial Relations*, 27, July (1987), pp. 247–66.

37. A.R. Ramaswamy, *Worker Consciousness and Trade Union Response* (New Delhi: Oxford University Press, 1988), p. 17.

38. R. Nagaraj, 'What Has Happened since 1991? Assessment of India's Economic Reform', *Economic and Political Weekly*, 32, 8–14 November (1997), pp. 2869–79.

39. S. Chaudhuri, 'Government and Transnationals: New Economic Policies since 1991', *Economic and Political Weekly*, 30, May (1995), pp. 999–1012.

40. A. Sen, 'Economic Reforms, Employment and Poverty: Trends and Options', *Economic and Political Weekly*, 31, September (1996), pp. 2459–78.

41. S. Deshpande and L.K. Deshpande, 'New Economic Policy and Response of the Labour Market in India', paper presented at a seminar on 'Labour

Markets and Industrial Relations in South Asia: Emerging Issues and Policy Options' (New Delhi: India International Centre, 18–20 September 1996).

42. Ibid., p. 18.

43. P. Visaria and B.S. Minhas, 'Evolving an Employment Policy for the 1990s: What Do the Data Tell Us?', *Economic and Political Weekly*, 26, April (1991), pp. 969–79, see especially p. 978.

44. A.N. Mathur, 'The Experience of Consultation during Structural Adjustment in India (1990–2)', *International Labour Review*, 132, (1993), pp. 331–45.

45. S. Muralidhar, 'Slipping through the Holes in the Safety Net', *The Economic Times*, Calcutta (26 December 1993), p. 7.

46. Venkataratnam, 'Industrial Relations in India'.

47. Mathur, 'The Experience of Consultation during Structural Adjustment in India (1990–2)', p. 344.

48. A. Bhaduri and D. Nayyar, *An Intelligent Person's Guide to Liberalisation* (New Delhi: Penguin Books India, 1996), p. 139.

Labour Activism and Women in the Unorganized Sector[*]

SUPRIYA ROYCHOWDHURY

The impact of economic reforms on the labour market in terms of informalization of the workforce has been well documented. Informalization is frequently seen as a double-edged sword: in the informal sector, workers lack both the legal entitlement to fair wages and other benefits, and at the same time in a labour surplus context, lacking security of employment and a basis for unionization, the workforce is increasingly disempowered. Casualization of women's employment has received particular attention. It is generally acknowledged that globalization has opened some new avenues of employment for women, such as in export zones. But low wages, insecurities and complete lack of organizational strength have characterized the quality of employment.

In the recent past, there have been several efforts to 'organize the unorganized'. The decline of the organized sector and the weakening of the trade union movement have provided the backdrop in which new unions have emerged to organize the informal sector. To an extent, the perceived limitations of the traditional trade unions—such as over-politicization—have shaped the politics and discourse of the unorganized sector. Thus, a studied distance from political parties characterizes the activities of new unions (for example, the National Centre for Labour, Self-Employed Women's Association). Second, this

* Originally published as 'Labour Activism and Women in the Unorganized Sector', *Economic and Political Weekly*, 28 May–4 June 2005, pp. 2250–5.

new activism is frequently expressed around issues that are marked by the sharp edges of the capital labour conflict. Thus for example, beyond employment and wages, the emphasis of the new activism is on a range of issues, like housing, health, education, street lighting, water, sanitation, and so on.

One significant feature of this activism, then, is that the community, rather than class, has become the protagonist and the potential recipient of welfare. Also, of course, in the context of casualization, where employment is scattered, decentred and frequently self-generated, it is the State, rather than private capital that becomes the sole target of welfare activism. The shift in labour activism from a class-based discourse is thus the result of many factors.

This shift is perhaps most clearly highlighted in the issues and activism around women's work. Here, the most prominent initiatives have been around themes such as self-help groups, credit, entrepreneurship, and so on. By and large the underlined emphasis has been on enlarging the scope of benefits, working both on state agencies and on the idea of self-generated initiative, thrift, credit worthiness, developing entrepreneurial abilities, and so on. There is a pronounced absence of a conceptualization of conflict-based struggle, in terms of clearly defined protagonists and antagonists.

And yet, it needs to be underlined that the critical issues of women's deprivation revolve around questions such as unequal wages, lack of maternity-related benefits, discrimination in the workplace, lack of child care facilities. While there are ILO guidelines as well as national legislation on equal pay for comparable work, these remain unimplemented in many sectors where women are employed in large numbers, for example, plantations, construction, and increasingly in the new export-oriented zones such as the readymade garment industry. Historically, trade unions, whether of the Left or of other parties, have been singularly unable or disinclined to address these issues, or to promote women as leaders within their organizations, as a basis for a more focused drive on these issues. This is not only because numerically women have had low representation within unions, but also importantly because trade union leaders, functioning within patriarchy-dominated paradigms, have not viewed women in terms of equal partners or in terms of their particular needs. This failure of the trade union movement as far as the rights of women workers are concerned is well documented.[1]

This chapter examines the shift from traditional unions to a new genre of activism and the implications thereof for women workers. Does the new activism perceive itself as addressing the issues left unaddressed by the traditional trade unions? To what extent does the new activism—centred on self-help groups, credit and so on—address the core issues of women's deprivation? What indeed are the fundamental dynamics underlying women's deprivation in the context of marketization? What are the effects of the union-political party distancing in the new era?

In order to address these questions, the chapter will look at women employed in the garment manufacturing industry in Bangalore, and at an activist group engaged in articulating the interests of these women. Following this introduction, the first section will provide a brief overview of the garment industry in Bangalore. The next section presents a brief history of unionization in this sector in Bangalore. In the next section we discuss the emergence and genesis of Civil Initiative for Development (CIVIDEP), a group of activists engaged in working for women workers of about 15 garment factories in the Mysore Road area of Bangalore. The next section focuses on women workers in a particular unit, Vidya Creations, in order to highlight CIVIDEP's beliefs in the context of the concept of international labour rights. The last section provides a conclusion looking at the dilemmas that beset worker-related activism in the current era.

WOMEN AND THE GARMENT INDUSTRY IN BANGALORE

India's readymade garment industry contributes around 16 per cent to total export earnings and is the largest foreign exchange earner in the country. Most of the growth in the industry occurred from the decade of the 1980s onwards, the growth chart being something like from $2 million in 1960–1 to $696 million in 1980–1, and then sharply rising to $2,236 million in 1990–1, and to $4,765 million in 1999–2000. As is well known the driving force behind the globalization of the garment industry is indeed the vast disparity in wage levels. In the starkest terms, whereas the hourly wage of a British worker is about Rs 420, a garment worker earns about Rs 8 an hour.[2]

Next to the *beedi* industry, the garment industry employs the largest number of women in Karnataka. The distinctive feature of the garment industry here is that it is relatively well organized in factory-based production. In Delhi and Mumbai, the two other large centres of garment manufacture, production is predominantly home-based and piece-rated. Officially, there are 788 garment-manufacturing units in Karnataka, of which 729 are in Bangalore. The total number of workers statewide is 153,978 out of which 146,835 are located in Bangalore units. The number of women workers in the industry statewide is 110,019 out of which 103,039 are in Bangalore.[3]

The exploitative nature of the employment of women in the garment industry is well documented, and needs no elaboration here. Briefly, the large majority of women, whether they are working as skilled tailors or as unskilled helpers, do not even get the legally stipulated minimum wage. They are frequently required to work overtime, but since this is set against production targets, workers are not paid for overtime work. Insecurity of work is one of the most widely reported problems, as employers frequently terminate a woman's service just before completion of five years in order to avoid payment of gratuity. Harsh production targets, sexual and verbal abuse, lack of maternity and other leave, lack of accident insurance, absence of toilet and crèche facilities, are some of the commonly stated and widely known features of female employment in garment manufacture. This misery underpins the production of high fashion garments sold in chic stores in the First World and worn by middle and upper class women who pay for a single dress a price that exceeds several times the monthly income of a woman who produces it.

BACKGROUND OF UNIONIZATION

Given the abject conditions of employment and wages, it is indeed puzzling that unionization has been almost non-existent in this sector. Bangalore has a long tradition of trade union activism, with several national level trade union leaders, belonging to the different federations, based in the city. Both in the public and private sectors, workers are given to unionization, collective bargaining, and so on. Most garment factories employ more than 100 workers, thus in principle falling within the framework of the Factories Act and the Industrial Disputes Act. Thus one would expect not only a far more stringent application of minimum wage and other regulations in this sector, but also unionized activities to ensure worker interests.

The predominantly feminine profile of the workforce has indeed worked against unionization, but the lack of unionism in this sector, also reflects that mainstream trade unions in the city have shown a certain marked apathy towards this relatively new and predominantly female-oriented sector. Given the high export earning capacity of the sector—which is underwritten, unfortunately by its low wage cost—state incentive to implement labour regulations in this sector have been low. This unfortunate alignment of forces underlies the misery of labour in this sector.

In Bangalore, in the 1960s and 1970s the industry was concentrated in the Lalbagh area (a crowded commercial-industrial neighbourhood) in the proximity of other industrial establishments, and with a predominantly male worker profile. This structure possibly had a potential for unionization. Following the industry's shift into a predominantly export-oriented zone, and the entry of a larger number of enterprises, it became much more decentred geographically. The industry is now spread over three areas in the city: Boomsandra, Peeniya and Mysore Road. Both Boomsandra and Mysore Road are close to outlying rural areas, attracting a large number of rural women to these units. The physical spread of the industry as also the presence of a large number of rural women are both factors that underpin the weak unionization in the industry. The nature of the industry, which requires low capital investment in physical infrastructure has also worked against unionization. Individual companies have adopted the strategy of spreading out units to outlying areas. Thus for example, Gokuldas Images is one of the largest garment-manufacturing units in the country. In Bangalore the company has no less than 45 units, spread over many parts of the city.

In the mid-1980s, management-worker problems erupted in a particular unit of Gokuldas Images located in Magadi Road. The workers became unionized and affiliated to the Hind Mazdoor Sabha. During this time, however, the company decided to shift location of this unit to Hebbal, a neighbourhood at a distance of several kilometres from the original location. Many employees were unable to work in the new location and so dropped out. This broke the basis of the emerging unionism in the unit. Subsequently, the unit was sold, although it remained within the owner's family. Under the new management, a large number of the older workers were retrenched, and some compensation was given to them. Thereafter the company decided to close down this particular unit, and at that time workers were given no compensation. Some of the women workers went to court. The case, which came up in 1987, dragged on till 2003, when the final verdict went against the workers.

In the case of Samrat Asoke garment manufacturing unit, Confederation of Indian Trade Unions (CITU) was involved in organizing a strike in 1996. The strike, however, led to the closure of the company. Approximately 10,000 workers lost their jobs. This was the last time that the CITU was seriously involved in organizing garment workers. But the closure leading to loss of jobs demoralized the workforce greatly and destroyed the tentative steps that had been taken towards unionization. Workers are not only sceptical about strikes but are suspicious of anyone who they see as attempting to organize them into unions.

CIVIDEP: GENESIS AND EMERGENCE

It is in the context of this apparent distance between the trade union movement on the one hand, and garment sector workers on the other, that one needs to view the alternate kinds of activism which have begun to emerge in this sector. This section discusses an organization called Civil Initiatives for Development (CIVIDEP), which came into existence in the year 2000 as a registered society under the Societies Registration Act. CIVIDEP is concerned solely with women workers in the garment industry in Bangalore. CIVIDEP is, on the face of it, an NGO. And yet, the fact that an organization solely concerned with workers interests describes itself as an NGO rather than as a trade union highlights certain significant features of this industry, as also of the political space of activism in the current context.

A former Left activist leads CIVIDEP, a group of over dozen full-time members, and several part-time consultants.[4] His shift from political party to NGO was underlined both by a general disillusionment with party politics and with the Left movement in particular. As part of the anti-Emergency movement, he had associated with a large number of pro-democracy forces, particularly the Janata Dal. Subsequently, the splitting of the Janata Dal into several factions and many important Janata Dal politicians shifting their party affiliations left a sense of disillusionment. The Left parties, on the other hand, had hardened into highly bureaucratic organizations, with little space for new thinking and unable to attract the youth. More specifically, Left organizations such as the CITU had developed expertise in particular areas of activism, such as public sector companies. But PSU-related issues were now only marginal to the issues that face industrial labour. The pronounced thrust in industry towards shrinking the organized sector of the workforce and the completely unregulated and unprotected character of the unorganized sector had created a need for trade unions with a new social base. This need was largely unmet within the traditional trade union movement. Unionists disenchanted with the scope and methods of the traditional trade unions moved towards the informal sector.

Two other members of this organization are former garment industry workers, who had a long history of attempting to organize workers in unions, and who ultimately lost their jobs. They bring to the organization their long experience in the industry, but also the lessons that they have learnt of the possible inappropriateness of trade union activity in this sector.

It was to fill the vacuum created by the inactivity of mainstream trade unions in the informal sector that organizations such as CIVIDEP came into existence. But a singular ambivalence marks their self-definition, as they see themselves operating at different times at different levels. Currently the principal modus operandi is what is described as the 'campaign-mode', were the main focus is on bringing to the notice of the state and of civil society the plight of women garment workers. But the group hopes that in the future it may be possible to shift to the 'union mode'—that is collective bargaining, negotiation and pressurizing the management.

A close look would reveal, however, that to the extent that CIVIDEP has been able to capture the workers' imagination, it is as a non-trade union outfit. The reluctance of workers to have anything to do with a trade union has already been discussed above, CIVIDEP activists stressed that wage bargaining at the firm level is completely out of bounds for them because they never present themselves as union leaders to the firm management. Thus as far as wages are concerned, their efforts are confined to lobbying with the government to raise the minimum wage in this sector.

It appeared that the central philosophy of the group was to create a sense of organization and unity amongst the women, without placing them in a conflictual mode with management. This organizational framework and the sense of unity created, could, in the future, be used for shifting the women to a union-mode of activism. Until such time, it appears that the activities of the group are directed towards micro activities which can to an extent address the workers' problems of economic insecurity and at the same time create a sense of solidarity whereby they can resist the everyday degradations that appear to be part and parcel of their workday/lives.

CIVIDEP's activities are confined to 15 factories in the Mysore Road area. The women workers in these factories are organized into small solidarity groups, largely on the basis of the localities in which they live. The main activity of these is to act as self-help groups (SHGs) for the organization of micro credit. Thus each member of the group contributes Rs100 at the start of each month, and member can take small credit amounts from what is collected. The purposes for borrowing are usually festivals, school admissions for children, and so on.

The other part of CIVIDEP's activities is to organize training camps in order to raise awareness of issues which affect women workers. These camps are held in local school auditoriums, and are typically addressed by labour activists, labour advocates, occasionally officers from the labour commissioner's office. Camps attract up to 500 participants. The camps are designed to inform the workers of labour laws and their rights, so that they learn to have an awareness of their situation.

CIVIDEP AND VIDYA CREATIONS

It was at a camp organized by CIVIDEP that set off a chain of events in Vidya Creations in the Mysore Road area. Workers in this unit, numbering about 600, worked under a particularly harsh production manager. Their workday easily extended to 7.30 or 8 PM every day, and they were not paid overtime. Working against heavy targets, they also had to contend with lack of toilet facilities, no maternity or other leave, and a harsh regimen where late comers were sent back or fined heavily. Many of the women also suffered sexual harassment by the production manager, many were grossly underpaid, and so on.

An awareness camp and pamphlets distributed by CIVIDEP brought a few workers in touch with CIVIDEP's activists. They recounted their plight in the factory, and particularly the inhuman methods of the production manager. CIVIDEP organized a visit to the unit by state-level members of the National Commission for Women (NCW) and the assistant labour commissioner. This visit led to the removal of the production manager and the appointment in his place of a more humane manager. Thus the intervention of the NCW highlighted to the owners not only the misbehaviour of the production manager, but also the fact that the system of oppression within the factory was no longer as opaque as it had been before and that they could, in fact, be subject to public scrutiny.

In an interview conducted with around 30 women belonging to this particular factory, it appeared that the intervention by the NCW, through the mediation of CIVIDEP, is looked upon as a watershed in the occupational lives of these women. After the visit to the NCW, their toilet facilities improved, they were being paid for overtime work, their working hours were typically limited to eight, it was easier to get leave, and so on. For each of these questions, the before and after conditions of the NCW visit was systematically highlighted.

For CIVIDEP this case has been a vindication of their strategy, which is that instead of adopting a confrontational posture vis-à-vis management, it is better to adopt a variety of other indirect means, such as highlighting the women's sufferings in the public eye, and particularly to draw the attention of concerned agencies. Thus recently, CIVIDEP has taken to writing to the labour commissioner's office, attempting to elicit its support in certain extreme cases of exploitation in particular units.

This particular incident also highlights, however, the limits of this kind of activism. In an industry whose geographical spread is considerable and in which quick locational shifts are more than possible, the vigilance of women's commissions and labour officials can at best be extremely limited. This kind of intervention is also highly contingent on the particular inclinations of individuals who happen to be involved in any given situation, their sympathies, their relative incorruptibility and so on. It is therefore fairly clear that this methodology of activism can be effective only in the preliminary stages of struggle and in extreme cases of abuse, but can hardly be an overall strategy of change.

In interviews with the women workers, it was found that most of the women were receiving monthly wages in the range of Rs 1,900 to Rs 2,100. This corresponds to the minimum wage in this sector, fixed by the Karnataka government of Rs 72 per day. The women spoke strongly of the inadequacy of the wage and their need for a higher minimum. On the questions of wages, however, the plight of workers in this sector is up against a variety of odds. In fact, in Karnataka, the minimum wage for garment workers was raised to Rs 78 in 2001. The Karnataka chapter of the Cloth Manufacturers' Association of India took up the matter with the high court, and the court subsequently reduced the minimum wage by Rs 6.30.

How do the women perceive activism, their future, their children's future? Many of the women head households, having been abandoned by their husbands. Most were married to men working in the unorganized sector, in work even more insecure and irregular than the work of the women themselves. The men in these household were frequently employed as skilled or semi-skilled labour in the small-scale industry sector. But given the rapid decline of the SSI sector in Karnataka in the last decade, many factories were closed[5] and the men rendered jobless. Almost every one of the women said that they worked in 'garment', (the local word for the industry), only because they had no option. The only possible option would be to work as domestic help. In terms of status, this was considered worse than garments,[6] but, many women, unable to bear the physical strain of working in a garment factory, leave and take up part-time domestic jobs. Thus garments and domestic jobs are the two options available to these women, with not much to choose between the two.

Each of the women described the pressure of work as unbearable. They said that they would be willing to settle for even less pay if the production target was lowered. For each, it seemed, the dream job was one in a government, where they would be able to work with 'free minds'. Thus the pressure of work combined with the harshness of the supervisors was what constituted their major source of anguish. Many said that their jobs in other units had been terminated for the smallest of mistakes. Permanent job was another dream. Each of the women said that they did not know what a trade union meant, either the English word or its Kannada equivalent. They had not even a vague concept of what a trade union might be. They knew about CIVIDEP for its positive intervention in bringing in the NCW, and they were comfortable discussing their individual problems with CIVIDEP activists. There was, however, in the discussions, no sense of a collective goal-seeking with regard to the problems which they had stated.

WORKERS' RIGHTS BEYOND THE NATION

The CIVIDEP seems to have taken the position by 2001 that factory-based action on the question of wages would not be a strategically appropriate choice of action. In their perception, the industry is essentially part of a long supply chain, and the freedom of manufacturers is to that extent extremely limited. There are, in fact more than a hundred operations between the designer and the final consumer. In this chain, only 15 are in the hands of the manufacturer. Any serious agitation for a rise in wages would lead manufacturers to shift their operations to other localities, beyond the reach of unionists. Essentially, in a production system of this kind, the most powerful voice is that of the retailer's. The state's control over the retailer is all but non-existent. At the same time, the state is highly appreciative of the industry's foreign exchange earning capacity. Therefore, the state's incentive to prod the industry to pay higher wages to a palpably powerless class of women workers, is understandably low. It is in this sense that CIVIDEP has all but ruled out the question of pressuring firms to come up with higher pay packets.

An important direction of CIVIDEP's current thinking, thus, is that for serious changes to come about, retailers abroad, manufacturers and the state must work together. Activists stressed that the buyer's pressure has so far been perceived to be most effective in ensuring minimum wages. Thus the fairly large number of units in Bangalore which supply to Nike, Gap and Wal-Mart, are subject to regular checks by the local agents of these companies. It is in these units that the minimum wage is being paid, while it is being clearly flouted by other units. But whether it is the payment of the existing minimum wage, or its substantial revision upwards, what is important is to enlist the support of the retailer in order to create the necessary pressure upon government and local agencies for a higher wage structure and its effective implementation.

Thus the vision here is that of the creation of an international opinion forum. Thereby consumers as well as producers abroad—who are the major beneficiaries of the low wages paid in this industry—

can be persuaded to extend their support and sympathies towards the workers for better wages and working conditions. This, it is assumed, will provide the necessary teeth for the implementation of these measures. In other words, given the nature of the supply chain in this industry which places the greatest leverage in the hands of retailers located abroad, the push for improvement in employment conditions must come from this external source, rather than from domestic sources.

In this vision, there is an indication of what the future of labour rights activism might look like in an increasingly globalized context. Thus what is envisaged is that an internationally created and monitored set of rights might emerge in this sector, and the fear of losing the orders of retailers abroad will force domestic producers to guarantee certain rights to their workforce. This is being attempted in the sphere of child labour in particular industries, where products must be marked as not having been produced by child labour in order to be fit for exports.

* * *

This then is an activism that has defined itself predominantly outside the factory. Its organizational strategy aims at awareness raising, group solidarity and building of credit groups. The targets of lobbying or pressure are the government, state and national level women's activist groups, international retailers, and consumers. It should be noted that worker-related activism which adopts a non-conflictual mode and is developed outside the factory is an emerging phenomenon that has been studied before. Kalpagam's study of the discourse and practice of informal sector politics noted that for both SEWA (Ahmedabad) and the Working Women's Forum (WWF) (Madras) the fundamental philosophy was a distancing from political parties, a developmental approach (that is thrift, entrepreneurship, credit) rather than a confrontational approach, belief in a mutual self-help approach, and using credit as an entry point for mobilization.[7] In the author's own research on the Karnataka Koligeri Nivasa Sangathana (KKNS) in Karnataka, I have pointed out that the KKNS, while working with the unorganized sector (construction workers, marble workers), has turned towards organizing the poor within their residential localities. Thus, slum-based welfare groups have come up under the leadership of the KKNS which work to solve a range of problems, such as street lighting, better roads, water, electricity, schools and so on. The thrust then is to lobby with the state for improvement in living conditions rather than to struggle with employers for better wages.[8]

This activist thrust is particularly noticeable in the case of women workers. One important reason for this has of course been that a large number of women in the unorganized sector are self-employed, and as such the exploiter-exploited relationship is not readily visible. This understanding of the informal sector as one in which the employer-employee, or capital-labour relationship is opaque, if not absent, is widely shared. It has underlined, on the one hand, trade union indifference to the informal sector. On the other hand, this understanding has to an extent justified the use of developmental activism rather than confrontational struggles.

The self-employed, of course, remain an important part of the informal economy. It needs to be said, however, that in the changing context of the economy, the capital-labour relationship is not found exclusively within the classically defined formal sector, that is, in large scale factories where a large number of male workers work in assembly-line operations, and are given to unionization. The predominant thrust in a globalizing economy has in fact been to recast this workforce, both within and outside the factory, as, irregular, underwritten by temporary contracts rather than permanent employment, putting out systems, outsourcing, ancillarization, and so on. The use of a large number of women workers in the garment industry is only an expression of these tendencies. Thus instead of using highly paid, unionized, possibly male workers in the First World, capital has relocated part of its activities such that it may use underpaid, non-unionized, female workers in the Third World. The capital-labour relationship, and the highly exploitative edge to it, is fairly clear in these contexts and is not opaque.

In the present context, the questions that face activists are perhaps different from those that faced SEWA in the 1980s when it was formed primarily as a trade union for self-employed women. The question, clearly, is whether a development ideology—around self-help, credit, entrepreneurship, and so on—should exclude a focus on what constitutes the core of exploitation in this context, that is, the extraction of surplus value from a disempowered populace, in this case doubly disempowered, by class and gender. Should the 'class' dimension of the context be relocated to the background, focusing attention on immediate needs of credit, housing, schooling, and so on.

The philosophy of organizations such as CIVIDEP is possibly more complex than what is highlighted by this either/or dilemma of developmentalism versus confrontational struggle. Thus the main thrust appears to be to build solidarity amongst completely powerless women, to bring to them a sense of economic security and self-sufficiency by promoting credit societies, and perhaps to use this organizational framework in the future as a tool of collective action.

On the other hand, what is absent here really is a clear conceptualization of the contenders in the conflict. Thus the focus on the retailer, and on the consumer as possible targets of campaigning and awareness raising, and the hope that pressures from these sources may indeed provide the cutting edge to changing the conditions of employment in this sector, has a unreal note in it. In a sense also, this strategy clearly belongs to the broad pattern adopted by mainstream trade union where the effort is to improve the conditions of workers within the framework of capitalism without challenging its basic premises. This trade union philosophy has indeed worked effectively in order to gain for workers in the West not only decent levels of wage but also a wide range of welfaristic measures that ensure them decent and secure standards of living.

But this strategy worked in a context where capital was clearly seen as an opponent from which concessions had to be wrenched, and where the support of rapidly democratizing states and social democratic parties could be enlisted in this battle. In the current context, where capital is located beyond national boundaries, and therefore far more inaccessible, where states are powerless against internationalized capital, the battle lines have changed irrevocably. The focus on influencing the opinion of retailers and consumers may therefore mean little in a context where the debate on international organizations such as the ILO in implementing labour rights is arguably inadequate,[9] and where the broader ideological environment now clearly prioritizes profits over welfare. In such a context, there may in fact be no alternative to waging micro battles in order to raise wages and working conditions at the factory level, and at the same time to pressurize the state to turn away from economic policies that pitch international capital against domestic workers.

NOTES

1. Nivedita Menon, 'Women in Trade Unions: A Study of AITUC, INTUC and CITU in the Seventies', in Sujata Ghotoskar (ed.), *Struggles of Women at Work* (New Delhi: Vikas Publishing House, 1992).
2. M. Roopa, 'Garment Workers; Identifying Legal Issues and Strategies', paper presented at the Consultation on 'Labour Standards in the Indian Garment Industry' (Bangalore, 29–30 September 2003).
3. Ibid.
4. This paragraph draws on two interviews with Gopinath, founder-director of CIVIDEP (Bangalore, February 2004).
5. A study of the small-scale industries (SSI) sector in Bangalore Division

highlights the rapid rate of erosion of the SSI sector. Between 1993–4 and 1998–9, 3.339 units received a new capital investment subsidy. Out of these, only 66 per cent were working in 2001 and 33 per cent had closed down. Within Bangalore Urban district, which received 36 per cent share of the total subsidy, 82.46 per cent of units had closed down. K. Gayathri, 'Genuineness of the Capital Investment Subsidy: A Study of Bangalore Division' (Bangalore: Institute of Social and Economic Change, 2002) (mimeo).

6. Nirmala Banerjee, 'The More It Changes the More It is the Same: Women Workers in Export-Oriented Industries', in N. Banerjee (ed.), *Indian Women in a Changing Industrial Scenario* (New Delhi: Sage Publications, 1991).

7. U. Kalpagam, 'The Discourse and Practice of Informal Sector Politics', in Kalpagam (ed.), *Labour and Gender: Survival in Urban India* (New Delhi: Vikas Publishing House, 1994).

8. Supriya RoyChowdhury, 'Old Classes and New Spaces: Urban Poverty and New Trade Unions', *Economic and Political Weekly*, 38 (50), 13 December (2003).

9. Druscilla K. Brown, 'Labour Standards: Where Do They Belong in the International Trade Agenda?', *Journal of Economic Perspectives*, 15 (3), (2001).

Women's and Students' Movements

This section deals with social movements by and of two categories —women and (student) youth—which I designate as 'biological' collectivities. A word of caution about the term 'biological' is in order here because some may misunderstand it for genetic determinism. Although it is possible for one to undergo sex-change thanks to the advancement of technology, persons born as female or male will invariably continue in the same sex category till death; that is, gender remains constant. In contrast, all human beings who live up to a certain age will pass from one age group to another; age cannot remain constant, it is variable. Note that the diametrically opposite 'biological' characteristics of these categories are irreversible, the male cannot become female and the old cannot become young. Be that as it may their deprivations are rooted in the same social phenomenon, namely, powerlessness. Thus women and youth who belong to the same caste/class share the privileges or deprivations of the social categories they are born into and yet they are deprived of power. Thus the shared feature of irreversibility rooted in 'biology' and powerlessness anchored to social structure (patriarchy, in the case of women and generation gap in the case of youth) provide the rationale of putting them under the same rubric. And both the groups seek equity in sharing power and participation in decision making.

As in the case of peasant and labour movements discussed in Part One, the mobilizations of women and student youth too were inspired by the anti-colonial movement. The promises made to these social categories by the leaders in the pre-colonial phase could not be fulfilled by the national state. However, all social categories demonstrated their commitment to nation-building and mobilization against the state was kept at low ebb for sometime after independence. But discontent accumulated gradually and got ventilated eventually. The flash point was in the 1970s when the state became explicitly authoritarian through the declaration of internal Emergency. The orientation of civil society organizations, usually referred to as non-governmental organizations (NGOs) in the post-Emergency period affected the movements of most social categories, including those of women, although it is difficult to establish a clear causal link.

While in the post-independence, pre-Emergency period, women's mobilization was done mainly through the front-organizations of political parties, the post-Emergency period witnessed a certain amount of autonomy of women's movement vis-à-vis political parties. An important outcome of this is the occasional conjoint articulations of the women's issues in spite of political differences as exemplified by the demand for reserving one-third seats for women in the parliament. Indu Agnihotri and Vina Mazumdar trace the trajectory of the changing terms of discourse with reference to women's movement in Chapter 8. Three developments critically moulded the response of women's movement: (a) Camouflaging issues of patriarchy through projecting them as matters of religious identity. (b) Fostering reckless consumerism by the market forces in the name of providing freedom and an emancipated lifestyle to women. (c) The proclivity of middle-class women for combining traditional and modern values in spite of their patent incongruity.

Violence against women, which was earlier perceived as a private concern of the family was brought to the public gaze by the women's movement. In turn, the newfound inclination of courts to entertain public interest litigation also increased the visibility of women's issues. While the cognitive blackout regarding issues and contexts of violence against women gradually disappeared one issue which attracted considerable attention in urban north India was that of dowry. Not only that substantial documentation of the dowry problem was undertaken by researchers, considerable anti-dowry mobilizations too became frequent. Rajni Palriwala provides a narration of this with special reference to Delhi, situating the problem in the wider context, in Chapter 9.

Dowry existed as an economic transaction and a cultural practice in India for long. Everyday symbolic violence against brides/daughters-in-law who did not bring in adequate quantity and appropriate quality of dowry had been a theme of not only contemporary literary works but also ancient folklore. Similarly, the structural violence against women embedded in patriarchy manifesting in unequal laws of property inheritance and unfreedom to make choices in most contexts did exist in India for long. But what is new is the brute physical violence against brides/daughters-in-law as and when their in-laws are dissatisfied with the dowry they brought. While the tendency was to suppress such instances in the name of protecting the honour of the families involved, the women's movement articulated the view that private worries of this kind are indeed public issues.

The fact that an overwhelming majority of labour in India belongs to the informal/unorganized sector and a greater proportion of women as compared to men are in that sector is well known. Similarly, that there are issues specific to women workers is highlighted in this section. There are two possible approaches to address these issues. One is to make women aware of these issues, mobilize them into collective actions and approach the appropriate agencies (for example, women's commissions) in addition to other mechanisms for redressal. The second approach is to establish exclusive women's organization to cope with the specific problems faced by women. Chapter 10 by Martha Alter Chen is an analysis of the Self-Employed Women's Association (SEWA) in Ahmedabad which pursued the second approach.

It was noted earlier that the women in the garment industry in Bangalore adopted the campaign-mode (see Chapter 7) as against the usual union-mode. But SEWA to achieve its twin goals of full employment and self reliance for its members combine the campaign-mode and union-mode, faced as they are with acute insecurity from their employers who are individuals rather than established firms. Further, SEWA pursues the holistic welfare of its members, and not simply better employment conditions.

Having started as a local union in Ahmedabad, SEWA gradually became an all-India union with global affiliations. Similarly, the union has transformed itself into a movement linking two global alliances of home-based workers and street vendors. Instances of movements transforming into organizations and political parties are not uncommon but SEWA illustrates the reverse possibility. This unfolds the importance of understanding the reciprocal relationships between movements and institutions.

The remaining two chapters in this section discuss student-youth movement in India. The beginning of mobilization of this category can be traced to the 1920s and it was initiated as part of the anti-colonial movement. Civil Disobedience launched by Mohandas Karamchand Gandhi in 1930s witnessed intense participation of students leading to the closing down of several institutions of higher education and the incarceration of many students in jail. The formation of All India Students Federation (AISF) in 1936 sponsored by the Indian National Congress (INC), provided the much needed organizational base for the students' movement. Subsequently pro-Muslim and pro-Hindu student organizations, which supported the formation of Pakistan and Hindu Rashtra respectively, were formed. Thus the student movement in the first-half of twentieth century India reflected the then prevailing social currents.

The arrival of freedom brought about a radical change in the orientation towards student movement as they were advised to undergo the required training to be participants in 'nation-building' as citizens of the newly emerging national state. But students' movements started manifesting themselves in the form of apolitical associations anchored to linguistic and religious communities. However, within a short span of time political parties realized the strategic importance of 'catching them young' and they floated their respective student-front organizations. By the 1960s, participation of student wings in political mobilizations became intense manifesting in confrontations between students and those who managed higher education as well as conflicts between different student associations. The phenomenal expansion of higher education, the decline in the quality of education and the anxiety associated with post-education unemployment were all contributory factors to the highly visible new student activism which was christened as 'indiscipline'. Philip G. Altbach traces this transformation of student activism from colonial to post-colonial India in Chapter 11. And I take forward the story of student activism in independent India in Chapter 12. But the central concerns of all varieties of student youth activism is inter-generational equity.

I interrogate the prevailing tendency to approbate student participation in the anti-colonial struggle and stigmatize party-linked student politics in the post-colonial period. It is suggested that while the structure of student power remained the same, the historicity of context and consequently the attitude of political parties to student participation in political processes have changed. Political parties patronize student unions affiliated to them and tend to deprecate the actions of those student unions which function as a countervailing force to their political clients. The acute internal divisions of the other two organized categories—faculty and *karamcharis*—and their cross-cutting affinities and enmities based on political-ideological orientations, ignoring their respective interests, led to the creation of a political battlefield in the domain of higher education. The fact that appointments to leadership positions in universities and colleges (vice-chancellors, principals) are invariably based on political affiliations and loyalties renders the situation singularly inhospitable to the production and diffusion of knowledge, the intended purpose of higher education. Admittedly, the nature and types of student mobilizations are conditioned by the prevailing social milieu of higher education in India.

ADDITIONAL READINGS

A. Basu, *Two Faces of Protest: Contrasting Modes of Women's Activism in India* (New Delhi: Oxford University Press, 1992).

T.K. Oommen (ed.), *Social Movements I: Issues of Identity* (New Delhi: Oxford University Press, 2010).

Raka Ray, *Fields of Protest: Women's Movement in India* (New Delhi: Kali for Women, 1999).

Kalima Rose, *Where Women are Leaders: The SEWA Movement* (New Delhi: Vistaar, 1992).

A.D. Ross, *Student Unrest in India: A Comparative Approach* (Montreal: McGill University, 1969).

Viswa Yuvak Kendra, *The Dynamics of Student Agitation in India* (Bombay: Somaiyya, 1972).

Changing Terms of Political Discourse
Women's Movement in India, 1970s–1990s*

INDU AGNIHOTRI AND VINA MAZUMDAR

The twentieth century promoted the cause of gender justice by internationalizing women's struggles for equality by women and other oppressed people. Women's struggles against their subordination were intertwined in varying degrees with ideologies and movements based on the values of freedom, self determination, equality, democracy and justice. The defeat of fascism and the forced retreat of imperialism around the mid-century paved the way for social advance of which gender relations was a key component along with the other broad objectives of human rights and the end of iniquitous social orders. The revolutionary changes which followed the two world wars also created the fora and structures that promoted debates on women's rights. The International Women's Decade was initiated during this period of hope which also posited a New International Economic order. By the end of the decade, however, this hope was already shaky.[1] In the mid-1990s, the context in which the international struggle for the advancement of women's rights is being waged has been transformed and debates promoted today twist the very premises on which the movement had been based. Terms like empowerment, choice, reproductive freedom, spiritual autonomy, etc., are being appropriated by forces inimical to the goals of the women's movement. Can the movement ensure the

* Originally published as 'Changing Terms of Political Discourse: Women's Movement in India, 1970s–1990s', *Economic and Political Weekly*, 30 (29), 22 July 1995, pp. 1869–78.

continued existence of fora to mount pressure for intervention in favour of more equitable gender relations—both at the level of international realpolitik, as well as at the ground-level processes?

It is important to note these international developments since they have significantly influenced the movement in India. If we were to spell out the parameters within which the movement developed in recent years, these would be (a) the decadal thrust provided by preparations for the UN Conference in Mexico, 1975 and the initiatives coming from the Non-Aligned movement in this context; (b) the history of and relationship between earlier movements for freedom, equality and democracy, values—which were subsequently enshrined as basic political tenets in the Constitution of India, and the constraints felt towards achievement of these in Independent India; and (c) the influence of ideas coming across through various streams of the women's liberation movements in the West.

THE INDIAN MOVEMENT

Although in India colonial rule and the freedom struggle marked the beginning of an awakening among women, differing streams within the anti-imperialist, anti-feudal struggle posited different, even contentious images of identities for women.[2] But the nationalist consensus symbolized in the Fundamental Rights Resolution of the Indian National Congress, 1931, postulated freedom, justice, dignity and equality for women, and the Constitution assured these rights. In the post-independence period, however, women exploring avenues for socio-economic and political mobility came up against limitations of a Third World ex-colonial state which posed conflicts between their new rights and the values carefully promoted by a long-standing patriarchal social hierarchy. Social disabilities and gradual isolation from the politico-ideological struggles that were shaping the nation-building process led to the fragmentation of the women's movement and the women's question faded from the public arena.[3] This is not to imply that no struggles were waged during this period. But, with the exception of the tempo built up before the passage of the Hindu Code Bill, 1956, these could not form the basis of spurring agitations which could catch the public imagination, cutting across sectional demands and organizations.

In contemporary India the resurgence of the women's movement and its contours have to be seen in the light of (a) the crisis of state and government in the 1970s going into the Emergency; (b) the post-Emergency upsurge in favour of civil rights; (c) the mushrooming of women's organizations in the early 1980s and the arrival of women's issues on the agenda; (d) the mid-1980s marked by a fundamentalist advance; and (e) the 1990s, when the crisis with regard to state, government and society has deepened.

The women's movement in India is one of the many burgeoning efforts at reassertion of citizen's claims to participate as equals in the political and development process. This places it in a situation of direct confrontation with the forces of conservatism and reaction. The fundamentalist onslaught in one country after another has exposed the vulnerability of women's advance in most places. In the Third World as well as in erstwhile socialist states, the combination of these with the onset of free market capitalism has both strengthened the powers of the oppressors, as well as created new instruments for hegemony, by weakening the balancing mechanisms and ideologies that sought to place limits on their rapacity. In India the mid-1980s have seen an onslaught on even existing rights of women through a harking back to 'tradition' and 'culture' and the positing of images which emphasize women's reproductive role as the only natural, historical one. The fundamentalist/ revivalist face of many social movements today is directly opposed to the radical demands and upsurges coming from below.

These decades in India have marked the end of the age of complacency, apathy and acceptance of the existing social order. Shifts in foci and awareness of problems that impinged on women's lives, the social construction of gender relations and the identity of women from different classes in their attempts to resolve the problems of the national economy and polity occurred during a period of dissolving certainties that characterized local, national or global systems.

This changing character and the contradictions are reflected within the governmental structures and in a shifting attitude towards the women's movement. A major question facing all governments in office has been how to respond to the movement and its demand to place the women's question on the political agenda. While the government's response has been teetering between responding to the conservative or the radical forces the women's movement, in turn, has mounted pressures from the opposite end of the spectrum. Itself experiencing major transformations, it has grown immensely despite pressures from diverse areas. Within the movement diversities manifested themselves in the form of ideological cleavages, fragmentation and regionally uneven growth. But the issues on which women first articulated their visible opposition covered a vast terrain—ranging from those which were gender-specific to those which impinged on citizen's rights, class formations, and the direction of social transformation.

Some of the main concerns of the movement, as it emerged, were spelt out by the report of the Committee on the Status of Women in India (CSWI) which drew attention to the wide diversities in 'culturally' prescribed gender roles in India's plural society. The committee raised serious doubts about the 'development' or 'modernization' models that not only ignored the real differences that revolved round caste, class and ethnic history but also exaggerated the influence of religion, culture and 'social attitudes' on gender role prescriptions. Questioning the continued 'invisibility of women' in areas/sectors where they were largely involved, the CSWI pleaded for a renewed concern that would reflect real life issues and aspirations of the majority of women.[4]

This disenchantment of women with the post-independence 'development' scenario was not a stance dictated by exogenous political considerations. Demographic indicators like the accelerated decline in the sex-ratio, increasing gender gaps in life-expectancy, mortality and economic participation, or the rising migration rate were disturbing enough. Combined with this was the utter failure of state policy to live up to its constitutional mandates in any field of national development. The CSWI noted clear linkages between existing and growing social and economic disparities and women's status in education, the economy, society and the polity.[5] It also formed a starting point for women's studies.[6]

In this chapter we confine ourselves to the movement's responses to violence, fundamentalism and the debate on economic role and processes. This is not only because of limitations of space, but because we see a close link between the marginalization of women as economic beings—a trend which continues to be on the rise—and the rising trend of violence targeting women. In India today the most modern techniques of propaganda are used to project women as consumers and reproductive beings rather than as producers; and, above all as members of one or other particular community which seeks to establish its political identity by right of birth, religion or culture. Fundamentalism provides an ideological framework while globalization and glorification of the market provide the operative instrument to demolish women's claims to equality, freedom and dignity as individuals. This awesome combination poses a challenge to the movement.

The chapter does not attempt to write a history of the movement. It only focuses on some of the issues, trends and challenges that emerged even as it locates women in the overall context of the complexity of India as a social and political entity; a democracy-in-making, as well as a democracy endangered.

VIOLENCE: CASE OF EXPANDING ARENAS

From the late 1970s, the contemporary women's movement perceived growing violence as a major issue, bringing 'visibility' to the movement itself. This identification of violence has also been interpreted in many ways, by analysts of the movement, primarily of course as a 'rallying cry' or a 'rallying point'.

Violence, however, is perpetrated through the given institutions of the state, community, the family and society at large. It draws sustenance from prevailing ideologies which advocate 'falling-in-line', in response to transgression of social norms or laws, which are defended in the name of age-old customs and tradition, religious or caste identities, or even political dissidence. Those in support of the status quo perceive the movement's focus on violence as a threat to basic social institutions like the family, community and construction of gender roles developed by the elites.

Rape

It was the widespread, national-level campaign, in the course of 1979–80, on the Mathura case which brought women's issues onto the public agenda. The Supreme Court's acquittal of two policemen involved in the rape of a minor tribal girl brought to the fore several crucial aspects of women's oppression, namely, the roles of class and caste in oppression of women, and the issue of accountability of public servants and the judiciary. These were pointedly raised by four law teachers in their protest to the Chief Justice: must illiterate, labouring, politically mute Mathuras of India be continually condemned to their pre-Constitutional India fate?[7]

The agitation sparked off by the Mathura case led to significant changes in the Evidence Act, the Criminal Procedure Code and the Indian Penal Code, including the introduction of a category of custodial rape, though these were insufficient. The concept of power rape was resisted and has only recently been admitted through an amendment in the Civil Rights Act. Significant loopholes nevertheless remain, both with regard to the law and lack of will to implement it. While the movement's understanding of the issue has widened, success has been limited due to both lacunae in the conceptual definition as well as monitoring of procedures. The definition of rape does not extend to marital rape and anomalies exist between the Child Marriage Restraint Act and the rape law in that consent is not required for intercourse in marriage before the age of 18. Also, whereas the character of the victim is not supposed to be a consideration in determining rape, even the Supreme Court has at times violated the principle of custodial rape on this count. In recent cases the courts even gave concession to the element of 'provocation' and 'temptation' in what was described as a 'crime of passion'. As has been highlighted in the case of rape of nuns in Gujraula, Uttar Pradesh, the law leaves sufficient loopholes for agencies such as the police and medical personnel to not act, with perfect impunity. Of late, the movement is emphasizing the rising trend in child rape and demanding new legislation to combat the trend.

The Anti-Dowry Agitation

Of all the agitations focused on violence the one that touched the public imagination the most and emerged as a rallying cry was that against dowry and dowry-related violence. The slogan 'Brides are Not for Burning' attracted media attention—both in India and abroad—on the torture of young brides for dowry. For those who became crusaders in the fight against dowry the movement transmitted a pulsating sense of energy which, over time, got transformed into a brand of activism which asserted women's agency for social change.

This public assertion shook older organizations from a seemingly unending slumber. Section 498-A, the Criminal Law amendment passed in the wake of the agitation, encompassed for the first time, a definition of cruelty which included not just physical but mental cruelty as well. The Dahej Virodhi Chetna Manch, formed in 1982 in the wake of the widespread anger, kept up a mass public campaign along with sustained pressure for legal reform leading up to the amendment of the Dowry Prohibition Act in 1984 and again in 1986. The campaign threw up many questions and different perspectives, some of which are discussed in greater detail in Chapter 9.

Amniocentesis and Sex Selection

In 1974 the department of human cytogenetics, All India Institute of Medical Sciences (AIIMS), New Delhi, started a sample survey with the aid of amniocentesis to detect foetal abnormalities. By 1975 it realized that the tests were being followed by abortion of female foetuses and discontinued them. By 1979, however, reports came in from Amritsar in Punjab where medical entrepreneurs openly advertised their services referring to daughters as a 'liability' to the family and a 'threat' to the nation's population problem. Expectant parents were exhorted to avail of the services of clinics to rid themselves of the daughters to come. At a meeting convened in New Delhi in July 1982 a three-point position was arrived at wherein: (a) the government was requested to restrict use of amniocentesis to only teaching and research establishments; (b) the Indian Medical Council was requested to take severe action against members indulging in unethical practices; and (c) women's organizations were to remain vigilant against the spread of the practice for commercial purposes.[8]

While government did issue some circulars to this effect, not much action followed. In the meantime the sex determination business had come to stay. Today the business flourishes more rampantly in north India. From the South, alarming reports have come in of the prevalence of female infanticide among the Kallars in Tamil Nadu which did not historically adhere to this 'tradition'.

In 1985, The Forum Against Sex-Determination and Sex-Pre-Selection (FASDSP) was formed in Bombay. The Forum addressed itself to the entire spectrum of new reproductive technologies. It sought wider alliances, undertook surveys, and filed a public interest litigation. A private member's bill introduced in the state assembly was finally adopted by the Maharashtra government in 1988. This had several lacunae as did the central government's bill passed in July 1994. A question that has arisen from these long campaigns and the debate is, what about women who practise female foeticide or infanticide? The new law treats them as guilty and punishable. But does a woman in India have the right to choose or decide?

Population Policy

Ironically, both sex-selection followed by female foeticide and female infanticide cite national population concerns as the instigation for these anti-women acts. The Government of India's current efforts to formulate a new population control policy in consultation with or at the behest of its international benefactors, include a series of measures foisted on women after the initial attempts at vasectomy during the Emergency period met with stiff resistance. The notable features of this policy are that (a) it is premised on the assumption of the population bomb theory; (b) women feature as the main targets since they are the agency of reproduction; (c) the contraceptives include steroids and hormonal injectables, with long-term effects on the health of the user; (d) no provision/consideration for monitoring of impact.[9]

Women's organizations have been fighting for several years against the entry of these hazardous contraceptives which 'exploit women's desperate need for "safe" contraception', and proposals for coercive, 'fascist' punitive measures such as changes in the People's Representation Act to disqualify those with more than two children, and in the Maternity

Benefits Act to restrict the benefits up to two children, while increasing leave provisions for abortions. These concerns were articulated forcefully before a recent expert committee appointed by Government of India to draft a new national population policy.[10] The committee's report has also stirred up a public debate.

Political Violence

In a highly charged political environment, violence against women too is viewed through coloured lenses. Whereas the movement has attempted to contextualize the woman victim on the basis of prevalent social inequalities, divisions in society take the edge out of the condemnation of the crime *per se*. Thus in every incident of violence against women, the attempt is made to underplay the crime itself by focusing on the identity/position of the perpetrator as well as the victim in order to mobilize support on the basis of defined parameters of polarization in the specific context. These can be caste, community, regional or even politico-ideological. Thus rape and other atrocities inflicted on women and others in Nagaland, Manipur, Assam, Tripura, Punjab, or Kashmir by the armed or paramilitary forces can be condoned by the administration as well as government under cover of action taken to put down subversive activities. A more perverse definition of pro-national activity in complete violation of constitutional guarantees, human rights as well as women's rights would be difficult to find. This 'teaching a lesson' to curb dissidence (whatever its shape or form) is disturbing. Given the trend of growing criminalization of politics in India, this form of violence can be crucial in keeping women away from public life.[11] In fact this also reflects a cynical societal response to transgression by women of given norms of social behaviour, which in turn are defined along lines of caste, class, and status. This violence is limited neither to the personal sphere nor to the framework of man–woman relationships.[12]

There is also an increasing social acceptance of violence against women in recent years with an increase in incidents of stripping, rape and other forms of humiliation inflicted on Dalits as well as other women in different parts of the country. This is in addition to earlier instances of lynching of women on suspicion of being 'witches'. Many have seen in these the reflection of new political configurations and conflicts arising out of the aspirations of upwardly mobile backward castes. This comes along with reassertion of authority by traditional community and religion-based structures, claiming sanction and power to wield authority on the basis of various brands of identities. There is, in contemporary India, a powerful ganging-up of conservative and reactionary forces which aggressively impose moral prescripts. Where other processes fail, gender equality and women's rights to freedom is opposed through intimidation, humiliation and violence, in complete violation of norms of civil society.

The response from social scientists on the subject of violence in general and specific to women has not been very illuminating and there are very few studies of the patterns of violence or even causal analysis.[13] While the movement itself defined and identified violence against women in many different ways, analytical perspectives from social scientists are singularly lacking. Within the movement, while there is a shift away from the earlier emphasis on domestic violence alone, there is also a simultaneous trend of subsuming other arenas of conflict—communal conflicts, fundamentalism, even economic conflicts within 'violence against women'? Conceptually, while this may give primacy to a gender perspective, it oversimplifies conflict in other spheres and different levels of societal existence, by reducing them to a one-dimensional affair. Such conceptualization also ignores differences in perception and impact of these varied conflicts among diverse groups of women.

FUNDAMENTALISM AND COMMUNALISM

The wave of fundamentalist xenophobic upsurges sweeping across the world threatens the international women's movement as a whole. In India the complex social structures, economic constraints and political opportunism have provided ample breeding ground for the growth of revivalist ideologies and identity politics. These have adopted aggressive postures, showing scant regard for the fundamental rights the Indian Constitution guarantees. All religious, ethnic or cultural fundamentalists are increasingly hostile to gender equality whatever the rhetoric they profess.

As early as 1983, 'a deal' was reportedly struck between the Government of India and the Akali Dal, spearheading the agitation for a Sikh state, to withdraw the agitation if the Government of India accepted a separate personal law for Sikhs. The draft bill would have deprived Sikh women of their rights to a share in their fathers' property (provided under Hindu Succession Act 1956); of right of divorce except through the dispensation of the religious heads (against the provision of the Hindu Marriage Act), and would have legitimized polygamy through the custom of *chadar andazi*, claimed as a 'Sikh custom'.[14] Protests from national women's organizations and others, backed by several Sikh women, including five village *mahila mandals*, apparently compelled the Government of India to change its mind and no bill was introduced.

The year 1985, however, marked a shift in Indian politics. Pro-liberalization statements and measures by the government on the economic front began to be combined with compromises with fundamentalists. People's disenchantment with the nature and pace of India's development was sought to be offset by successive governments playing the 'communal card' to win community support.

May 1986 witnessed a total surrender by the government to Islamic fundamentalism with passage of the Muslim Women's (Protection of Rights of Divorce) Act 1986, which deprived divorced Muslim women of their right to seek maintenance under Section 125 of the Criminal Procedure Code, a secular law open to all communities.[15] The Act came in the wake of a year-long debate on the Supreme Court judgement in the Shah Bano case. While upholding a Muslim woman's right to this legal remedy, the court observed that it was high time for government to think of a uniform civil code. In the months that followed, Muslim fundamentalists organized themselves for a show-down accusing the government of interference with Muslim Personal Law. It is no coincidence that the campaign proceeded alongside protests against the reopening of the gates of the Babri Masjid which Hindu fundamentalists claimed was the birthplace of Lord Rama. Women's organizations campaigned against the bill, drawing support from large numbers of Muslim women especially from the poorer sections, intellectuals and reform groups from within the community. While the Bharatiya Janata Party suddenly espoused the demand for the uniform civil code, Muslim fundamentalists responded with the hysteria of 'Islam in Danger'. Despite sharp differences within the ruling party and the resignation of a Muslim minister (who had opposed the bill), the bill was enacted.[16] Petitions were filed in the Supreme Court challenging the new law as anti-constitutional and discriminatory. Meanwhile, organizations report that many more Muslim women come to discuss their problems and participate in other campaigns for women's rights.[17]

In September 1987 in Deorala, a village in Rajasthan, Roop Kanwar, a young bride burnt to death sitting atop the funeral pyre of her dead husband, while several thousands of people watched and even chanted slogans glorifying Sati. Though a few in the media came out with strong statements against the event, many played it up as a return to pristine glory, likening Roop Kanwar to a *devi* (goddess), who presented a sharp contrast to the urban elite, westernized feminist women who had disowned their traditional values. Sati was sought to be projected as a sort of ethnic re-assertion of indigenous womanhood.[18]

The state government remained paralysed, despite massive protests by women's group, and a court order to stop the celebrations of the event. The public outcry forced the Government of India to intervene, belatedly, with an unnecessary and ineffective law against both the act and the glorification of Sati. A strange feature of this law is to make the victim, if she escaped death, culpable for attempted suicide, even as women's organizations, some scholars and legal experts argued that Sati was murder, that its worship in Rajasthan and elsewhere was being encouraged by the rich Marwari business community and the landed Rajputs. They also argued that glorification of such heinous crimes would encourage violence as well as the positing of a family and community-bound identity for women.

The Nineties

In December 1992 when aggressive Hindu fundamentalists demolished a 500-year old mosque in Ayodhya, claiming that it was a *mandir* (temple) which marked the birthplace of Lord Rama, the government's paralysis was fully exposed. The demolition also sparked off riots in several parts of the country.

The overtly political manipulations of fundamentalists also found other victims. Several scholars were threatened or harassed for not adhering to fundamentalist versions while writing cultural, religious or even literary histories with a gender focus. These incidents of growing intolerance were not confined to any single community. The need to counter communal politics and fundamentalist perceptions emerged repeatedly as the greatest challenge during discussions on the movement. Activists pointed to the rupture with progressive movements of the nineteenth and twentieth centuries, the growth of a metropolitan culture and continued use of English as the lingua franca of officialdom which made the non-English speaking feel alienated from the cultural ethos of the emerging elite. This disjunctive situation, they argued, was capitalized upon by communal parties who stepped in to fill the void. Some pushed for a dialogue with reform movements and women's groups working within a religious framework.[19]

There is also an ongoing debate regarding retrieving religion from fundamentalists and highlighting the progressive aspects of socio-religious reform movements. Some argue that given the politicization of religion this may reinforce the notion that reform can come only through pre-ordained idioms, in denial of secular space. Respecting people's faiths is one thing, but preoccupation with religion quite another. Some say it may endanger the fragile solidarity the movement has achieved. At the same time women from the minority community argue forcefully that they can advance only if the majority does so.

The movement has sought to counter communal propaganda amongst women. Organizations have intervened in riot situations to provide relief as well as to start a process of dialogue between women of different communities. Apart from several local initiatives, at least two massive mobilizations of several thousand women each were organized in Ayodhya 1989 and Lucknow 1992 to focus on secularism and communal harmony. Nevertheless, whenever a confrontation took place between women and fundamentalism, the inaction of the government on the plea of neutrality was a stance which itself constituted an active intervention. Meanwhile taking advantage of women's attachment to religion, fundamentalist organizations amongst both Hindus and Muslims are today floating new organizations and fronts such as the Durga Vahini, wherein women's role as mothers, progenitors and defenders of the faith are highlighted along with exhortations to act against the 'other'. Realization of the global nature of this threat only increases the need to understand the basis or reasons for the spread of fundamentalist or communal ideologies, and their persistent hold on many women. The connections between state, government, and communal forces within the country are apparent. But what are the global forces that lie hidden behind this phenomenon?

Given the patriarchal ideology of family and community honour during riots women were invariably the primary targets of attack by the other group and were subjected to rape and humiliation in order to devalue and demoralize members of the 'other' community. Further, women's role as instigators of violence requires careful analysis which can only emerge from developing greater insights into the way in which caste, community, and gender intersect. This challenges an essentialist construction of the feminine identity. At the same time, instances abound of women playing a compassionate role in protecting members of the other community, often incurring personal risk. Such acts were often also in contravention with the stated intent of ideologues and the wishes of their own family or community groups.

Post-Emergency India has seen many communal riots but the nature of violence witnessed since 1992 was marked by the specific targeting of women for sexual attacks and perversities inflicted primarily on women from the minority community. A joint delegation of national women's organizations which visited three of the riot-affected cities in February 1992 found that (a) women were the most affected in the riots yet their needs were the 'least attended to' and relief itself had become a cause for 'further exploitation, corruption, poisonous propaganda'; (b) over the years 'some amount of communal relocation of populations' had taken place as an outcome of urban housing schemes, contributing to alienation and growth of suspicion along with lack of communication between groups; (c) nowhere had women been included in the peace committees set up to restore normalcy; and (d) no thought was given to the psychological rehabilitation of traumatized children, who witnessed acts of violence against their families. The delegation also came up with some questions about the politics of women's organizations in this context for, 'even the most committed work among vulnerable sections of women is not capable of enabling such women to liberate themselves from the pressures of divisive identity politics, without a conscious direction to confront this type of politics which is so inimical to women's rights and the movement for equality.[20]

WOMEN AS ECONOMIC BEINGS

If violence was the rallying issue for women's organizations, the marginalization and impoverishment of the majority of women within the changing economy became the entry point for academics into the movement. The CSWI's initial analysis was based more on inferences, the deposition of thousands of poor women across the country before the committee and demographic evidence of a secular trend of decline in women's value in the economy and society as a whole. The complexities of the relationship between macro-economic changes and women's status issues—at different levels of society—had been neglected by social analysis till then. The committee appealed to the social science community to study this relationship on a continuous basis.[21]

Meanwhile, large organizations of poor women in the informal sector had emerged.[22] The dynamism in struggle demonstrated by these groups became a major focus in the search for alternative strategies of development—with organized groups of women from the grassroots as primary agents of change.

Coinciding with the increasing intensity of critiques of the dominant model of economic growth emanating from various parts of the Third World, women's studies in India began and grew rapidly in its initial stages to study this interaction.[23] The Women's Studies Programme of the Indian Council of Social Science Research helped to start off a research process heavily biased in favour of 'invisible' women, that is, poor working women in rural and urban areas. The focus on economic themes by the Indian Association of Women's Studies in its National Conferences facilitated the interaction between academics and activists and policy makers. A new national government in 1977 opened up various development policies for review.

The combined pressure of a group of women members of parliament (MPs), some concerned bureaucrats and leading social scientists led to research as well as the constitution of several working groups at the behest of the Planning Commission, to search for alternative strategies to arrest the marginalization of the majority of women—especially the poorer—through prevalent development policies. A memorandum authored by the ICSSR's Advisory Committee on Women's Studies highlighted the problems of increasing devaluation of women in the economy and society, and recommended special strategies for employment, health, and education.[24] These documents, along with the CSWI's report and some of its major recommendations were to form the initial thrust of demands by a network of national women's organizations that came into existence, informally in 1980. The memorandum, *Indian Women in the Eighties: Development Imperatives*, one of the first joint statements by women's organizations, stated that:

...unless explicit provision for the imperative developmental needs of women is made in the Sixth Five-Year Plan, the conditions of women will continue to decline notwithstanding constitutional pledges of equality and justice and the parliamentary mandate for removal of disparities and discrimination.[25]

It recommended that the family/household approach in programme thrusts be replaced by 'explicit mention of women as a target group', since the 'invisibility' of women to planners and administrators was rooted in the 'tendency to view women only through the screen of families and households and not as individuals in their own right', which reinforced the perspectives of seeing women's economic role as 'marginal and supplemental'.[26] The demands included a special component approach with earmarked resources and separate monitoring arrangements in each of the sectoral programme thrusts; inclusion of child care centres within the Minimum Needs Programme; and the demand for joint *pattas* (land titles) for women and men already voiced by poor peasant women. Some of these demands led to a 'sharp exchange' with official representatives with regard to the 'philosophy of the family-household approach', which, women activists maintained, reflected the planners' status quo-approach in the name of 'defence of the family'.[27]

Despite government's reluctance—this dialogue, backed by several women MPs from opposition parties who were members/leaders of a network of national women's organization resulted in the appearance of a chapter on 'Women and Development' in the Sixth Five-Year Plan for the first time in the planning history of India. Acknowledging government's failure to achieve gender equality, the Plan stated explicitly that without economic independence, equal access to education, skill-training, and family planning services, the constitutional guarantee of equality would remain a myth.[28] Henceforth all anti-poverty programmes were directed to include women as targets, along with the promise to 'endeavour to provide joint titles to husband and wife' in cases of asset-distribution by government (productive/homestead land, technology, etc.) along with priority to 'female headed households'.[29]

Women have comprised a crucial component of those struggling for land and forest rights, against the havoc wrought by the construction of large dams and ecological disaster, struggles for fishing rights in coastal waters, for recognition as workers in governmental networks of health and child care services, as urban unorganized labour, migrant labour, and rural workers.[30] In all these they have fought for basic rights as workers, for equal wages and better working conditions. Micro studies have highlighted the role women play in all these sectors though a full and detailed history of these numerous and multifarious struggles is still awaited.

The women's movement also consistently demanded implementation of genuine land reform even as 'defenders' of the 'family' accused women's organizations of arresting 'distributive justice' by demanding women's right to a share of productive resources. A study of land ceiling laws enacted by different states brought out clearly that many of the ceiling laws were discriminatory and thus unconstitutional. State procedure/rules for redistribution were even more so. While in one case, a group of peasant women challenged their exclusion from getting title to redistributed land in the Rajasthan Canal Area in the Rajasthan High Court, the issue of land rights featured consistently in discussions in the movement from different perspectives.[31]

The closing year of the Women's Decade marked a high tide. The Rajiv Gandhi government announced in January 1985 that women would receive greater priority than before. The same year Government of India hosted the second NAM Conference on Women and Development, and the official delegation included several leaders of the national women's organizations. Not content with this, the Delhi-based network of organizations held its own review a week before the NAM Conference and separately distributed their report to all delegations.[32]

But the tide receded fast. The widening divergence between the perspective of the Government of India and movement-based initiatives on gender roles, issues and participation became clear with the release of two documents in 1988.

Shramshakti, the Report of the National Commission on Self-Employed Women and Women in the Informal Sector, to an extent represented the voice of a substantial section of the women's movement and of women's studies' scholars, who were inducted into its various task forces.[33] Yet, there were shades of divergence in approaches to the problem of women in the informal sector. While some went along with the government in its active promotion and special emphasis on the role of women in the self-employed and home-based sectors, others disagreed. The latter felt that this reinforced the process of marginalization and was a retreat on the government's earlier commitment to bringing women into the 'productive' sphere. The dilemma was a genuine one. No one disputed that the limited opportunities for economic earnings should be expanded and work conditions in this sector be improved. The point at issue was whether one should settle for little 'bits and crumbs'. As one economist put it, 'the women's movement should have fought harder for gender equality in the labour market/force'.[34]

Meanwhile the National Perspective Plan for Women (NPP), up to the year 2000, was prepared by with no interaction with activists. The draft, placed for endorsement before a National Committee headed by the prime minister faced opposition from some members who found the absence of women's organizations' representatives inexplicable and demanded a national debate before adoption of the document. With no response from the government, the organizations proceeded to organize a debate in Delhi, followed by several state-level discussions. The women's organizations critique of the NPP pointed out that the proposed plan's recommendation to bring women 'into the mainstream of development' ignored 'the reality of women's marginalization being the result of such "mainstream" development'.[35]

The NPP's approach omitted the earlier thrust for convergence of economic and social services with organization for collective strength and participation, and demonstrated a trend towards centralization, disregarding ongoing debates on the need for decentralization and democratization of the planning process. The proposed reservation of 30 per cent seats for women in elective bodies, to be filled by co-option or nomination in the initial stage, revealed the government's interest in subverting the representative process. Another real danger came from the 'preferential emphasis' to be given to the unorganized sector. Rejecting all these anti-democratic proposals, women's organizations demanded: (a) the constitution of statutory, autonomous women's commissions at the centre and in the states with a broad-based, representative composition; (b) inclusion of child-care as a priority within minimum needs from the next plan onwards; (c) ratification of CEDAW; and (d) due recognition of national organizations of women at all levels of the planning and decision-making processes.

The movement has adopted a multi-pronged strategy on these issues. While the specific skills of women's studies' scholars have been directed at evolving a critique of the macro-level policies of government, grass-roots level initiatives to develop alternatives have been stepped up. One of the biggest mobilizations of women in Delhi from all over the country, in September 1989, was of over 20,000 women demanding the right to work.

Women's organizations have mushroomed: sometimes combining issues at the workplace and family environment; sometimes as sub-committees within existing trade unions or joint fronts. The critique of macro-policies basically adopts three thrusts: (a) that they would enhance inequalities among the people in general; (b) that this would make the majority of women already struggling for survival in the informal sector still more vulnerable; and (c) they would contribute to the social turbulence and violence, of which women and children are the major victims. Critiques have also condemned violence stemming from the promotion of consumerist lifestyles through the mass media as such lifestyles trap women into the stereotype of being objects and subjects of consumerism.[36] It is important to note that the few important concessions wrested from the government in the poverty alleviation through economic development programmes provided some space up to the early 1990s for urban poor and rural women to use the opportunities to organize and articulate their demands. However, the macro-policies adopted, continued with the processes of marginalization.

The issue facing the movement today is about the relevance of these debates and efforts. The earlier critique of macro-policies was from a standpoint of introducing a pro-women approach within the given parameters, using constitutional guarantees as the basic reference point. Today, Indian women feel that the Structural Adjustment Programmes (SAPs) and the package of economic 'reforms' threaten not only earlier gains, but also the stated national goals by successive governments. While the movement was critiquing the development model, SAP has now removed the few regulatory/compensatory aspects of India's mixed economy, leaving 'global market forces' as the sole players in the field. The processes bear significant resemblance to what happened to the Indian economy, and to women's role in the economy in particular, during the colonial period.[37]

This realization has made unity amongst differing organizations easier to achieve today. In a joint statement women's organizations argued that: 'discussions on the impact of the new economic policies usually focus on the impact on the organized sector, since women make up only a small percentage here it is assumed that the impact is minimal. We need to unitedly and forcefully correct the picture. In our multidimensional roles, as workers, as peasants, as producers, as citizens, as mothers, wives, daughters, as women, the economic policies hit us the hardest'.[38]

The overall impact of SAP has to be understood in the context of the overbearing reality that already 94 per cent of the women workers are part of the informal sector and that they constitute half the labour force in the unorganized sector. What is the future lying ahead for women in an economy which itself shall be struggling to find a space within the model of 'sustainable development' under the aegis of a carefully orchestrated Structural Adjustment Programme?

* * *

The contemporary women's movement in India spans a large canvas. There are small groups as well as large national level organizations.[39] While some are recent, having been formed only over the last two decades, others go back to over 50 or even 100 years. Some focus on a single issue while mass organizations cover a vast range. Their organizational structures, as well as activities undertaken, differ.

The movement has been fraught with tensions, rifts and differences, reflecting differing notions of what are women's issues or how to proceed to focus on these. Nevertheless, in comparison with the early years of the decade, today it is much easier to come together. With an experience of working together for over a decade-and-a-half women's groups in the country are fairly well aware of the issues they agree on and where they differ. However, neither the agreement nor the differences should be seen as static, or in a frozen-time frame. Whereas ideological differences remain and perspectives differ, the overall thrust is in favour of unity in action.[40] The same attitude is reflected in the issues being taken up. In the 1970s the movement took off as part of an overall build up against the authoritarian regime symbolized, ironically, by a woman prime minister. It then got fragmented and even perhaps insulated. For a while even overtly political statements were resisted. Today it is much easier to come together even on a platform to denounce the economic and other policies of the government. The 1990s represent a trough in the political graph, where the need to join hands and build alliances with other forces is ever greater.

The women's movement has undoubtedly grown. Its outreach is far beyond the figures of enrolled membership of organizations. Nothing illustrates this better than the response to the literacy campaigns in several states. Whereas earlier attempts to reach women had been abysmal failures, today it is estimated that two-thirds of the neo-literate learners as well as two-thirds of the volunteers are women.[41] The impact of the literacy movement came to be highlighted in the context of the anti-arrack movement in Andhra Pradesh. Another remarkable achievement in recent years has been the process set in motion by the implementation of the 73rd and 74th Constitutional Amendments which provide for 33 per cent representation for women in local bodies in rural and urban areas. Whereas observers rightly see in this a qualitatively new dimension that has been added to the women's movement through this development the depth and complexities of these linkages are yet to be understood. In rural India, as also in the cities, it is the new found articulation and confidence which is coming into conflict with the consolidated combine of conservative social forces which draw strength from the regressive steps taken by government as well as political representatives of reactionary forces. The latter are today preparing to mount an onslaught through the political process to check women's halting steps to advance and strengthen democracy in India.

Movement politics, as it has developed in India, shows up elements which are unclassifiable. Ideological differences exist—but within a continuum—and tend to get blurred when strategic choices have to be made between priorities. But the debates continue and the questions persist. Is the movement's decentralized structure and its multiple arena a point of strength or weakness or both? Is the movement's 'excessive preoccupation' with the state's development policies and legislation 'welfarist' in its objective rather than 'feminist' or 'radical'? Does extension of the issue of violence against women from the domestic to the social and political spheres indicate a backsliding or an advance? Does this successfully combat the dichotomy posed between 'economic welfarism' and 'body politics'? Should the women's movement get involved with issues related to environment, population, child rights, globalization/marketization, international debt burden, all of which arise from its widening base at the grass-roots level or should it retain its autonomy while restricting its focus?

Clearly, as it has developed, the focus could not be confined to the issue of interpersonal relationships. The limits to creating an essentialist, biological entity as well as identity of 'woman' have become only too obvious. While the ideological outreach of 'feminine' identity politics has widened, this spread has also demolished the fossilized image sought to be created. From different starting points, organizations have moved towards a more holistic vision. As the proto-fascist undertones of political events/processes become clearer along with the state's surrender to them, the need to join hands is felt ever more deeply, lest we come out with a *cri de coeur*—'we have the movement but they (the other?) have the women'. While the movement is aware of these challenges the strength of its grass-roots support base provides a ray of hope that counter-actions and counter-ideologies are not impossible.

NOTES

1. Lucille Mathurin Mair, *International Women's Decade: A Balance Sheet* (New Delhi: CWDS, 1985), pp. 2–4.
2. Kumkum Sangari and Sudesh Vaid (eds), *Recasting Women: Essays in Colonial History* (New Delhi: Kali Press, 1989).
3. *Towards Equality, Report of the Committee on the Status of Women in India* (Government of India, 1974), p. 301; V. Mazumdar (ed.), *Symbols of Power* (Allied Publishers, 1978).
4. Government of India (1974), p. 3.
5. Ibid., p. 234.
6. See Susie Tharu and K. Lalitha (eds), *Women Writing in India*, Vol. II (New Delhi: Oxford University Press, 1994).
7. 'Open Letter to the Chief Justice of India, 1979', *Supreme Court Journal*, 4, (1979), pp. 19–22.
8. V. Mazumdar, *Amniocentesis and Sex Selection*, Occasional Paper, no. 21 (New Delhi: CWDS, 1994).
9. 'Perspectives from the Women's Movement: Health and Population', in *Some Issues in the Struggle for Women's Equality*, 1994 (henceforth, *Some Issues*); a joint document published by the Delhi Network of Six National Women's Organizations, pp. 10–17. S. Vaid and K. Sangari, 'Institutions, Beliefs, Ideologies: Widow Immolation in Contemporary Rajasthan', *Economic and Political Weekly*, 26 (17), 27 April (1987), WS 2–18.
10. Joint Memorandum to Swaminathan Committee by 12 women's organizations, 12 November 1993, also see Open Letter to Swaminathan Committee, *Indian Express*, 9 July 1994. Also see, National Population Policy, Perspectives from the Women's Movement, CWDS, New Delhi, 1996.
11. Cf. resolution adopted in meeting to plan Joint Action against Criminalization of Politics and Sexual Abuse of Women (Delhi, 22 October 1994) (unpublished).
12. B. Karat and I. Agnihotri, *Violence Against Women*, Vol. 6, Proceedings of Sixth National Conference on Women's Studies (NCWS) (Mysore, 1993).
13. V. Das (ed.), *Mirrors of Violence* (New Delhi: Oxford University Press, 1990); C. Datar (ed.), *The Struggle Against Violence* (Stree Publications, 1993).
14. A common custom among peasant communities, aimed at preventing partition of property by making a widow marry her brother-in-law. For more on this see Prem Chowdhry, *Contentious Marriages, Eloping Couples:*

Gender, Caste and Patriarchy in Northern India (New Delhi: Oxford University Press, 2007).

15. Asghar Ali Engineer (ed.), *The Shah Bano Controversy* (Orient Longman, 1987).

16. Zoya Hasan, 'Minority Identity, Muslim Women Bill Campaign and the Political Process', *Economic and Political Weekly*, 24 (1), 7 January (1989), pp. 44–50; R. Palriwala and I. Agnihotri, *Tradition of the Family and the State: Politics of the Contemporary Women's Movement* (Nehru Memorial Museum and Library, Occasional Paper, New Series, 1993).

17. Information received in conversation with AIDWA activists in Delhi; also *The Times of India*, Research Fellowship, *Study of Muslims in India* (unpublished).

18. *Janasatta*, editorial (18 September 1987); also see Ashis Nandy, 'Human Factor' in *The Illustrated Weekly* (17 January 1988), pp. 20–3. For debate on 'voluntary' *sati* see 'From the Burning Embers', A Film on Sati by Mediastorm and, Lata Mani, in Sangari and Vaid (eds), *Recasting Women*.

19. See, Confronting Myriad Oppressions Report of a Consultation on the Women's Movement in Bombay (New Delhi: CWDS, 1995). Also, see report of Plenary session, V National Conference on Women's Studies (NCWS) (Jadavpur, January 1991). The theme of the conference was 'Religion, Culture and Politics'.

20. YWCA, *Women against Communalism, Report of Joint Women's Delegation to Ahmedabad, Surat and Bhopal* (YWCA of India, 1993), pp. 23–4.

21. Government of India (1974).

22. SEWA Ahmedabad, the Working Women's Forum, Madras, the Annapurna Mahila Mandal, Bombay etc.

23. It was the first priority area in the Indian Council of Social Science Research's sponsored programme of women's studies, See, *Critical Issues on the Status of Women*, 1977, ICSSR.

24. Ibid.

25. All India Women's Conference, *Indian Women in the 1980s: Development Imperatives* (All India Women's Conference, 1980).

26. Ibid.

27. Vina Mazumdar to Lotika Sarkar, M-6/80, (CWDS Files, 12 September 1980) and Vina Mazumdar to Ashok Mitra, M-6/80, (CWDS files, 1 October 1980).

28. *Sixth Five-Year Plan 1980–85*, Chapter 27.

29. Ibid.

30. Lotika Sarkar, *What Price Constitutional Equality? Peasant Women and Land Reform in India* (CWDS, 1995).

31. For more on this issue see B. Agarwal, *A Field of One's Own: Gender and Land Rights in South Asia* (Cambridge: Cambridge University Press, 1994).

32. Charter on Employment, 8 March 1983 Also, Tomsic, Vida, 4th J.P. Naik Memorial Lecture (CWDS, 1986); Government of India, *Women in Development, Report of the Non-Aligned Ministers' Conference* (New Delhi, 1985).

33. Government of India 1985.
34. Nirmala Banerjee, *Report of Calcutta Consultation* (CWDS, unpublished 1995); also see Banerjee, 'Analyzing Women's Work Under Patriarchy', in K. Sangari and U. Chakravarty (eds), *From Myths to Markets: Essays on Gender* (New Delhi, Shimla: Manohar Publications, IIAS, 1999).
35. Joint Press Statement by National Women's Organizations, 6 July 1988.
36. K. Bhasin and B. Agarwal (eds), *Women and the Media* (Kali, 1984).
37. M. Krishnaraj, *Women and Development* (Bombay: RCWS, SNDT Women's University, 1988); Utsa Patnaik, 'The Likely Impact of Economic Liberalization and Structural Adjustment on the Food Security System in India' (unpublished, 1993); J. Krishnamurthy, *Women in Colonial India, Essays on Survival, Work and the State* (Oxford University Press, 1989); Asok Mitra, 'Introduction', in *Status of Women: Shifts in Occupational Participation* (Delhi: Abhinav, 1979).
38. 'Why We Need to Struggle against the New Economic Policies?' in *Some Issues*, p. 3.
39. Some of these may even have a membership going up to a few million: AIDWA—3.5 million. NFIW, 1 million, YWCA 15,000.
40. This point came across from consultations held by the CWDS with activists across the country in 1994. A greater readiness and felt need to act together is also reported from state-level Consultations of Women NGOs preparing for the World Conference on Women (Beijing, 1995).
41. Government of India, *Total Literacy Campaign Evaluation Report* (National Literacy Mission, Ministry of Education, Government of India, 1994).

The Anti-Dowry Movement in Delhi*

Rajni Palriwala

In this chapter I look at the anti-dowry movement which emerged around 1979, continuing through till 1984. It was largely urban-based, yet nation-wide in scope—not just in rhetoric, but also in the active participation of women across classes and the country. In documenting the movement, I focus on Delhi, where it was perhaps at its strongest. I consider the political context in which the movement took root, its relation to earlier activities of women's organizations, the forms of action adopted and the various perspectives it encapsulated. The anti-dowry movement did not emerge from women's spontaneous actions, but was a result of campaigns by women's organizations. Data was obtained through participatory research, newspaper clippings for the years 1980–5, interviews with representatives of women's organizations, group discussions with members of a few organizations, reports, pamphlets and other written material available with different organizations and the few articles which touch on the movement.

THE SPREAD OF DOWRY AND BRIDE BURNINGS

Why did dowry bring women onto the streets in the 1970s in various forms of collective protest? Dowry was not after all a new phenomenon. I

* This is an edited version of the paper presented in November 1985 at the symposium on 'Anthropological Perspectives on Women's Collective Actions: An Assessment of the Decade 1975–85' organized by the Wenner-Gren Foundation for Anthropological Research in Mijas, Spain. It has not been updated.

suggest that the shifts in dowry practices resulting from socio-economic changes following colonial and post-colonial capitalist development led to an intensification of violence against wives. It was this rather than the dowry system itself which spurred the movement. People were responding to the symbol of the burning bride.[1] Dowry murders drew a much stronger public response than had earlier campaigns against dowry or for reform of the Anti-Dowry Law.

I do not attempt here a detailed analysis of the dowry system in India. However, it is necessary to make a few comments. In the pre-colonial period, dowry was limited largely to the Hindu upper castes. The exchange of goods in the context of a marital alliance between two kin groups took the form of dowry. It was tied to the exclusion of women from ownership of the most valuable economic resource, land, and thus enabled the control of women. Dowry and hypergamy[2] were empirically linked and tied to Brahmanical ideology. The latter entailed the seclusion of women, their apparent exclusion from productive work and categorization as economic burdens as well as status asymmetry between husband and wife. Dowry helped 'ease' the entry of women into their marital homes.

In 1974, the Committee on the Status of Women in India (CSWI) and later the Parliamentary Joint Select Committee found that dowry had spread to all castes, communities, religions, and regions. With dowry has been carried the caste-gender ideology. Not only has dowry increased in the quantum and variety of goods given by the bride's parents, it has come to encompass the entire character of gift exchange between the two kin groups.[3] Simultaneously, the network of kinship, caste and political relationships which provided a check on social behaviour, expectations, and the treatment of wives has weakened, especially in urban spaces. The daily violence of 'traditional' marriages has increased and women find themselves with nowhere to turn in times of crisis. Social values stress marriage as the only acceptable status for women, obliging the bride/wife to 'adjust', telling her that only on her funeral bier may she permanently leave her marital home.

Thus, if a bride's parents are unable to meet the demands for dowry, increasing harassment can drive a young married woman, with the active connivance of her husband and in-laws, to 'suicide'. If she does not take this step herself, they can burn her to death. Neighbours, friends, and her natal kin are informed that she died in a cooking accident or had committed suicide. The way is then open for the unencumbered widower to find a new bride with a new dowry; socially he is as eligible as on his first marriage, but richer; the death of his first wife allowed him to retain her dowry.

Most deaths of young married women in Delhi were registered as suicides or accidents, rather than murders. Prior to the anti-dowry movement, people were not ready to interfere in 'internal domestic matters'. This was especially true of Delhi which as a city had no recent history of collective struggles.[4] Neighbours were afraid of harassment if they got involved. Due to the nature of the crime, witnesses were unlikely and evidence was destroyed. Laxity and connivance on the part of the police was common. The cases brought to court usually resulted in acquittal of the accused.

By 1982, women's organizations were insisting that the majority of deaths of young married women by burning were dowry murders or suicides. It became increasingly difficult to pass them off as accidents. The scale and immediacy of the problem moved women to mass collective action.

THE POLITICAL CONTEXT TO THE MOVEMENT

Women were politically active in the national movement,[5] but there was a hiatus in the decades after independence. A renewal of women's activism was witnessed in the 1970s, accompanying a nation-wide political ferment. Velayudhan notes that during this time women participated in varied demand-based and sectional movements, including anti-corruption, price-rise, and workers' rights.[6] Through these struggles, not only were questions of women's oppression directly tackled, the relationship between the women's movement and other movements was debated as also what constituted 'women's issues'. The struggle for civil liberties and the fight against the growing authoritarianism of the ruling party marked the entire decade, bringing together people with diverse viewpoints. The issues of political prisoners and police atrocities, including on women, became a major focus of mobilization, especially after the withdrawal of the internal Emergency in 1977.[7] For the first time, the Indian National Congress lost the elections and was not the party that formed the government at the centre.

The press took on a new activist role in the aftermath of the Emergency. Reports were filed on sensational cases of mass rape, administrative lapses and police negligence and collusion in the rising atrocities on women. The report of the CSWI (1975) and the International Women's Decade generated a discussion among the educated middle classes on the situation of women in India.[8] These various movements and associated shifts in collective conscience laid the basis for a renewed women's movement. A number of new women's organizations and groups emerged, while older organizations reactivated themselves. The issue of rape and atrocities became the first focus of nationwide agitations by women. These agitations pinpointed the need to amend laws related to criminal assaults on women. It was in this context that women's organizations and groups and the press came to highlight the number of young women being burnt to death for dowry.

WOMEN'S ORGANIZATIONS AND THE ANTI-DOWRY MOVEMENT

The nature and direction of the anti-dowry movement has been determined, to an extent, by the history of the participating women's organizations. It will therefore be useful to outline this history, while documenting the early days of the movement and the activities of these groups.

The Mahila Dakshata Samiti (MDS), formed in 1977, included women who had long been active in social democratic politics. Some of the founders had been among the leaders of the militant agitation by women in Bombay—protesting price rise—and in anti-corruption movements in various parts of the country. A link had been made in the latter between corruption and dowry.[9] Of the four sub-committees it formed, one was an anti-dowry committee. In 1979, it presented a report of the cases of victimization for dowry and abandonment it had handled over two years. The press highlighted its findings that many of the so-called accidental or suicidal burnings of young women were in fact murders. Despite links with the then ruling government, MDS had limited success in bringing dowry cases to the court, legal lacunae being the main reason, it suggested.

The All India Women's Conference (AIWC) founded in 1927 and the Young Women's Christian Association (YWCA) formed in 1875 are organizations of predominantly middle and upper class women. Their emphasis had been on social work and institution-building, particularly in education, and not on agitation as was true of many organizations in the decades after independence.[10] In its early years, the AIWC had been active in demanding equal rights for women in property, education, and employment, with a constant tension between social reform activities and political struggle. Closely linked to the Congress Party, it became an advisory body to the central government on women's status.[11] By 1981, both organizations were speaking of the need to study the dowry law and set up legal aid cells and wished to cooperate with other groups active on the issue of dowry deaths and involved in remedial action around women's issues.[12]

The National Federation of Indian Women (NFIW) is a mass organization formed in 1954 by women who broke away from the AIWC aiming to build a more militant and Left women's movement. Many NFIW members had been active in agrarian, working class and student movements. However, after the spurt of agitation in the 1950s around the reform of personal law, it lost much of its militancy and became engaged in vocational training and literacy activism.[13] The atmosphere in the 1970s, the impact of the CSWI report and the issue of bride burnings reactivated the organization.

The All India Democratic Women's Association (AIDWA) was formed in 1981 through the merging of a number of new and old organizations. These included some which shared a common history with the NFIW but had separated from it in the 1960s due to its lack of militancy and reluctance to confront the government. AIDWA, unlike the AIWC or YWCA, explicitly sees itself as a political organization. In its perspective, the women's movement is 'inextricably linked with all democratic struggles for a society free from exploitation' (Interviews). The membership of the Delhi unit (Janvadi Mahila Samiti—JMS) is concentrated in working class areas and resettlement colonies[14] as is the Delhi unit of the NFIW. Not only had dowry and dowry harassment spread to poorer sections, administrative negligence and police connivance were particularly blatant where they lived. AIDWA stressed area-level membership and discussions on the need for organized, mass, collective struggles to confront and change women's situation at home, at work and in society.

A number of small Delhi-based groups emerged through the movement. The Nari Raksha Samiti (NRS) and Kalyani, with social work orientations and origins in Congress politics, addressed individual cases of harassment, suicides and murder. The NRS held neighbourhood demonstrations and took delegations to the home minister and lieutenant-governor of Delhi. Stree Sangharsh and Karmika, more overtly feminist, stimulated middle-class women of south Delhi to protest cases of dowry harassment in their localities. Another Delhi-based and consciously feminist organization, Saheli (female friend) was also formed during this period, with the aim of being a referral and resources centre for women, including survivors of burnings and not just as a consciousness-raising group.[15] It began a training/production centre for readymade garments, took up cases for survivors of burnings, and conducted a study of young burn victims in Delhi hospitals.

In looking at the various organizations and groups that were active, it has to be noted that many which would be categorized as feminist in Europe or North America refuse(d) to call themselves so in India. The reasons are varied, including a strategic building of bridges, an insistence that women's issues are tied to and require struggles along varied lines of oppression, and/or a desire to distance themselves from positions perceived as too militant, exclusionary, or anti-men. This refusal also points to the need to encompass the multiplicity of feminisms which run through women's movements.

THE DVCM (FORUM FOR CONSCIOUSNESS AGAINST DOWRY)—A COALITION OF WOMEN'S GROUPS

Initially most groups acted separately, taking up individual cases, demonstrating, approaching the police, following cases through the courts, counselling, holding discussions, organizing performances of anti-dowry street plays,[16] as well as seminars. There were occasions when they came together, notably on 8 March 1981, when Delhi's women's organizations jointly observed International Women's Day in protest against rape, dowry murder, and other atrocities against women. Men also participated and university students were particularly visible. Slogans read; 'Women are not for burning, Women are human beings' and 'Let not the marriage fire become a funeral pyre'. Two street plays were performed on that day.

It was in focusing on anti-dowry agitation to draw the attention of the state in terms of law, administration and government responsibility that India's women's groups and organizations came together in a collective effort nationally. In the 1980 elections the Congress Party returned to power, but leading members of all-India women's organizations (some of whom had been MPs earlier) were also elected. They moved a private member's bill on amendments to the Dowry Prohibition Act of 1961[17] and in December, due to the persistence of opposition MPs, the two houses decided to refer this Act to a Joint Select Committee (JSC) to recommend amendments. A joint petition was submitted, demanding the immediate establishment of an autonomous commission on women with statutory powers and vigilance committees in all areas, including members of women's organizations.

The JSC became a point of mobilization. When its report was not placed by the government before Parliament months after it had been submitted, it was decided to take the agitation to a new level. At a meeting of five national women's organizations (AIDWA, AIWC, MDS, NFIW and YWCA) and seven other groups, the Dahej Virodhi Chetna Manch (Forum for Consciousness Against Dowry) was formed. The five national groups were named as convenors. Despite differences, their concerns converged on the particular issue of dowry. A record of limited but positive united action in the past helped to consolidate the DVCM. The specificity of their focus and their concretized demands also promoted unity.

Though individual organizations did not agree with its entire content, the JSC Report formed the basis for the DVCM programme. Recommendations included broadening the definition of dowry; ceilings on presents and expenses of all ceremonies related to the engagement and wedding; the recording of gifts; a distinction between givers and takers of dowry on the question of punishment; making dowry a cognizable, non-bailable and compoundable offence; enhancement of punishment and the establishment of vigilance committees with representatives of women's organizations as members and Dowry Prohibition Officers.[18]

At first reading, this national social movement is ideologically similar to earlier protests against dowry and to the mainstream pre-independence women's movement. Manifestations of women's oppression were described as 'social evils', in essentially liberal terms. A DVCM memorandum stated that 'dowry was not an isolated phenomenon', but an aspect of the 'inferior female condition' and the 'corrosion of moral values'. However, this was partly to do with choosing a language which wide sections of people could relate to and partly to do with the plurality of views within the DVCM. The categories of 'moral' and 'social evil' were given a structural context, as the memorandum noted that 'the continuing erosion of women's status' was 'related to the worsening social-economic crisis within which structural inequalities have accentuated, and black money power has grown to fuel greater human oppression'.

Not all member organizations agreed with this analysis and in the interests of unity some issues were barely touched on in joint campaigns. While public support for the anti-dowry movement was in response to bride burnings and other atrocities against women, the DVCM tried to draw attention to the wider issues surrounding dowry and domestic violence. DVCM slogans called for a transformation of family relations and society in India. It was understood that dowry was related to women's economic dependence and their legal rights in both their natal and marital homes. It viewed legal changes as an instrument of social change, aware of inadequacies in the law and the collusion and connivance of the police and local administration. Its efforts were directed at changing public consciousness, in order to build the necessary political and social will to ensure action that would be effective in eradicating both the practice of dowry and increasing brutality against brides.

ACTION STRATEGIES OF THE ANTI-DOWRY MOVEMENT

The perspectives within the DVCM and the movement are evident in the types of actions undertaken. These may be grouped into five broad types.

1. The struggle within parliament, largely through opposition MPs who were members of women organizations. They mobilized the support of other MPs from opposition parties. Women's organizations tapped this forum by lobbying and placing their experiences and views before the JSC. Women MPs who were members of the latter ensured that their suggestions were incorporated into its report.

2. Legal aid and counselling were activities that most of the women's groups and organizations were involved in. The intention was both to try for immediate relief for harassed women and a 'consciousness-raising' exercise. Throughout the movement, events in the courts were a barometer of the impact of various agitations (see below).

3. Collective action that was by design knowledge-creating and consciousness-raising, including studies and surveys, public seminars and discussions, and elocution and poetry contests about the issue. Other than corner meetings and street plays, some of these actions allowed for only minimal participation of illiterate and working-class women. Their impact on the broader public and on the government was largely dependent on press coverage, but they succeeded in mobilizing support and triggering other actions.

4. A fourth category of activity involved signature and postcard campaigns. These allowed extensive participation, particularly of women who were unable to overcome familial, cultural or other constraints to feminine public activity. Signatures (or thumb prints) and postcards were collected from all over the country by national organizations such as the AIDWA, MDS and NFIW, drawing government attention to the fact that dowry harassment, suicide, and murder was a pan-Indian phenomenon.

5. The fifth form of action consisted of *dharna*s (sit-ins), rallies, and marches. Neighbourhood actions were a sub-type. These actions were undertaken by individual organizations, by several coordinating groups, and by the DVCM. Sometimes they involved courting arrest en masse. They all brought women into public spaces as political actors in larger or smaller numbers.

Neighbourhood action had its origins in, and characterized, the anti-dowry movement in the capital. In May 1979, the burning of a middle-class woman close to the University of Delhi was publicized in newspapers. This case activized many feminists (Stree Sangharsh) and women of the Left (JMS) on the issue of bride burnings. A large number of local residents and neighbours joined the demonstrators, swelling their numbers to about 300. However, contrary to reports,[19] the neighbours did not join spontaneously. Women lecturers, with their experience from the teachers' movement, distributing a leaflet in the neighbourhood, talked to residents and persuaded them of the need to join the protest and shame the victim's in-laws. Such an incident and mobilization also underlay the origin of Karmika in south Delhi.

These demonstrations, held in front of the house of a murdered or harassed bride, were directed at social ostracism of the victims' in-laws. They also drew attention to police collusion and often ensured police registration and follow-up. Stories of confrontations between women activists and local residents indicated that a few concerned outsiders could not just enter a neighbourhood and demonstrate.[20] Women's organizations repeatedly had to tackle public apathy and even the outright hostility of local residents who had social ties with the harassers. Leafleting, canvassing their views, and involvement of other local organizations—trade unions, youth and residents associations—were steps taken by organizations such as the JMS. It emphasized that neighbourhood actions must be preceded by house-to-house campaigns and that the bride's natal family should join the demonstration and mobilize support from within their kin and social circle, including neighbours of the harassers. The first success in retrieving the dowry of a harassed victim was a result of JMS following such a strategy.

Demonstrators, in effect, were stating that domestic violence and the harassment of women were no longer private family matters. They helped to create an atmosphere wherein the victim's husband would be unable to remarry for another dowry. The demonstrations underlined the need for neighbourhood social responsibility and the necessity to intervene where injustice is seen. They played an important role in building up public opinion not only around the individual cases but against dowry and the harassment of wives in general. Other demonstrations were calculated to attract the attention of the broader public and, more specifically, of the government. In fact, legal action, corner meetings and mass demonstrations as consciousness-raising events and to build political pressure were among the movement's central and successful strategies.

The first major action undertaken by the DVCM was a mass demonstration on 3 August 1982. Organizers had appealed to all citizens of Delhi to march to Parliament to press for the tabling of the JSC Report. Street-corner meetings in lower and middle-class neighbourhoods, in markets, at factory gates, and in office areas and colleges were held. By now the cooperating organizations were over 25, including trade unions such as the AITUC and the CITU, student and youth organizations such as the AISF, AIYF, DYFI and the Students Federation of India (SFI), civil liberties platforms such as the PUCL, welfare organizations, consumer organizations, women's groups such as Karmika, Nari Raksha Samiti, Stree Bal, Solidarity with Women and the University Women's Association of India. Three to five thousand people, mostly women, joined the march. A national newspaper reported that 'the number of persons who had responded to the march convened by 5 women's organizations were overwhelming. Casual labourers, mill hands, housewives, students, professionals all braved the scorching afternoon sun and walked the 4 km stretch from Jantar Mantar to Boat Club carrying banners and demanding a better deal for women'.[21] Within a few days, the Delhi Administration promised to establish a special cell to investigate dowry cases, while the government tabled the JSC report in Parliament. One newspaper report had also indicated that the judiciary was granting bail in fewer cases of dowry deaths.[22]

Some six months later, trying to go beyond dowry and broaden the analysis of women's oppression the DVCM held a mass meeting on women's employment on International Women's Day. However, there was less unity among the women's organizations and groups than when dowry deaths alone were the target issue, the campaign was weaker and the action was not as well planned. Some groups insisted that rather than employment, the focus ought to be on the depiction of women in the media and this was added to the agenda. A popular street play, *Aurat*, was performed. On the same day a DVCM delegation met with the prime minister to urge her to introduce proposed amendments to the Dowry Act.

A notorious case of dowry murder became a rallying-point for the movement when in November 1983 the High Court overturned the conviction and death sentence to the husband, mother-in-law, and brother-in-law of Sudha Goel. Women's groups issued protest statements immediately and JMS and NFIW organized high-publicity demonstrations outside the courthouse. As a result three groups were cited for contempt of court. However, a joint appeal of the High Court judgement was eventually filed in the Supreme Court by the victim's brother, the Delhi Administration, nine women's organizations, lawyers' associations, and a family welfare organization. The accused husband and mother-in-law were ultimately found guilty.

Political pressure was kept up through continued street corner meetings, DVCM open meetings, campus agitations, and another delegation to the prime minister. A bill to amend the criminal and evidence codes was finally placed before Parliament in the summer of 1983.[23] Though these amendments fell far short of the comprehensive legislation hoped for, they have been widely used by women's organizations and groups and by individual women experiencing harassment. A sit-in was organized by DVCM on the last day of Parliament, but only the five convening organizations participated. The women blocked city traffic at a major intersection, knowing they were liable to be arrested, in order to symbolize their lack of faith in the present legal system. They were arrested and released after a few hours in custody. For the first time public expression of differences among organizations occurred at the sit-in, reported by the press. It centred on whether women MPs of the ruling party would be allowed to address the *dharna* when their government was not taking any action in Parliament. In fact, the session closed without the government moving any legislation on the Dowry Law amendments. In January 1984, mothers of some of the dowry murder victims went on hunger strike outside the prime minister's house. It drew no response and the mothers were persuaded to give up their strike before their health deteriorated drastically.

By early 1984, the willingness to espouse militant mass action was waning among some of the DVCM members. The MDS, YWCA and the AIWC favoured holding a press conference, but AIDWA and NFIW pressured for a sit-in. Prior to the sit-in, JMS members marched to the prime minister's house and members of NFIW courted arrest outside Parliament. This split over forms of action undermined the effectiveness of the DVCM, and the coalition was not sustained following passage of the dowry amendments. The bill amending dowry laws was introduced in Parliament on the last day of the April session in 1984 and passed in the following session during a walk-out by opposition members. The rules were not framed till October 1985, further delaying its implementation. Though it fell far short of the JSC's recommendations and the movement's demands, it represented a significant legal step in the struggle.[24] Subsequent national events[25] overshadowed the anti-dowry agitation and the major activity returned to its initial focus on legal counselling on individual cases.

The nature of anti-dowry mobilization, particularly in terms of the class composition of women participants, marked it as unlike the mainstream women's movement before and immediately after independence. The heterogeneous organizational strategies and perspectives on movement goals of the various women's groups reflected the differing economic and social bases of their membership. Public forms of protest such as marches, mass courting of arrest and sit-ins were disliked by the AIWC and the YWCA, whose middle and upper class members preferred delegations, hall meetings, seminars and workshops—activities thought to be 'more constructive and ladylike'. Demonstrations were deemed 'too political' and unnecessary, because in their understanding of the national movement and independence, women had gained constitutional equality without recourse to militant agitation. On the other hand, the NFIW and AIDWA, with their largely working class membership, advocated, mass public agitation and intensive canvassing. They viewed these actions as learning processes, means of promoting solidarity and a sense of collective struggle, and as having a higher public impact. Participation required overcoming physical and social barriers as well as psychological inhibitions to engaging in this form of public action. In India, and in Delhi particularly, it was unusual for large numbers of women to assert themselves in public, marching and shouting. When such action occurred, it drew much public comment. Participants felt a sense of exhilaration which increased their determination. This form of political action created new spaces for women.

PERSPECTIVES WITHIN THE ANTI-DOWRY MOVEMENT

The earlier discussions have indicated that there was no uniform under-standing within the movement. Diverse perspectives were reflected in the speeches given by representatives of various organizations at public meetings and in the emphases placed on different points in their writings and interviews. Controversies over whether the movement was political or apolitical, what its relationship to the government should be, whether women MPs from the ruling party should be allowed to address a sit-in, or whether only women lawyers should be hired for a case came up at various moments.

The last issues suggest questioning of notions of 'natural' sisterhood. They point to the need to examine the real and not-so-real divisions among women and the assertion of solidarity among women as a political construction. The nature of dowry murders themselves raised this issue. The structure of kinship and family in most communities in India, together with the economic and social dependence of women tends to place the daughter-in-law and mother-in-law in opposition.

The hierarchy within the household places the young bride in subservience not only to her husband, but under the direct supervision and control of her husband's mother. The mother-in-law and sister-in-law of the bride are directly involved in many of the murders or suicides which organizations deal with. It thus creates the appearance of women as the main oppressors of women, a point which those who wished to counter the women's movement were quick to suggest. At times campaigners came across as fighting for the rights of daughters-in-law, as their vitriolic attacks on mothers-in-law in their speeches suggest. Focusing on roles and individuals, rather than structures appeared to be easier in mass campaigns. Activists spoke of the need to find ways to cross the tension, rather than obscure or exacerbate it; the difficulties in explaining at the popular level the process whereby women are made the instruments of their own oppression, while also reflecting the real divisions among women.

Linked to this was a varied critique of the self-sacrificing, all-accommodating image of the wife-mother role. Some attacked the institution of the extended family, others that of marriage, while still others confined their attack to notions of female self-sacrifice. Again, a counter viewpoint was heard, which accused women's organizations of being anti-family and this had to be addressed. In their discussions, activist women argued that for the vast majority of Indian women, their families and their marriages were of primary importance—their one form of social and economic security. This has to be accounted for but without forgetting the violence they experienced within them. Some organizations talked of how marriage and the family must be put on a new 'democratic' basis in which women were given their rights as equal partners and only then could 'the family' survive.

An explicit aim of the DVCM and member organizations was to create the political will for determined action against dowry, as also to educate women regarding their rights. However, the AIWC argued that that the women's movement must concentrate on the ways in which, through its own efforts, it can change social consciousness and end dowry. The MDS, NFIW, and AIDWA placed the onus for ending dowry and dowry deaths on the government, given its responsibility for legislative reform and its control of the police, the administration, the mass media, and the education system. AIDWA and NFIW saw this as inherent in the nature of the present state, highlighting government policies which had led to curtailment in women's employment rather than their economic independence. MDS, on the other hand, spoke more of the lack of concern on the part of the government. Members of the YWCA agreed with them, but also with the AIWC, which said this was an attempt to 'politicize' the issue and that the women's movement should remain 'above politics'.

For the AIWC and the YWCA the meaning of politics was limited to party and electoral politics; perhaps a reflection of their links with the ruling party. Some leaders of the MDS, NFIW, and AIDWA belonged to opposition parties. The MDS and NFIW also called for the movement to remain 'above politics', meaning that it should not be linked to any one party. The AIDWA agreed with the last, but said that women's oppression and the women's movement were inherently political; politics was not only in elections, but related to the power structure and governance of society as such.

The different approaches were reflected in whether an organization expected that the anti-dowry movement would succeed in eliminating dowry, indeed what they hoped to achieve through the movement, and in their post-facto assessments of the DVCM. In their interviews, the AIWC members were the most negative as they looked back at the movement, expressing the view that nothing was achieved and remembering the tensions which arose because of differences within the movement. Organizations such as AIDWA were the most positive, arguing that while tangible achievements have been minimal and that the movement need to go much further, there has been a sea change in the political and social discourse on women and gender. The issues facing women are viewed in a different light as compared to a decade earlier. Many more women are ready to fight for their rights, to join the struggle in support of other women. This is a huge step forward.

THE IMPACT OF THE MOVEMENT

Dowry-related harassment and deaths of young women has not ended, leave aside the domestic violence that they experience. Contrarily, in the subsequent decade, the practice of dowry seemed to spread and grow spectacularly. Yet, there had been a widespread public response to the movement. The apparent contradiction is made understandable when one notes the essential ambivalence of this response, as was reflected in newspaper articles and letters to the editor. The deaths would be condemned by all, most in support of the women's organizations, but some would question whether they were murders. Others put forward the view that this was a result of daughters-in-law being unwilling to 'adjust', being bad housewives or just a case of women oppressing women. Some suggested the impossibility of change, while many raised the debate of legal reform versus a change in social attitudes, saying the former had to come first. The national print media put forward the opinion of the movement which insisted that this was not a case of either/or. Legal reform and the campaign for it could shape public opinion and vice versa. However, as noted earlier, much of the public support was directed against the deaths and did not question the dowry system or other issues related to women's oppression. This was true even at times of families who had suffered themselves.

Trade unions and student and youth organizations, as indicated earlier, also joined the agitations quite regularly. Some set up anti-dowry sub-committees. In most cases this was a result of common struggles with women's organizations. Caste, community and resident associations reacted to the issue of dowry deaths and some even tried to regulate the giving of dowry. Thus the Jat leaders of Rajasthan, UP, Haryana, and Delhi invoked the *sarvakhap panchayat* to establish rules for gift exchange and entertainment at engagements and marriages.[26] Opposition to dowry and to dowry harassment of women was in consonance with social reform agendas

While active public support to demands to end dowry was not intense, there was a widespread awareness that women were marching in the streets to demand rights. The conditions of women in Indian society became a matter of public discussion. Not just the movement, but the various processes which had enabled the movement were part of the new discourse. Plays, films, and magazines focused on women and on dowry. In buses, markets, and offices, stories, jokes and comments indicated this new awareness, whether in support of or in opposition to incompletely understood demands of the women's movement. As already outlined the impact of the movement was seen most dramatically in the law courts, both positively and negatively.

Women's organizations found their offices flooded by women who wanted to know their rights, who wanted advice, who were ready to talk of their most private problems and act to change their situation. An increasing number of women are refusing to accept harassment and refusing to be driven to suicide. The collective actions in response to the symbol of the burning bride created new social and political spaces for women and gave them public recognition as political beings, as participants in collective struggles.

NOTES

1. The Parliamentary Joint Select Committee on the Dowry Prohibition Bill (JSC) reported that incidents of 'wife burning', excluding 'suicides of new brides', had increased from 670 in 1975 to 1,676 in 1979 (all-India).
2. Hypergamy is the rule where women marry into groups higher in status

than their natal family. Due to lack of space, most of this section as well as references pertaining to kinship, marriage, and dowry have been omitted.

3. M.N. Srinivas, *Some Reflections on Dowry* (New Delhi: Oxford University Press, 1984).

4. Other than the open and secret agitations during the Emergency (see below), when their homes were being demolished in the name of beautification of the city, slum dwellers, particularly the women, battled the police and the bulldozers to stay where they were and save their homes.

5. See A. Basu, 'Gujarati Women's Responses to Gandhi, 1920–42', *Samya Shakti*, 1 (2), (1984), pp. 6–20; R. Chakravarty, *Communists in Indian Women's Movement* (New Delhi: People's Publishing House, 1980); K. Chattopadhyaya, *Indian Women's Battle for Freedom* (New Delhi: Abhinav Publishers ,1983); N. Desai, 'From Articulation to Accommodation: Women's Movement in India', in L. Dube, E. Leacock, and A. Ardener (eds), *Visibility and Power: Essays on Women in Society and Development* (New Delhi: Oxford University Press, 1986); G. Forbes, 'The Women's Movement in India: Traditional Symbols and New Roles', in M.S.A. Rao (ed.), *Social Movements in India Vol. II* (New Delhi: Manohar Books, 1979); 'From Purdah to Politics: The Social Feminism of the All-India Women's Organizations', in H. Papanek and G. Minault (eds), *Separate Worlds: Studies of Purdah in South Asia* (Delhi: Chanakya Publications,1982); 'In Pursuit of Justice: Women's Organizations and Legal Reform', *Samya Shakti*, 1 (2), (1984), pp. 33–55; K. Jayawardena, *Feminism and Nationalism in the Third World in the Nineteenth Century* (Hague: ISS, 1982); V. Mazumdar (ed.), *Symbols of Power: Studies on the Political Status of Women in India* (Bombay: Allied Publishers, 1979); G. Minault, (ed.), *The Extended Family: Women and their Political Participation in India and Pakistan* (Delhi: Chanakya Publications, 1981); B.R. Nanda (ed.), *Indian Women: From Purdah to Modernity* (New Delhi: Nehru Memorial Museum and Library, 1976); G. Omvedt, 'Caste, Class and Women's Liberation in India', *Bulletin of Concerned Asian Scholars,* 7 (1), (1975), pp. 43–8; U. Rao and M. Devi, 'Glimpses: UP Women's Responses to Gandhi', *Samya Shakti*, 1 (2), (1984), pp. 21–32; M. Velayudhan, 'Women Workers and Struggles in Alleppey, 1938–50', *Samya Shakti*, 1 (2), (1984), pp. 63–73.

6. Velayudhan, 'The Crisis and Women's Struggles in India (1970–77)', *Social Scientist*, 13 (6), (1985), pp. 57–68.

7. During the period of the Emergency, 1975–7, all civil rights were suspended and no public, let alone collective protests against government actions were allowed.

8. Committee on the Status of Women in India, *Towards Equality, Report of the Committee on the Status of Women in India* (New Delhi: Department of Social Welfare, Government of India, 1975).

9. Escalating demands for dowry were linked to the motivation to make 'under the table' money, which would supplement salaries and be untaxed. In the J.P. movement (1973–5) directed against the 'authoritarian and

corrupt Congress government', the connection between the fight against corruption and against dowry was explicitly made.

10. P. Caplan, *Class and Gender in India: Women and Their Organization in a South Indian City* (London: Tavistock Publishers, 1985).

11. M. Anjum, *Social Status and Social Work: A Sociological Study of Non-Professional Women Social Workers in Delhi* (unpublished PhD thesis, University of Delhi, 1985).

12. See Annual Reports of the AIWC, Report of the 21st Annual Convention of the YWCA India and other YWCA publications such as Action Now and PIB.

13. Anjum, *Social Status and Social Work*.

14. During the Emergency of 1975–7, slum dwellers were removed from the city centre to resettlement (housing) colonies. The class composition remains, by and large, working class, petty middle class, and the lumpen proletariat.

15. Saheli, *Saheli—The First Four Years* (New Delhi, 1985).

16. In late 1980, Karmika and Stree Sangharsh reported that together they had performed a street play, *Om Swaha*, in 22 different localities. The play, based on specific cases, challenged the existing cultural image of women. After a performance, people would relate their own experiences and in one area this resulted in a demonstration. The JMS held many performances of a play *Aurat* which depicted women's multiple oppressions and was scripted and enacted by the Jan Natya Manch.

17. In the Dowry Prohibition Act, 1961, dowry was a non-cognizable, non-compoundable, and bailable offence and punishment was imprisonment for a maximum of six months. The definition of dowry was vague, it being equated to property or valuable security given 'at or before or after the marriage as consideration for the marriage of the said parties', that is, this excluded marriage expenses and demands during the life of the marital relationship. The giver and taker of dowry were not distinguished in terms of offence.

18. Recommendations of the JSC included comprehensive legal reform, not only of the 1961 Dowry Act, but also on registration of marriages, inheritance rights for daughters, custody of children, legal aid, family courts, a common civil code, and the use of mass media and school textbooks for public education, as well as the establishment a national commission on women.

19. M. Kishwar and R. Vanita (eds), *In Search of Answers: Indian Women's Voices from Manushi* (London: Zed Books, 1984), p. 223.

20. Ibid., p. 225.

21. *The Times of India* (4 August 1982).

22. *The Statesman* (2 August 1982).

23. The amendments were introduced on the basis of the 91st Report of the Law Commission (1983) on Dowry Deaths and Law Reform. Recommendations in this report included that any death of a married

woman within five years of marriage, by burning, and behind closed doors may be presumed to be either homicide or abetted suicide; that demands for dowry be deemed to be matrimonial cruelty, punishable by imprisonment for a period up to three years.

24. In the Dowry Prohibition (Amendment) Bill, 1984, while dowry was made a cognizable offence, it remained bailable and non-compoundable. Provisions were made to record gifts to the bride, associate women's organizations with the registration of the cases and punishment was enhanced. Dowry received by any person other than the bride had to be transferred to her either on her turning 18 years of age or within three months of receipt or marriage. However, the definition remained vague, no ceiling was placed on presents given or expenses incurred and no distinction was made between givers and takers of dowry (AIDWA, *A Criticism on the Present Amendment Bill to Dowry Prohibition Act* (1984) (mimeo); *Letter to Prime Minister on the Dowry Prohibition Bill* (1984) (mimeo); Centre for Women's Development Studies, 'The Dowry (Prohibition) Act, 1961: The Struggle for an Amendment', *Samya Shakti*, 1 (2), (1984), pp. 131–4. A further amendment to the Act in 1986 provided for the appointment of area-wise Dowry Prohibition Officers with advisory boards of not more than five persons (at least two women) to assist them. The burden of proof of not having demanded or taken dowry was placed on the accused (K. Singh, 'The Dowry prohibition Act', *Equality*, Inaugural issue [1987]).

25. The developments in Punjab, the assassination of Indira Gandhi, the anti-Sikh pogrom, and then the General Elections.

26. *Hindustan Times* (19 June 1983).

The Self-Employed Women's Association

MARTHA ALTER CHEN

SEWA HISTORY AND PHILOSOPHY

SEWA Story Begins

In 1920, inspired by Mahatma Gandhi, Ansooya-ben Sarabhai (the daughter of a textile mill owner) started a union of textile workers called the Textile Labour Association in Ahmedabad City, western India. For the next 60 years, the textile industry—including the Textile Labour Association (the TLA) and its institutional counterpart, the Ahmedabad Mill Owners Association (the AMA)—dominated the economic and political landscape of Ahmedabad. In 1955, a young woman lawyer named Ela Bhatt joined the TLA. In 1968, after working for more than a decade on labour issues, she was asked to head the women's wing of the TLA. The mandate of the women's wing was to provide training and welfare services to the wives of textile mill workers.

But in 1971, a small group of migrant women cart pullers in the wholesale cloth market of Ahmedabad (India) approached the women's wing to ask whether the TLA might be able to help them find housing. Ela Bhatt accompanied the women to the wholesale cloth market where she met another group of women who were working as head loaders, carrying loads of cloth to and from the wholesale market. The head loaders described to Ela Bhatt their work, including their low and erratic wages. The head loaders were paid on a per-trip basis by the merchants—not according to the distance travelled or weight carried. Because no records were maintained of how many trips they made, they were often not paid the full amount they were owed.

Under the auspices of the women's wing of the TLA, Ela Bhatt decided to organize a public meeting for the head loaders in the cloth market to discuss their problems. During the meeting, she told the women that they should organize if they wished to address their problems: the women agreed to organize themselves into a group and each paid 25 paisa (quarter of a rupee) as a membership fee. Following the meeting, Ela Bhatt wrote an article for a local newspaper detailing the problems of the head loaders. The cloth merchants countered with their own news article in which they denied the allegations and claimed that they treated the head loaders fairly. The TLA Women's Wing responded by reprinting the merchant's claims of fair treatment on cards which they distributed to the head loaders to use to hold the merchants accountable: thus turning the merchant's rebuttal to the head loaders' advantage.[1]

Word of the head loaders' moral victory spread quickly. Soon, a group of used-clothing dealers approached the TLA Women's Wing with their complaints. Again, Ela Bhatt called a public meeting to which over 100 used-garment dealers and other women came. During that meeting, a woman from the crowd suggested they form an association of their own. Thus, on an appeal from the women and at the initiative of Ela Bhatt and the TLA Women's Wing, the Self-Employed Women's Association (SEWA) was born on 3 December 1971. The rest, as the saying goes, is SEWA's history.[2]

Although she was not able to negotiate housing for the cart pullers, Ela Bhatt arranged to have the TLA Women's Wing provide a hot meal to the cart-pullers at the end of each day near where they worked. Supa Goba-ji, the leader of the migrant cart pullers from Maharashtra who first approached Ela Bhatt, became one of the founding members of SEWA.[3]

Ela Bhatt, a labour lawyer by training, soon began organizing two other overlooked and largely female segments of the textile industry— home-based garment makers and quilt-makers (who made patchwork quilts from textile waste called *chindi*)-—as well as street vendors. By 1975, membership in the SEWA Union had grown to 2,750 women from 15 trade groups of which the largest was that of street vendors (400 members) followed by head loaders, garment makers, used-clothing dealers, and *bidi* rollers (300 members each). In 1975, SEWA also began organizing agricultural labourers in several villages in Ahmedabad District. But it was only in 1989 that SEWA began to significantly expand its rural operations in Gujarat. And it was only in the early 1980s that SEWA began to significantly expand its operations outside of Gujarat. By end-2006, there were about 500,000 SEWA members in Gujarat state and another 500,000 SEWA members in six other states of India: a total of one million members in India. In 2006, given its size and the scope of its operations, SEWA was officially recognized as a national trade union federation. As a recognized national trade union federation, it became a founding member of the new International Trade Union Confederation (ITUC) established in November 2006.

Gandhian Roots

As its overarching goal, SEWA is committed to the pursuit of what Mahatma Gandhi called India's Second Freedom: that is, economic freedom or freedom from poverty and hunger. After the First Freedom—political freedom—was attained in 1947, the founding fathers of modern India disregarded Gandhi's notion that economic freedom should be based on agriculture and small-scale cottage industry. But, 25 years later, Ela Bhatt adopted Gandhi's notion of economic self-reliance as a basis for SEWA's work.

In SEWA's interpretation of Gandhi, the two key components of economic freedom are Full Employment and Self-Reliance. Unlike mainstream economists who use the term 'full employment' to refer to the level of employment in a country as a whole, SEWA uses the term to refer to the level of employment at the household or individual level. Further, SEWA defines full employment as employment that assures security of income, food, and social security (defined, by them, to include health care, child care, and shelter). SEWA also uses the term 'self-reliance' in a holistic sense to refer to economic or financial self-sufficiency as well as to control and autonomy as workers. Moreover, SEWA believes that collective self-reliance is as, or more, important as individual self-reliance for its members. 'With collective strength the woman is able to combat the outside exploitative and corrupt forces like traders and moneylenders. Also her respect in the family and community follows soon'.[4]

In articulating its philosophy, SEWA evokes two overlapping sets of Gandhian principles. The first is a set of goals, namely: economic self-reliance as well as truth, non-violence, and unity or integration. The second is a set of guiding principles, namely: being truthful, being non-violent, being honest, retaining minimum possessions, controlling one's desires, using one's own labour, rejecting caste divisions, being free from fear, promoting local livelihoods (*swadeshi*), adopting a simple lifestyle (including diet), practicing equality of all faiths (*sarvadharam*).

These 11 Gandhian principles serve as SEWA's 'moral compass' which all SEWA organizers and members are encouraged to follow.[5]

SEWA draws its inspiration from sources other than Gandhi as well. SEWA shares a commitment to promoting democratic representative membership-based organizations of workers with the international labour movement; a commitment to women-centred development and women's empowerment with the international women's movement; and a commitment to building the financial and physical assets of the poor with the international micro-finance movement.

Practical Grounding

World-renowned for its practice, not only its philosophy, SEWA has translated its Gandhian vision and values into concrete operational goals and strategies. And it has done so through on-going consultations and deliberations with its women members. To promote its vision and values, SEWA pursues a dual but integrated strategy of what it calls Struggle and Development: that is, union-style collective bargaining and campaigns to raise awareness, air grievances, and demand change; and development interventions to promote alternative economic opportunities and build assets. To promote this joint strategy, SEWA engages in 'organization, capacity building, asset building, and empowerment'.

In terms of benchmarks, the key operational framework guiding SEWA's work is what it calls the Eleven Points. Developed and distilled by SEWA organizers and members over the years, these Eleven Points

---

Box 10.1: SEWA's Eleven Points

The Eleven Points—or standards—by which SEWA measures its progress can be grouped under the two of its overarching goals:

Full Employment requires that each woman has:
  employment which generates sufficient
  income for living with security and dignity. This, in turn, requires
  ownership of productive assets; sufficient
  nutrition, and the fulfilment of other basic needs such as
  health care,
  housing, and
  child care.

Self-Reliance of each woman is achieved through:
  organizing in groups, achieving
  leadership as a SEWA member,
  self-reliance as a group, and
  education.

are valued as ends in themselves as well as means to the overarching goals of Full Employment and Self-Reliance. As shown in Box 10.1, points 1–7 are linked to the goal of Full Employment while points 8–11 are linked to the goal of Self-Reliance through organized strength.

Two final notes on SEWA's philosophy are in order. First, SEWA's philosophy and practice are clearly centred on the working conditions of its members: all low-income working women from a myriad of trades and occupations. SEWA remains focused on issues that its members face as workers and related trends in markets, in government policies and procedures, in legislation and regulation. They do so through on-going inquiry and deliberation with their members and on-going policy dialogues with government officials and other stakeholders on work-related problems and issues.

Second, although guided by the principles outlined above, SEWA is quite pragmatic in its approach. It does not take strong ideological positions. It is not, for instance, against globalization, liberalization, or modernity per se. Rather, it seeks to minimize the negative impacts and maximize the positive opportunities associated with these forces for its members. Reflecting this pragmatism, SEWA is willing to work with government, international donors, and the World Bank: so long as they listen to its perspective and that of its members. Similarly, in working with various international movements—labour, women, and micro-finance—SEWA seeks to reform from within: influencing the labour movement to organize informal workers (not just formal workers), the women's movement to focus on women as workers and on market relations (not just on gender relations), and the micro-finance movement to focus on housing and consumption loans, savings, and insurance (not just investment loans).

SEWA INTERVENTIONS AND INSTITUTIONS

In pursuit of its twin goals, SEWA offers its members a range of organizing strategies and development services. First and foremost, as a trade union, SEWA offers all of its members some combination of the following, tailored to their main occupation or trade:

Organization: into trade groups or cooperatives or producer groups.
Local leadership development: opportunities and training to become local leaders.
Collective bargaining: trade-wise or issue-based.
Policy advocacy: trade-wise or issue-based.

Organizing is the central strategy of SEWA and takes several forms. In addition to organizing its members by trade into its Union, SEWA helps its members to form cooperatives and other local associations. All members of SEWA belong to a relevant trade group and are voting members of the SEWA union; many also belong to one or more membership-based organizations—cooperatives, producer groups, and (in rural areas) savings-and-credit groups. All members of these primary organizations are represented through elected leaders in the governance structure of the SEWA Union. Two types of these primary organizations—cooperatives and rural groups/associations—are also federated into separate state-wide organizations.

In addition, SEWA offers the following development services to all interested members on an on-going basis:

Financial services: savings, loans, and insurance.
Social services: health, child care, and education (adult literacy).
Infrastructure services: housing plus water, sanitation, electricity, and (in remote areas) transport.
Capacity-building services: training in technical skills, leadership, and other skills.

Also, for its members who are self-employed working either on their own or in groups—in handicraft production, agriculture production, animal husbandry, salt production, gum collection, or other productive activities—SEWA offers:

Enterprise development services: skills training and product development.
Marketing services: local, state, national, and export-marketing services.

While most of these services are offered on an on-going basis to as many members of SEWA as possible, some services are targeted to specific groups of SEWA members in specific areas of its operation through special (often time-bound) schemes. For instance, SEWA joined a public-private partnership scheme to provide slum infrastructure services to some of its urban members in designated project slums; and SEWA has collaborated with government schemes to provide water resources to its rural members in designated project sites and to organize rural producers into local producer groups under a specific government scheme.

Over the years, to provide these various services and make these various interventions, SEWA has built a sisterhood of institutions, as follows:

1. SEWA Union (Swashree Mahila SEWA Sangh): recruits and organizes SEWA's urban and rural membership and organizes campaigns around issues of concern to its membership.
2. SEWA Bank (Shri Mahila SEWA Sahakari Bank Ltd.): provides financial services, including loans and savings (including a long-term savings account for old age).
3. SEWA Cooperative Federation (Gujarat Mahila Cooperative Federation): organizes SEWA's membership into several types of cooperatives and provides support services to these cooperatives.
4. SEWA District Associations: provide services to SEWA-organized village groups and link members to other units within SEWA for other services.
5. SEWA Marketing (Gram Mahila Haat, Kutch Craft Association, and SEWA Trade Facilitation Centre): help cooperatives or associations of women producers to reach local, domestic, or international markets.
6. SEWA Social Security: provides health and child care services and oversees SEWA Vimo.
7. SEWA Vimo: provides insurance services.
8. SEWA Housing (Gujarat Mahila Housing SEWA Trust): provides housing services.
9. SEWA Academy: provides research, training, and communication services.

The first four—the Union, Bank, Cooperative Federation and District Associations—are membership-based organizations, governed by elected representatives of SEWA members. The others are service units. But, reflecting SEWA's commitment to building sustainable local institutions, some of the services provided by these units are delivered, managed, or owned by membership-based organizations: Gram Haat and the Trade Facilitation Centre are owned and managed by SEWA producers; cooperatives of SEWA members provide health and child care services; the insurance scheme developed by SEWA Security has been structured to become an insurance cooperative; and SEWA Academy provides communication services through a cooperative of SEWA members trained in video technology.

SEWA MEMBERSHIP

Any self-employed woman in India who is 15 years or older is eligible to become a member of SEWA. In SEWA's use of the term, 'self-employed' refers to all economically active persons who are not in formal salaried jobs.[6] Eligible women are recruited variously: by SEWA members (who encourage a relative, neighbour, or co-worker to join SEWA), by local SEWA leaders (who canvass for new members in their neighbourhoods or hold local meetings for interested members), by SEWA organizers (in the course of their routine work or through special recruitment drives) or simply by word-of-mouth. Most commonly, the recruitment channel is through a given trade group or occupation: with a SEWA member or leader speaking to other women in her particular trade.

Identity through Work

SEWA members are engaged in a wide variety of occupations or trades which SEWA classifies into four broad groups:

1. *Hawkers and vendors*, who sell a range of products including vegetables, fruit, and used clothing from baskets, push carts, or small shops.
2. *Home–based producers*, who stitch garments, make patch-work quilts, roll hand-made cigarettes (*bidis*) or incense sticks, prepare snack foods, recycle scrap metal, process agricultural products, produce pottery, or make craft items.
3. *Manual labourers and service providers*, who sell their labour (as cart pullers, head-loaders, construction workers, or agricultural labourers), or who sell services such as waste collecting, laundry services, or domestic services.
4. *Rural producers*, including small farmers, milk producers, animal rearers, tree nursery growers, salt farmers and gum collectors.

The members of SEWA are generally very poor. Available evidence suggests that half of SEWA's urban members live in households where income per capita is below the US dollar-a-day poverty line. More than one-third lives in households that are above that line, but where the per capita income is below two dollars a day. The rest (around 15 per cent or so) are only slightly better off.[7] The wider environment—economic, regulatory, and social—makes it difficult for SEWA members and their families to improve their living standard.

Drawn from different religious communities, castes and tribes—not only from different occupations—SEWA members face discrimination at work and in their daily lives by reason of their gender, caste, religion, and/or social class. SEWA seeks to build the identity and solidarity of its members (all women) as workers—as members of the working class and of particular trades or occupations—not as members of a particular sex, caste, religion, or social group. The primary channel through which SEWA members are recruited and the primary identity around which they are organized is their occupation or trade (a community of interest). But SEWA members are often first recruited by neighbours in their own locality (a community of place).

Agency through Organization

Organizing and capacity building provide the essential foundation—organized local groups and trained local leaders—for all that SEWA does. As its central on-going strategy, SEWA recruits new members, organizes them into local groups, and convenes regular local group meetings to identify needs as well as the strategies to address needs. In the process, local grass-roots leaders emerge: just as Kamla-Ben and Madhu-Ben emerged. Some leaders are trained and deployed as members of spear-head teams or as para-professionals to help carry out SEWA activities; while others are elected to serve as representatives of the general membership on the governing bodies of the Union Bank, Cooperative Federation, District Associations and other member-based organizations of SEWA.

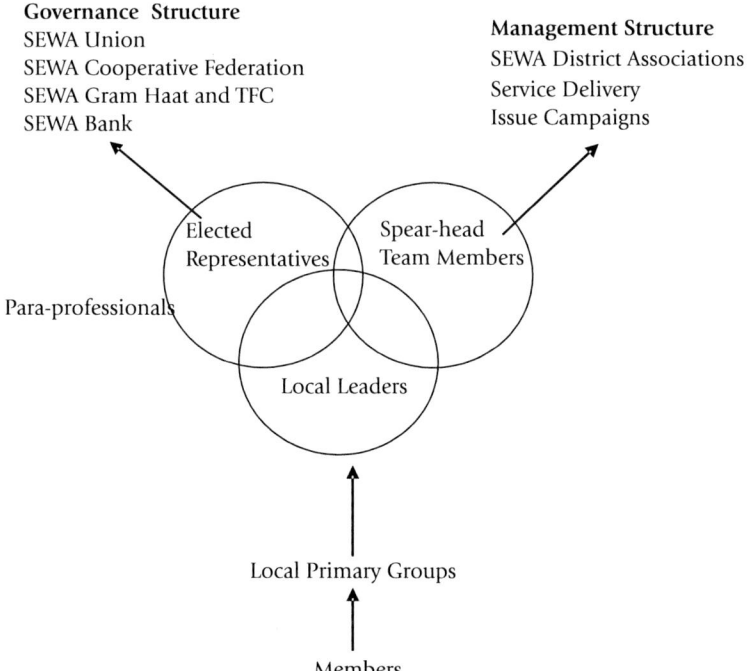

Governance Structure
SEWA Union
SEWA Cooperative Federation
SEWA Gram Haat and TFC
SEWA Bank

Management Structure
SEWA District Associations
Service Delivery
Issue Campaigns

Elected Representatives

Spear-head Team Members

Para-professionals

Local Leaders

Local Primary Groups

Members

Figure 10.1: Organizing Strategy of SEWA

SEWA's step-wise organizing process is summarized below and its organizational structure is illustrated in Figure 10.1.

Step 1: Recruiting and mobilizing members to build awareness and solidarity; to identify needs, constraints, opportunities; and to undertake activities.

Step 2: Organizing members into one or more local primary groups (trade group, cooperative, producer group, savings and credit group, village associations, campaign committee).

Step 3: Promoting and building the leadership that emerges out of the local organizations.

Step 4: Training and deploying leaders to help implement SEWA activities through decentralized management systems: as members of local spear-head teams (who implement projects or undertake campaigns) or as para-professionals (who provide technical services).

Step 5: Convening elections of representatives from among the leaders to serve on the executive committees of the SEWA Union, the SEWA Bank, the Gujarat Mahila Cooperative Federation, the District Associations, and other member-based organizations in the SEWA family.

While all of SEWA's members belong to the SEWA Union, many also belong to other membership-based organizations established by SEWA, including:

1. SEWA Bank (Shri Mahila SEWA Sahakari Bank Limited): all depositors are shareholders in the bank and elected shareholders serve on the governing board of the Bank.
2. SEWA Cooperatives: SEWA has organized over 100 cooperatives of various kinds, including service cooperatives (for example, child care providers and office cleaners), producer cooperatives, and marketing cooperatives.
3. SEWA Cooperative Federation (Gujarat Mahila SEWA Cooperative Federation): comprised of the various SEWA cooperatives.
4. Rural Membership-based Organizations of Various Kinds: trade groups, cooperatives, producer groups, savings-and-credit groups, and other local member-based associations.
5. SEWA District Associations: comprised of rural membership-based organizations that are not in the Union or Cooperative Federation, such as savings-and-credit groups and producer groups.[8]
6. SEWA Marketing Organizations (Gram Mahila Haat, Kutch Craft Association, and SEWA Trade Facilitation Centre): in which

individual SEWA members and SEWA-organized producer groups and cooperatives are shareholders.

Each of these member-based organizations has its own constitution, by-laws, and governance structure depending on whether it is registered as a cooperative or some other legal form. For example, SEWA Bank is registered as a primary cooperative. The Gujarat Mahila SEWA Cooperative Federation is a registered federation of primary cooperatives; while the district associations are registered federations of other types of primary membership-based groups, such as savings-and-credit groups. The Trade Facilitation Centre is a registered for-profit company with SEWA members as shareholders. In each of these member-based organizations, elected SEWA members serve on the executive committee or governing body.

Governance of SEWA Union

SEWA Union is the mother institution, so to speak, of the sisterhood of SEWA institutions. Established as a trade union in 1972, SEWA is registered under the Indian Trade Unions Act of 1926. Union members pay an annual membership fee of 5 rupees and are organized into various trade groups. An additional fee is levied on trade groups which have benefited from struggles supported by SEWA. The Union is governed by three tiers of elected representatives: Trade Committees, Trade Council and Executive Committee. Every three years, the members of each trade group elect representatives to trade committees (called *Dhandha Samities*); the various trade committees elect their representatives (called *Pratinidhis*) to a central trade council; and the trade council elects an executive committee of 25 members who, in turn, elect the office-bearers of the Union. The executive committee also includes five elected SEWA organizers as honorary members: one of whom serves as general secretary and two of whom serve as secretaries. Since 1981, the president of the SEWA Union has been elected from the trade group with the largest membership. At the last election in 2008, Ramilaben Jayantibhai Rohit, a tobacco farmer from Kheda District in Gujarat State, was elected president of the SEWA Union.

The trade committees meet once a month to discuss the problems faced by women in their respective trades and to plan strategies to deal with these problems. They serve as the 'nerve centre' of SEWA sending out signals as to what is happening locally and what the organization needs to do. The Union hires paid organizers for each trade group who serve as member-secretaries of their respective trade committees.

Management of SEWA

In addition to or instead of serving as elected representatives in the governance structure of SEWA, local leaders are also recruited and specially trained to help SEWA implement its various activities. Every activity or programme of SEWA is managed by a local spearhead team comprising of four local leaders and one SEWA organizer. Local leaders who have worked with SEWA for some time are trained to become spearhead team leaders. The goal is to have local leaders and members of SEWA assume the management and responsibility for all activities over time.

ADVOCACY OF SEWA

Informed by its members and through the organized strength of its membership, SEWA pushes for structural changes in the wider environment. Some of these structural changes relate to the informal economy as a whole, such as legal recognition of the informal economy; legal recognition of SEWA as a trade union; and representation of informal workers in mainstream institutions at the local, state, national and international institutions. Other structural changes relate to specific trade groups, such as increased wages or piece rates; worker benefits and social protection measures; licenses to buy and sell goods; access to new and improved markets. And some of these relate to specific issues of concern to SEWA members such as housing; infrastructure services (water, electricity, transport); land and other natural resources.

In shaping the wider policy environment, SEWA also seeks to change public understanding and appreciation of working poor women and their work and, thereby, to change the values, norms, and practices within society. This change may and should take place at different levels: husbands, families, and communities learn to value the contributions and understand the views of their wives, mothers, sisters, and neighbours; employers learn to value the contributions and understand the needs of their wage workers or their sub-contracted workers; and society learns to value the contributions and understand the needs of working poor women.

In SEWA's work, the wider environment is seen to include policies, institutions, and norms. Policy is interpreted quite broadly by SEWA to include: formal policies adopted by government or other institutions; guidelines and procedures for official schemes or programmes; laws and legal decisions; informal 'rules of the game' governing market transactions; and collective bargaining agreements. Institutions are seen to include rule-making institutions of various kinds, both formal and informal, in the economic, political and social arenas. And norms are seen to include public perceptions and social norms as well as the dominant neoliberal models of labour markets and the economy more generally.[9]

Of particular concern to SEWA is the fact that the working poor, especially women, do not have voice in most of the institutions that set the rules that affect their lives and work. This lack of voice—this exclusion from decision-making—has translated into lack of visibility in mainstream policies. Some of the relevant fora from which SEWA's members, other working poor women, have been excluded include: local councils; municipal, state, and national planning bodies; tripartite boards; minimum wage and other advisory boards; economic sector-specific business associations; local, state, and national labour federations. Thus, SEWA's strategy to impact policy includes gaining representation in key relevant institutions and, thereby, giving voice to the policy needs of its members and other working poor.

A GLOBAL MOVEMENT

From a Local to a National Union

During the 1970s and 1980s, SEWA's membership grew slowly but steadily from just under 4,000 in 1975 to nearly 20,000 members in 1988. Although SEWA began organizing rural women on a limited scale from Ahmedabad in the mid-1970s, it established a full-fledged field-based rural wing only in 1989. Since then, its membership has grown dramatically. During the 1990s, SEWA's urban membership grew nearly five-fold while its rural membership grew more than 14-fold. The dramatic increase in membership between 2000 and 2002 was due to a membership drive and to SEWA's relief and rehabilitation efforts in areas badly hit by the 2000 cyclone and 2001 earthquake: many of the new members came from affected households in those areas. By late 2006, SEWA's membership in Gujarat state had stabilized at just under 500,000.

In the early 1980s, SEWA began expanding the scope of its operations to other states in India. Established in 1982, SEWA Bharat (literally, SEWA India) is the registered federation of SEWA organizations nationwide. With support and guidance from SEWA Bharat, eight SEWA organizations in six other states have been established over the last 20 years. By late 2006, membership in these eight SEWA organizations had reached nearly 500,000.

Given the numerical size and geographical spread of its membership, representing women workers all over India, SEWA is now an officially recognized national trade union federation. In 2006, SEWA became a founding member of the new International Trade Union Confederation (ITUC).

From a Union to a Movement

Over the past two decades, an international movement has emerged in support of the working poor, especially women, in the informal economy. Much of the impetus and inspiration for this growing movement has come from SEWA

During the 1980s, SEWA began establishing linkages with membership-based organizations of home-based workers and street vendors and NGOs working with these groups of workers. In the mid-1990s, at two separate meetings in Europe, these organizations under SEWA's leadership came together to form two international alliances: one of organizations of home-based workers, the other of organizations of street vendors.

From its inception, the alliance of home-based worker organizations was centrally involved in the campaign to pass an International Labour Organization (ILO) convention on homework. To help with the campaign, in particular to highlight the extent and contribution of homework, SEWA and its allies requested a researcher (this author) to compile and analyse existing data on homeworkers worldwide. With the passage of the ILO Convention on Homework in 1996, SEWA and HomeNet recognized the power of statistics and of 'the joint action of activists and researchers'. This recognition led to the creation in 1997 of the global action-research-policy network called Women in Informal Employment: Globalizing and Organizing (WIEGO) which serves as a think-tank for the growing global movement of informal workers.

In 1995, SEWA organized a meeting at the Rockefeller Foundation Study and Conference Centre in Bellagio, Italy of representatives of street vendor organizations from a dozen cities around the world as well as activists and lawyers working with street vendor organizations. At that meeting, the participants drafted the Bellagio International Declaration of Street Vendors which calls for action at four other levels: by individual traders, by traders' associations, by city governments, and by international organizations including the United Nations, the ILO, and the World Bank. The participants also called for the establishment of an international network of street vendor organizations to be called StreetNet. In early 2000, a StreetNet office was set up in Durban, South Africa. In November 2002, after several regional meetings of street vendor organizations, StreetNet International was officially launched. The aim of StreetNet is to promote the exchange of information and ideas on critical issues facing street vendors, market vendors and hawkers (that is, mobile vendors) and on practical organizing and advocacy strategies.

Membership-based organizations (unions, co-operatives or associations) directly organizing street vendors, market vendors and/or hawkers among their members, are entitled to affiliate to StreetNet International. As of late 2008, StreetNet International had 30 members affiliated from 27 countries, including: local associations or trade unions, national federations or associations, and regional alliances.

Over the past decade, SEWA has also co-founded or inspired national and regional branches of homeworkers and their allies (called HomeNets) in South-East and South Asia; and national alliances of street vendors in India and Kenya. It also serves on an international coordinating committee that has organized three regional and two international conferences of organizations of informal workers; and as advisor to an international steering committee that is organizing the first international conference of organizations of waste collectors to be held in Columbia in early 2008.

Together, these organizations have helped foster a global movement of workers in the informal economy that now includes local trade unions and other membership-based organizations of informal workers, national and global trade union federations that have begun organizing informal workers, several national federations of workers' education associations, the International Federation of Workers' Education Associations (IFWEA); eight national and two regional HomeNets, StreetNet International, and the WIEGO network. Drawing inspiration and guidance from SEWA, this movement continues to identify and network organizations of informal workers and to inform and influence policy debates on the informal economy.

NOTES

1. J. Sebstad, *Struggle and Development among Self-Employed Women: A Report on the Self-Employed Women's Association, Ahmedabad* (Washington, DC: USAID, 1982).
2. The most recent history of SEWA, full of telling stories and profound insights, has been written by Ela Bhatt, *We are Poor, But So Many* (New York and London: Oxford University Press, 2006). Two earlier, also engaging, histories of SEWA were written by Jennefer Sebstad (1982) and Kalima Rose, *Where Women are Leaders: The SEWA Movement in India* (New Delhi: Vistaar Publications, 1992).

3. Three of the meeting halls in the SEWA Reception Centre are named after founding members of SEWA who have died, including Supa (the cart puller), Zora (a *chindi* quilt-maker), and Kapila (a vegetable vendor).

4. Ela Bhatt, *Cooperatives and Empowerment of Women* (Ahmedabad: SEWA, 1992).

5. SEWA, *Annual Report* (2002).

6. SEWA's membership includes women workers who are (a) fully independent self-employed; (b) semi-dependent self-employed; (c) disguised wage workers; and (d) casual wage workers who do not have a fixed employer. None of them are salaried workers and few of them are fully dependent wage workers: hence, SEWA's choice of the term 'self-employed'.

7. Martha Alter Chen and Don Snodgrass, *Managing Resources, Activities, and Risk in Urban India: An Impact Assessment of the SEWA Bank*, Assessing the Impact of Micro-Finance Services (AIMS) Project (Washington, DC: USAID, 2001).

8. In Banaskantha District, working in collaboration with a national government programme called Development for Women and Children in Rural Areas (DWCRA), SEWA has organized a large number of local producer groups—called DWCRA Groups—which are federated into the Banaskantha DWCRA Mahila SEWA Association.

9. For more details on how SEWA influences the wider environment, and for a summary of the influence it has had on the wider environment, see Martha Alter Chen, *Towards Economic Freedom: The Impact of SEWA* (Ahmedabad, India: SEWA, 2005).

The Transformation of the Indian Student Movement[*]

PHILIP G. ALTBACH

S tudents constitute a key element in the economic and political development in many of the new states of Asia, Africa and Latin America. In some nations they have toppled governments, in others they have played a significant role in nationalist struggles. In almost all of the developing nations, the student community constitutes a primary source of technologically trained manpower, and an important impetus to the process of modernization. The elites, who have a major responsibility in shaping the affairs of the emerging nations, are, to a large degree, recruited from the student community. In many nations, the student movement—that segment of the student community, which has organized itself for political or social action—has, made significant contributions to political development. In several of the new states, student movements have been involved in revolutionary political struggles, in educational and cultural reforms, and in a range of political and social concerns. Students have gained valuable training in political methods and ideology through the student movement. In many instances, the student political movements have been instrumental in shaping political and social attitudes of the emerging (and occasionally the incumbent) elites in the developing nations. These student organizations, often the largest Western-oriented groups

* Originally published as 'The Transformation of the Indian Student Movement', *Asian Survey*, 6 (8), 1966, pp. 448–60; published by University of California Press.

in the nation, have proved to be a spiritual and ideological 'home' for those individuals who seek to engender Western values and methods.

Student organizations have often provided an important adjunct to the formal education which emerging elites receive in schools and colleges. The extra-curricular role of the student movement, as well as the views of this movement on educational issues can provide a valuable source of information on educational policy and development in the new nations. It is a fact that much of the student 'discontent' so much discussed by educators and politicians has its roots in grievances directly related to education.

India offers a particularly interesting model for examining the role of the student movement. Its long tradition of Western education has built up a sizable Westernized class. It has seen indigenous organized political activity at least since the founding of the Indian National Congress in 1885. The long struggle for independence from the British, which went through a number of significant stages and ended in the non-violent mass movement led by Gandhi, also provided a training ground for political activists and forced the Westernized middle classes to build a broad-based movement. Almost two decades of independence has allowed indigenous political institutions to develop and problems of economic development, educational reform and political stabilization to reveal themselves.

The Indian student movement has been intimately concerned with most of these developments, and was deeply involved in and committed to the nationalist movement. It can be divided into two distinct phases, which mirror some of the important changes which have taken place in Indian society. Prior to independence in 1947, the students took an active part in the political life of the nation, and were organized into a number of powerful movements. Political groups were quite influential in the student community and provided strong support to the nationalist movement. Since independence, the student movement in India has all but collapsed. Most of the organizations, which exercised so strong an influence on the students have disappeared, and the spirit of nationalism and sacrifice has left the campus. Indian students exhibit something of an ambivalence about the society in which they must take their place, and there is a notable lack of enthusiasm for the vital tasks of nation-building.

THE STUDENT MOVEMENT AND THE INDEPENDENCE STRUGGLE

Prior to 1920, the small Indian student community had little experience with politics, and concerned itself primarily with its academic programme and with cultural affairs. But as the nationalist movement grew and was gradually transformed under Gandhi's leadership from a middle-class 'debating society' into a militant mass movement, the students took an increasingly active role in politics. The impact of nationalism was combined with Western intellectual influences—particularly the ideas of the British Fabian socialists and later the Russian Communists. During the 1920s, many student groups were formed which took an interest in politics. The nascent Indian Communist movement, as well as the Left-wing of the Congress, were active on the campuses, and discussion groups devoted to politics were popular. The Right-wing Rashtriya Swayamsevak Sangh (RSS), which emphasized Hindu nationalism and cultural regeneration was also born during this period and had a strong element of student support.

Gandhi's Non-Cooperation movement of 1920 was the first political struggle in which students were involved on a substantial scale. The call for students to quit their colleges and support Congress-sponsored 'national colleges' received substantial backing. Although the national colleges were short-lived, the traditional educational structure was temporarily thrown into confusion. Students helped with Congress campaigns and meetings, and when Congress leaders were arrested, students assumed the leadership of the movement.

INDIAN STUDENT MOVEMENT

The 1920 movement provided the students with valuable political experience and established the student movement as a part of campus life in India. The organizations formed in the course of the struggle continued to exist, and politically minded students involved themselves in 'constructive' social service projects and in study circles. Youth Leagues were formed in major educational centres with the help of Leftist Congress leaders, and the first annual All India Student Conference was held in 1920 to provide coordination to the growing student political movement. The dominant trend among the politically minded students was radical, and Gandhian traditionalism and non-violence had much less influence than socialist ideologies. The annual student conferences, which normally attracted more than 3,000 student delegates from all parts of India, provided Left-wing congressmen with a platform and with support for their views.[1]

While only a minority of the Indian student community was politically active during the 1920s, it was during this period that the movement established itself and gained both organizational experience and some degree of ideological sophistication. Student cultural associations also came into their own and became an important part of campus life. Organizations devoted to debating, drama, literature and other subjects blossomed at many colleges, often with the support of the college authorities. For the first time, students were involved in large numbers in the planning and administration of extra-curricular activities. While unrelated to politics, such activities gave students a sense of confidence as well as training in organizational matters.

The 1930s brought an intensification of the political struggle in India and along with it a growth in the student movement. Students participated in Gandhi's militant Civil Disobedience movement of 1930 on an unprecedented scale, and in many of the activities calculated to impair British administration in India. Colleges were closed, agitations launched, and illegal publications distributed. Hundreds of students were dismissed from their colleges or were sent to jail. While the struggle died down after almost a year, the student movement continued its activity, and the All India Students' Federation (AISF) was organized in 1936 to provide a unified voice for the student movement. From the beginning, the AISF was strongly nationalist and radical in its political views.[2] Communists, socialists, and Gandhians worked harmoniously within the AISF and provincial affiliates were organized in all parts of India. The annual AISF conferences, held at the same time as the sessions of the Indian National Congress, attracted upwards of 3,000 delegates and the top Congress leaders addressed the students.

In this period, the newly formed Congress Socialist Party had a strong influence on politically minded students, as did the small but articulate Communist Party. Study groups trained cadres in ideology as well as in organizational tactics. Many committed student leaders became active in the growing trade union movement or in the cultural organizations sponsored by the Leftist political groups.[3] In addition to the 'mainstream' nationalist student movement, a number of other important trends existed within the student movement. Many Muslim students, previously apathetic or pro-Congress, were influenced by Mohammad Ali Jinnah's call for a separate Muslim state in India and joined the Muslim League's All India Muslim Students' Federation (AIMSF). This organization did not participate in the independence movement, but instead pressed for Muslim rights and defended Muslims when they were attacked. Muslim student organizations also shaped the political ideologies of a whole generation of Muslim leaders, and were particularly important because of the relative backwardness of the Muslim community in India.

The Hindu Right-wing also gained strength. The RSS appealed to militant Hindu nationalism and to anti-Muslim and anti-Christian sentiments among the Hindus. By upholding traditional Hindu values, then under attack from Westernized elements in India, the RSS was able to attract many students, particularly in smaller colleges. Its para-military programme which emphasized physical training and discipline, appealed to many students. The Hindu Students' Federation was similar in ideology to the RSS, although its approach was somewhat more sophisticated. As a counter to the RSS, secular-minded Leftists organized the Rashtra Seva Dal (RSD), which also sponsored a paramilitary programme in addition to other cultural and social activities. The RSD was devoted to secular values and did much to overcome the communalism of both Hindu and Muslim extremists. Its strength was mainly in Maharashtra, while the RSS drew most of its support from the Hindi-speaking areas of north India.

By 1938, the Indian colleges were highly politicized. While the 'mainstream' Leftist student groups had a dominant position, they were by no means unchallenged. As the nationalist movement gained strength and militancy, students took a more active part in the struggle, and many voluntarily left the colleges to work in the labour movement or with Gandhian constructive programmes. The increasing ideological sophistication of the student movement also created problems, and the factional in-fighting, which has become characteristic of Indian politics, grew rapidly.

The split in the All India Students' Federation in 1940 was indicative of this trend. The differences between the Communists on one side and the socialists and Gandhians on the other came into the open in 1940. The Communist faction was able to impose its support for the Soviet Union and its strong criticism of the Congress on the AISF. The socialists led a walk-out, and two separate student organizations were formed as a result. The bitterness engendered and the energy wasted during these disputes weakened the student movement, sowing the seeds of further factional problems later. During the 1942 'Quit India' movement, students played a key role; the nationalist student movement (the Communists at this time were actively supporting the British war effort) succeeded in closing most of India's colleges for extended periods, and involved masses of students in the struggle. Students who had got previously been involved in politics worked for the Congress and participated in almost all daily demonstrations. Committed student cadres took part in sabotage campaigns and tried, with some success, to disrupt British administration. When the adult Congress leadership was arrested, the students took over much of the leadership of the struggle and acted as a liaison between underground leaders and the movement. Student groups published illegal newspapers, and even operated a clandestine radio station. The 1942 struggle was the apex of the student involvement in India, involving for the first time, a majority of the students. Thousands were jailed, and many thousands were dismissed from their colleges. The militancy of the 1942 movement was retained, if on a reduced scale, until the end of the independence struggle. The nationalist student movement had achieved substantial influence on the campus, and many of the best students participated in the struggle.

By 1946, however, the student movement had lost much of its impetus. While the Students' Congress (the nationalist wing of the movement and successor to the non-Communist wing of the AISF) remained a large and active organization, its emphasis returned to campus issues or the Gandhian constructive programme. Many radical student leaders were disillusioned by the compromises, which the Congress leadership found it necessary to make in order to achieve independence without further bloodshed. The 1946 Mutiny of the Indian Navy was a further shock to them, since the Congress ordered the militant sailors to surrender to the British in the interest of a compromise.[4] A large number of active student leaders participated in the movement, and this event marked the end of the politically significant phase of the student movement in India.

A number of important factors had contributed to the growth of a militant student movement in pre-1947 India. The student community itself was fairly small and homogeneous. Most students came from upper middle or upper class and caste backgrounds, and the educational emphasis was strongly on the liberal arts. Higher education usually insured a fairly high status job after graduation, and most students did not have to worry about financial problems while studying. The colleges themselves were relatively compact, and communication between colleges was not too difficult. From the beginning, many of the best students were involved in the student political movement, particularly in the Left-wing groups, and this helped to make the movement more 'respectable'.

In the 1930s and 1940s, India was a highly politicized nation, particularly in the cities and towns, where most of the colleges were located and from which the vast majority of the students were recruited. The heady revolutionary atmosphere had its effect on the students, and it was not difficult to create interest in the student movement. Western political ideologies had a powerful influence on the students and stimulated much thought and discussion. Thus, the immediacy of the nationalist struggle was combined with an ideological ferment, thereby creating a politically conscious student movement.

THE STUDENT MOVEMENT SINCE 1947

By 1947 the student movement had lost much of its momentum, and many of the key student organizations had all but collapsed. With a few isolated exceptions, the student movement was never able to regain its militancy and has been steadily weakened. The causes for this decline are complex; it is only possible to mention some of them briefly here.

Perhaps the most important factor was the end of the independence struggle. Prior to 1947, political issues were clear and dramatic—the British had to be driven from the subcontinent. Respected nationalist leaders, such as Nehru and Jayaprakash Narayan, encouraged students to take an active part in the political struggle. Following independence, the Congress leaders reversed themselves and urged students to stay out of politics.

Furthermore, students learned that compromise was a necessary ingredient of practical politics; the issues were no longer obvious. The spirit of self-sacrifice, which had marked the independence struggle almost, disappeared, and many political leaders and others were more concerned with their own careers than with ideology or national development. As the student movement lost its main *raison d'etre*, the attitude of government and educational authorities changed drastically. The powerful Congress and socialist student organizations were abandoned by the adult leaders and ignored by most of the students. The Communists retained their interest in the student movement, but embarked on a disastrous programme of violence against the government, thereby losing most of its support.[5] The student community and the educational system were also undergoing substantial changes during this period. Between 1950 and 1960, the number of arts and science colleges in India grew from 498 to 1,039, and the enrollment doubled, from 310,000 to 691,000 students.[6] Higher education became available to young people from rural or lower middle-class backgrounds, and unemployment of graduates, always a problem in India, assumed substantial proportions. The quality of instruction declined as the number of students increased. The homogeneity of the student community was shattered by this influx of students. Thus, the physical and sociological composition of the student community made the creation of a movement much more difficult. Higher education was no longer a preserve of the elite, but became a necessity for many middle-level government or private jobs.

As a result of these and other pressures, the student movement has substantially changed its role and function since 1947. The mass political organizations of the pre-independence period have either collapsed or have become debating societies of modest proportions. The most active student groups on the Indian campus today are the local organizations devoted to cultural or social concerns, most of which are sponsored by the college or university. The various elected college unions, again under official sponsorship and supervision, are often able to coordinate the various extra-curricular activities. The interest of the student community has shifted from the political realm to cultural and social activities.

Among the most popular organizations on the Indian campus are the various linguistic associations, organized as separate groups. A typical college in Bombay will have a Marathi Literary Society, a Hindi Mandal, a Gujarati Dramatic group, an English Literary Society, and others. While these groups probably tend to limit the social contacts of the students to members of their own linguistic community, they do provide an outlet for student energy and are valuable in an educational system conducted in a language, which is only imperfectly understood by many of the students. Religious and communal student groups also continue to exist, although they are less important than the linguistic associations. Christian, Sikh, Muslim, Parsi, and other minority religious communities have organized their own student groups, which have some following on the campus. Most of these groups have no political interests and are intended to provide a social centre for the students involved. Debating clubs, film societies, and discussion groups are popular at most colleges, and an attempt has been made to provide an adequate athletic programme for the students.

A number of the all-India student organizations still exist, and retain some degree of influence. The largest of the pre-independence student movements, the Students' Congress was disbanded in 1948. Congress leaders expressed interest in the formation of a non-political student organization, and the socialists agreed to unite with them in the formation of the National Union of Students (NUS). Founded at a large congress in Bombay at which Nehru and the socialist leader Jayaprakash Narayan spoke, the NUS proved unable to rid itself of the heritage of external political manipulation and soon floundered.

The National Union of Students remained fairly active for several years after its formation, but eventually, political infighting together with a negative attitude by most educators destroyed the organization. An attempt was made to make the organization representative, but when less than half of the universities in India joined, financial problems made NUS operations precarious. After an initial burst of enthusiasm, the NUS found itself virtually leaderless and forced to rely on students more interested in their own personal advancement than in building a student movement. Factional disputes caused a split, and by 1958 the NUS was, for all practical purposes, dead.

Another group, the National Council of University Students of India (NCUSI), was formed subsequently to fill the vacuum created by the disappearance of the NUS. But this new group has faced many of the same problems as its predecessor—opposition from educators and political leaders, student apathy, and careerism among its own leaders. The Cold War brought the problem of foreign subsidies, for both the East and the West were interested in gaining as much influence among the Indian students as possible, for which they were willing to support student organizations. The Russians traditionally supported the Communist-sponsored All India Students' Federation, while the NCUSI reportedly received funds from Western sources, further removing it from the campus. It seems quite unlikely that the NCUSI will be able to build a representative student association in India even though it has generally stayed out of partisan Indian politics. By the 1960s, the organization had branches in less than one-third of the universities, with a few ongoing programmes to prove its usefulness to the student community.

The political parties in India have had a rather ambivalent attitude toward the students in recent years. The Congress Party, for instance, has sponsored its own youth affiliate; moreover, it has vacillated between encouraging student participation in politics and warning against such participation. The Youth Congress was formed in 1949. Despite its claims to be the largest youth organization in India, it has not succeeded in making any impact on the campus and has served mainly as a 'front group' for aspiring Congress politicians. Its few social service projects have attracted some interest; yet, the Youth Congress had almost no active chapters in India because of internal political conflicts. The organization took part in Congress election campaigns and saw a short burst of activity during the Chinese invasion of 1962, when it was responsible for obtaining support for the government from the youth and students. The oldest student organization in India still in existence is the AISF, founded in 1936. Under Communist control since 1940, the AISF claims to be the largest representative student group in India. In fact, however, it is almost non-existent outside of the major centres of Communist strength in India—Bengal and Kerala.[7] Furthermore, the recent split in the Indian Communist Party has aligned many sections of the AISF with the 'Left' Communists, thereby arousing the opposition of the 'Right' faction. The AISF does continue to have major influence in the colleges of Calcutta, although much of its activity has been more in the cultural and social area than directly concerned with politics. The

AISF has also failed to attract the kind of dedicated and able leadership that it did in the past years, and the organization faces both political and organizational crises. It is doubtful if it has more than 1,000 active members in India by the 1960s (compared to more than 50,000 two decades ago) and probably boasts less than 25 affiliates, out of a total of more than 1,000 colleges.

The Samajwadi Yuvak Sabha (Socialist Student Organization) was founded in 1953 by the Socialist Party when the NUS experiment failed. The SYS has been adversely affected by the various splits within the Indian socialist movement in the past decade. Never intended as a militant movement, the SYS has acted as an educational arm of the socialist groups in some areas, although it has only a small number of affiliates limited mostly to northern India. The strength of the SYS has declined along with the viability of the socialist parties; it can probably boast of less than 500 active members. Its discussion groups have provided some of the few forums for serious political debate among students, but even these have been too limited to make any real impact on the campus.

One of the most important of the student organizations in India today is the Akhil Bharatiya Vidyarthi Parishad (All India Students' Organization). This group, usually called the Vidyarthi Parishad, has maintained that it is non-political, but there is strong evidence to suggest that it is the youth wing of the Rightist Hindu communalist parties. The Vidyarthi Parishad concentrates on a culturally oriented programme and scrupulously avoids broader political issues. The association claims that teachers, students, and administrators should cooperate and not oppose one another. Professors serve with students on various governing bodies of the Parishad.

The Vidyarthi Parishad was founded in 1955 by students and teachers who had been involved in the militant Right-wing RSS. The organization, under a competent and dedicated leadership, has grown steadily and now has strong roots in the Hindi-speaking areas of northern India. With a sprinkling of members in other parts of India, the Vidyarthi Parishad comes close to being an all-India organization. The organization has strongly stressed patriotism, but has also engaged in a good deal of social service work such as textbook libraries for needy students and a limited scholarship programme. Its programme, which has emphasized cooperation with college administrators, has succeeded in gaining the sympathy of many principals. The political composition and emphasis of the Parishad is, however, quite clear. A large proportion of its members were formerly in the RSS, including a majority of the National Council. The communalist views of many of its members are evident, even though the Parishad has refrained from making inflammatory statements.

The reasons for the limited success achieved by the Vidyarthi Parishad are simple. Competent leaders have provided an active programme which has relevance for the student community. Social service and cultural activity has been combined with occasional demonstrations for student rights. Although the Vidyarthi Parishad claims 50,000 members, it is unlikely it has more than five thousand active supporters and it is certainly true that the association lacks broad campus support. That it is probably the most active student organization in India is more than an indication of the general weakness of the student movement than of the strength of the Vidyarthi Parishad.[8]

These are the main national student organizations. There are other groups, such as national associations of religious groups like the National Council of Catholic College Students, but these generally make little impact on the student community. The government has made several attempts to foster constructive work among students. The Bharat Sevak Samaj (Indian Social Service Association), a semi-official group, has sponsored social service projects in various parts of India and has succeeded in involving students in its work. The scope of this work has, however, been limited and student potential for service has not been adequately tapped. The Congress Party as well as local colleges have also sponsored service projects and students have enthusiastically responded when asked to participate in village uplift work and other projects.

STUDENT INDISCIPLINE—THE BOGEY OF INDIAN HIGHER EDUCATION

While the problem of student 'indiscipline' in India has received much attention in recent years, educators and other officials have probably exaggerated its seriousness. 'Indiscipline' has been variously defined; the term is often used to describe any student action, which does not meet with the approval of the government or of educational officials. Actions ranging from violent demonstrations protesting an examination or a fee increase to peaceful meetings or petitioning have been labelled 'indiscipline'. If one takes into account the poor conditions of a large proportion of the student community, the attitude of many administrators toward student grievances, and the falling standards in much of Indian higher education, it is surprising that there has not been more indiscipline. For, in fact, student indiscipline has been limited to a relatively small number of educational institutions and is not characteristic of the student community.

Among the most famous examples of student indiscipline are Banaras Hindu University and Aligarh Muslim University, two of India's most venerable institutions. At both of these schools, faculty politics had succeeded in lowering the standards of the institution and the morale of both teachers and students. The Banaras incidents, which caused the university to be closed temporarily, were investigated by a government commission, which found evidence of mismanagement and favouritism.

Other examples of indiscipline which give some indication of its scope and impact were the linguistic rioting in Madras state in 1965, in which students took a leading role in agitating against the imposition of Hindi as a national language, and the 1964 student demonstrations in Orissa which led to the resignation of the chief minister on charges of corruption. Calcutta has traditionally been politically volatile and is one of the few places in India where the student political movement has continued almost unabated. Student protests against stiff examinations, bad instructors, or other real or imagined injustices related to university administration have been widespread. Students in Bombay have demonstrated recently against a college principal against increases in university fees, and against poor living conditions.

Thus, student indiscipline is more often than not directed against a specific administrative policy rather than at broader educational issues or matters of political importance, although politics has provided an important undercurrent to post-independence student agitation. Another characteristic of student indiscipline is its generally spontaneous nature, for most student agitations are not planned by politically motivated student agitators or by non-students, but are the result of spontaneous student action. Lack of organization is a hallmark, and there have been many instances when self-appointed student leaders have prepared lists of demands only after the agitation had been launched. While political parties have tried to exploit student demonstrations, and sometimes with success, they have rarely initiated them.

The causes for student unrest in India are not difficult to perceive. The educational system is characterized by poor standards of instruction, especially in the liberal arts (where most of the indiscipline seems to originate), by inadequate facilities such as libraries and laboratories, by an outmoded curriculum, and by poorly trained teachers. Students have few outlets for their energy, and demonstrations are perhaps such an outlet. Many students begin their collegiate careers at the age of 15 or 16 and lack the maturity that a few extra years would give. Furthermore, students living in hostels and away from their families for the first time are probably affected by their freedom, particularly in view of India's strict family system. The generational problem, present in almost every society, lies somewhat below the surface in India, although it probably influences the students. Finally, the economic uncertainty of many Indian students is clearly a cause for ambivalence and indiscipline. Many students must hold part-time jobs, and a survey of students in Calcutta pointed out that a substantial number were undernourished. It is difficult for graduates, especially in the liberal arts, to obtain suitable employment, adding a further factor of uncertainty to the plans of many students. The amount of 'wastage' (the number of students who do not finish their college educations) in India is quite high, and many of these former students remain at the universities.[9]

Despite these factors and the everyday frustrations to which the student in India is subjected, the amount of indiscipline is surprisingly small. Most of India's 1,500 colleges have never witnessed any agitation. And while many institutions have been subjected to an occasional isolated demonstration, such actions are the exception rather than the rule. The centres of student unrest in India which have received so much attention in recent years—Aligarh, Lucknow, Calcutta, Banaras—offering interesting case studies, but are by no means typical of educational institutions in India.

THE FUTURE OF THE STUDENT COMMUNITY

The age of the student movement in India seems to have ended, and ideological politics play a very small part among the students. Almost all of the national student organizations are bureaucratic structures rather than functioning movements. No one, the government, politicians and educators included, have been able to arouse the students. In essence, the Indian student community is without direction and without ideology. Life remains difficult on the subcontinent, and students are much involved in the day-to-day struggle for existence and future employment.

But political or educational interest among students is not dead. On the contrary, strong movements can be launched when the students feel involved with a particular issue. The Orissa agitations and the Madras riots are indications of this fact. Fee increases or arbitrary administrative action can mobilize the students into a well-organized campaign. But these are ad hoc and essentially directionless movements—aimed at a specific goal. When the aim has been achieved (or soundly defeated) the students retreat into their apathy and no ongoing movement is created. It is almost certain that students will continue to play a sporadic although occasionally significant political role in India. The creation of a movement similar to that, which characterized the student community during the independence struggle, is very unlikely.

It is impossible to predict when or where student unrest will occur in India. Students in Madras, for example, have a tradition of serious scholarship and a notable lack of unrest, yet they participated in one of the most volatile student agitations in post-independence India. There are, however, some parts of India which have retained a tradition of student activism, notably Calcutta, Delhi, and some of the northern cities in which indiscipline is more likely to occur. It is also possible to state with some degree of accuracy, that student unrest is more likely to occur in the arts colleges, and hardly ever constitutes a problem in the technological institutions. Missionary-administered colleges have had less trouble than other institutions, perhaps because there is often a more satisfactory teacher-student relationship at these institutions. Some pattern does exist—traditions of student activism, poor educational opportunities, or a particularly important political event *can* trigger a student movement. What is lacking is any ideological or organizational base in the Indian student community.

The Indian experience may have some relevance to other developing nations. India has been independent for almost two decades, and has had a chance to develop stable institutions and patterns during that time. In India, the small 'modern' segment of the society moved from a high awareness of politics and participation in an all-encompassing mass movement to the more mundane and difficult tasks of building a modern nation.

The tension and commitment of the independence struggle has not been maintained. The idealism of the independence period has also been muted by the responsibilities of family and the awareness of caste and linguistic particularism. Corruption in government and private enterprise has become widespread. The students have been affected by these changes. They have high expectations of the society, and when utopia seems very far off, they often give up the fight. Furthermore, the educational system itself has changed. While during the pre-1947 period, college students constituted something of a presumptive elite, this is no longer true.

The future of the student community in India is uncertain. It is likely that the current trend towards apoliticization and a lack of social concern; could continue along with increasing problems for both the educational system and the individual student. The harnessing of the student community remains a challenge to the government and the educational authorities.

NOTES

1. M. Muni Reddy, *The Student Movement in India* (Lucknow: K.S.R. Acharaya, 1947), p. 30.
2. Myron Weiner, *The Politics of Scarcity* (Chicago: University of Chicago Press, 1962), p. 163.
3. Interview with Raja Kulkarni, Secretary, Indian National Trade Union Congress (Bombay, 13 March 1965).
4. Philip G. Altbach, 'The Bombay Naval Mutiny', *Opinion*, 6 (17), 31 August (1965), p. 35.
5. Gene Overstreet and Marshall Windmiller, *Communism in India* (Bombay: Perennial Press, 1960), p. 398.
6. 'Progress of Education in India', *Economic and Political Weekly*, 17 (32), 7 August (1965), p. 1249.
7. Sagar Ahluwalia, 'Student Movement in India: A Historical Background' (unpublished paper, 1963), p. 23.
8. 'The More Important Youth Festival in Nagpur', *Organiser* (7 December 1964), p. 6.
9. A.R. Kamat and A.G. Deshmukh, *Wastage in College Education* (Bombay: Asia Publishing House, 1963), p. 12.

CHAPTER
12

Student Power
Mobilization and Protest*

T.K. Oommen

THE INDIAN SCENARIO

One way of assessing student power in society is to locate the significance of students in the formal as well as informal political processes and for this their numbers may be relevant. Broadly speaking, most university students in India belong to the 16–23 years age group. And 21 being the age (now it is 18) at which one attains political adulthood in India by becoming a voter, the number of voters in the student category is not significant enough to influence the electoral process.[1] Further, it is extremely unlikely, that one can be significantly associated with the decision-making process in the country at this stage in one's life. In other words, the possibility of students getting involved and therefore influencing the formal process and structures of society is extremely limited. Viewed from the angle of numerical strength, which is of crucial relevance in the democratic political set-up, students do not occupy any significant position in society. However, one may view the significance of number from another angle. Universities are huge student aggregations which can be easily mobilized through a nominal amount of communication and this renders them a power to be reckoned with in many contexts.[2] The visibility of any group is considerably enhanced and their

* Originally published as 'Student Power in India: A Political Analysis', *Political Science Review*, 14 (1 and 2), 1975, pp. 10–38.

bargaining power great when they can be collected in large numbers with relative ease.

One may, however, argue that what matters is not the number involved but the attributes of the category concerned. Students, particularly in a country like India, are a privileged group in so far as only a small section of the population can take to higher education. Further, most university students are drawn from the elite stratum of society and therefore the linkages and networks in which they are involved give them access to power. While this argument sounds persuasive, a closer analysis would show that in reality the situation is different in that students who are endowed with the network resource are infinitesimally small. Yet another way of assessing student power is the potency of the causes they champion to influence societal processes. But most of the issues for which students agitate are closely linked to their immediate needs and environment. In cases where Indian students have agitated over extra-educational issues, they have rarely been ones to initiate them.[3] In contrast the French students did revolt for the dissociation of knowledge and power.[4]

I do not know of any significant movement initiated and led by students in India for the eradication of untouchability, illiteracy, unemployment, corruption or distributive justice, save the student upsurges in Gujarat and Bihar.[5] But in both cases, the students were dependent on leaders drawn from political parties or the Sarvodaya movement. It is legitimate and natural for students to be involved in the problems of their immediate environment, however trivial they might appear from the angle of elders. But to argue that such involvement would render students a modernizing and change-generating elite is fallacious. In fact, the Indian student movement has always been a tributary movement and only an accelerating force to the movements initiated by elders. However, this is not to argue that a tributary movement does not influence the course of societal processes but to suggest that students are not the prime movers of change.

Another mode of viewing student power is to recognize it as a countervailing power in society. Most student activism in effect leads to a temporary suspension of the ongoing processes in society; the students may not always usher in changes in the direction they desire but can stop undesirable changes. In this sense, students have a veto power; their power is coercive in character. However, it cannot be denied that preventing changes in a certain direction may itself be positive. Similarly, it would be wrong to argue that student power is always coercive in nature; in fact it often combines the productive and coercive aspects. Viewed thus, it will not be difficult to appreciate the nature and role of student power. In my view a perspective which recognizes the two facets of student power—the coercive and the productive—is the most fruitful approach to the analysis of student power. In order to situate our analysis in its proper context we need to take into account two factors: the milieu in which student power originated and operated in India and the structural determinants which influence its functioning today.

The history of student activism in India can be traced to the early twentieth century,[6] and since then it has had a continuous history.[7] In the pre-independence era, when the colonial ruler was the natural enemy, when those in authority were status quo oriented and those in opposition were heroic, moral and agents of change, to be in the mainstream of opposition did not pose any serious dilemma. Mobilization of the student population was easier in the pre-independence period, as freedom was the common cause, the target was clear and compelling, political variations were limited and the homogeneity of the then student-youth population, drawn as it was from a similar background, was great. Further, although most parents did not encourage or openly approve of their sons and daughters getting involved in the freedom movement, they felt that the cause was legitimate. The fact that Mohandas Karamchand Gandhi called for the open and total immersion of students in the freedom movement rendered the student freedom fighter at once a charismatic object and an altruistic being imbued with a heroic mission.

After independence the task at hand—nation-building—is pursued by different political parties and ideological groups keeping different blueprints ahead. To be involved in nation-building activity, keeping in view the values embedded in the Indian constitution, would mean, to a large extent, to be with the establishment. Parenthetically, to be in the opposition would raise questions of legitimacy. To complicate this, political parties follow an ambivalent attitude with regard to the students' involvement in politics. While they announce from rooftops that one should not exploit students for narrow political ends, all of them privately practice the policy of 'catch them young' thereby concentrating their attention on universities.

It is not surprising then that the 'heroic' and 'patriotic' young student freedom fighter is replaced by a group of 'indisciplined', 'insubordinate', 'belligerent' and 'deviant' students, according to the party or parties in power. As is well known, almost all political parties have their youth/student wings and the student knows (whatever may be the epithets used to describe him in public) that he gets encouragement, help and admiration privately from the political bosses of the party to which he is attached. What is expressed publicly is an impersonal description of somebody who is distantly placed, what happens privately is a warm, intimate and affectionate appreciation of real persons. No wonder, the young student prefers 'private rewards' rather than 'public reprimands'.

The point I am making is this: Student power has not undergone basic transformation from the legitimate and productive force of the pre-independence era to an illegitimate and coercive force in Independent India; what has changed is not the nature of student power, but its characterization and evaluation by political parties in power against whom students operate as a countervailing force. Needless to say, the exact manner in which student power operates today is substantially different from what it was earlier. When the student body was involved in the freedom movement, it was a 'national' cause, and, hence, praiseworthy. Today, students are occasionally goaded into action to grapple with 'here and now' problems—be it the location of a nuclear plant in a specific state, the 'imposition' of a particular language, the underdevelopment of a particular region, the spiralling of prices of essential commodities, the construction of a huge dam. Involvement in such issues will not be universally acclaimed; they are 'legitimate' or otherwise depending upon the perspectives of particular ideological groups, political parties, or deprived categories. Thus, others may label what one group defines as regional 'chauvinism' as 'discrimination' or 'domination'. Such clash of values will also be found in student involvement in international issues. In a political democracy with a multi-party system a wide spectrum extending from the radical Left to the radical Right exists. It is inevitable, then, that student perspectives on several issues will vary tremendously and this, in turn, will be reflected in student politics and their understanding of the role of student power.

The exercise of student power in India is constrained by several structural factors. Student politicians are rarely, if ever, autonomous. They depend on political parties or other outside agencies for ideas, finance and organizational support.[8] It is but natural that this investment by outsiders is based on expectations of political pay-offs. Often this takes the form of the student politician becoming their agent or propagandist on the campus. Naturally, he has to abide by the instructions of his patron; the relationship between political parties and student political organizations is a hierarchical one and the latter is usually at the receiving end. What happens in the party will immediately be reflected in student political wings and even student cultural associations.[9] The splits in the Congress, Socialist, and Communist parties were immediately followed by splits in the corresponding student political organizations. This amply illustrates the pattern of dependence in the relationship between the two. Further, student leaders often aspire for a political career and therefore they cannot afford to displease their political mentors.[10] In order to get a ticket to contest from an assembly or parliamentary constituency or in order to secure a position in the party hierarchy it is necessary that they should keep the local party bosses in good humour.

However, the reverse side of the picture cannot be completely ignored. Through the radicalization of its youth wing a party may try to change its image or at least outwit other parties in verbal radicalism. The radicalization of the Chhatra Parishad in West Bengal and the Kerala Students Union, partly to curb the influence of the Marxist-led Student Federation of India and partly to impart a radical orientation to the Congress is an interesting case in point. Further, radicalization of student/youth wings may serve the functions of an internal opposition within a party and may be systematically and successfully used by the radical section of the party leadership either to legitimize its policies or to accelerate the implementation of its programmes. In both these events student politicians assume great significance and they come to be pampered and protected in all possible ways; even their indulgence in socially undesirable activities is condoned. Indeed, students have power and they may dictate terms to their political elders in such situations.

The confrontation of students takes place at various levels and with several groups. Student power may be pressed into service by them or by their patrons for dealing with problems in society at large, or within the student government itself. In each of these cases the confrontation is with specific groups and presently we will identify the groups outside the campus.

Students frequently speak of their opposition to the 'establishment' or 'authorities'. On close questioning, it will be clear that they tend to confuse the two categories of persons/officials. Occasionally, by authorities they mean the government (specially, ministry of education or the chancellor), those who manage public facilities (that is, the transport system) or the formal agencies of social control (for example, the police). Often student confrontations with such authorities take place, particularly the latter two, when the issues involved are not concerned with education or matters regarding the campus, or due to an excessive deterioration in the relations between students and those who manage university affairs, leading to an occasion for outside intervention.

In a democratic political system with a multiplicity of political parties, student power can but be an accelerating force of change in society. This is particularly true in India where all student organizations with political orientations operate as adjuncts to political parties. Student power can be a major source of structural change only if it operates as a united force. It is widely known that only a small minority among the student populace is politically articulate and it is sharply divided in its ideological and political loyalties. Students express their unity only through intermittent collective actions tinged in violence. But when the crisis event is over, their strength is diluted. And in the very nature of things conflict and violence are discontinuous in their occurrence.

In a system where students are not organized into a movement rooted in their own consciousness there cannot be any student power which is constructive in character. What we have in India is intermittent student rebellions against specific personalities, institutions or issues. The coercive power the students exercise through the temporary alliances and alignments of the politically articulate among them is realized by the momentary mobilization of the vast apathetic majority into action. But once the immediate 'enemy' concedes or persists the rebellion becomes meaningless. The system continues with all its defects; only the career of a few activists and the fortunes of a few officials and organizations is affected.

THE SOCIO-POLITICAL MILIEU

Broadly speaking, the population of a university belongs to three distinct occupational categories: the administrative staff, the teachers and the students. In turn, each of these categories can be divided into two broad sections, that is, the elites and the masses, from the perspective of distribution of formal power. Thus, only the top few in the administration actually exercise authority in any significant manner, the majority—the *karamcharis*—being a powerless lot unless they unionize. Similarly, among the teachers it is 'by and large', the dons and deans who exercise power, the part-time or junior lecturers are relegated to the other end of the continuum with no opportunity for participation in the decisional processes of the university. Finally, it is a handful of student leaders, particularly student union leaders, office-bearers of student wings of political parties and student voluntary associations who exercise student power. In our attempt to comprehend the nature of student power in the universities, we should keep in mind both the horizontal and vertical cleavages between these three major sections. Logically, we should also expect the possibility of alliances among the deprived and combines among the powerful.

Several structural factors influence the exercise of student power in Indian universities. First, the autonomy of university, although formal, is not actual. Dependence of Indian universities on the government, or of colleges on private managements for finance and hence, for directives, is well known. Often universities are incapacitated to deal with issues on the basis of merit as the instructions 'from above' cannot be ignored and these may often be based on non-educational considerations. In the appointment of vice-chancellors political considerations are patently present. This situation creates a series of problems. The university authorities cannot often effectively deal with student power and this is for two main reasons. First, they cannot ignore the wishes expressed from above, usually the ministry of education or the chancellor, who is also often a high political dignitary. Second, given this situation students occasionally tend to ignore university authorities and directly enter into communication (negotiation and bargaining) with extra-university authorities, leading to the erosion of power invested in university administrators. Adding complexity to these is the dependence of student leaders on political leaders and the consequent lack of autonomy, a point I noted earlier.

In the final analysis, the confrontation that takes place in Indian universities is between the two semi-autonomous entities—the university authorities who are dependent on the government and student politicians who are dependent on political parties. Of course, the involvement of the real powers—the government and political parties—in campus affairs is often invisible and hence intractable. This involvement and the manner in which it takes place renders the confrontation between university authorities and student leaders enormously complicated.

Another important structural determinant of student power is the character of student government itself.[11] By its very nature, student government is almost always coalitional. While it is true that different political parties sponsor their candidates for student union elections, it is extremely unlikely that all the elected candidates would belong to the same political party. This means the possibilities of factional alliances, floor-crossing, infighting, dissensions, backbiting, and so on, are ever present in student government which impairs its smooth functioning, particularly because the number which can tilt the balance one way or the other need be only very small.

Finally, the kind of participation that students can realize in a university under any circumstances is limited and therefore the possibility of sharing power is also limited. It is extremely unlikely that in several vital decision-making processes such as faculty appointments or evaluation of student performance, students can ever participate fully without doing gross violence to the professional autonomy of the faculty[12] and reducing the educational system to a mockery. Admittedly then, democratization of the university will be realized only partially and therefore the possibility of students sharing power with the administration and faculty will always remain limited. Indeed, university '…is a graded community, inevitably hierarchical by virtue of difference in age and competence'.[13]

Although student participation in university governments is increasingly being recognized in principle in India, it is rarely practised.[14] For instance, the response of universities to the University Grants Commission's (UGC) suggestion in 1969 for the progressive association of students in the management of universities was not very favourable. While most universities favoured student participation in bodies looking after student welfare, library facilities, hostels and discipline, considerable opposition to the presence of any student representative in statutory bodies like the Syndicate, the Senate and the Academic Council or the Board of Studies was expressed.[15] Even today, with the exception of a few institutions, student involvement in university governance is nominal. This being the situation, it is difficult to consider student power as an effective force of change in the near future. Usually, the context in which student power is exercised in the universities is provided by confrontation between the students and the authorities. University authority is constituted by vice-chancellors, deans, registrars, proctors, and heads of department. Invariably student leaders tend to develop antagonistic relationships with these office-holders and it is purposeful because unless they develop and maintain hostile relationships with them and prove their ability to flout the establishment, no large-scale mobilization of students for their 'rightful cause' in the 'hour of crisis' would be possible. Usually the conflicts between students and university authorities stem from issues relating to the immediate issues—be it the postponement of examinations, supply of hot water in hostels, or withdrawal of punishment meted out to their deviant fellow students.

As noted earlier, in most Indian universities an overwhelming majority of teachers do not have any opportunity to participate in university governance. Deprived as they are, they tend to align with students, often invisibly, in the context of student-authority confrontation. One can assert with a high degree of confidence that in any confrontation between students and university authorities the teachers play a very important role. However, this should not be surprising to any keen observer of the campus situation as the socio-economic, intellectual and ideological variations among the faculty are incredibly high. The ideologues who always hanker for populist appeal, the party workers who constantly educate students along party lines and strategies, the foreign-trained and pompous who are out to exhibit their intellectual superiority, the rural-bred who privately nurse a grudge and an inferiority complex vis-à-vis those who show off, the intellectually unequipped with an exalted aspiration level, the 'progressives' with long hair who feel uninhibited to go on a 'trip' with students, the radical who rejects the prevalent academic norms, the 'tradition-minded' steeped in primordial loyalty structures such as caste, region, religion, and so on, form an unbelievably heterogeneous group which can rarely be united on any issue. Consequently, a section of the faculty will invariably be 'at the service' of students in the event of any confrontation. It is not suggested that the situation is as complex and heterogeneous in all campuses, but the difference in complexity and mix vary from university to university. Admittedly, in the event of any conflict with the authorities, the students invariably get advice, information and help from one or the other section of the faculty. Often this 'service' may be extended to the students by the faculty members to wreak vengeance against their colleagues with whom they do not get along well.[16] Thus, the university system is one in which students and teachers are both cooperative and intimate as well as hostile and impersonal. Needless to say, the association of faculty with students in the event of a student-authority confrontation in the university adds immensely to student power.

More importantly, faculty association and involvement lends legitimacy to student activities. Even when the faculty plays only an advisory role, it boosts the morale of students tremendously. Often such 'radical' teachers of the Right or Left are hailed as pro-student and anti-establishment in the campus by one or the other section of students, while the majority of the faculty may consider them as opportunists, blacklegs or traitors. But, as it often happens, the radical teacher runs into trouble soon when he realizes that there is a point of no return in his intimate parleys and association with students for the latter are rarely satisfied with his peripheral and indirect involvement in the rebellion or 'revolution'. Caught in the dilemma of being pressurized by students and disowned by his colleagues, the erstwhile radical teacher, almost instinctively and emotionally, turns anti-student, to be labelled—by the very same students who hailed him a hero till the other day—as a 'traitor', 'revisionist', 'dishonest' and, of course, all those 'epithets' which are usually not printed.

Another section of the university community, the *karamchari*s, is also instrumental in realizing or suppressing student power, depending upon the nature of specific situations. Generally speaking, in most university campuses students tend to sympathize with the 'cause' of *karamchari*s in their eagerness to project themselves as the champions of the 'poor'. In the Indian university context, the slogan, 'students and workers unite' often manifests itself in student–*karamchari* alliances. Indeed, there is nothing like a class identity between them—the students are usually drawn from the middle class and the *karamchari*s most often from the lower middle and lower class. Further, their problems are quite different. The *karamchari*s are usually worried about service conditions, eager to better their economic prospects, whereas the students invariably face a different set of problems.

Thus, the alignment between students and *karamchari*s is bipolar in character in that they are socially and economically differentiated with differing orientations and objectives, entering into a temporary alliance with the limited objective of pressurizing university authorities to get things done. However, given the fact that both students and *karamchari*s experience deprivations, although of different types, the alliance between the two is often successful and provides the greatest threat to the university establishment. In the context of student–authority confrontation, the *karamchari*s may often play the role of the mercenary—usually the Class IV staff—to terrorize and publicly insult the bigwigs in university administration. Therefore in most student–authority confrontations, the *karamchari*s also provide the muscle component as against the faculty who provide the brain component.

Student heterogeneity is another important constraint in student mobilization. Even when students are drawn from a relatively similar background, their motivations to enter the university are so varied that it is impossible to expect that most of them will be attracted to power politics. But in reality students are drawn from a variety of backgrounds and enter the university with varying motivations. They comprise: the affluent urban elite groups and the new-rich business class with no economic anxieties; the socially disinherited who come from disorganized families; the anxious middle-class climbers who prepare for competitive examinations; the first-generation rural migrants who lack the social skill to date a girl or to pick up the 'right accent'; the scheduled caste and scheduled tribe students who get into the university on bonus marks and, hence, nurse an intellectual inferiority complex; those from the urban lower middle-class families—the proverbial *dada*s of Indian campuses; the ideologically oriented, the anarchists, the Trotskyites, the Maoists, the Marxists, the free lovers and the like; the hardworking and intelligent careerists; the confused and politically enthused ideologues; those who are out for a little fun and frolic; the girl who waits in the campus till she gets married; the Bengalis, the Tamils, the Punjabis with differing degrees of primordial attachments; the Brahmans, the Jats, the Dalits, the Adivasis, among others, with different self-images; and finally, the Muslims, the Hindus and the Christians with varying involvement in religion. All these cannot be make for a unity of any sort.

Admittedly, student heterogeneity is an important constraint in achieving student mobilization. How is it, then, that at least occasionally the entire student body is united and mobilized against university authorities? Before we attempt to answer this question we must consider another crucial category in the context of student power in universities.

The 'non-students' constitute an important force in university politics. Broadly speaking, they are of two types: those who are on the rolls of the university, that is, those who qualify technically to be called students, but whose actual activities and interests differ from those of the 'regular' students. They are usually referred to as 'professional students' who continue in universities by shifting from one course to another for a long period, sometimes even for 15 years. These 'marginal students' are in the university but not of it; often they are the paid or voluntary workers of political parties and propagate ideas and ideologies specific to the parties they represent.[17] In the context of any confrontation they suddenly assume the role of self-appointed leaders who champion the cause of students but by advocating the strategies and tactics the party bosses have instructed them to follow. They may be drawn from political families or from those families where considerable inter-generational conflict exists.[18] They may be calculating politicians to be, consciously assuming leadership positions which will facilitate their entry into the political arena of the state, or they may be self-styled messiahs posing to be altruistic and out to reform the world.

The second category of non-students is so, even technically. They may be political workers associated with parties or simple muscle-activists, the *dadas*. Most of those in the latter category hail from urban slums or the rural periphery of the university town. These semi-literates are interested in body-building and indulge in eve-teasing and are present in the campus to 'serve' the student unions or student political groups. Usually, they are found in university commercial establishments such as coffee houses, cooperative stores, and the like, invariably lending 'a helping hand' to the contractors in return for the 'subsidy' they receive. In the event of an agitation, most, if not all, of the destructive tasks are either assigned to them by the student leaders or they voluntarily undertake to do them. Often they play the role of agent provocateur and indulge in physical violence. The successful mobilization of student power in many situations is directly related to the number of 'toughs' the union can field.

It is widely known that the activists, either of the Right or the Left, are a minority and their major task is to mobilize the passive majority. But inciting the majority into collective action without raising the level of its political consciousness is fraught with many dangers and this is precisely what happens in Indian universities most of the time. Therefore, the real task of the politically oriented student activist is to transform the latent discontent and vague rebelliousness into a coherent 'revolutionary vision'.[19] Usually the passive, indolent, dull majority is 'provoked' through the offering of an occasion to be involved in a demonstration. Here, what is important is not the cause for which students agitate but the fact of their involvement in agitation.[20] Once this involvement occurs, an interest develops and an intimacy grows vis-à-vis the issues of the agitation. Human psychology seems to be such that when one gets into an activity, even if by accident, one tries to develop an interest in it.

Sometimes the zeal and commitment of the passive many is greater than that of the routine activists, once they are involved. Often physical violence will be deliberately planned by student leaders by destroying public property or by assaulting some higher official of the university.[21] Once this happens, usually the formal agencies of social control, particularly the police and the press, step in. To get the police inside the campus is a strategic step in the acceleration of the revolt. At the very sight of the police, slogans against police repression will be raised and the university authorities will be accused of deliberately calling the police in the context of a 'peaceful' situation to brutally assault the students. The newspapers will highlight the 'catchy' and 'juicy' aspects of the agitation and will print versions justifying the actions of either students or authorities, depending upon the political interests and faith they pursue.

If the attempt of student leaders to 'manufacture' a couple of student martyrs succeeds they are at the height of their glory. The martyrs are those who get shot, injured, arrested, dismissed or suspended. There then follows an instant mobilization of the student community on the campus, which is, of course, usually not informed of any kind of ideology. Suddenly students come to assume the characteristics of a homogeneous group, however short-lived this solidarity might be, and large-scale, if not total mobilization follows. In such a situation student power triumphs as several of the 'demands' so far vehemently refused by the university authorities are suddenly conceded, in part due to the orders they may get from above. Once the sound and fury disappear, the campus returns to normalcy and the desirability or otherwise of what had happened will be debated, the strategies and tactics used will be criticized or appreciated, the political motives associated with the agitation discovered, the 'traitors' and 'revolutionaries' sifted out and the student population again becomes a divided house.

What I am suggesting is this: student power is often effective only through violent agitations and this is for three reasons. First, violence is the most effective means of focusing attention on issues and this invites the sudden intervention of higher authorities. Second, violence is the medium through which the passivity, which envelops the majority, is at least temporarily effaced, galvanizing it into action. Third, it is violence, which makes the hitherto unwilling university authorities concede demands which they have been continuously refusing. Whether or not violence actually erupts is at least partly dependent on how student issues are handled by the university authorities.

THE IMPACT OF PROTEST

It is not unusual that the demands bluntly refused are readily conceded in the face of student mobilization. Conceding demands as a response to student pressure serves as an incentive for the general body of students to further intensify their agitational activities.[22] The implications of this are several and varying for different categories of students. First, the students in general could come to believe that university authorities would make concessions in the face of student violence and aggression. Second, the inactive majority comes to recognize participation in violence as a 'legitimate' activity. Third, for the activists, it provides a new base to proceed further with new demands and to convince the student-mass of the meaning of student 'unity'. Fourth, the activists, despite their marked indulgence in criminal activities suddenly become heroes or martyrs of the 'movement' which comes to be labelled 'radical'. Fifth, the university authorities' ideological position weakens vis-à-vis the activists since the former has conceded student demands under pressure. It is easier to suppress student violence completely thereby refusing to recognize the coercive student power than accept student demands under pressure once and then refuse similar demands on successive occasions.

The manner in which students put pressure on university authorities, including teachers, varies. The typical procedure is that a charter of demands is presented to authorities along with an ultimatum that 'we will be compelled to resort to direct action unless these demands are accepted by….[date]'. Usually, the authorities will initiate negotiations, proposals and discussions on the demands and the acceptance of at least some of the demands automatically follows. But in accepting or rejecting demands, rarely can one discover any principle. From the point of view of the authorities it is a device to postpone the threatened disturbance: from the perspective of student leaders, to gain something in order to harp on it as their success and a step towards 'reform' and 'revolution'. Even when principles are involved and accepted, they are not respected in practice.

If their requests are not met, students often allege 'victimization', 'partiality' and 'corruption'. Further, they may make written representations, allegations or complaints which are usually channelled through their union. The net result of all this is that the decision-making processes get highly bureaucratized and the authorities are compelled to conform to the letter of the rules, ignoring its spirit. Undoubtedly, they will become very cautious in their actions as the rationale of every decision is to be made visible and acceptable for an eventual scrutiny and inspection. In such a situation the eagerness to help genuine marginal cases will be replaced by the tendency to develop defence mechanisms or to present matters in such a way that they 'look alright'. Thus, an unanticipated consequence of students exerting pressure on the decisional process is the growth of bureaucratization in universities. On the other hand, the way in which student leaders interfere with faculty autonomy and intimidate fellow students who oppose their viewpoints often creates the impression that they are not genuinely interested in true democratization but only in creating a countervailing power in the university either for meeting their personal needs or furthering the sectional interest they represent.

So far I have analysed the nature of student power in India with reference to society and university. We have listed several structural obstacles in the way of any permanent student unity. The leading among these obstacles are: (a) their general political apathy; (b) dependence on the political parties for ideas, strategy and finance; (c) the heterogeneity of student composition and motivations; (d) the transitory character of the student population and their leaders; and (e) vulnerability of most of the student leaders to manipulations by political leaders and academic administrators.

The familiar pattern the students resort to for exerting pressure on the decisional process is collective action, which can take two different forms. It can either take the form of a student movement with a clear-cut ideology visualizing alternate systems and arrangements, thereby forcing structural changes on the system. Alternatively, due to a variety of systemic conditions, listed earlier, students may intermittently resort to short-lived rebellions, usually concentrating on certain immediate targets. Which of these mechanisms students take to is at least partly dictated by the recognition accorded to the potential of student power to bring about desirable changes in society and university by the top political decision-makers. Depending upon their perception of the situation, whether or not student mobilization is favourable to them, the politicians may resort to one of the following mechanisms, in one or the other situation:

1. Suppression of student opposition to the establishment or neutralizing their impact by creating divisions among them. The assumption underlying this approach is that student power is coercive in character; students are incapable of responsibility and therefore they should be kept out of the decision-making process.

2. Incorporating students into the decision-making structures and providing them with the opportunity of expressing their opinions, feelings and ideas and registering their differences and articulating their protests. The assumptions here are that student power is productive in nature and that students are capable of responsible participation.

The coercive or productive dimension of student power is reflected both in the movements initiated for the realization of student power and through participation in structures inducted for the purpose. Thus we can conceive of four distinct response patterns: (a) student power used as a coercive force through violent agitations; (b) student power used as a coercive force by putting pressure on decisional processes surreptitiously; (c) student power translated into a productive force through participation in movements with clear ideological orientations and alternate visions of society; and (d) student power converted into a productive force through direct participation in the decision-making processes at appropriate levels.

In India the expression of student power usually takes place through the first two forms as students are treated as 'outsiders' to the university system and to society, congenitally relegated to the receiving end. Inevitably, they develop an alienation vis-à-vis the very system in which they are, and the alienated need not be apologetic in destroying the system. Understandably, the difference between 'we' (student) and 'they' (the faculty, administration and the elders) is continuously sharpened and the possibilities of head-on collisions between them are ever present.

While a beginning has been made in some universities to transform the coercive student power into a productive force by incorporating it into the university government, no serious effort has yet been made on a countrywide basis to harness student potential for basic changes in the society at large. And the situation is far from satisfactory even in those universities where a beginning has been made, since the authorities and the students are confused about the legitimate boundaries of student involvement in the decisional process. Therefore, whether or not the purpose for which the changes are introduced will be achieved depends at least partly on the spirit with which the faculty and administration work the arrangement and the willingness of students to cooperate with them. If the former view student participation as a ritual and/ or a concession to student belligerence and if the latter feel that the authorities only want to crucify them on the cross of responsibility by increasing their accountability,[23] the prospects of student participation and hence student power, are, indeed, bleak.

NOTES

1. In 1968–9 there were 25 lakh students enrolled in the higher education category in India. Of these, very few fall in the age category 21 plus since most students complete their Master's degree by the time they reach this age. For instance, in 1965–6, out of 605,445 students in the Arts, only 51,305 were in post-graduate classes.

2. Feuer writes: 'A student audience or crowd is the easiest in the world to assemble. They are not dispersed over distance as peasants are, and their studies are rarely so demanding that they do not have time on their hands. They are not bound and exhausted by work schedules as workers are and usually have no families to support.' (L.S. Feuer, *The Conflict of Generations* [London: Heinemann, 1969], p. 14). In India, student union leaders frequently boast of their power to call a strike not only in their universities but also to initiate a successful *bandh* or '*hartal*' in the cities and towns in which their universities are located and to stop the operation of public utilities such as transport or to paralyze the activities of several institutions. For details see T.K. Oommen, *Student Unions in India: An Introduction* (New Delhi: Vishwa Yuvak Kendra, 1970).

3. See Vishwa Yuvak Kendra, *The Dynamics of Student Agitation* (Bombay: Somaiya Publications, 1972).

4. See A. Touraine, *The May Movement: Revolt and Reform* (New York: Random House, 1971).

5. Ghanshyam Shah, *Protest Movements in two Indian States* (Delhi: Ajanta Publications, 1977).

6. Muni Reddy claims that the revolutionary movements of 1906–19 and 1920–32 were mostly led by students (M. Muni-Reddy, *Whither Students?* [Nidubrolu: Kisan Publishers, 1949]).

7. See P.G. Altbach, 'The Transformation of the Indian Student Movement', *Asian Survey*, 6 (8), (1966), pp. 564–84; and M. Weiner, *The Politics of Scarcity* (Bombay: Asia Publishing House, 1962), pp. 170–99.

8. Almost all students' political organizations originated as youth fronts of political parties and this continues even today. For details, see Muni Reddy (1949), p. 12.

9. Apart from student wings of political parties, even student cultural associations originate and spread on the basis of political orientations. For an understanding of the situation in one university, see Oommen, 'Nature and Types of Student Voluntary Associations in Delhi University', *New Frontiers in Education*, 2 (2), (1972).

10. It is interesting to note here that 54 per cent of the students interviewed in a Maharashtra study expressed political aspirations, with most of them wanting to be ministers at that. See Shinde, *Political Consciousness Among College Students* (Bombay: Thacker and Co. Ltd., 1972), pp. 111–12.

11. See Oommen, 'Student Politics in India: The Case of Delhi University', *Asian Survey*, 14, (1974), pp. 777–94.

12. Cf. Ben-David and Collins, 'A Comparative Study of Academic Freedom and Student Politics', in S.M. Lipset (ed.), *Student Politics* (New York: Basic Books Inc., 1967), p. 150. Feuer is categorical in his assertion: 'Wherever student movements have flourished academic freedom has consequently declined', *The Conflict of Generations*, p. 44.

13. S.M. Lipset, 'University Students and Politics in Underdeveloped Countries', in S.M. Lipset (ed.), *Student Politics* (New York: Basic Books Inc., 1967), p. 5.

14. In November 1970, Dr V.K.R.V. Rao, the then education minister in the Union Cabinet, expressed the view that students should have a voice in matters like change in courses, textbooks and the syllabus. He said: 'Today the student community has reached a state of adulthood which we did not reach when we were students' (*The Times of India*, 19 November 1970). The Committee on the Governance of Universities appointed by the University Grants Commission under the chairmanship of P.B. Gajendragadkar recommended several structural reforms in universities, such as a student advisory committee for each faculty with the right to express its views on such important academic issues as the structure of course, the content of the syllabus, the pattern of examination, inclusion of student representatives in University Courts (Senates), etc.

15. *The Times of India*, 24 March 1969.

16. For example, it was reported that the BHU was a hotbed of intrigue, nepotism and even crime and the eastern Uttar Pradesh teacher-politicians were said to be actively involved with students in planning violence. See, Government of India, *Report of the Banaras Hindu University Inquiry Committee* (New Delhi: Ministry of Education, 1958).

17. Perhaps this situation is inevitable in a democratic political system where universities play an important role in the process of political socialization. A study of college students in Bombay revealed that 47 per cent supported

one or the other political party, 17 per cent were members of politically oriented organizations, and 28 per cent worked for a party or candidate during elections. T.C. Eakin, *Students and Politics: A Comparative Study* (Bombay: Popular Prakashan, 1972), p. 135.

18. Activist students the world over are said to be drawn from maladjusted families. Ideological orientations and institutional identification or alienation are said to be associated with early socialization experience. See A. Kornberg and M.L. Brehm, 'Ideology, Institutional Identification and Campus Activism', *Social Forces*, 49 (3), (1971), pp. 445–99.

19. The task of involving the passive majority in agitation is assigned to the active minority of students by Cohn-Bendit, the well-known student activist. See Richard Johnson, *The French Communist Party versus the Students* (New Haven and London: Yale University Press, 1972), p. 168.

20. As Kakkar and Chowdhry write: 'The periodic violent and destructive agitations by the students are thus not only rejection of a "dirty" "authority" but also serve as communal "purification" rituals for the young' (*Conflict and Choice* [Bombay: Somaiya Publications, 1970], p. 24).

21. G.F. Bereday, 'Student Unrest in Four Continents: Montreal, Ibadan, Warsaw and Rangoon', in Lipset (ed.), *Student Politics*, p. 20.

22. This seems to be the situation the world over. Even in Latin American universities, where student participation has already reached a high pitch, there does not seem to be any saturation point in demand-making and demand conceding. See A. Liebman, K.N. Walker, and M. Glazer (eds), *Latin American University Students: A Six Nations Study* (Cambridge: Harvard University Press, 1972).

23. The ultra radicals consider student participation as a subtle and devious means of making them a part of the establishment, an attempt to castrate them of their revolutionary élan. See Glen S. Dumke, 'Bad Days of Generation Gap', in G.R. Walker and J.H. Weaver (eds), *The University Revolution* (New Jersey: Prentice Hall, 1969), pp. 165–73.

Ecological and Environmental Movements

The two previous parts in this book analysed social movements of different social categories. This short part consisting of three chapters discusses movements which affect the entire population sharing a common habitat, although they impinge on different categories and dimensions with varying intensity. The ecological/environmental movements are relatively recent in origin, indeed they are offshoots of the latent functions of the models of development that are adopted. Equity and justice among fellow human beings are the central concerns of movements discussed in Parts One and Two. Ecological/Environmental movements, in contrast not only endeavour to pursue inter-generational equity but also provide security to future generations; they search for peaceful co-existence of humanity and nature.

Although ecology movements as a phenomenon surfaced only recently in the West, their roots can be traced to the cosmocentrism of ancient India. Mohandas Karamchand Gandhi revived that value orientation in the twentieth century through his advocacy of a humane model of development which disapproved the capital intensive, labour displacing, and high-tech driven paradigm of development in vogue. The grass-roots ecology movements such as Chipko (hug-the-tree) emerged in mid-1970s in Garhwal region of then Uttar Pradesh, now in Uttaranchal. Vandana Shiva situates the movement in the context of ancient India's values and Gandhian philosophy in Chapter 13.

The Chipko movement triggered off to counter the exigencies created by reckless felling of forest trees for commercial purposes by contractors, resulting in soil erosion and floods endangering the livelihood of the people of Garhwal. Viewed in terms of the issues involved Chipko is an ecological movement par excellence. But it is to the credit of the peasant women who prevented the felling of trees by hugging them. Analysts are often inclined to label movements (see, the general introduction) based on *who* are the initiators and principal participants. But this poses problems because the collectivities involved have multiple identities. In the present case there are three identities—regional (people of Garhwal), gender (women), and occupational (peasantry). And yet there ensued a fierce but pointless controversy; some analysts designated Chipko as a peasant movement and others labelled it as a women's movement. While analysts highlighted one of the identities, the ecological issue was the shared concern of all movement participants irrespective of their identities.

The movement was also subjected to a controversy based on the centrality of leadership versus that of participants. Some analysts insist that the peasant women who initiated the act of hugging were the prime movers, but others argue that the movement could not have been sustained for long with out the involvement of the local charismatic leaders who articulated the ideology behind the movement and provided the required connectivity of the deprived participants dispersed across the region, through an organization. The controversy ignores the imperative need to have an appropriate ideological vision of the leadership, relevant organizational weapon and motivation and commitment of participants to achieve the material and symbolic goals of a movement.

Apart from the well-known Chipko movement and the Narmada Bachao Andolan (see Chapter 15), there have been numerous mobilizations initiated by non-governmental organizations (NGOs), singly or conjointly to preserve and protect environment. One concrete achievement of these mobilizations manifested in maintaining national parks and wild life sanctuaries as protected areas (PAs). These PAs have been increasing steadily; in 1975 there were only 130 PAs in India but by mid-1990s the number of PAs increased to 520. The PAs were made possible through several legislations passed by the government responding to the pressure exerted by environmental NGOs.

Chapter 14 by Ranjit Dwivedi provides a narrative of one such mobilization—the Jungle Jivan Bachao Yatra (Journey to Save Forests and Forest Lives) by a conglomerate of NGOs in mid-1990s. The Yatra was conceived as an event to sensitize the rural people about the importance of conservation of nature and environment. To the extent the Yatra represented a shift from pursuing only the interests of the urban environment encapsulating the rural situation it was a welcome development. However, the possibility of such mobilizations imposing the value orientation and aspiration of a section of romantic urban middle class on the rural hinterland ignoring its basic infrastructural needs, which are pre-requisites for improving the quality of life in the rural areas, the required caution needs to be administered.

Independent India has launched a massive programme of high-tech driven industrialization which has resulted in substantial displacement of people in the name of development. The tribal population constitutes only 8 per cent of India's population but 60 per cent of the displacees are tribals which endangered their livelihood and devastated their habitats. Of the numerous mobilizations against displacement the most well known, well documented and highly controversial is the Narmada Bachao Andolan (NBA). The NBA is at once perceived as anti-development and pro-development depending upon the manner in which development is conceptualized. Those who consider it as anti-development stand for sustainable development and insist on protecting the integrity of the habitat of those threatened by displacement.

Displacement is an all-India phenomenon but it is particularly acute in some states. The economically backward state of Orissa with 40 per cent of its population drawn from the most socially backward segments—22 per cent STs and 17 per cent SCs—had launched a programme of industrialization since the 1950s which was intensified in the 1980s culminating with the introduction of the Special Economic Zones (SEZs) in 2005. The substantial displacement of the rural poor in Orissa threatening their livelihood security and violating the integrity of their environment led to massive mobilizations against the state and the corporates. In Chapter 15, I discuss displacement caused by 'development' and protests prompted by displacement in India with special reference to NBA and the state of Orissa. The analysis leads to two suggestions: one, minimize displacement and rehabilitate the displacees before the projects are launched and two, nurture a cosmocentric value-orientation as against the prevailing homocentric value orientation which ignores the integrity of the relationship between humanity and nature.

ADDITIONAL READINGS

Amita Baviskar, *In the Belly of the River: Tribal Conflicts Over Development in the Narmada Valley* (New Delhi: Oxford University Press, 1995).

W. Fernandes and E.G. Thukral (eds), *Development, Displacement and Rehabilitation* (New Delhi: Indian Social Institute, 1989).

Ramachandra Guha, *The Unquiet Woods: Ecological Change and Peasant Resistance in the Himalaya* (New Delhi: Oxford University Press, 1989).

L.K. Mahapatra, *Resettlement, Impoverishment and Reconstruction in India: Development for the Deprived* (New Delhi: Vikas Publishing House, 1999).

Haripriya Rangan, *Of Myths and Movements: Rewriting Chipko into Himalayan History* (New Delhi: Oxford University Press, 2000).

Ecology Movements in India*

Vandana Shiva

The 1970s witnessed the emergence of grass-roots ecology movements searching for a new kind of peace—peace with nature. Despite the differences in the stage and in the actors, these movements shared the common objective of a search for an alternative development that is more in harmony with nature's rhythms, patterns and processes. In India, ecology movements went a step further. They emerged as movements for a just peace. The simultaneous search for justice and peace through a restructuring of man's relationship with nature has been a characteristic of India's ecology movements because of her cultural, historical and natural heritage. India is a large country, with a large population and an ancient history. Every ecological niche is occupied in one way or another. The balance between nature's productivity and people's needs is a delicate one and can be easily upset in such a context. The replication of the industrialization patterns of the countries of the North in countries like India cause rapid resource depletion and the diversion of resources from people's basic needs to industrial raw materials. Ecological disruption and economic exploitation are intrinsically linked; and this linkage stares everyone in

* This chapter was originally commissioned by the Committee for a Just World Peace for presentation at its Lisbon Conference in March 1985. It was subsequently revised and published as 'Ecology Movements in India', *Alternatives*, 11, 1986, pp. 255–73.

the face when resources are scarce, people are many, and new modes of production are resource-intensive and resource-wasteful, and consume resources needed for survival.

The ecological implications of resource-intensive and labour-displacing production forms were understood in ancient India. This understanding was revived by Gandhi in modern India. And it has been revitalized by the contemporary ecology movements.

In India, to be civilized is to practice 'Dharma' (the Sanskrit word for right conduct). Etymologically, Dharma means the stabilizer. It is the source of stability of human societies. And this social stability is related to stability of natural resource and of ecology. According to the Indian cultural heritage, the three values of life which guide human activity are Artha (which stands for resources), Kama (which stands for needs and desires of human beings), and Dharma (which denoted right conduct or the proper utilization of resources to fulfil or satisfy the needs and desires of human beings). According to the *Isavasyopanishad*, Dharma consists in restricting use of resources to satisfaction of basic needs, because using resources beyond one's needs would be appropriating the resources of others. According to the *Isavasya*, a selfish man utilizing others' resources to satisfy his own ever increasing wants is nothing but a thief. Justice and ecological and social stability are therefore intrinsically interlinked in the Indian world view.[1] 'Dharma' is the mediator between resources and needs and is thus a secular category, not a religious one. It is equivalent to rational economic and technology choice. 'Dharma', as technology choice, involves a conscious rejection of resource-wasteful production. As Gandhi pointed out, the Indian civilization opted for another mode of development not because of technological inadequacy, but because of ecological sophistication. 'We have managed with the same kind of plough as existed thousands of years ago....It was not that we did not know how to invent machinery'.[2]

This relationship between restraint in resource use, ecological stability and social justice was also repeated by Gandhi who said, 'Earth provides enough to satisfy every man's need but not for every man's greed'.[3] This creed of political economy, in which restraint in resource use is a precondition for justice and peace is best substantiated in land use. If we cooperate with nature's processes and its cycle of life, the soil renews its fertility indefinitely and provides sustenance. But when the exploitative and predatory attitude takes over, nature's balance is upset and there is an all-round biological deterioration. Upon the balance between man and nature, depends the stability of and peace in society. The philosophical recognition of the nexus between ecology and a just peace is contained in the concepts of Dharma and Ahimsa (non-violence) on which the ancient civilizations of the East were based.

Contemporary ecology movements in India are informed by this philosophy, which is vivified by the existential reality of the wanton destruction of the life-support system of a very large number of people. They realize that the criteria of choosing lifestyles and matching technology inherent in the Indian heritage are today the only criteria that can assure survival, which is the elementary fundamental right of every human being—as much of the poor (who have to suffer the gruesome consequences of the pillage of nature) as of the rich (who perpetrate this outrage in pursuit of a wickedly affluent lifestyle, inimical to justice and peace).

Ecology movements in India are struggles of the dispossessed, the marginalized, the victims of discrimination, among whom can be counted women, tribals and the non-commercial farmer. These movements are aimed at conserving nature's balance in order to conserve their means of survival. In this sense they are the keepers of the residual Indian cultural and economic heritage.

Although grass-roots ecological struggles are seemingly local episodes, their reverberations are global in import, if only because survival on the local plane is impinged upon by forces that are non-local in origin—such as the dominant proselytizing scientific and technological culture; the development paradigm forcibly imposed through conditionalities of loan and aid and trade; and overarching all this, the hard national-scientific state. The local struggles are part of the process of global transformation currently under way. They are modest manifestations of a search, non-theorized and non-verbalized, for an alternative scientific and technological culture; an alternative development paradigm; an alternative concept of state and security; and, with their stress on non-violence and justice and peace, an alternative civilization.

THE SURVIVAL IMPERATIVE AND ECOLOGICAL MOVEMENTS

For all the long tradition of ecological consciousness in India, instances of ecological abuse were not wanting; but they invariably provoked people's resistance. To take an example, some three centuries ago the entire Jain community of Vishnois of Rajasthan sacrificed their lives to prevent felling of green trees by the royal forces of Jodhpur.

Systemic large-scale destruction of forests for commercial-industrial purposes and misuse of other natural resources began, however, in the colonial era; but they almost invariably met with resistance. A confrontation that became a landmark in the history of the national struggle for freedom from colonialism occurred in the Champaran district of Bihar in 1917. In Champaran every tenant was bound by law to plant indigo on three out of twenty parts of his holding for the landlord (the British planter). The simmering discontent came to a boil when Gandhi (made well-known by his historic struggle against racism in South Africa and now plunged into Indian public life) was persuaded to take up the cause of the oppressed, exploited, farmers of Champaran; and he led them to victory: indigo planting was abolished. Gandhi had scrupulously avoided giving the struggle a political colour by keeping the Indian National Congress and non-Bihari Congress leaders out of it. But another struggle in 1930, centred on the use of commons and the people's right of access to them, was frankly political. It was an open countrywide defiance of the salt law which, for the first time in the history of India, had made it illegal for the citizens to collect salt on the sea shore or make it anywhere in the land. It had vested total monopoly of making and marketing salt in the state. What began as an assertion of the people's right of access to the free gifts of nature became the assertion of people's right to independence.

India did become independent; but even in Independent India ecological abuse has not ceased, neither have the struggles for ecological conservation. In fact, the intensity and range of the ecology movements in independent India have kept on increasing as predatory exploitation of natural resources has increased in extent and intensiveness in consequence of the huge expansion of energy-intensive and resource-consuming industrialization and development projects, and the concomitantly narrowing resource base of the economically poor and powerless. Ecology movements came up as people's response to this threat to their survival and as demands for conserving vital natural resources. The most vital resources that were being destroyed are soil, water and vegetation systems, and these have therefore been at the centre of ecology movements in the last few decades.

The Chipko movement is the most well-known ecology movement in the country. It is a movement of the forest dwelling communities to save the forest cover from destruction. Movements with the same end, though not with the same means, have been occurring in other vulnerable mountain systems like the Western Ghats, the Aravallis and the Vindhyas. They have occurred in all tribal belts of the country. Most notable among them are the Singhbhum (Bihar) and Bastar region (Madhya Pradesh) where people's movements were aimed against the conversion of mixed natural forestry into the monoculture of commercial species such as teak or pine, a sure recipe for the destruction of the tribal modes of life.

There has been resistance wherever forest and agricultural lands have been threatened by inundation, waterlogging, salinity resulting from the construction of large dams and large irrigation projects—for example, in Tehri in the north, Koel Karo in the east, Sirsi in the South, and Inchampalli in central India. Another significant ecological

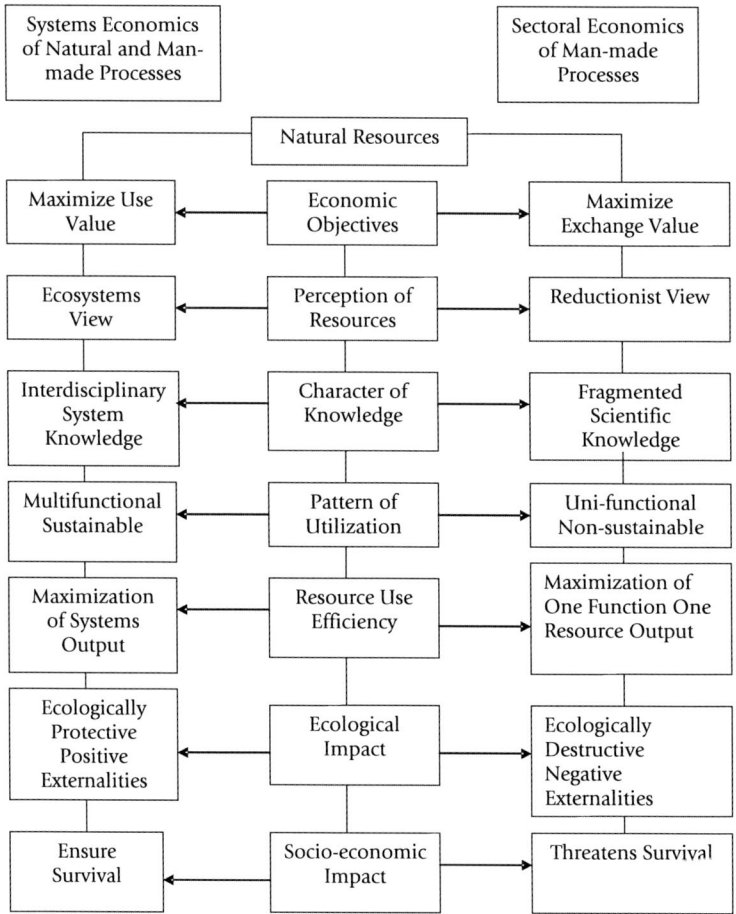

Figure 13.1: Structural Linkage of Economic Objectives with
Scientific Knowledge System and Ecological Impact

movement has revolved round the threat to marine resources as well as to indigenous fishing from mechanized fishing. It has surfaced all along the Indian coastline. The one in Kerala has received much wider notice because of the involvement of the radical section of the Catholic clergy.

Ecological conflicts, regardless of where they take place and how they are conducted, have things in common: they all centre around the right of access of the poor to natural resources, and they all have three aspects:

1. Economic conflict between two types of economic activity—one aimed at ensuring survival for the people in a sustainable manner through a genuinely collective management; and the other aimed at maximizing the growth rate even at the cost of bare survival of many.
2. Technological: conflict between two types of technology—vernacular and labour-intensive, one aimed at minimizing ecological costs to ensure survival; and the
3. Other borrowed from abroad regardless of its suitability in the local context, aimed at 'modernization' of the productive process.
4. Scientific: conflict in the politics of knowledge—one open to all, non-dogmatic, not ruling out other ways of acquiring knowledge; and the other a closed system, drawing a sharp dividing line between the expert and the non-expert.

The three are, of course, closely interlinked. Figure 13.1 is a schematic presentation of the linkages between growth economics, ecologically destructive technology and reductionist science, on the one side, and sustainable economics, ecologically sound technology and ecological science, on the other side.

'CHIPKO' MOVEMENT

The 'Chipko' (hug-the-tree) movement,[4] which derives its name from the novel method it invented, is the most powerful ecological movement of India. An analysis of Chipko shows that it is a civilizational response to a threat to survival. Beginning as a grass-roots local movement, it has spread into the national and the transnational arenas, challenging global paradigms of resource use. While the first global environment meeting of the elite was taking place in Stockholm in 1972, the first grass-roots ecology movement was emerging in remote villages in the southern foothills of the Himalayas. The villages were totally unaware of the global event. Their awareness was born of their own existential experience of increasing floods and landslides caused by deforestation; it was rooted in their cultural heritage that has instilled in them a deep respect for the lofty, luminous, awe-inspiring, Himalayas as also for its magnificent forests and sparkling frolicking streams. The first Chipko action occurred in March 1974 in Reni village of the Garhwal Himalaya. A group of village women led by one Gaura Devi hugged the trees, challenging the hired sawyers, about to cut down trees for a sports-goods company, to saw them alive first. In July 1970, the Alaknanda valley, in which Reni village is located, had experienced a disastrous flood, when the Alaknanda inundated 1,000 sq kms of land and washed away a large number of bridges and roads. The cause, they knew was deforestation. The women resorted to the novel method to protect their forests in order to protect themselves from future landslides and floods. The occurrence of landslides had increased dramatically through the 1970s largely as a result of road expansion and timber extraction. In 1977, the Alaknanda disaster was followed by the Tawaghat tragedy. In 1978, the holy Ganga was blocked at Kanodiagad, 50 km downstream from Gangotri, by a massive landslide. When the dam burst, the entire Gangetic plain was flooded all the way down to Calcutta.

These ecological disasters had prepared the ground for a grass-roots popular movement to protect the forests; the Chipko movement spread rapidly in the valley. In February 1978, Chipko activists in Henwal valley saved the Advani forests; and in December 1978, the forests of Badyargad were saved through Chipko. The news spread beyond the geographical boundaries of Garhwal; and in 1983–4, the Chipko strategy was used by environment activists of the Western Ghats to save the forests of the other ecologically vulnerable mountain systems of India.

Ecological World Views and Chipko

The ecological crises to which these village communities responded were new, yet the ecological perception with which they responded was centuries old. The illiterate women of the hill villages did not need professional forest hydrologists to tell them of the role of forests in protecting the land and water stability of mountain watersheds, they had drunk this knowledge with their mothers' milk, and had it reinforced as they grew with religious myths and folklore. One of the best descriptions of the hydrological role of the Himalayan forests is contained in the myth of the descent of the mighty and sacred Ganga. Reiger, the eminent Himalayan ecologist, describes the rationality of the myth in the following words:

In the scriptures a realization is there that if all the waters which descent upon the mountain were to beat down upon the naked earth, then earth would never bear the torrents. In Shiva's hair we have a very well known physical device which breaks the force of the water coming down...the vegetation of the mountains.[5]

The Chipko strategy draws on these ecological modes of perception by readings from the scriptures. Tactically, too, this mode of mobilizing people by appeals around the ecological messages from the religious heritage is effective because it uses an ancient and spontaneous form of gathering village communities together. Another tale from the scriptures which communicates the ecological value of trees and is used in Chipko mobilizations is from the *Bhagwad Gita*; it drives home the life-sustaining role of forests.

Chipko and Conflicts over Forest Resources

The conflicts and tensions from which the famous Chipko movement has emerged can be historically traced to the far-reaching changes in forest management introduced in India during the colonial period. Forest resources, like other vital natural resources had been till then managed as common resources with strict, though informal, social mechanisms for controlling utilization to ensure sustained productivity. Besides the large tracts of natural forests that were maintained through this careful husbanding, village forests and woodlets were also developed and maintained through careful selection of appropriate tree species. Remnants of commonly managed natural forests and village commons still exist in pockets and these provide knowledge of the scientific basis underlying traditional land management.[6]

Colonial impact on forest management undermined these conservation strategies in two ways. First, changes in the system of land tenure through the introduction of the zamindari system transformed common village resources into the private property of newly created landlords. People who satisfied their domestic needs from the collectively owned village forests and grasslands had to now turn to natural forests. Second, large-scale felling of trees in natural forests to satisfy non-local commercial needs—such as shipbuilding for the British navy and sleepers for the expanding railway network—created an extraordinary force of destruction. After about half-a-century of uncontrolled exploitation the need for controlling it was felt. The colonial response to this was two-fold: vesting ownership in the state and setting up a forest bureaucracy to regulate commercial exploitation and to conserve forests. What the bureaucracy in practice protected was forest revenues, not the forest themselves. This typically colonial interpretation of utilization, the new management system catered only to commercial demands which, after prolonged struggles, were occasionally granted as favours.[7] On the conservation level, since the new forest management was concerned solely with forest revenues, ecologically unsound silvicultural practices were introduced. This undermined biological productivity of forest areas and transformed renewable resources into non-renewable ones.[8]

With the reservation of forests and the denial of the people's right of access to them the villagers created resistance movements in all parts of the country. The Forest Act of 1927 sharpened the conflicts, and the 1930s witnessed widespread forest *satyagraha*s as a mode of non-violent resistance to the new forest laws and policies: Villagers ceremonially removed forest produce from the reserved forests to defy forest laws that denied them their right to forest products. These *satyagraha*s were specially successful in regions where survival of the local population was intimately linked with the access to the forests for example, the Himalayan foothills, the Western Ghat and the central Indian hills. These non-violent protests were suppressed with the might of arms. In central India, Gond tribals were gunned down for participating in the *satyagraha*. In the Himalayan foothills dozens of unarmed villagers were killed and hundreds injured in Tilari village of Tehri Garhwal on 30 May 1930, when they gathered to protest against the forest laws. After enormous loss of lives, the *satyagrahi*s were finally successful in regaining some of the traditional rights of the village communities to various forest produce. But the forest policy and its revenue-maximizing objective remained unchanged.

From Forest Satyagraha to Chipko Movement

In independent India the same colonial forest-management policy was continued but enforced with greater ruthlessness, which is justified in the name of 'national interest' and 'economic growth'. The threat to survival having become more sinister, the response of the people has changed: sporadic protests have become organized and sustained movements. Chipko is the most spectacular of these.

Global Implications of the Chipko Movement

Ecology movements like Chipko call into question the dominant paradigm of thinking and living in all its aspects: ontological, epistemological, scientific, technological, social, economic. They call, in effect, for a redefinition of the criteria of science and rationality, criteria of technological choice, criteria of economic development and, overarching all this, criteria of good life.

Since the dominant world view is global in spread, any question relating to its validity and appropriateness, even if raised by events in a remote corner, has global implications. The guardians (who are at the same time beneficiaries) of the status quo, both at the centre and at the peripheries, look at even local conflicts over access to natural resources with suspicion and disapproval, because they appear to be incipient threats to the status quo.

From Chipko to Alternative Science

Chipko has generally been viewed merely as a forest movement, and sometimes as an environment movement. A deeper insight will reveal that Chipko carries within it the seeds of a movement for an alternative science.

Scientific and technical knowledge of forestry in the existing model of forest management teaches that forests are nothing more than so much timber—for industrial-commercial use, of course. This inevitably leads to manipulations of the forest ecosystem for furtherance of those species of trees that yield commercial wood. Hence, the encouragement given to replacement of ecologically valuable oak forests by commercially valuable conifers. Result: the destruction of other biomass forms that have low commercial value but very high use value for the people. Scientific forestry, is, in its present form, an essentially reductionist system of knowledge that ignores the complex relationships within the forest community and between plant life and other resources like soil and water. By ignoring the systems linkages within the forest ecosystem and its multiple functions this pattern generates instabilities in the ecosystem and leads to irreversible soil erosion and uncontrollable floods. The Alaknanda disaster in the Garhwal region was an exceptionally grim reminder of this. The lesson was lost in the reductionist science; but the people of Garhwal rose to the defence of forests because their life-support system was at stake. The two conflicting perceptions corresponding to two conflicting interests were all brought out in the two slogans used in the Chipko movement. The establishment perception of the forests went as follows:

> What do the forests bear?
> Profit, resin and timber.

The people's perception was summed up as follows:

> What do the forests bear?
> Soil, water and pure air.

It is this conflict of interests and of perception that lies at the heart of the Chipko movement, which has now turned into a national movement, spreading into forest areas of Karnataka, Himachal Pradesh, Rajasthan, Bihar, etc., laying the nebulous foundation for an alternative science and technology and an alternative development strategy for sustainable and equitable development.

ECOLOGY MOVEMENT IN DEHRADUN

The twin conflicts between interests and between perceptions of the functions of nature is reflected in the case of mineral resources in Doon Valley at the base of the Himalayan foothill. An ecology movement has sprung up there and it is growing; it is directed against limestone quarrying. The Doon Valley is well known for its rich water resources as well as rich limestone deposits. In the reductionist view of a market economy (where the only value that matters is exchange value), the most efficient use of the limestone deposit is its extraction for the satisfaction of commercial-industrial demands, in the ecological view (where 'man is the measure of all things'), limestone in its fractured form provides the best and largest aquifer that sustains the rich water resources of the valley. The most efficient economic use of the mineral in this perspective is its conservation for the sustenance of the water resources on which the whole economic life in the valley is dependent. The reductionist view of minerals is blind to their other functions and therefore destroys them for maximizing short-term benefits.[9]

The Dehradun movement has emerged from the ecological perspective of the people whose survival depends on the continuing ecological functions of natural resources. It carries within it the seed of an alternative knowledge system. In the words of Feyerabend:

…in a free society intellectuals are just one tradition. They have no special rights and their views are of no special interest (except, of course, to themselves). Problems are solved not by specialists (though their advice will not be disregarded) but by the people concerned, in accordance with the ideas they value and by procedures they regard as most appropriate.[10]

THE POLITICS OF FORESTRY SCIENCE AND THE DIALECTICS OF NATURE

Ecological perceptions of nature provided by Chipko and other ecology movements are based on the recognition of interrelationships and interdependence among the various material components of nature as well as on the awareness that these relationships are crucial and have therefore to be preserved to ensure survival of plant and animal life. A direct implication of this ecological perception is that the properties of individual components of the ecosystem will differ according to the other components it is seen to be related to. Relationships thus define the context for knowing the properties of nature. What properties are perceived depends on the context, which, in turn, is fixed by priorities and values that govern the pattern of the use of natural resource. The context is therefore created by a value system. It is thus that values get built into scientific facts about nature. There is nothing like an objective property possessed by natural systems independent of the value injected into it by human cognitive and economic activity. Properties perceived in nature depend on how one looks at nature; and how one looks depends, in turn, on the economic interest guiding the use of nature. If one looks at them as ecosystems, one sees their productive role in soil, water, fertility, nutrition.

Looking does not itself create properties in a causal sense. It creates them by creating conditions for perception.[11]

The thesis that there are no objective facts of nature independent of their context of perception is not peculiar to ecology movements for preservation of nature's resources. It is also supported by the ontological implications of the new physics of quantum mechanics which establishes that the properties of systems change when the context of their observation is changed.[12] Quantum mechanics merely articulates at the micro level the ontological implications of an ecological world view, which tells us that the determination of the properties of nature are built into human knowledge about how nature works.

Reductionism creates a particular context in which the components of a system are perceived in isolation from their interrelationships. Properties and facts about nature arrived at through the reductionist approach are therefore specific to the context created by reductionist ontology and epistemology. Since the context is not explicitly mentioned in reductionist claims about nature, such claims are presented as neutral factors about nature independent of the contextual value. The dominant system of knowledge of forest resources is epistemologically linked with the wood-based industry such as paper. However, its value commitment is implicit, and it is called 'scientific forestry'. Forestry science practised by forest dwellers, such as tribals, who see trees as living entities providing them with conditions of life are declared unscientific in the reductionist framework. In spite of being restricted by their particular context, reductionist knowledge of 'scientific forestry' is projected as universal and objective. However, as Feyerabend has pointed out: 'The appearance of objective that is attached to some value judgements come from the fact that a particular tradition is used but not recognized; absence of the impressions of subjectivity is not proof of "objectivity" but an oversight'.[13]

This oversight leads to the exclusion of the possibility of alternative contexts of perception of nature. A non-reductionist ecological perception of nature, as provided by Chipko, leads to the awareness that reductionism is a particular way of looking at nature, in which only certain facts of nature are picked out while denying the existence of the others. Ecology provides the foundations for an alternative philosophy that recognizes that there is a plurality of ways of knowing nature; it provides the ontological possibility of an alternative framework for science and technology.

Ecology also provides an epistemological framework that shows that alternatives to reductionist science and technology are preferable because, unlike the exclusive reductionism, they provide a holistic view of nature. Reductionist forestry is silent about the hydrological role of tree species. The rejection of the reductionist view of forestry is not an advocacy of a materially vacuous philosophical position. The survival issues from which Chipko has emerged is fundamentally a materialist issue. On the other hand, reductionist 'scientific forestry' in practise becomes a prescription for desertification.[14] Ecologically based alternatives in science are an imperative because they alone ensure human survival by preserving the life-support system.

Reductionism is not, however, an epistemological accident. It is the answer to the need of a particular form of economic organization. The reductionist world view, the industrial revolution and the capitalist economy were the philosophical, technological and economic components of the same process. This nexus is substantiated in the dominant paradigm of forestry. Reductionist forestry was born with the increasing need for transportation and communication in an emerging global capitalist economy. Teak was exploited for ship-building, sal and deodar were felled for the railway network. The purpose of forestry science was, and still is, to generate revenue for the state and profits for industry. Trees ceased to be seen as vital parts of a living and essential ecosystem; they became commodities. This economic value is built into the very concepts, basic terms, and definitions, of the science of forestry.

Social groups generate the conflicting economic objectives guiding the utilization of natural resources with conflicting economic interests; and they are reflected in conflicting perceptions of nature. And it is in this sense that Chipko as an ecology movement converges with movements for alternative sciences.

THE POLITICS OF DEVELOPMENT

The earlier forest *satyagraha*s as well their contemporary form, the Chipko movement, should be seen as civilizational responses to a development model based on ecological destruction, on the one hand, and poverty creation, on the other. They have been inspired by the Gandhian world view which recognizes that prosperity of the ordinary citizens of India can only be based on an ecological development that is just and sustainable. The imitation of a pattern of development, which had evolved elsewhere in a different socio-economic and historical context, could not, in Gandhi's view, solve India's economic problems:

Why must India become industrial in the Western sense? What is good for one nation situated in one condition is not necessarily good for another differently situated. One man's food is often another man's poison. Mechanization is good when hands are too few for the work intended to be accomplished. It is an evil where there are more hands than required for the work as is the case in India.[15]

The demand for wood of forest-based industry has been the major source of conflicts to which ecology movements like Chipko are a response. In the Himalayas, at the heart of the conflict over forest resources is the need of forest-based industries for species like pine, on the one hand, and the basic need of local villagers for species like oak, on the other. Responding to the needs of organized industry, the forest department has been planting pine at the expense of oak. Pine, unlike oak, is not useful for fodder or fertilizer; it upsets the hydrological balance of the mountain slopes, leading to increased floods and erosion, and decreased infiltration into subsoil and ground water sources. The drying up of springs and water sources has been a major cause of changes in vegetation. Chipko activists have been removing pine seedlings from forest department nurseries and replacing them with seeds of oak and fruit-bearing trees.

In other regions of India, too the demands of forest-based industry have led to drastic changes with severe ecological consequences. In the Western Ghats rich natural forests were felled to plant eucalyptus for the pulp industry. This was justified on the grounds that eucalyptus planting would increase the 'productivity' of the site—productivity for the cellulose-based industry. For the village communities the cultivation of eucalyptus was counterproductive. Large-scale eucalyptus monoculture upset the ecological equilibrium, since in the tropics stability is related to biological diversity.[16] Eucalyptus plantations in the Western Ghats, raised after clearfelling dense evergreen and moist deciduous forests, have themselves been devastated by fungal diseases; and the consequent low productivity has defeated the very purpose for which they were raised. In the Western Ghats the movement, known as 'Appiko', aims at stopping the destruction of natural forests which are critical to the survival of the agricultural community.

The needs of pulp-based industry cannot be satisfied without turning renewable land and vegetational resources into non-renewable ones. It may be noted that the conversion of fertile croplands into wasteland has the official sanction and international funding for so-called 'social forestry' programmes. Here is a glaring example of collusion between politicians and private interests to undermine the equitable and sustainable use of resources for development! A campaign called 'Munna Rakshana Koota' (Save the Soil) has been initiated to counter the threat posed to people's survival.

TECHNOLOGICAL DEVELOPMENT AND RESOURCE UNDER-DEVELOPMENT

Technological modernization is sold as a means of increasing productivity. Productivity here means productivity of labour (more production with less labour); it does not care for increasing the production of raw materials (that is, natural resources) which are an indispensable input for even the most sophisticated industry, nor does it care for making increasing production sustainable; it cares less for an equitable sharing of what is produced.

This limited definition of productivity, evolved in a specific context, has, however, been universalized, and the ruling elites in entirely different societies avidly subscribe to it in the name of 'national interest'. Labour-saving and resource-guzzling technology has been introduced in societies where labour is abundant and resources scarce. The development-planner has been brainwashed by education and training to believe that resource and resource processes that are not produced through excessive technological and capital inputs are valueless. This economic doctrine leads to a thoughtless destruction of natural resources which is the survival base of millions. The assertion in action of the simple truth, not self-evident to the planner, that human survival is a precondition for development is the central contribution of Chipko and other ecology movements to development alternatives. Chipko stresses the fact that for survival, satisfaction of two basic needs is enough: (a) the need for food and water, quantitatively and qualitatively enough for healthy biological survival, and, (b) the need for clothing and shelter necessary for physical survival.

Traditional economies with stable ecology, share with affluent economies the ability to use natural resources to satisfy these basic needs. The difference between them is two-fold: (a) in affluent societies the same needs are satisfied through longer technological chains requiring higher energy and resource inputs; and (b) affluent societies generate new and artificial wants to create a demand for increasing production of industrial goods and services. Traditional economies may not be advanced in the creation and satisfaction of non-basic needs; but in regard to the satisfaction of basic needs they are, barring natural disasters, what Marshall Sahlins calls 'the original affluent society'.

Economies based on indigenous technologies have been viewed as having lower productivity because of the distorted concept of productivity. With a sensible view of productivity as optimum use of natural resources and adequate labour these traditional technologies are usually very productive and efficient. The destruction of these technologies, along with the destruction of their material base, is generally the reason behind the poverty in societies which have been made to bear the cost of resource destruction for economic growth.

New technologies and new production processes are often merely new ways of satisfying basic needs or generating new non-basic needs. In societies where most resources are already being utilized for satisfaction of basic needs, diversion of resources to new uses for the satisfaction of non-basic wants threatens survival and therefore generates conflicts between the demands of growth and the demands of survival.[17] When, for instance, forest resources are already being fully utilized to stabilize soil and water, and to provide for the basic needs of food, fodder, fertilizer, fuel, etc., their diversion to the pulp industry makes no sense.

Growth or Destruction?

The much-used metaphor in the current paradigm of economic development is that the national cake must grow bigger if everyone is to get a bigger slice. Modern technologies are believed to increase the size of the cake, never mind if it does not achieve justice and peace.

Ecology movements challenge this paradigm by showing that modern technologies involve high ecological and social costs. In actual instances—such as in forestry—it is plain that the cake is actually shrinking because of the spread of resource-intensive, resource-wasteful, resource-demanding technologies.

The assumption of the technological solution to underdevelopment and poverty is related to the historical metaphors guiding the received view of economic development. Development is equated with economic growth, which is then reduced to the growth of technologies and hardware. Linear progression is the guiding principle; resource endowments, resource scarcity and resource conflicts are just ignored.

The paradigm of development guiding conventional policy and politics is based on the Rostowian model of stages of economic growth which assumes limitless resources. The first stage in this model is the traditional society whose structure is developed within: 'Limited production function, based on pre-Newtonian science and technology and on pre-Newtonian attitudes towards the physical world....The central fact about the traditional society was that a ceiling existed on the level of attainable output per head'.[18]

The fact that such societies had consciously chosen to adopt limited production functions to ensure sustainability and justice is not recognized. The second stage of growth, according to the Rostowian model, embraces societies in the process of transition from the traditional to the take-off stage. During this period of transition, it is assumed, the traditional society persists side-by-side with modern economic activities. It is this stage of transition which provided the backdrop for the common characterization of contemporary India as a 'dual sector' economy. The third stage is the take off 'When the old blocks and resistance to steady growth are finally overcome. The forces making for economic progress, which yielded limited bursts and enclaves of modern activity, expand and come to dominate society'.[19]

The Rostowian model of economic growth assumes that the process of modernization can ensure economic development for all groups because 'the economy exploits hitherto unused natural resources'. The new methods of production are therefore viewed as generating increased employment and consumption in an absolute sense. Growth, therefore is supposed to symbolize development in this model.

However, it is only in very exceptional cases that the natural resources consumed by modern production processes have been 'hitherto unused'. Their traditional utilization has remained invisible to modern technologists, economists and planners for two reasons.

1. Traditional utilization of natural resources has been predominantly for use and not for exchange. Since it is only the exchange value that gets noticed in modern economics, resources are declared unused or useless if they do not have exchange value, even if they have high use value. The role of forests as a common resource providing fuel, fodder, fertilizer etc., is not internal to forestry science or forestry economics; only their commercial yield is.

2. The traditional utilization of natural resources is calculated, not only by the extent of their consumption but also by their ecological function in maintaining the productive processes of nature which make sustained supply of resources possible. The failure or refusal to recognize these ecological functions of natural resources leads to their being viewed as unused even while they are being utilized economically in conservation. The invisible function of forests in soil and water conservation had to be made visible by the Chipko movement. It was not perceived by foresters.

Modernization based on resource-hungry processes materially deprives communities which use those resources for survival, either directly or through their ecological functions. The growth of pulp industry does not ensure development for all. On the contrary, it hits those communities who need water and land for agriculture. It causes underdevelopment of those affected negatively by resource diversion or destruction. Conflicting demands on resources lead to economic polarization through growth brought about by modern technology. It is therefore necessary to evaluate the role of new technologies in economic development on the scale of their resource demand. The productivity of a technology in the perspective of human survival must distinguish between basic and non-basic needs, because on the satisfaction of basic needs depends human survival. As Georgescu-Roegen points out:

There can be no doubt about it. Any use of the natural resources for the satisfaction of non-vital needs means a smaller quantity of life in the future. If we understand well the problem, the best use of our iron resources is to produce plows or harrows as they are needed, not Rolls Royces, not even agricultural tractors....[20]

Indicators conventionally used for measuring economic growth rate are insensitive to the difference between the satisfaction of vital and non-vital needs as well as to the differential contribution of economic growth to the diverse social groups and classes. These indicators focus on increasing the total consumption of non-vital commodities irrespective of how this increased consumption is linked with a decreasing availability of resources for the satisfaction of vital needs. In forestry, for example, while the major thrust in economic growth is towards production and consumption of non-vital industrial products like pulp, cement or steel, there is no serious attempt to stop the alarmingly quick rate of the destruction of natural water resources, for drinking or irrigation. In a world of finite resources, if the emphasis is on the satisfaction of non-vital needs, it can be done only at the cost of satisfaction of vital needs.

Civilizations that have survived without denying others the right to survival have always been guided by the criteria of technological choice which are sensitive to nature and man. The unit of assessment of technological productivity is the entire chain of technologies that transform natural resources into goods and services for human needs. Contemporary technology, however, leaves both nature and man out of the growth calculus. Technologies are considered fragments of value in themselves, never as a means for satisfying human needs. The technological shift that has taken place is a shift based on changing the value referents for human activity. Accelerating erosion of resources and poisoning of ecosystems are the inevitable outcome of this self-serving technology. The values of 'Artha' (resources) and 'Kama' (needs) are no longer primary. And there is no place for 'Dharma'—the stabilizer.

Ecology movements are an attempt to shift value back to nature and man. They are also an attempt to revive the earlier criteria for choosing technology. Peoples' ecology movements like Chipko attempt to do just that by redefining development in terms of different concepts of 'economic value' and 'productivity' in which symbiotic survival of man and nature is the central consideration.

The underdeveloped societies are not those that have yet to fall prey to the ideology of growth and development. The really underdeveloped societies are those in which a small section appropriates whatever benefits accrue from growth and a much larger section is made to pay for it. Rostow's take-off is integrally linked to this syndrome. Its forcing three continents into a state of underdevelopment made Britain's take-off at the end of the eighteenth century possible. The destruction of Indian textiles industry and Indian agriculture and much else besides, the slave trade from Africa and the genocide of the indigenous North American people provided the scaffolding for building modern industry in Britain. The Rostowian fiction of take-off for the whole society with improved quality of life for all appears seductive because under the historical conditions of colonialism the costs of growth were borne by the colonies while the entire population of the ruling countries benefited from the gains, notwithstanding the internal inequities in distribution. The vast geographical spaces separating the benefiting and the losing countries in the process of colonial exploitation made the resource destruction of the colonies invisible and led to the superficial impression that absolute growth was taking place. The model however, has been invalidated by the experience of countries which have attempted to follow the model: increasing poverty alongside economic growth. In the process the odious features of colonialism have emerged: interior and resource-rich interior areas of the country bear the costs of destruction of their resources while a small minority appropriates all the benefit. Communities living in these regions and supporting themselves on local resources are pushed to the wall. Ecology movements are a warning that when life is at stake even those on the margin can fight—non-violently, of course—with their backs to the wall. They are a reminder, too, that a radical shift in the received wisdom about economic development is overdue.

Societies have not always progressed on the Rostowian linear path. Societies that have been careless about their resource base for sustenance have collapsed after an initial spurt of prosperity. The collapse of the Mayan and the Mesopotamian civilization was associated with a collapse of their life-support systems. The threat to the survival of the sub-Saharan countries is again rooted in the destruction of life-support systems. History falsifies Rostow.

The ecological consciousness of ancient civilizations was based on cyclical progress, not along a linear path. But just as classical physics is incapable of explaining or understanding the motion of the electron, so is conventional economics incapable of understanding stable and ecologically sound development. It interprets stability as stagnation and ecologically sound development as 'limited production functions' (that is, without any movement whatever). Capturing this civilizational conflict between stable and unstable societies, Gandhi observed:

….It is a charge against India that her people are so uncivilized, ignorant and stolid that it is not possible to induce them to adopt any changes. It is a charge really against our strength. What we have tested and found true on the anvil of experience, we dare not change. Many thrust their advice upon India, but she remains steady. This is her beauty, it is the sheet anchor of our hope.[21]

The contemporary ecology movements like Chipko are a new Gandhian attempt in the Gandhian spirit to establish that steadiness and stability do not mean stagnation, and that balance with nature's innate ecological processes is not technological backwardness but technological sophistication. At a time when a quarter of the world's population is facing starvation due to erosion of soil, water and genetic diversity of living resources, running for the mirage of unending growth is a major source of genocide. Killing people by murdering nature is no longer an invisible form of violence. Claude Alvares has called it the Third World War—'a war waged in peace time, without comparison but involving the largest number of deaths and the largest number of soldiers without uniform'.[22]

Ecology movements are a non-violent intervention in this Third World War which threatens the survival of humanity, including even the victors. They are political movements for a non-violent world order in which nature is conserved for conserving the options for survival. They are movements on which issues of peace, development and environment converge.[23] These movements are local, but their impact is bound to be felt far beyond their small geographical boundaries; for the right of survival that they are demanding can be ensured in a just and peaceful world. That is how these grass-roots movements are linked with the global issue of peace. Unless the world is restructured in its lifestyle, peace and justice will continue to be elusive. As the Vedic poet realized, peace for man cannot be isolated from peace in the universe. He prayed 'Peace of sky, Peace of earth, peace of waters, peace of plants, peace of trees, peace of the universe, peace of peace, may that peace come to me'.[24]

Grass-roots ecology movements are basically striving for the realization of the old concept of 'Vasudhaiva Kutumbakam' (earth-family), in which peace means peace not only for man but for all living organisms.[25] Such a peace is not inconsistent with development; it is a precondition for a just and sustainable development.

NOTES

1. Mohamopadhyay Laxmithatachar, 'Srivaisnavite Precepts and Practice Concerning Environment', paper presented at a seminar on social and religious basis of environment policy (Bangalore, 1984).
2. M.K. Gandhi, *Hind Swaraj* (Ahmedabad: Navajivan Publishing House, 1938), p. 61.
3. Pyarelal, *Towards New Horizons* (Ahmedabad: Navajivan Publishing House, 1959), p. 12.
4. J. Bandyopadhyay and Vandana Shiva, 'The Evolution, Structure and Impact of Chipko', paper prepared for the UNU Himalaya–Ganges project (1984); and Sunderlal Bahuguna, *Chipko: A Novel Movement to Re-establish Cordial Relation between Man and Nature*.
5. H.C. Reiger, 'Whose Himalaya—A Study in Geopiety', in T. Singh (ed.), *Studies in Himalayan Ecology and Development Strategies* (New Delhi: The English Book Store, 1980).
6. M. Moench and J. Bandyopadhyaya, 'Dynamics of Resource Degradation in the Himalaya', paper presented at a seminar on Ecological Crises and Legislative Safeguards (New Delhi, 1984); and Bandyopadhyay and Shiva, 'The Evolution, Structure and Impact of Chipko'.
7. Bandyopadhyay and Shiva, 'The Evolution, Structure and Impact of Chipko'.

8. C.T.S. Nair, 'Crisis in Forest Management', paper presented at a seminar on Ecological Crises and Legislative Safeguards (New Delhi, 1984).
9. J. Bandyopadhyay, et al., The Doon Valley Ecosystem (1984) (mimeo).
10. Paul Feyerabend, Science in a Free Society (New York: Schocken Books, 1978), p. 10.
11. See, Ibid., p. 70.
12. Vandana Shiva, 'Hidden Variables and Nonlocality in Quantum Mechanics', Ph.D. thesis, University of Waterloo, Ontario, Canada.
13. Feyerabend, Science in a Free Society, p. 83.
14. J. Bandyopadhyay and V. Shiva, Ecological Audit of Eucalyptus (EBD, 1984).
15. M.K. Gandhi, Young India (25 July 1929), p. 2444.
16. Bandyopadhyay and Shiva, 'The Evolution, Structure and Impact of Chipko'.
17. J.Bandyopadhyay and V. Shiva, 'Political Economy of Technological Polarisations', Economic and Political Weekly, 18 (45), (1982), pp. 1827–32.
18. W.W. Rostow, The Stages of Economic Growth (Cambridge: Cambridge University Press, 1979), p. 4.
19. Ibid.
20. N.Georgescu-Roegen, The Entropy Law and the Economic Process (Harvard University Press, 1974), p. 2.
21. M.K. Gandhi, Hind Swaraj, p. 61.
22. C. Alvares, 'Deadly Development', Development Forum, 11 (7), (1973), pp. 3–4.
23. S. Bahuguna (personal letter).
24. Krishna Chaitanya, A Profounder Ecology: The Hindu View of Man and Nature (mimeo).
25. E. Lott, 'India's Religious Resources for Developing a Global Eco-Theology', paper presented at a seminar on social and religious basis of environmental policy (Bangalore, 1984).

Parks, People, and Protest
The Mediating Role of Environmental Action Groups*

RANJIT DWIVEDI

THE CONTEXT: PROTECTED AREAS AND THE CRITICAL DISCOURSE

Since the early 1970s, there has been a steady rise in the number and size of protected areas in developing countries, notably national parks and wildlife sanctuaries. In India, there are now about 520 protected areas (PAs), compared to 130 in 1975, spread over 148,700 sq kms. An estimated 3 million people live inside these PAs.[1] Although in some protected areas limited human interventions are allowed, people living in and around these areas face a systematic restriction of access rights and usufruct which in turn affects their entitlement portfolio. Further, people are frequently displaced from their original settlements, with or without adequate compensation, to make way for the PAs. Such actions are justified by the official conservation discourse, which regards local communities as the principal threat to forests and wildlife. The major preoccupation of forest authorities has been to limit human interference. This attitude has generated stiff resistance from the affected people. Thus protected areas become arenas of resource struggles.

To accommodate the subsistence and natural resource requirements of the local people the Government of India and aid agencies have devised a number of measures. The creation of buffer zones in the

---

* Originally published as 'Parks, People and Protest: The Mediating Role of Environmental Action Groups', *Sociological Bulletin*, 46 (2), 1977, pp. 209–43.

1970s, as part of the UNESCO's 'Man and Biosphere Programme' between strictly preserved areas and human settlements, was one such step.[2] Such programmes, too have been biased towards conservation objectives. Attempts to promote agricultural and rural development programmes alongside conservation measures have yielded poor results because of their largely experimental character, designed principally to reduce conflicts at the local level, rather than to generate sustainable livelihood opportunities and alternatives.

Their policy of conservation has enjoyed support from a sizable number of environmentalists located in urban areas. They believe that without state intervention, deforestation and wildlife depletion would be accelerated, given the pressures on forests from local communities on the other. Sustained lobbying by this group has influenced stringent legislation such as the Wild Life Protection Act (1972 and 1991), the Forest Conservation Act (1980) and the Environment Protection Act (1986).

In recent years, however, with the intensification of resource conflicts around protected areas, a new discourse of conservation has gained ground. It is highly critical of the government and the environmentalists who support the government. The government's strategies have been seriously questioned, for their top-down, non-participatory character and the urban environmentalists have been dubbed elitist for their failure to take cognizance of the social roots of environmental use and abuse. This critical discourse has largely bred on local-level struggles over access and use of resources and on the mediation of non-governmental organizations (NGOs) which are actively involved in such peoples' struggles for forest resources and environmental protection. This is a recent trend in conservation movements; it accords importance to grass-roots activism and demands that attention be given to human rights along with animal rights.

OBJECTIVES AND METHOD

The focus in this chapter is on a collective action programme—a campaign march called Yatra, traversing through several national parks and sanctuaries in central and western India. Organized by a conglomerate of NGOs, conservation groups, grass-roots organizations and environmentalists, the aim of the march was a critical assessment of official conservation policies and practices. It also attempted to initiate a dialogue among a wide range of actors affected by and associated with conservation to facilitate the participation of local people in evolving new strategies of conservation. A major part of this study is based on the participation in the campaign march. This technique of participatory research involved participation in informal discussions and group meetings, complemented by participatory observation and follow-up discussions with some of the principal organizers of the Yatra. To assess the public face of the march and its perceptions of nature and environment, the speeches made by the leaders of the Yatra from different platforms, documentation of some press briefings, and published material distributed by the organizers during the march are also analysed.

The chapter consists of four sections. The first section introduces the objectives and constituents of the Yatra. The second section identifies the major issues confronting the local communities that surfaced during the Yatra. The third section analyses the march as representing the critical discourse and examines its problems and prospects. The final section consists of some concluding remarks.

CONSTITUENTS OF THE YATRA

The Jungle Jivan Bachao Yatra

In the early months of 1995, the Jungle Jivan Bachao Yatra,[3] passed through several national parks and sanctuaries in western and central India. In September 1994, at a meeting of grass-roots—mostly NGO—activists held at the Indian Institute of Public Administration, New Delhi, a view was expressed that people living in and around national parks and sanctuaries had no forum to voice their concerns and that no attempt has been made to bring together these people and the officials of the forest and wildlife department, with the purpose of initiating a dialogue between them. The meeting highlighted the need to go 'beyond an articulation of the problems into an exploration of alternative strategies at conservation'.

Yatra: Form and Content

The use of the peaceful march as a strategy for mobilization dates back to the early days of the Indian freedom struggle. During the independence struggle, Gandhi used the *yatra* as an instrument of learning from the people and mobilizing them to protest against the state. Since those days the *yatra* has become an established political strategy in the country.[4] This mode of campaigning has been used in the environment movement as well. The Jungle Jiven Bachao Yatra bears legacy to a series of similar marches—the Save the Western Ghat March, the Sangharsh Yatra in the Narmada Valley to protest against the

Sardar Sarovar Project, and the Save the Aravalli Padyatra undertaken by different actors of the environmental movement in India.

The purposes of the Yatra were to ascertain the conditions of wildlife and human habitat in protected areas and to learn about the perceptions of different social actors and their experiences. Thus, it was a 'journey of discovery'. But this learning process was part of a wider mobilization strategy geared towards bringing together hitherto isolated and localized organizations, groups and grass-roots activists into a wider network, for synthesizing shared experiences as well as formulating strategies. Therefore the Yatra was also a protest campaign over existing conservation thinking and management, documenting and voicing evidence of their non-participatory, elitist and ineffective character. Representing, as it was, various social actors articulating and mediating resource conflicts emerging from state conservation practices, the Yatra was to 'help form bridges between such persons and groups so as to secure the future of these habitats (sanctuaries and national parks) and the wildlife they contain'.[5]

The Yatra, being the brainchild of a group of NGOs and individuals actively involved in conservation, was endowed with an *a priori* understanding of causes of the continuous decline of the protected areas. This understanding was meant to be sharpened with the marshalling of concrete experiences and evidence across states, so as to build up strong bases for demanding more effective and participatory conservation.

Constituents

The participants in the Yatra were members of conservation groups, NGOs and representatives of local communities living in and around the protected areas.[6] The latter were drawn primarily from the areas on which a few of the organizers had some influence. These community representatives were directly or indirectly involved in the activities of their respective local NGOs. Overall, the *yatris* comprised a group of urban conservationists, researchers, activists and representatives of affected rural communities.

Four NGOs were assigned the task of organizing the Yatra; the Tarun Bharat Sangh of Rajasthan, the Centre for Environment Education of Gujarat, the Maharashtra Arogya Mandal and the Ekta Parishad of Madhya Pradesh. These NGOs undertook to organize the march in their respective states. Local grass-roots organizations were also mobilized. In a few places, particularly in Gujarat, the forest and wildlife department of the government played host. The modus operandi of the Yatra was to exchange ideas and discuss problems with local NGOs and concerned officials, visit the protected areas, campaign at the village level and discuss problems with the local communities.

Itinerary

Using two jeeps, a mini-bus and a car the Yatra covered a distance of about 14,000 km over a period of 50 days, traversing 18 national parks and sanctuaries in Rajasthan, Gujarat, Maharashtra, Madhya Pradesh, Uttar Pradesh and Delhi. On an average the Yatra consisted of about 30 people although this number swelled on occasion as local community organizations and activists joined it.

The itinerary included Sariska Tiger Reserve, the Keoladevo National Park in Bharatpur, Ranthambore National Park in Sawai Madhavpur, Jamwanagar Sanctuary near Jaipur and Phulwri Ki Nall near Udaipur all located in Rajasthan, the Gir National Park, the Girnar Reserve, Hingolgarh Sanctuary and Shoolpaneswar Sanctuary, and some Joint Forest Management Schemes undertaken by the forest department in Gujarat, the Borivelli Reserve in Bombay, Koyna Sanctuary, Radhanagari Sanctuary, the Melghat Tiger Reserve and the Bhimashankar Sanctuary in Maharashtra, the Kanha Tiger Reserve and the Pench Reserve in Madhya Pradesh and the Shivpuri and Rajaji National Parks of Uttar Pradesh. The Yatra culminated in Delhi after a visit to the Delhi Ridge. A concluding two-day convention was held in Delhi to evaluate the achievements and plan follow-up actions.

MAJOR ISSUES DURING THE YATRA

Contours of Resource Conflicts

The following summaries reflect the nature of resource conflicts in some of the protected areas covered during the Yatra.

Pastoral Rights

One of the most frequently voiced demands that the yatra documented and supported was the restoration of the traditional grazing rights of the local pastoral communities. The ban on grazing has been overtly resisted in Bharatpur and Ranthambore (Rajasthan), and in Rajaji National Park (Uttar Pradesh) where the local Gujjar community has carried on a protracted agitation against it. Resistance is also visible in routine everyday forms, subverting official regulations and sanctions. Bribing forest guards is the common practice. Very often cattle just stray into the parks, especially during the monsoon seasons. The popular belief is that cattle instinctively run towards the forest at the onset of monsoons.

The ban on grazing has indeed affected the pastoral community. In Melghat, for instance, where officials had sanctioned allotments for fodder development programmes in the buffer zones, it has not altered the reluctance of local communities to carry head loads of grass to feed their cattle. 'Why should one carry head-loads when the cattle can just walk in and eat?', ask the villagers from Merhat in the Melghat Sanctuary, referring obviously to the thick growth of grass which has been the consequence of the ban on grazing. This reluctance, however, has earned them the epithet of 'lazy people' who function in a 'zero cost economy'.

Fuel-Wood Crisis

For rural communities living in and adjacent to sanctuaries and parks the availability of fuel wood itself is not as acute a problem as it is for their rural counterparts elsewhere; their problem is one of access because of the stringent regulations governing the protected areas. In many of these areas, to get fuel wood people bribe forest guards. The system has become institutionalized in many places in the form of fixed rates per head-load. For the poorer households, such illegal collection is also a source of income; they can sell fuel wood in the nearby villages and towns. Such collection and sale of fuel wood is entirely carried out by women and children. Local communities also face difficulties in procuring fuel wood for special occasions like funerals and weddings when large quantities are required, and hence they resort to bribing the forest guards. Their representatives have pointed out that although the wood brought for funerals is prohibited for other uses, quantities much in excess of the requirement for such occasions are collected because a bribe is paid.[7] Local activists support such arguments and even suggest that free access to such resources will have a less damaging impact, because people would then take only what they require. This view is contradicted by the official position according to which free access causes inefficient use of resources and could lead to denudation of forests and acute scarcity of fuel wood.

The middle ground between these contending positions is now being explored under the Joint Forest Management (JFM) schemes being implemented by some state governments. Under the JFM scheme, the forest department takes on the protection, regeneration and plantation of forests with the help of the local communities so as to primarily cater to the fuel wood and fodder needs of the communities. There are also direct economic benefits. When dense patches are periodically loomed, cleaned and the timber sold, the local community gets 25 per cent of the sale. After 25 years, when the forest matures for harvesting, 50 per cent of the sales proceeds' would accrue to the local community.

In Mandvi village, where this scheme was in operation, the panchayat leader explained its mechanics. The area had dense forests 50 years ago, but pressures largely from the local communities led to depletion and degradation. Facing severe crises of fuel wood, fodder and logs for house repair, the communities agreed to the JFM scheme which was initiated with 65 members on 25 hectares of land. Today, all the village households are covered under this scheme and the entire forest area in the region (of about 500 hectares) has been brought under it. The villagers have access to fodder and fuel wood from these areas and their requirements are regulated by the JFM village committee.

Despite its innovative features and its relative success the scheme has been viewed with suspicion for several reasons. First, with the initiation of JFM schemes on pasture land under the forest department, their character as village commons with open access has changed to controlled access only for the members of the JFM committee in the village.[8] Often the poorer inhabitants, backward tribal communities and women of the villages are left out of such committees.[9] This means that the rural male elite who already own and control agricultural land would extend its control to forests and forest products as well. Second, these schemes prove to be environmentally unsustainable because they promote monoculture of the species which have high market value, thereby reducing biodiversity. The proposed harvest of the forest in 20 years implies that nothing of the 'forest' would remain after the harvest. Thirdly, the participatory element of the scheme is very much restricted only to protection of the forests and is in no way demonstrative of any joint 'management'. All the major decisions are taken by the officials of the forest department. Although the plan was to hand over the forest for local management after the first five years, the tardiness in registering the JFM committee have led to delay in its implementation.

Minor Forest Products

Although government resolutions and legislation on the collection, harvesting and trading of MFPs (minor forest products) differ from state to state, it is well known that most of the states prefer to retain monopoly rights over profitable MFPs. Usually *kendu/bidi* leaves[10] form the maximum share—about 45 per cent—in the returns from MFPs. In the financial year 1993–4, the Madhya Pradesh government's annual turnover from this sector was Rs 200 crores. Other MFPs yield less but their contribution is nevertheless substantial. In the Balaram Sanctuary in Banaskantha District in Gujarat, the turnover from gum is estimated to be roughly Rs 15 lakh per week during the peak season. Where the states have allowed private trading of MFPs, big monopolies have emerged. In Gujarat, the *bidi* business is controlled by three traders, one of whom controls the trade in 40 of the 120 units that constitute the Gujarat forests. This is despite the fact that the monopoly over MFPs lies with the Gujarat Forest Development Corporation.

However, the collection and petty trading of MFPs are crucial for the survival needs and income augmentation of the poor, particularly in the tribal areas. Fruits, roots and berries are added to the survival portfolio in the most vulnerable months; vegetables are collected usually after two months of rain. Gum, *mahua*, lac, honey and *saag* seed are other major MFPs that provide additional income to the local forest communities.

The collection cycle of MFPs suggests that income from these is crucial for survival during the dry months until the agriculture season begins after the rains. The demand for access to and control over MFPs was clearly articulated in the Vasava villages in Shoolpaneswar where the Gujarat Vanavasi Sangathan has been demanding the abolition of the monopoly of the Gujarat Forest Development Corporation, a free market, and fair prices for the MFP. In at least two other parks representatives of the local communities demanded access to MFPs and expected the Yatra to take up this issue with the officials in Delhi.

Commercial and Industrial Pressures

While local communities have systematically experienced curtailment of usufruct and access rights to forests and in many places have been displaced from their original habitats, all in the name of conservation, in the majority of the parks, commercial and industrial activities which are detrimental to the cause of conservation have been allowed. As these areas gradually become degraded, pressures from powerful interest groups lead to their denotification. Many national parks and sanctuaries such as the Melghat and Rahanagari in Maharashtra, the Narayan Sarovar in Gujarat, Bhitarkanika and Balukhand in Orissa have either been denotified or face denotification. The Narayan Sarovar Sanctuary in Kutch, for example, has recently been denotified to make way for a cement factory, while the Gulf of Kutch marine national park faces denotification because of a proposed oil refinery by the Reliance industries.

The Yatra came across several ongoing commercial activities in the protected areas. Large-scale bamboo extraction from the Shoolpaneswar Sanctuary by the Central Pulp Mills has been allowed, while the forest officials harass local villagers wanting fuel wood or small timber for house repairs. Open-cast marble mining is also carried out in and around the Jamva Ramgarh Sanctuary in Rajasthan. In Ranthambore, the Geological Survey of India is now carrying out a prospective survey of mineral areas adjacent to the park.

Such activities are nevertheless supported by conservation officials. For instance, bamboo extraction was justified on the ground that it allowed sunlight into the park which the herbivorous animals liked! Mineral exploration and mining were justified for their economic benefits and for providing employment opportunities to the local population. And when the issue of general corruption was taken up for discussion in the context of illegal logging in the park areas, the response was that the entire system is corrupt and it was unfair to isolate the forest department for criticism. As one official put it, 'So long as a sleeping berth in a railway train is available for (a bribe of) Rs 100 the problem of corruption will continue to exist'.

Crop Damage by Wild Animals

Crop damage by the wild animals led to a direct clash of interests between the local communities and conservation groups. The loss to the local economy at places is computed to be 50 per cent of the total crop output. In 1987, the Maharashtra Arogya Mandal attempted to quantify the extent of crop damage by wild boars. A survey conducted in 25 hamlets that year revealed that about 96,000 kgs of grain was destroyed by wild animals, resulting in a loss of Rs 232,000. In 1993, the survey was repeated and the damage computed was 90,820 kg of grain valued at Rs 453,000.

While state governments offer compensation for attacks on people and cattle and humans by wild animals, crop damage, which is more rampant, has been kept out of the purview of compensation. In fact, officials claim that compensation schemes for crop damages do not exist because of the difficulties in devising and implementing them.[11] Preventive measures which could minimize the damage, such as translocation of wild animals, fencing of parks and sanctuaries, financial allocations for employing watchmen and even (as one local group suggested) castration of the male animals, require more funds. The officials also have to shed their apathy to such problems.

Extensive crop damage usually occurs because of over breeding among herbivores. Of course, park officials attribute the increase of herbivores to successful conservation strategies. But this increase could well be due to a sharp decline in the number of carnivores. It is not coincidental that in protected areas where there is reported merciless poaching of leopards and tigers, crop damage from herbivores is simultaneously reported and has become a serious problem.

Forest Land and Forest Wage Labour

'Encroachments' on forest land, and the demands for regularization of such lands have been contentious issues for the conservation movement. Cultivation of forest land is an age-old and widespread practice primarily, though not exclusively, in Adivasi areas. In some areas in western India, the forest department itself has leased out land for a specific tenure for cultivation. Even then, major portions of forest land under cultivation are deemed to have been 'encroached' upon by the state agencies. The fact that population pressure and the consequent ecological pressure on the local communities forces them to bring more forest land under cultivation is, however, entirely ignored.

Within the conservation movement itself, demands for regularization do not find much support and are treated with suspicion. The Yatra revealed the uneasiness of conservationists when confronted with such demands. The struggles in the Dangs and in Shoolpaneswar over 'encroachment' received almost no attention compared to other elements of conflicts that the Yatra chose to highlight. The issue of exploitative labour regimes in the forests was also left out of the Yatra's discourse. Given that these regimes are hidden from the public gaze, the Yatra could at least have brought to light the high-handedness of the forest officials in interpreting labour laws.

Standard Environmental Narrative

The Yatra represented several organizations and action groups with differing perspectives on and approaches to conservation. The minimal consensus that prevailed over the issue of conservation related to the resource conflict between urban/industrial and local needs. Throughout the Yatra the leaders took recourse to populist rhetoric on the rural-urban divide by highlighting the rising consumption demands of the urban industrial enclaves, condemning the urban way of life and eulogizing the virtues of rural living and its customary bond with nature and environment. The rationale of the Yatra to a village gathering was explained thus by Rajinder Singh:

When governments talk of forest destruction they state that people living in villages are irresponsible and they destroy forests. They keep attaching this stigma on us, whereas actually they are the ones who have played a major role in the destruction process. We want to bring this truth to light before the world, before the nation and the people that those who have been hitherto accused (by the government) of destroying forests do not actually do so....In this yatra we... want to erase this stigma attached to villagers as destroyers of forests. Villagers do not cut forests, for they know that their lives are dependent on it.[12]

In an encounter with some forest officials Singh claimed; 'I do not, for one, believe that people for whom forests are an integral part of their lives, a base for their livelihood, are not worried about them. There is no evidence whatsoever to prove that something that gives the people air, food, medicines and milk is being ignored by them'. Kusum Karnik of the Maharashtra Arogya Mandal, another leader, said in one of her speeches:

We (people living in villages around forests) are poor people, we only bring minor products and other such items from the forests. We never destroy the forests. Is it possible for us to cut those huge trees and carry them to our homes? Small twigs and branches are enough for us. The forest is our mother. We have lived with it. It is an age old bond. If the government wants us to break this relationship, we will not do so. The fact is that the wood from the forests are required by the rich, the urbanites, because they need huge cots, tables and chairs. They even need their handkerchiefs to be made out of paper. They care little about our forests getting depleted. We, the people who live in the forest, know it like we know our mothers. We live by drinking its milk and not its blood.[13]

Such a projection of the rural community was not just a strategy of consciousness-raising nor was it a confidence-winning measure. It reflected the Yatra's understanding of the problems and prospects of conservation, which can be summed up as follows:

1. People living in and around forests are critically dependent on the forests for their livelihood. Because of this dependency they share an integral bond with the forests and live in harmony with them. Age-old traditions and customs guide the manner in which people in these communities use the forest resources. This relationship is neither extractive nor exploitative.

2. Conservation policies adopted by the government in recent years have alienated the local people from their traditional resource base while privileging urban industrial needs. This has resulted in the wanton destruction of wildlife habitats.

3. Despite the alienation most of the people in these communities are inclined towards conservation and protection of the forests. Hence conservation policies must address the question of participation, making use, in the process, of traditional conservation methods and practices.

4. Participation also implies sharing in the benefits of conservation by granting the local communities access to and control over the distribution of forest resources so that their livelihood needs are met.

CRITICAL DISCOURSE OF THE YATRA

Public Face of the Yatra

The Yatra's understanding on conservation apart, it was important for it to define the interests that it represented. With a fair share of urban nature lovers and environmentalists participating, it was almost compelled to magnify its rural orientation, in order to live up to the image it had come to project of itself.

The Yatra was therefore projected as representing the interests of those village communities which have experienced the adverse effects of official conservation practices. It provided a platform for communities living in and around protected areas to come together and exchange their ideas and experiences with each other. On several occasions the leaders, who were themselves NGO activists, projected the Yatra as representing rural communities hailing from different parts of the country.[14] The names of these *yatris*—Nanak Ram, Sedu Ram, Prabhu Gujjar, Mohammad Khan and Bechain Das—were repeatedly mentioned, particularly in village-level meetings and press conferences. The fact that the Yatra had a sizable (more than two-thirds) contingent of urban environmentalists and 'urban' NGO activists—interacting with but certainly not belonging to the grass-roots, was deliberately sidelined.

Towards this end, Nanak Ram Gujjar, a community leader of Haripura village in Sariska, played a significant role and served as a symbol *par excellence* for the Yatra's public face. He had been in the forefront of the Sariska struggle against mining along with the Tarun Bharat Sangh and had also participated in the Save the Aravalli March from Sariska to Delhi. These experiences made Nanak Ram conversant with the prevailing critical discourse on conservation, as was amply demonstrated when he spoke during the Yatra:

We have a bond, a relationship with the forests and we have to work towards their protection. Nothing can be left to the government. (If so) it will only result in the depletion of the forests. Forests and tigers are fast dwindling. The local communities need to get united and organized to save their forests.[15]

In Nanak Ram's view, the Yatra represented the voice and perception of the rural subaltern, essentially the nature loving, and those working against all odds to protect forests and lives from the destructive designs of the state. His dramatic rendition of the 'Sariska story' only reiterated this fact:

During early days there were a lot of tigers and wolves in the forests and they would eat a lot of our cattle. But we never bothered about such loss. For we know that the tiger is the king of the forests [sic] and is also a predator....When the tiger project in Sariska was initiated, the government first formed the sanctuary and then later on converted it into a national park and occupied it. The laws enabled them to kill the tigers, skin them, bury their flesh and sell the skin in the big cities. All this while, we were deprived systematically of our customary rights. While initially the government said that nothing would happen to us, in about two years it cut our throat with such force that we did not even get a place to urinate.[16]

As well as telling the story well, there was an acknowledgement of the dominant role of Rajinder Singh ('Bhaisahab') and his Tarun Bharat Sangh in the struggle at Sariska. Thus not only was Nanak Ram making the Yatra's claim of rural representation legitimate, he was also effectively endorsing the activities of conservation groups and NGOs at the grass-roots.

The ruralization of the Yatra's image was in many ways necessary. How else could it differentiate itself from the nature lovers among the urban middle-class elite, who were the early actors of the conservation movement in India? The contribution of this section of the movement for nature preservation notwithstanding, the emergence and articulation of new social actors with a strong grass-roots base has exposed such conservation policies and strategies as elitist. However, this difference in perceptions between the old and the new actors has not prevented them from coming together. The success of the Yatra demonstrates the growing ties between these two sets of actors. The Yatra in its conception, objectives and its protagonists, reflected the growing bond between the two sets of actors. Yet the new actors of the conservation movement have staked claims to a new constituency of rural interests. The rural face of the Yatra was therefore a prerequisite if its claim to speak on behalf of the rural subaltern was to be justified. Nanak Ram's contribution was to render this claim legitimate.

This trend is characteristic of almost all major environmental movements in India. As grass-roots problems begin to dominate the environmental agenda, a struggle over representation of rural interests ensures in which different social actors, including the state, claim to be working in the interest of this new constituency. Persons such as Nanak Ram symbolize these new claims. The example of the famous Narmada Bachao Andolan (NBA) against the Sardar Sarovar Project is illuminating. In Narayan Bhai Tadvi, the sarpanch of Manibeli, the first village facing submergence in Maharashtra, the NBA has found a spokesperson well-conversant with its lexicon. In NBA's public disposition, Narayan Bhai Tadvi constitutes the subaltern. While the leaders claim representation of the subaltern, Tadvi, like Nanak Ram, ratifies these claims.

It is important to underscore the fact that the state agencies, on their part, have also begun to adopt similar strategies in order to gain legitimacy for their actions at the level of the grass-roots. The Joint Forest Management sites in Gujarat highlight this point well, with forest officials presenting the local panchayat leaders to speak about the success of the scheme in their areas and the benefits they have derived from these projects. Of all the meetings that the Yatra attended those connected with JFM and involving forest officials became the most vociferous and unpleasant. The point is that the clash of the Yatra leadership and the forest officials was as much over the functioning of the JFM scheme as over the government agencies' claim to represent the interests of the grass-roots.

Private is Political

While significant efforts were directed towards projecting the rural face of the Yatra as its authentic face, the rural participants had very little role to play in organization and decision-making during the Yatra. The majority of them—relatively well-off and elderly, with less familial responsibilities—were just happy to be a part of it. For them, it was a sort of a pilgrimage, an opportunity to visit different places.[17] For the leadership, rural participants were precious cargo, whose comfort was to be ensured. Input from them was however, deemed unnecessary.

The decision-making, of course, was the prerogative of its leaders. But they often had sharp differences. In fact, at one point the Yatra was to split into two; one faction wanted to go to Narayan Sarovar Marine Park, and the other to Gir forests. Timely interventions prevented a serious split. While these incidents could be dismissed as insignificant—dissent being integral to democratic practice—they are indicative of the character of the Yatra leadership. For any protest movement, leaders are important, as is the case with the environmental movement. There is a tendency to rely heavily on charismatic leaders, to mobilize people and resources for such movements. But this may prove adverse to institution-building. The split which the Yatra faced was the outcome of a clash of personalities rather than a dispute over issues at hand.

Empowerment: Class Blind, Gender Sensitive

Despite reflecting a few disturbing trends within the environmental movement, the Yatra established that social actors working at the grass-roots can achieve significant success in mobilizing and organizing people. In Sariska and Shoolpaneswar, the Tarun Bharat Sangh and the Arch Vahini respectively, organized the local population to articulate their demands and intervened through socio-economic projects to alter the prevalent conditions and perceptions of the people. Thus if Sariska can boast of a 'Sanchuri', a sanctuary declared and maintained by the local people, with locally set rules and sanctions, the mobilization at Shoolpaneswar has resulted in a strong people's movement, which not only demands the denotification of the sanctuary but also the infrastructure facilities: irrigation, power and access to markets.

The limitations, however, have been in the conceptualization of rural people as homogeneous entities. In making the rural–urban divide the central problem, the disparities that exist within the rural population get neglected. While this may not be a major problem in tribal areas where land holdings and other means of livelihood are more evenly dispersed between regions, the village population is sharply divided along class lines. For instance, in the villages around the Sariska Reserve, land distribution is very uneven. Among those gathered at Mallena to send off the Yatra were people who owned as little as 3 *bigha*s of land while others owned more than 150 *bigha*s. For the marginal farmers and the landless in this area, small cattle holding and non-farm occupations are vital for sustenance. During visits to some mine sites, the local, largely landless people, confessed that the closure of mines in the area has severely affected their economic conditions, and even asked some of the *yatri*s to ensure their resumption.[18] The assumption, therefore, that the benefits from local access and control will accrue equally to all sections often turns out to be erroneous.

The gender divide within the rural population was also glossed over though the Yatra revealed more sensitivity to it as a problem. In the sites visited, the collection and sale of fuel wood and MFPs were women's jobs. Women also worked as forest wage labourers for private contractors or under government schemes. The specific nature of their problems necessitated not just a degree of sensitivity but a well-formulated strategy to properly document their perceptions. Apart from Shoolpaneswar, where women turned up in large numbers and spoke about their problems, in other places the Yatra heard only male voices. Women, though encouraged to speak, seldom did so. During dialogues with forest officials, government schemes under the eco-development projects were scrutinized for gender sensitivity. In one such encounter, the Yatra had to account for its own under-representation of women. During a meeting with the forest officials and beneficiaries of the JFM schemes at Jara village in Gujarat, some *yatri*s were critical of the lack of representation of women among the people who were gathered. The District Forest Officer, while explaining the difficulties in mobilizing women, in turn wondered why there were so few women in the Yatra!

What needs to be clarified here is the fact that the Yatra had no specific agenda or action plan to document problems specific to women, a fact that may be attributed to the lack of an informed women's perspective on conservation-related resource conflict. Unlike the class question though, which it deliberately ignored, it did demonstrate a general awareness of the women's question and expressed a need to incorporate it in the agenda of the conservation movement.

* * *

New Politics and Populism

The Yatra reflected the general political trend of the conservation movement. Conservation politics has witnessed a shift in agency from urban environmentalists to grass-roots activists. The central focus of the agitation has moved from conservation of wilderness to integrating human needs into conservation. The agitational mode/form no longer relies predominantly on lobbying but on grass-roots activism. These shifts have decisively redefined the boundaries of conservation politics. While it would be appropriate to welcome such shifts towards community rights of access and control, one needs to be cautious, particularly in lending support to movements which turn out to be populist in form and content. In the discourse of the Yatra, rural communities were projected not just as having a unified set of interests but also as essentially conservationist in their approach to nature and environment. Activities of the rural people which were detrimental to the cause of conservation, were considered as proof of their alienation from their productive resources, which was seen as the consequence of a 'non-participatory, elitist' conservation agenda. The existential realities amidst which rural communities live and within which they demand roads, water, irrigation facilities and employment opportunities, quite apart from their grievances over deprivation of forest resources, were suppressed to focus on a seemingly broader set of contradictions between local usufruct and access on the one hand and state-led conservation strategies on the other.

End as the Beginning

In the concluding convention held in Delhi on 28 February 1995 some of these tenets of the Yatra were critically reviewed by a group of invited environmentalists, activists, intellectuals and researchers. The use of the 'rural-urban divide' was singled out for its erroneous implications. As one of the invitees pointed out: 'To understand that all is well in the urban areas is naïve, for about 70 per cent of the population in these areas is in acute poverty, struggling for sustenance'.[19] The Yatra's lack of understanding of the industrialization process was also debated, with some participants expressing dissatisfaction with the piecemeal approach: that is, tackling each problem in each sanctuary, be it mining or bamboo extraction, in isolation from others, and without considering wider trends and ramifications.

The self-evaluation of the Yatra was, however, generally positive. It was considered to have been an important event, full of experiences, which should be followed up by devising strategies to bring together different grass-roots organizations and radical platforms 'under one roof, with unity and common principles'. The need was felt to work towards ensuring a people's movement on conservation and to have 'links with other similar movements on water, forests and land', with the final objectives of 'forming a strong people's organization in the country and a composite people's plan on water, forests and land'.[20] The end of the Yatra, therefore, was considered to be the start of a long, and difficult road ahead.

Revising the Critical Discourse

The optimistic note on which the Yatra ended raises some questions regarding the future of conservation in India and the scope for resolution of natural resource conflicts around protected areas. It is now widely accepted that existing conservation policies cause resource conflicts. At one level they have failed to yield the desired results—wildlife habitats over the years have dwindled and become degraded due to inefficient forest management and inability to resist industrial and commercial pressures. At another level, they have alienated local communities, depriving them of resources and therefore generating resource conflicts. Therefore, the conservation movement should attempt to reverse both the degradation process and the alienation of local communities. To succeed in meeting these twin objectives it is necessary to properly assess the clash between animal rights and human rights on the one hand and between industrial needs on the other. But the preconceived notion that rural communities are conservationist, prevents effective intervention. The very fact that the Yatra concluded with a series of policy recommendations[21] in which the state was assigned a crucial role underscores a tacit lack of faith in the local communities and the NGOs, and their ability to undertake conservation operations. There is a need to shed populism and to engage in community awareness and empowerment projects. To date, the new protagonists of conservation have only demonstrated their capability in raising community aware-ness. Given the undemocratic relationships between them and the local communities which were amply evident during the Yatra, the empowerment project could well be a pipe dream.

In conclusion, it can be said that the Yatra, in representing the recent trends within the conservation movement, exhibited both hope and concern. While it pointed out the hurdles blocking the resolution of conflicts over conservation it also highlighted the opportunities to resolve them. A major cause for concern revolves around the manner in which rural communities and their interests are projected. Unless the tendency to reify the grass-roots is overcome, the new agents of the conservation movement are unlikely to become agents of change and empowerment, no matter how hopeful the prospect may seem in the beginning.

NOTES

1. A national survey conducted in 1989 showed that about 70 per cent of the surveyed protected areas had people living within their boundaries and about 65 per cent of the areas were involved in leases, concessions, and community rights. For more details see A. Kothari *et al.*, *Management of National Parks and Sanctuaries in India: A Status Report* (New Delhi: Indian Institute of Public Administration [IIPA], 1989).
2. A task force set up by the Indian government in 1982 recommended a multiple use zone in the PAs in which eco-development measures such as land and water conservation could be promoted.
3. The rather awkward but literal translation in English is 'Journey to Save Forests and Forest Lives'.
4. The groups represented were Tarun Bharat Sangh based in Alwar district in Rajasthan, Maharashtra Arogya Mandal based in Pune district in Maharashtra, Ekta Parishad from Madhya Pradesh. The Adivasi Ekta Vikas Mandal and the Centre for Environment Education in Gujarat, Kalpavriksha from Delhi, the Bombay Natural History Society, and the Keoladeo Research Foundation from Bharatpur, Rajasthan.
5. The convoy also included a film crew that recorded the entire march—proceedings of meetings, press briefings—as well as the conditions of the protected sites, the wildlife therein and the ongoing activities inside the parks pertaining to conservation and deforestation. The crew also interviewed government officials, NGO activists, and local community representatives.
6. For the purpose of this research the yatra was covered only till Bhimashankar. The participation in its proceedings was resumed again at Delhi, after the *yatris* left the Rajaji National Park.
7. A testimony to this affect was given in Ranthambore where an educated

young man claimed to have brought wood worth Rs 500 after having paid a bribe of Rs 50 on the excuse that he needed to cremate a body.

8. The JFM schemes are also being undertaken on private revenue land.

9. In fact, forest department officials openly admitted that they have made no attempt whatsoever to accommodate these sections. The DFO of the eastern division of the Bhruch-dang Circle in Jara village, clearly stated that to attempt to integrate all the communities in the village is a futile exercise and one would only 'burn one's fingers' if such attempts were made.

10. The *kendu* leaves are dried and use to roll tobacco for smoking.

11. In Ranthambore, the *yatris* were asked by government officials to suggest ways in which the department can put in place a compensation scheme for crop damages.

12. Speech, Village Mallana, 14 January 1995.

13. Speech, Village Bodhal, 18 January 1995.

14. The range of actors who use this mode of campaigning is quite wide. At one level, mainstream political parties have used it to mobilize support for their politics. The Rath Yatra of the Bharatiya Janata Party, used for mobilizing support for building the Ram Temple in Ayodhya, is a good example. On the other hand, individual actors—politicians, philanthropist and social workers—have also undertaken such journeys. The Bharat Jodo Yatra of the noted social worker, Baba Amte, was undertaken to raise awareness on nation-building and national integrity.

15. Speech, Village Bodhal, 18 January 1995.

16. Ibid.

17. The simple vegetarian meals, the early morning prayers and the preference for politically correct music actually served to create the atmosphere of a pilgrimage.

18. At one place, where some of the *yatris* had gathered for tea, a small group complained about the closure of mines in the area and asked if something could be done. When others present warned those who were complaining that the Yatra was actually full of people instrumental in closing the mines, the topic of conversation, immediately thereafter changes to the benefits of mine closure for the local people!

19. Dunu Roy, 'Proceedings of the Concluding Convention of the Yatra' (Raj Ghat, Delhi, 28 February 1995).

20. Ibid.

21. The following policy recommendations were made at the end of the Yatra:

   (a) A clear and strict national policy which prohibits industrial, urban and commercial encroachment on protected areas, including a ban on denotifying protected areas for such purposes.

   (b) An official recognition of the legitimate resource rights and needs of local traditional communities and measures to meet these needs.

   (c) A central role for local communities in the planning, protection and monitoring of protected areas, including in the determination and enforcement of inviolate core zones and sustainable-use buffer zones.

(d) Planning the management of protected areas based on a healthy interaction between formal ecological science and traditional knowledge, learning especially from traditional practices which have helped to conserve and promote sustainable use of natural resources.

(e) Greater sharing of the benefits of the protected areas, including biomass rights, tourism income, employment in wildlife/forest related work and alternative livelihood opportunities. See, *JPM Update No.3* (New Delhi: Indian Institute of Public Administration [IIPA], March, 1995).

Protests against Displacement by Development Projects

T.K. Oommen

Development, driven by high technology and sponsored by the State, was the refrain of post-colonial societies of Asia and Africa. India was at the forefront of this endeavour. However, the unanticipated consequences of this process gradually surfaced, and civil society organizations and social movements started interrogating this route to development. Protests against displacement caused by development projects have become common in India in the last couple of decades. This chapter traces the trajectories of different types of mobilizations in Independent India, with a focus on the well-known Narmada Bachao Andolan (NBA), and one of the resource-rich but economically backward states in India, namely, Orissa.

THEORY AND RESEARCH: FILLING THE GAP

Displacement is widely perceived as inevitable in the course of development. Thus, the rural is to be displaced by the urban; agriculture by industry; low, simple, or traditional technology by high, complex, or modern technology. But the obsession with a particular pattern of 'development' and displacement it entails is playing havoc with people and, hence, the need to turn the spotlight on it. However, it may be noted here that crystallization of protest is intense now because of two reasons: (a) the unanticipated consequences of displacement became visible only gradually; and (b) the legitimation accorded to high-technology-driven development rendered interrogating it particularly problematic.[1]

Having acknowledged this, let me address the 'trained incapacity' of both the development social scientists and social movement theorists. Some writers have already pointed out that despite the convergence between studies in social movements and policies, the estrangement between them persists.[2] Let me amplify.

Those who did research on the sociology of social movements (which needs to be distinguished from psychological accounts of social movements) initially viewed them as anti-systemic eruptions. Their commitment appeared to be getting the system back to equilibrium, without bothering about the quality of it: consensual or coercive equilibrium. The impression they conveyed was that they were eager to help the state to contain the disequilibria and to maintain status quo. In contrast those who elected themselves to be 'radical' formed a demolition squad, as it were, to squash the State system, without realizing that the State will not wither away and it cannot be wished away. For them social movement was the solution to cleanse the system of its evils. But neither asked the question: what kind of research will produce usable knowledge for those who lead social movements? That is, they conjointly produced a sociology *of* social movements, although of differing value orientations, but did not produce a sociology *for* social movements, leaving a tremendous knowledge gap for social activists involved in social movements.[3]

In contrast, those who did research on social policy thought it to be an instrument of conflict management and negotiation between the state and various interest groups, be it labour or business. The ultimate commitment of social policy researchers was to system stability by conceding concessions to the contending parties so as to bring about changes in the system.[4] However the possibility of social policy measures gradually bringing about an incremental revolution was scarcely recognized. That is, the social policy researchers produced a sociology *for* social policy, and did not even attempt a sociology *of* social policy.[5]

Extrapolating from this let me suggest that we have a sociology *of* protest movement and a sociology *for* the resettlement of displacees. Although scarce beginnings have been made towards a sociology *for* protest movement and a sociology *of* displacement policy, we need to move forward fast in both contexts. The persisting estrangement between them has harmed both sound theory construction and relevant empirical research because they are really complimentary.

THE GENESIS AND SPREAD OF PROTESTS AGAINST DISPLACEMENT

With these clarifications, let me look at the Indian situation. Planned economic development was the refrain of the Indian Republic from 1950 till 1990, when economic liberalization was launched. The first four decades witnessed the coexistence of state-owned public sector and the private sector owned by corporations. The 'mixed economy' that emerged out of that arrangement was widely acknowledged as an appropriate model, which combined the positive aspects of capitalist and socialist economies, and was christened as the 'Third Way'. Neither the public sector, that is, the State, nor the private sector, that is, the market institutions, paid much attention to displacement, although they did pay lip service to resettlement and even rehabilitation. India's Planning Commission, almost exclusively manned by economists, did not consider displacement as an issue. And given the over-enthusiasm of the first charismatic prime minister (who occupied that office for 17 years) for technology-driven rapid development, who labelled huge projects as 'temples of modern India', protest movements against displacement could not crystallize easily.

However, as the number of displaced people soared, as the civil society gained strength, and as the legitimacy of the State eroded, the discontents of development manifested in numerous protest movements against displacement gradually surfaced. The estimates of displacement vary vastly. According to one such estimate some 35–55 million people have been displaced in Independent India. Of these, displacement due to large projects according to the government, between 1951 and 1985, is 16.5 million. But critics estimate that the figure for 1951–90 is little over 21 million.[6] Even if one endorses the most conservative estimates, the numbers are huge, and the population affected is larger than the total population of the majority of member-states of United Nations. It needs to be underlined here that only 8 per cent of India's population is tribal, the First Nations if you will, numbering 80 million. And 60 per cent of the displacees are tribes, as the huge projects, be it dams or industries, are located in their ancestral habitats.

The state in India wanted to retain its centrality not only in initiating planned economic development, but also in promoting and sustaining civil society.[7] This meant that civil society functioned in a subdued manner. But the aberrations of the state rendered civil society alert and assertive. The internal Emergency during 1975–6 was the most crucial event which eroded the democratic credentials of the Indian state, and the struggle against it provided the decisive break between state and civil society. Therefore, it is no accident that the 'temples of modern India' got de-sacralized and the 'destructive development' pursued by the Indian State came to be intensely interrogated by late 1970s.

As one reviews the trajectory of protest movements against displacement, three broad and overlapping patterns emerge. All the three have several stages, some common and some different. In the case of the first trajectory the following stages may be identified.

1. Stage one: The government (federal or provincial) grants the permission for the corporation (which may be in the public or private sector) to launch the project. Invariably this is shrouded in secrecy and the public will not have any information, not even the population likely to be affected by the project.

2. Stage two: Engineers and bureaucrats arrive on the project site to survey the area and do the markings, the enterprising media (print and/or electronic) spies on these activities and flash the news about the impending project to the public.

3. Stage three: Non-governmental organizations working in the area attempt an assessment of the negative and positive consequences (both short and long term) for the local people and the exploitative designs of the corporations. Large-scale mobilizations of the agitated future victims follow.

4. Stage four: Expert committees are appointed by the government to understand whether the claims made by the NGOs are correct and the mobilizations initiated by the activists sustainable. If the experts' opinion is to stall the project, even if the vested interests support the project, it is likely to be stalled. Such a trajectory is likely only if the civil society activists involved in protest movements have a common perspective and/or the experts take a consensual view. Even when the provincial government is eager to launch the project (because the project can be cited as an achievement for electoral gains), the federal government may stop it. Such happy conjunctions are extremely rare but not unheard of. One such case is that of stalling the Silent Valley Project in Kerala in the 1970s.[8] Today, the Valley Project area is a world heritage site for rare species recognized by UNESCO.

The second trajectory shares the first three stages, but if differences among the civil society activists surface and are forcefully articulated, the victims themselves are likely to be confused about the contradictory impact assessment available. In fact, the local people may get differentiated into 'winners', 'losers', and the 'unaffected' which affects the texture of stage four. The situation gets further exacerbated because of a lack of consensus among experts. It is not uncommon for experts to be sharply divided regarding their impact assessment. Such a scenario gives birth to a sharp division between the opponents and supporters of the project, giving birth to stage five.

5. Stage five: During this stage those civil society activists who are convinced about the largely negative consequences of constructing the project will continue their protest. The project initiators will try to weaken the mobilization by bribing, threatening, and intimidating the leaders of the protest movement. If the movement persists in spite of all these, agents provocateurs will be pressed into service to spur violence. Should the participants who opposed the project fall prey to this by indulging in counter-violence, the state seizes the opportunity to deploy police and paramilitary forces to control the law and order situation. This may lead to the use of firearms by state forces to control the 'unruly crowd', resulting in death and injury of civilians.

6. Stage six: This stage witnesses the third entry of the state (the first two being sanctioning the project and deploying the forces to maintain law and order) via a judicial commission to enquire about the violent incidents. The commission will condemn violence; invariably reprimanding the State bureaucracy and police, which did not acquit themselves well in managing the law and order situation. However, the commission will also highlight the imperative of continuing the project in the 'national interest'. A few officials will be transferred, some of the movement activists will get punished and/or stigmatized. The protest will whittle down, and after a lapse of time the project will be re-launched. Those who get displaced are demoralized; they do not have the requisite resources to continue with the protest, and invariably accept the adjudications of the project authorities as compensation. This imaginative reconstruction of the trajectories of protest movements is not isomorphic with particular cases, but largely tallies with most cases in India and is constructed on the basis of information available in several studies.[9]

There is a third trajectory possible as exemplified by those projects physically located at the border of two or more provincial states. The classic case in contemporary India is that of the NBA, that is, Save the Narmada movement. The provincial state of Gujarat enthusiastically supports the construction of the highest dam possible, the state of Maharashtra is mildly opposed to it, and the state of Madhya Pradesh is largely ambiguous. Similarly, there are both opponents and supporters of the protest movement among civil society activists, bureaucrats, and experts. It may be noted here that the protest is not against the construction of the dam as such, but to its height and the consequent possible geometrical increase in the number of displacees it may cause. The opponents argue for a series of small dams instead of one giant dam.

The negotiations by international agencies such as the World Dam Commission and the pronouncements by the Supreme Court of India have not led to the resolution of the problem, and the protest movement continues unabated. The supporters and opponents of the Sardar Sarovar Project (SSP) are stuck with their respective ideological orientations, which is the characteristic feature of the third trajectory I am referring to. The credo of supporters is developmentalism; they advocate 'development' at any cost even if millions of people are uprooted and rendered 'ecological refugees'. On the other hand, those who insist that the project should be abandoned even if only limited displacement occurs because the integrity of the environment is to be maintained in its pristine purity are indulging in environmentalism. If blind supporters of the dam are advocating 'mal-development', the opponents are championing 'anti-development', and both are unsustainable positions. And the knowledge generated through the analyses of protest movements is not amenable to be used in such situations. Why?

Typically, social movement studies are post-event enterprises; these are studies of terminated movements unless of course there is an inextricable relationship between research and movement as exemplified by the case of women's movement. Ongoing movements are rarely studied by researchers, either because their course may change drastically, or because their duration could be too long. Further, the emotional identification of participants in the protest movements and the opponents' utterly negative attitude towards it make it extremely difficult to arrive at an objective evaluation of the impact of these movements. While knowledge generated through analysis of protest movements may be useful for theory construction, it is not as helpful to be invoked for policy formulation to rehabilitate the victims. Of course, such knowledge may be useful to be applied in subsequent similar cases, but this rarely happens.

In contrast, the impact assessment of displacement is to be done before the event occurs; it is a *pre-event* analysis. Policy makers rarely initiate such studies; even if they do, they relate to material compensation to be provided to the oustees. It is widely believed that economists are better equipped to undertake such studies. Here, the real issue is not only the *quantum* of compensation, but also the *type of compensation*. The resources to be provided to the oustees to rehabilitate themselves is a consideration rarely entered in the studies by economists. Further, theoretically oriented social scientists are not at ease with prescription, which leads to tension between them and applied social science. In contrast, economists are adept at prescription. Finally, social scientists in general are obsessed with the present, ignoring past–present–future inter-linkages. Once again, the orientation of economists is largely prospective and future-oriented. To put it pithily, the reluctance on the part of social scientists to engage in prescriptive and prospective studies rendered them incapable of making path-breaking policy analysis.

THE NARMADA BACHAO ANDOLAN: A CASE STUDY

The trajectory of protest movements portrayed earlier remains general and it is useful to discuss the specificities of a couple of cases. One most suited for this analysis is that of the NBA for three reasons. First, it has a history of two decades of active mobilization; second, it has global visibility; and, third, it is the most widely documented case of its type in India.[10]

1. The protest against dam construction at the SSP obtains at three levels. At the grass-roots level participants are concerned mainly with material compensation, at the second level the mobilization becomes norm-oriented; and at the third level it transforms into a value-oriented movement.[11] At the first level are those concerned about resettlement and rehabilitation, and the quantum and quality of compensation. These bread-and-butter issues enthuse the oustees who are the local participants. These mobilizations are not against dam construction, but for a better deal for the victims; these are local and micro mobilizations. These mobilizations do not make a movement in that there is no articulated ideological content to them. They are elementary collective behaviour caused by insecurity due to the feared loss of shelter and means of livelihood.

2. Next are mobilizations that go beyond the issue of fair distribution of compensation and raise the issue of displacement. They question the inevitability of displacement to achieve development, and often insist on reducing displacement to a critical minimum. They have an ideological content and, hence, this can be legitimately designated as a movement. The activists involved in the mobilization and the academics opposed to the construction of dams have a concern beyond mere resettlement of the oustees. The juxtaposition between 'national development' at the cost of local victims is often questioned by these participants; they are national in reach and meso in orientation. These are norm-oriented movements.

3. A third set is one that encompasses only a few mobilizations. They interrogate the very paradigm of development implicated in the construction of huge projects, including dams. They are concerned

with both culturocide (systematic dismantling of the lifestyle of people)[12] and ecocide (the destruction of their ecology). Local participants do not articulate these concerns. They may not even be conscious of them. The activists and academics involved in meso-level mobilizations are aware of these issues, but are not equipped to pose them. Therefore, these questions are to be raised by an intellectual community functioning at the national/international level. These are macro and global mobilizations; they are value-oriented movements.

The NBA-initiated mobilizations against displacement have all these three components coalesced into one. As one moves from the first through the second to the third level, consensus regarding the movement goal decreases. Thus, the very notion of development is contested at the third level. The electrifying notion of 'national' development is the refrain of those who support the project. Thus, a former chairman of the Narmada Valley Development Agency says:

No trauma could be more painful for a family than to get uprooted from a place where it has lived for generations…. Yet, the uprooting has to be done. Because the land occupied by the family is required for a development project which holds promise of progress and prosperity for the country and people in general. The family getting displaced thus makes a sacrifice… so that others may live in happiness and be economically better off.[13]

The domain assumptions in the passage cited are that: (a) the project will bring about progress; (b) it will generate happiness for the beneficiaries; and (c) the oustees will have to be patriotic. The assumptions, even if valid, do not hold for the people as a whole, much less to the victims of the project. The position taken by a sociologist is more disquieting. He asks rather rhetorically: 'Why should any one oppose when tribal culture changes? A culture based on lower level of technology and quality of life is bound to give way to a culture with superior technology and high quality of life. This is what we can call development'.[14]

Such a position stigmatizes tribal culture and quality of life; it holds that their displacement is development. Several questions need to be posed here. Should social scientists categorize cultures as inferior and superior although they should recognize the differences between cultures. Should an alien culture, even if presumed to be superior, be imposed on an unwilling people? Should such an imposition be called the process of development? These are value-loaded questions, and whether one answers these questions positively or negatively, depends on one's ideological orientation. That is, development is a contested notion.

The beginning of the NBA's mobilization may be traced to 1985. Its effort was to accelerate the process of fully implementing the excellent compensation package announced by the state, which included land in the command area of the project to the oustees, providing land even to the erstwhile landless in the project area, and the like. But gradually NBA leaders realized that none of these promises materialized and the government was indulging in diversional tactics through promises to avoid violent confrontations. Understandably, the ideological position of the NBA was reformulated and it demanded an end to all projects which devastate the environment and destroy people's livelihoods, and called for the adoption of a socially just and ecologically sustainable pattern of development. Its defiant message, to politicians and planners, was that people are no longer prepared to watch in mute desperation as project after destructive project is heaped on them in the name of development and progress.[15]

The metamorphosis in the NBA's position from facilitating rehabilitation, through questioning displacement, to rejecting the model of development implied in the Sardar Sarover Project (SSP) was gradual and was based on its experience in confronting the state. A movement is sustainable only when there is a confluence between the ideological visions of its leadership and the material needs and aspirations of the grass-roots participants.[16] Happily, such a confluence exists in the case of the NBA, which explains its continuation for more than two decades.

Additionally, goal inconsistency regarding a project may prolong the continuation of protest, as exemplified by the case of the NBA. In the case of the construction of big dams, two sets of actors and their goals pull in opposite directions. Those who define big dams as instruments of development perceive opposition to them as an 'anti-development' activity. These 'developmentalists' do not ask the question: development for whom and for what? Conversely, those who launch protests against the construction of dams insist that what will happen through the instrumentality of big dams is 'mal-development' and, hence, an anti-people project bringing about culturocide (the systematic destruction of culture) of the affected people and ecocide of their habitat, in addition to their material impoverishment. Thus, there is no consensus about the very purpose for which the dam is constructed. This explains the deep division between the supporters and opponents of the NBA.

A movement may terminate because of goal attainment, co-optation, discreditation, institutionalization, and repression.[17] In the case of the NBA its goal is distant yet, and neither co-optation nor institutionalization is possible because of the deep divide between its leaders and those who support the SSP—politicians, bureaucrats, technocrats, and a section of beneficiaries. No effort was spared to discredit the NBA, and it is labelled as 'anti-developmental' and ecologically fundamentalist.[18] And the state apparatus has been continuously pressed into service to repress the movement leading to numerous arrests, *lathi*-charges, and firings. The government also usually blacks out movement events from All India Radio and the Doordarshan, the media it controls. In January 1989 the government tried to contain the NBA's dissent by invoking the Official Secrets Act to prevent mobilizations in the project area. In spite of it all, the movement continues.

ORISSA: THE TRAJECTORY OF DISPLACEMENTS AND PROTESTS

The second case that I propose to analyse is that of Orissa, one of the provincial states in India, and this also for several reasons. One, Orissa is resource-rich but economically backward. Two, some of the earliest high-technology-driven development projects in Independent India were launched here. Three, the state government has launched a massive programme of industrialization recently. Four, Orissa has a tradition of protest movements against displacement caused by large projects. Finally, there is a fair amount of documentation regarding protest against this mode of development.[19]

Orissa is one of the poorest states in India with 47.15 per cent of the population living below the poverty line (BPL) as against the national average of 26.1 per cent according to the latest available estimate by National Sample Survey Organization (NSSO) for 1999–2000. According to the 2001 Census of India, 65 per cent of the workforce in the state is directly dependent on agriculture. The state also has a sizable proportion of the traditionally disadvantaged social categories of Indian society: SCs 16.53 per cent and STs 22.13 per cent, the national proportions being 16.2 and 8.2 per cent, respectively. While some states are comparatively developed (for example, Punjab, Maharashtra, Gujarat, Haryana, and Tamil Nadu), Orissa is one of the least developed one along with Assam, Bihar, Madhya Pradesh, Rajasthan, and Uttar Pradesh. Orissa had a population share of 3.6 per cent in 2001 and 4.7 per cent of landmass, but only 2.37 per cent of India's GDP in 1993–4 according to the Centre for Monitoring Indian Economy.[20]

This is in spite of the fact that Orissa did establish the Industrial Infrastructure Development Corporation (IDCO) in 1980, and the Industrial Promotion and Investment Corporation of Orissa Limited (IPICOL), with a foreign investment division, to attract investors.

The Orissa Industrial Policy Resolution (IPR) of 1980, and the subsequent IPRs of 1986 and 1989, were all meant to facilitate rapid industrialization. In July 1991 the Government of India announced a New Industrial Policy (NIP) in the wake of the economic liberalization superseding the Industrial Policy Resolution of 1956 when the State occupied a commanding position. The State of Orissa soon fell in line with the Industrial Policy of Orissa (IPO) 1992, which was reformulated in 1996.

While the main objective of the 1996 IPO was giving a big push to industrial development, it also wanted to strengthen the rural economy through development of agro-industries, small industries, village and cottage industries, sericulture, handloom, and handicrafts. It resolved to provide greater support to entrepreneurs drawn from among women, SCs, STs, and the physically challenged. It laid emphasis on generating large-scale employment. However, these provisions intended to bring about a just society were largely erased from the New Industrial Policy (NIP) formulated in December 2001, in the wake of accelerating acceptance of the Structural Adjustment Programme (SAP). The Government of Orissa signed Memorandum of Understanding (MoUs) with 43 companies—foreign and Indian—for the setting up of iron and steel plants, aluminium and alumina plants, and the like, which are facilitated by the state to exploit the vast raw material reserves in the predominantly tribal districts. The prominent among these corporations are POSCO of South Korea, Sterlite and Vedanta Aluminium Companies owned by a non-resident Indian located in London, Tata Steel, Jindal, and Bhusan Steel, which are Indian companies.[21]

As noted earlier the hi-tech-driven process of development was initiated in Orissa by the 1950s. For example, Hirakud Dam, one of the earliest big dams of Independent India, was constructed in Orissa. Till the mid-1990s more than 400,000 persons had been displaced by development projects in Orissa, out of which 75 per cent were dam outsees,[22] and among them 35 per cent were STs and some 15 per cent SCs. According to available evidence, the resettlement of the Hirakud Dam oustees is far from satisfactory.[23] Since the case of dam oustees has been dealt with earlier at some length through the analysis of the NBA, I shall not pursue it here.

One of the three steel plants set up by the Government of India in the 1950s with foreign collaboration was established in Orissa: the Rourkela Steel Plant (RSP). For establishing the RSP 19,557 acres (7,918 ha) of land was acquired, leading to the displacement of 2,467 households in 30 villages. Among the oustee households 67.23 per cent were tribals.[24] By the time RSP became fully operational, there was more involuntary displacement of families. The latest estimate is that 10,704 households have been displaced in Orissa due to the ongoing process of industrialization,[25] and their resettlement and rehabilitation have been far from satisfactory. It is against this background that the people's protest against the spree of MoUs signed by the Government of Orissa in the wake of the NIP formulated in December 2001 is to be understood.

Till such time as India endorsed SAP, the State was the main agent of economic development sought to be brought about through industrialization; indeed, it occupied the position of command in this regard. But with the ushering in of the SAP the State retreated from this role and became a facilitator of corporations, mainly private, to accelerate the process of industrialization. The new strategy was brought in through the passing of the Special Economic Zones (SEZs) Act 2005, which invokes the principle of 'eminent domain'. Instead of allowing the market principle to operate, that is, corporations buying land directly from farmers at the market rate, the state operates as a broker between them, acquiring land at a low price, invoking the obsolescent colonial Land Acquisition Act of 1894 for 'public purpose', and selling it to the corporations. For example, the Government of Orissa acquired around 12,000 acres of land in Kalinga Nagar, during 1992–4 at the rate of Rs 37,000 per acre and allotted 1,960 acres to Tata Steel in 2004–5 at ten times the rate at which the landowners were paid.[26] According to another estimate, Rs 25,000 per acre was paid to the farmers and the Industrial Infrastructure Development Corporation (IDCO), the nodal agency of the government at Kalinga Nagar sold the land to industrial houses at Rs 335,000 per acre.[27] In either event the point to be noted is that the government makes huge profits at the cost of farmers, and the corporations are willing to pay the demanded amounts because they are sure of making much greater profits.

The Board of Approvals, under the commerce ministry of the Government of India, has already granted formal approval for 237 projects, of which 63 have been notified, while hundreds of projects are still awaiting approval. A petition addressed to the Chairman of the Empowered Group of Ministers on SEZs, signed by over 100 civil society groups and individuals, demanded the scrapping of the SEZ Act 2005 as it displaces land-based livelihood, ignores environmental concerns, and leads to exploitation of labour.

It may be noted here that there are four patterns of response in the context of SEZs. First, that which exists in northern states such as Haryana and Uttar Pradesh wherein protests against acquisition of land by the government and its allotment to the corporations has not crystallized.

Second, that which exists in Goa, which led to the abandoning of the SEZs projects by the government because of the massive protest from civil society. Third is the West Bengal pattern wherein protests against SEZ are a conjoint expression of political parties, both in opposition and in the coalition government and the civil society. Further, there are also internal differences within the Communist Party of India (Marxist) with regard to facilitating the capitalist path of development. All these render the situation in West Bengal highly ambiguous and implementation of the SEZ policy tortuous. Finally, the Orissa pattern where in spite of substantial protest, and protest from both the civil society and opposition political parties the government seems to be impervious and is forging forward with its agenda of massive industrialization. This makes Orissa a suitable case for analysis in the context of protest against displacement.

The virulent opposition to displacement by the people is answered through state violence of which two examples are particularly gruesome. In 1995–6 the Government of Orissa acquired land for the Utkal Alumina International Ltd (UAIL) by paying Rs 20,000 per acre to the tribals. Before evolving a consensus regarding the rehabilitation package, the UAIL started evicting the tribals from the acquired land using muscle power and destroyed their standing crops. The infuriated victims unleashed a massive protest when the company started construction of the plant with police protection. In the confrontation that followed, three tribals fell prey to police bullets on 16 December 2000.

The second incident is even more ghastly. When the Tata Steel Company started the construction of a boundary wall on 7 October 2005, the tribals opposed it and demanded rehabilitation before displacement. The Tatas made tactical withdrawal to reappear on 2 January 2006 to continue the construction of the boundary wall with support of the massive paramilitary forces already stationed there. But the 3,000-odd tribals armed with bows and arrows were there as well, ready for confrontation. Scared by the beheading of a policeman on duty with an axe by one of the women protesters, the police started reckless firing, leading to the death of 12 tribals—10 men and two women between the ages of 14 and 40. The construction activity has been suspended for an indefinite period and the project is in limbo at present.

While these two instances are indicative of the intensity of the ongoing process of protest against forced displacement in Orissa, institutionalization of protests and mobilization can be discerned from the formation of People's Forum to Oppose Displacement (PFOD), which demands the following: (a) no fresh displacement on grounds of industrialization; (b) 5 acres of land in lieu of land acquired; (c) ownership of land in possession/occupied; (d) ex-gratia payment of Rs 2 million each to families of the dead and Rs 1 million for each of the injured; (e) withdrawal of cases slapped against tribals; (f) ban on entry of multinationals into the area; and (g) appropriate action against officials directly responsible for the firings.

While it cannot be established unambiguously that the flurry of new policy initiatives are caused by these events, the plausible connectivity between the two cannot be ignored either. Thus, setting aside its 2004 settlement policy, the Ministry of Rural Development of the Government of India formulated another policy in the summer of 2006. This parallels a policy document prepared by the National Advisory Council (NAC) chaired by Sonia Gandhi, leader of Congress Party, which leads the coalition government in power. To cap it all, in December 2006 the prime minister announced that within three months the government would issue a new national resettlement policy. Perhaps all these are indicative of the increasing audibility of civil society voice in India. But such hurriedly prepared and announced policies are of not much consequence, even if they are faultless, unless they are faithfully implemented, the Achilles' heel of India's governance. But a sound policy in this context cannot be evolved without robust inputs from social scientists.

As I have noted in the case of the NBA, three strands of ideas are articulated at three different levels—micro, meso, and macro—in the case of all the hi-tech-driven large projects in Orissa too. Thus, issues that the displacees are concerned with are related to livelihood security, appropriate and adequate compensation if displaced, and the preservation of their identity and culture within their traditional habitats. The meso-level articulations are made by the numerous NGOs that champion the cause of the displacees. Apart from the immediate welfare of the victims, they are also concerned with issues of sustainable development and, hence, their interest in environmental and ecological problems. They attempt to sensitize the displacees about the long-term consequences of the policy of rapid industrialization pursued by the government through private corporations. Finally, those who articulate the macro issues are concerned with the political economy of development, neo-colonialism/imperialism, the tension between the concept of private property held by the state and communal property internalized by the tribals, the illegitimacy of the very notion of profit, and the like. It is not very easy to mesh into one unified whole the ideas and articulations of the three levels and translate them into a programme of action. As I have argued at the beginning of this chapter by addressing the issues involved both in the sociology of as well as sociology for protest movements, this wedge can be largely bridged.

SUSTAINABLE DEVELOPMENT: TOWARDS A VIABLE POLICY OPTION

How can we steer the exit from this impasse? I suggest that we need to do two things. One, a new set of questions should be asked. Two, a new perspective about development should be developed. The new set of questions should shift the attention from resettlement and rehabilitation to displacement. In the case of resettlement and rehabilitation the social scientist enters the scene post-project, that is, after the displacement occurs due to the initiation of the development process. At this stage one can only argue about the nitty-gritty of compensation. But if the focus shifts to displacement, it is possible to start interrogating the inevitability thesis regarding displacement. The relevant questions here are:

1. Is displacement *always* inevitable?
2. If the answer is in the affirmative, can we reduce the quantum of displacement to the *critical minimum* and how?
3. What precautionary measures (legal, administrative, economic, cultural) are to be taken in advance so that the economic, psychological, social, and cultural costs of displacement can be minimized?

Such questions blend theoretical issues and practical concerns. Fortunately, such orientations are now becoming evident. For example, Michael Cernea observes: 'The optimal response to predictable impoverishment risks is to search for project alternatives that could *eliminate altogether the need to displace people, or could at least reduce the number of displacees'.*[28] The moot question is: why is it that these eminently practical issues have been neglected for long by social scientists? My hunch is that while professional peers devalue those who address practical questions, they applaud those who attempt theoretical analyses. But the paradox is that those who formulate and implement policies marginalize those who attempt abstract theory building devoid of practical use. To render knowledge more relevant, we need to blend theory and praxis. This may create some wedge initially between those who construct theory and those who apply it. But conceding autonomy to both and recognizing reciprocity between them can considerably narrow it.

The second suggestion I made earlier is to develop a new perspective about development. There are two elements in this, technology and environment, and these are inextricably intertwined. Much of displacement occurs because of the reckless application of modern high technology anchored to inanimate energy. Instead of endorsing either of the prevailing polar views that technology is necessarily and always an instrument of human emancipation, or it is an unmitigated evil, it is necessary to accept that technology is a conditional good. Such a perspective also renders the juxtaposition between high and appropriate technology irrelevant. In fact, all technologies—high, intermediate, low— are appropriate contextually. This calls for our endorsing technological pluralism.[29]

Experiences the world over have demonstrated that the degradation of physical environment is caused by the type of development in vogue today. The value orientation to nature is critical here; the prevailing tendency to exploit nature excessively for human welfare is rendering the earth sick. It is necessary to recognize that the health and well-being of humankind is possible only if the earth is nurtured. All elements on the planet should have their place and the right to Gaia.[30] I venture to suggest that the Green Project is an attempt to shift our focus from the prevailing homocentrism to cosmocentrism.

To conclude, displacements are caused by the rash application of high technology and result in degradation of the environment. I have attempted to analyse displacements caused by dam construction and rapid industrialization through reckless application of high technology to bring about 'development' and people's protest against it. In the course of this analysis I have suggested the need to endorse technological pluralism. Such an approach will render technology eminently usable for accelerating a process of development, which will reduce, if not eliminate, displacement. This seems to be the route to render social science more relevant in the context of bringing about humane development.

NOTES

1. See T.K. Oommen, *Development Discourse: Issues and Concerns* (New Delhi: Regency Publications, 2004).
2. See T.K. Oommen, 'Social Movements and Social Policies: A Misplaced Polarity in Social Research', in Willian V. D'Antonio, Masamichi Sasaki, and Yoshio Yonebayashi (eds), *Ecology, Society and the Quality of Social Life* (New Brunswick and London: Transactions Publishers, 1994), pp. 119–32, as an example.
3. C.A. Rootes, 'Theory of Social Movements: Theory for Social Movements?', *Philosophy and Social Action*, 16 (4), (1990), pp. 5–17.

4. E. Oyen, 'The Muffling Effect of Social Policy: A Comparison of Social Security Systems and Their Conflict Potential in Australia, the United States and Norway', *International Sociology*, 1 (3), (1986), pp. 283–95.

5. R. Sigg, 'The Contribution of Sociology for Social Security', *International Sociology*, 1 (3), (1986), pp. 283–95.

6. Jai Sen, 'National Rehabilitation Policy: A Critique', *Economic and Political Weekly*, (1995), pp. 241–4, especially p. 243.

7. T.K. Oommen, 'State, Civil Society and Market in India: The Context of Mobilization', *Mobilization: An international Journal*, 1 (2), (1996), pp. 191–202.

8. R. Herring, *Politics of Nature: Interests, Commons Dilemmas and the State* (Bangalore: Indian Institute of Science, 1991).

9. B. Baboo, 'Technology and Social Transformation: The Case of the Hirakud Multi-purpose Dam Project in Orissa' (New Delhi: Concept Publishing House, 1992); W. Fernandes and E.G. Thukral (eds), *Development, Displacement and Rehabilitation* (New Delhi: Indian Social Institute, 1989); S. Kothari, 'Development Displacement and Official Policies', *Lokayan Bulletin*, 11 (5), (1995), pp. 9–28; L.K. Mahapatra, *Resettlement, Impoverishment and Reconstruction in India: Development for the Deprived* (New Delhi: Vikas Publishing House, 1999); Hari Mohan Mathur and David Marsden (eds), *Development Projects and Impoverishment Risks: Resettlement of Project Affected People in India* (New Delhi: Oxford University Press, 1998); Narmada Control Authority (NCA), *Submergence of Villages in Gujarat, Maharashtra and Madhya Pradesh with the Construction of SSP* (Indore: NCA, 1991); A.B. Ota and A. Agnihotri (eds), *Development Induced Displacement and Rehabilitation* (New Delhi: Prachi Prakashan, 1996); V. Paranjpye, *High Dams on the Narmada: A Holistic Analysis of the River Valley Projects* (New Delhi: Indian National Trust for Art and Cultural Heritage, 1990); S. Parasuraman, *The Development Dilemma: Displacement in India* (New Delhi: Palgrave Macmillan, 1999); People's Union for Civil Liberties (PUCL), *The Terror of Development* (in Hindi) (Bhopal: PUCL, 1990); N. Ram, *Muddy Waters: A Critical Assessment of the Benefits of the Sardar Sarover Project* (New Delhi: Kalpavriksh, 1993); S. Sharma, 'The Vanquished Tribal World of Shifting Cultivation', in A. Bhalla and P.J. Bumke (eds), *Images of Rural India in the 20ᵗʰ Century* (New Delhi: Sterling Publishers, 1992); P. Sheth, 'The Politics of Ecofundamentalism', in *All About Narmada* (Gandhinagar: Directorate of Information, Government of Gujarat, 1991); Tata Institute of Social Sciences (TISS), 'Sardar Sarovar Project: Review of Resettlement and Rehabilitation in Maharashtra', *Economic and Political Weekly*, 28 (34), (1993), pp. 1705–14.

10. C. Alvares and R. Billorey, 'Damning the Narmada: The Politics Behind the Destruction', *Ecologist*, 17 (2), (1987), pp. 120–32; A. Baviskar, *In the Belly of the River: Tribal Conflicts Over Development in the Narmada Valley* (New Delhi: Oxford University Press, 1995); Centre for Science and Environment (CSE), *The State of Indiana's Environment 1984–85: The Second Citizen's Report* (New Delhi: CSE, 1985); V. Joshi, *Rehabilitation: A Promise*

to Keep: A Case of SSP (Ahmedabad: Tax Publications, 1991); Kalpavriksh, *The Narmada Valley Project: A Critique* (New Delhi: Kalpavriksh, 1988); Lawyers Committee for Human Rights (LCHR), *Unacceptable Means: India's Sardar Sarovar Project and Violations of Human Rights, October 1992 through February 1993* (New York: LCHR, 1993); Multiple Action Research Group (MARG), *Sardar Sarovar Oustees in Madhya Pradesh: What Do They Know?* (New Delhi: MARG, 1986); B. Morse and T. Berger, *Sardar Sarovar: The Report of the Independent Review* (Ottawa: Resource Future International, 1992); Narmada Bachao Andolan (NBA), *Towards Sustainable and Just Development: The People's Straggle in Narmada Valley* (1991) (Mimeo); Narmada Control Authority (NCA) (1991); Paranjpye, *High Dams on the Narmada*; Ram, *Muddy Waters*; Sharma, 'The Vanquished Tribal World of Shifting Cultivation'; Sheth, 'The Politics of Ecofundamentalism'; TISS, 'Sardar Sarovar Project', among others.

11. N.J. Smelser, *The Theory of Collective Behaviour* (London: Routledge and Kegan Paul, 1962).

12. T.K. Oommen, 'Insiders and Outsiders in India: Primordial Collectivism and Cultural Pluralism in Nation-Building', *International Sociology*, 1 (1), (1986), pp. 53–74.

13. Quoted in Alvares and Billorey, 'Damning the Narmada', p. 64.

14. Joshi, *Rehabilitation*, p. 68.

15. NBA, *Towards Sustainable and Just Development*, p. 4.

16. T.K. Oommen, 'Sociological Issues in the Analysis of Social Movements in Independent India', *Sociological Bulletin*, vol. 26, no. 1 (1977), pp. 14–37.

17. G.R. Rush and R.S. Denisoff, *Social and Political Movements* (New York: Meredith Corporation, 1971).

18. Sheth, 'The Politics of Ecofundamentalism'.

19. See, for example, B. Baboo, *Technology and Social Transformation: The Case of the Hirakud Multi-purpose Dam Project in Orissa* (New Delhi: Concept Publishing House, 1992); W. Fernandes and S.R. Anthony, *Development, Displacement and Rehabilitation in Tribal Areas of Orissa* (New Delhi: Indian Social Institute, 1992); N.C. Kar, *Socio-Economic and Cultural Impact of NALCO on Local Tribals in Damanjodi Project Area* (Bhubaneswar: Nabakrushna Choudhury Centre for Development Studies, 1991) (Mimeo); L.K. Mahapatra, *Resettlement, Impoverishment and Reconstruction in India: Development for the Deprived* (New Delhi: Vikas Publishing House, 1999); Rajkishor Meher, 'Degeneration of the Periphery under Hegemonic Development: The Case of Marginalisation of the Aboriginal in a Tribal Region', *Indian Social Science Review*, 3 (2), (2001) pp. 289–326; Rajkishor Meher, 'The Social and Ecological Effects of Industrialization in a Tribal Region: The Case of the Rourkela Steel Plant', *Contributions to Indian Sociology*, 37 (3), (2003) (n.s.), pp. 429–57; Rajkishor Meher, *Stealing the Environment: Social and Ecological Effects of Industrialization in Rourkela* (New Delhi: Manohar Books, 2004); Rajkishor Meher, 'Globalization, Industrialization and the State: A Sociological Study of Tribals' Reaction

to Industrial Development in Orissa'. Paper presented at the Seminar on Towards a Sociology of South Asia, New Delhi, 27–8 January 2006; A.B. Ota, *Resettlement and Rehabilitation Policies of Different Sectors for the Affected People in the State of Orissa* (Bhubaneswar: Department of Water Resources, Government of Orissa, 1999) (Mimeo); Balaji Pandey, 'Impoverishing Effects of Coal Mining Projects: A Case Study of Five Villages in Orissa', in Hari Mohan Mathur and David Marsden (eds), *Development Projects and Impovershment Risks: Resettlement of Project Affected People in India* (New Delhi: Oxford University Press, 1998), pp. 174–92; B. Pandey, 'The Kalinga Nagar Tragedy: Development Goal or Development Malaise'. Paper presented at the IAPS Conference on Environment, Health and Sustainable Development, Alexandria, Egypt, 11–16 September 2006; B.K. Roy Burman, *Social Processes in the Industrialisation of Rourkela*, Vol. I, Monograph Series, Monograph No. 1, Part XI-E, Census of India, 1961 (New Delhi: Registrar General and Census Commissioner, 1968); Bholeswar Sahu, *Development and Displacement: A Case Study of Rengali Dam Project in Orissa* (Bhubaneswar: Utkal University, 2000).

20. Centre for Monitoring Indian Economy (CMIE), *National Income Statistics* (Mumbai: CMIE, 2004).

21. Rajkishor Meher, 'Globalization, Industrialization and the State: A Sociological Study of Tribals' Reaction to Industrial Development in Orissa', paper presented at the seminar on 'Towards a Sociology of South Asia' (New Delhi, 27–8 January 2006).

22. A.B. Ota, *Resettlement and Rehabilitation Policies of Different Sectors for the Affected People in the State of Orissa*.

23. B. Baboo, *Technology and Social Transformation: The Case of the Hirakud Multi-purpose Dam Project in Orissa* (New Delhi: Concept Publishing House, 1992).

24. B.K. Roy Burman, *Social Processes in the Industrialisation of Rourkela* (vol. I, Monograph Series, Monograph no. I, Part XI-E, Census of India, 1961) (New Delhi: Registrar General and Census Commissioner, 1968).

25. Ota, *Resettlement and Rehabilitation Policies in Different Sectors for the Affected People in the State of Orissa*.

26. Biswamoy Pati, 'Tatas and Orissa "Model" of Capitalist "Development"', *Social Scientist*, 34 (2), (2006).

27. PUCL. *Police Firing and Kalinga Nagar* (Bhubaneswar: PUCL, 2006).

28. M.M. Cernea, 'Impoverishment Risks, Risk Management and Reconstruction: A Model of Population Displacement and Resettlement', in M.M. Cernea and Chris McDowell (eds), *Risk and Reconstruction: Experiences of Resettlers and Refugees* (Washington, DC: World Bank, 2000).

29. Oommen, 'Restructuring Development Through Technological Pluralism', *International Sociology*, 7 (2), pp. 131–9.

30. J. Lovelock, *The Age of Gaia: A Biography of Our Living Earth* (New York: Fantom Books, 1988).

Contributors

INDU AGNIHOTRI is Deputy Director and Senior Fellow, Centre for Women's Development Studies, Delhi.

PHILIP G. ALTBACH is Monan Professor of Higher Education and Director, Center for International Higher Education, Boston College, USA.

DEBASHISH BHATTACHERJEE is Professor, Indian Institute of Management Calcutta.

MARTHA ALTER CHEN is Lecturer in Public Policy, Kennedy School of Government, Harvard University.

D.N. DHANAGARE was Professor, Department of Sociology, University of Pune.

LATE RANJIT DWIVEDI was Research Scholar at the Institute of Social Sciences, The Hague.

LATE KATHLEEN GOUGH was Professor of Anthropology at Simon Fraser University, Canada.

VINA MAZUMDAR is National Research Professor, Centre for Women's Development Studies, Delhi.

PARTHA MUKHERJI was Professor, S.K. Dey Chair, Institute of Social Sciences, New Delhi.

T.K. OOMMEN is Emeritus Professor, Centre for the Study of Social Systems, School of Social Sciences, Jawaharlal Nehru University, New Delhi.

RAJNI PALRIWALA is Professor, Department of Sociology, Delhi School of Economics, University of Delhi.

LATE S.M. PANDEY was Senior Research Fellow, Sri Ram Centre for Industrial Relations, Delhi.

SUPRIYA ROYCHOWDHURY is Professor, Institute for Social and Economic Change, Bangalore.

VANDANA SHIVA is Director, Navdanya, New Delhi.

Name Index

Subject Index